Studies in the History of Medieval Religion

VOLUME XXXII

MONASTIC HOSPITALITY

The Benedictines in England, c. 1070–c. 1250

Studies in the History of Medieval Religion

ISSN: 0955–2480

General Editor
Christopher Harper-Bill

Previously published titles in the series
are listed at the back of this volume

MONASTIC HOSPITALITY

The Benedictines in England, c. 1070–c. 1250

JULIE KERR

THE BOYDELL PRESS

First published 2007
The Boydell Press, Woodbridge

ISBN 978-1-84383-326-0

CATHEDRAL AND ABBEY
CHURCH OF ST. ALBAN

THE HUDSON

MEMORIAL

LIBRARY

The Boydell Press is an imprint of Boydell & Brewer Ltd
PO Box 9, Woodbridge, Suffolk IP12 3DF, UK
and of Boydell & Brewer Inc.
668 Mt Hope Avenue, Rochester, NY 14620, USA
website: www.boydellandbrewer.com

A catalogue record of this publication is available from the British Library

This publication is printed on acid-free paper

Typeset by Carnegie Book Production, Lancaster
Printed in Great Britain by Antony Rowe Ltd

Contents

For mum and dad

List of Illustrations

The publication of this book has
been made possible by a grant from The Scouloudi Foundation in
association with the Institute of Historical Research.

Acknowledgements

I have received considerable support, encouragement and advice during my doctoral research and in subsequent years, in particular from friends and colleagues at the universities of St Andrews and Sheffield and attending the annual conferences at Battle and Leeds. I have benefited greatly from Miss Barbara Harvey who examined the thesis, read several chapters of the typescript and has generously shared her knowledge and advised me on a number of issues relating to the administration of the monastery and refectory arrangements. I am grateful to Professor Janet Burton and Dr Angela Montford who kindly read the typescript in its entirety and made valuable comments. Professor Christopher Holdsworth, Mr Peter King, Dr Michael Staunton, Dr Liesbeth Van Houts and Miss Lorna Walker have patiently answered my many questions over the years; Drs Sally Crumplin and Angus Stewart have helped considerably with modifying the monastery plans for publication. Irma Bowness and Berta Wales have been towers of strength during the doctoral process and since; my parents, Betty and Bob, my husband, Haki, and my feline friend, Saphy, have supported and encouraged me throughout. I am particularly indebted to Professor John Hudson and Dr Simone C. Macdougall who have tirelessly guided me from my undergraduate days and remained my mentors and friends. John supervised my doctoral work, survived the monastic customary experience, and has steered me on the course to converting the thesis into a book. Simone, who kindled my love of medieval monasticism, has been an inspiration ever since. She, fittingly, examined the doctoral thesis and bravely agreed to read a typescript of the book; her comments have been invaluable. Finally, and most especially, I would like to thank my father, whose enthusiasm, interest and support over the years have been quite overwhelming – and unmerited – and without whom this would never have seen completion.

I would like to acknowledge the financial support I received as a doctoral student from the British Academy, the Carnegie Trust and the Scouloudi Foundation, and to thank Caroline Palmer of Boydell & Brewer for her guidance and patience.

List of Abbreviations

AN Studies	*Anglo-Norman Studies: Proceedings of the Battle Conference* (Woodbridge, 1979–)
ANTS	Anglo-Norman Texts Society
Bury Customary	*The Customary of the Benedictine Abbey of Bury St Edmunds in Suffolk*, ed. A. Gransden, HBS 99 (Chichester, 1973)
Caesarius, *Dialogue on Miracles*	*The Dialogue on Miracles*, trans. H. von E. Scott and C. C. S. Bland, 2 vols (London, 1929)
Canivez, *Statutes*	*Statuta Capitulorum Generalium Ordinis Cisterciensis ab Anno 1116 ad Annum 1786*, ed. J. M. Canivez, 8 vols (Louvain, 1933–41)
Chronicle of Lanercost	*The Chronicle of Lanercost, 1272–1346*, trans. with notes by Sir Herbert Maxwell (Glasgow, 1913; Llanerch facsimile 2001)
CCCM	*Corpus Christianorum Continuatio Mediaevalis*
CFMA	*Classiques français du Moyen Age*
Chronica Majora	*Matthaei Parisiensis, monachi Sancti Albani, Chronica Majora*, ed. H. R. Luard, 7 vols, RS 57 (London, 1872–84)
CS	Camden Society
De Obedientiariis	'De Obedientiariis Abbendoniae', in *Chronicon Monasterii de Abingdon*, ed. J. Stevenson, 2 vols, RS 2 (London, 1858), 2, pp. 335–417
Dugdale, *Monasticon*	*Monasticon Anglicanum*, ed. Sir William Dugdale, rev. J. Caley, H. Ellis, B. Bandinel, 6 vols, in 8 (London, 1817–30)
EHR	*English Historical Review*
EYC	*Early Yorkshire Charters*, vols 1–3, ed. W. Farrer (Edinburgh, 1914–16); index to vols 1–3, ed. C. T. and E. M. Clay; vols 4–9, ed. C. T. Clay, YAS Rec. Ser., extra ser. (Edinburgh, 1935–65)
Eynsham Customary	*The Customary of the Benedictine Abbey of Eynsham in Oxford*, ed. A. Gransden, *Corpus Consuetudinum Monasticarum* 2 (Siegburg, 1963)
GASA	*Gesta Abbatum Monasterii Sancti Albani a Thomas Walsingham, regnate Ricardo Secundo, ejusdem ecclesiae Prae centore, compilata*. ed. H. T. Riley, 3 vols, RS 4 (London, 1867–69)
Gervase, *Chronicle*	*Historical works, the Chronicle of the Reigns of Stephen, Henry II, and Richard I, by Gervase, the Monk of Canterbury*, ed. W. Stubbs, 2 vols, RS 73 (London, 1879–80)
HBS	Henry Bradshaw Society
History of Abingdon	*Historia Ecclesiae Abbendoniensis: The History of the Church of Abingdon 2*, ed. and trans. J. Hudson, OMT (Oxford, 2002)
Idung, *Dialogue*	Idungus of *Prüfening*, 'A dialogue between a Cluniac and a Cistercian', trans. J. O'Sullivan in *Idung of Prüfening, Cistercians and Cluniacs: the Case for Cîteaux* (Kalamazoo, 1977), pp. 3–141
Instructio Noviciorum	'Instructio Noviciorum' in *The Monastic Constitutions of Lanfranc*, rev. D. Knowles and C. N. L. Brooke (Edinburgh, 2002), pp. 198–221

JEH	*Journal of Ecclesiastical History*
JMH	*Journal of Medieval History*
Jocelin	Jocelin of Brakelond, *The Chronicle of Jocelin of Brakelond*, ed. and trans. H. E. Butler (Edinburgh, 1949)
L/P Henry VIII	*Letters and Papers Foreign and Domestic in the Reign of Henry VIII*, arranged and catalogued J. S. Brewer, J. Gairdner and R. H. Brodie, 22 vols (London, 1862–1932)
Lanfranc, *Constitutions*	*The Monastic Constitutions of Lanfranc*, rev. edn D. Knowles and C. Brooke, OMT (Oxford, 2002)
Liber Eliensis	*Liber Eliensis: A History of the Isle of Ely from the Seventh Century to the Twelfth Century*, trans. with notes J. Fairweather (Woodbridge, 2005)
Materials for Becket	*Materials for the History of Thomas Becket, Archbishop of Canterbury*, ed. J. C. Robertson and J. B. Sheppard, 7 vols, RS 67 (London, 1875–85)
NLT	*Narrative and Legislative Texts from Early Cîteaux*, ed. and trans. C. Waddell (Cîteaux, 1999)
OMT	Oxford Medieval Texts
Orderic	*The Ecclesiastical History of Orderic Vitalis*, ed. and trans. M. Chibnall, 6 vols, OMT (Oxford, 1969–80)
PL	*Patrologia cursus completes, series Latina*, ed. J. P. Migne *et al.*, 221 vols (Paris, 1844–64)
PR	*Pipe Rolls*, published by Pipe Roll Society
PRS	Pipe Roll Society
RAC	*Reading Abbey Cartularies*, ed. B. R. Kemp, 2 vols, CS, 4th ser. 31, 33 (London, 1986–87)
RS	Rolls Series: *Rerum Brittanicarum Medii Aevi Scriptores, Chronicles and Memorials of Great Britain and Ireland during the Middle Ages*, 99 vols (1858–96)
Rule of St Benedict	*The Rule of St Benedict*, ed. and trans. D. O. Hunter Blair, 5th edn (Fort Augustus, 1948)
St Augustine's Customary (c. 1250)	'Consuetudines Monasterii Sancti Augustini Cantuariae compendiose notatae', in *The Customary of St Augustine's, Canterbury and St Peter's, Westminster*, ed. E. M. Thompson, 2 vols, HBS 23, 28 (London, 1902–4), 2, appendix, pp. 249–318.
St Augustine's Customary (fourteenth-century)	*Customary of St Augustine's, Canterbury, and St Peter's, Westminster*, 1
St Mary's Customary	*The Chronicle of St Mary's, York*, ed. H. H. E. Craster and M. E. Thornton, SS 148 (London, 1934), pp. 80–108
SS	Surtees Society
Thomas Marlborough, *History of Evesham*	Thomas Marlborough, *History of the Abbey of Evesham*, ed. and trans. J. Sayers and L. Watkiss, OMT (Oxford, 2003)
TNA	The National Archives
TRHS	*Transactions of the Royal Historical Society*
VCH	*Victoria County Histories*
Vita Anselmi	Eadmer, *The Life of St Anselm, Archbishop Canterbury*, ed. and trans. R. W. Southern, Nelson's Medieval Texts (London, 1962), 2nd edn OMT (Oxford, 1972)
Westminster Customary	*Customary of St Augustine's, Canterbury and St Peter's, Westminster*, 2
YAS Rec. Ser.	Yorkshire Archaeological Society Record Series

Introduction

> From receiving guests cheerfully the reputation of the monastery is increased, friendships are multiplied, animosities are blunted, God is honoured, charity is augmented and a plentiful reward is promised in heaven.[1]

Hospitality has been integral to society from time immemorial. Its significance in Biblical times is reflected in the Old and New Testaments, chiefly in Abraham's encounter with the angels in Genesis 18: 1–15 and Christ's injunctions to care for the stranger in Matthew 25: 40. Its importance in classical and medieval times is evident in contemporary writings such as the works of Homer and Cicero, the Anglo-Saxon poem, *Beowulf*, and the Arthurian romances.[2] Whether these writings reflect the ideals or the practices of the societies that produced them, they are a testimony to the place they accorded hospitality.[3] Of course, hospitality is not a Western phenomenon. Anthropological studies have highlighted its significance to other cultures, notably, Marcel Mauss' pioneering analysis of the gift-exchange which considers what compelled people to give, receive and reciprocate, and Julian Pitt-Rivers' study of honour in contemporary Mediterranean societies.[4]

---

1   'Of the hosteller', *The Observances in Use at the Augustinian Priory of Barnwell in Cambridgeshire*, ed. and trans. J. W. Clark (Cambridge, 1897), ch. 41, 'De hospitario' (pp. 192–3). The ordinances have been dated to the late thirteenth century.

2   For a useful overview see J. Kristeva, *Strangers to Ourselves* (New York, 1991), and for further discussion see M. T. Bruckner, *Narrative Invention in Twelfth-century French Romance: the convention of hospitality, 1160–1200* (Lexington, 1980); R. A. Greer, 'Hospitality in the first five centuries of the church', *Monastic Studies* 10 (1974), pp. 29–48; J. Kerr, 'The open door: hospitality and honour in twelfth- / early-thirteenth-century England', *History* 87 (2002), pp. 322–35, 'Food, drink and lodging: lay hospitality in twelfth-century England', *Haskins Society Journal* 18, ed. S. Morillo (forthcoming, Woodbridge, 2007), 'Welcome the coming, speed the departing guest', *JMH* (forthcoming); J. Koenig, *New Testament Hospitality: partnership with strangers as promise and mission* (Philadelphia, 1985); S. Reece, *The Stranger's Welcome: oral theory and the aesthetics of the Homeric hospitality scene* (Kalamazoo, 1993).

3   Note Jaeger's discussion of the educative and mimetic function of Arthurian literature, for example, in his *The Envy of the Angels: cathedral schools and social ideals in mediaeval Europe* (Philadelphia, 1994), p. 15.

4   M. Mauss, 'Essai sur le don', *The Gift: forms and functions of exchange in archaic societies*, trans. W. D. Halls (London, 1990); J. Pitt-Rivers, *The Fate of Shechem: essays*

Whilst hospitality has a long and enduring history, its significance in the twelfth century is of particular interest, both in a European and Anglo-Norman context. This was a dynamic period that gave rise to a number of religious, social and economic developments. The institution of a new ruling class in England following the Conquest of 1066 strengthened links with the Continent, for it brought greater access to foreign ideas, practices and texts. This would have generated more traffic, with a number of lords now travelling to their familial lands across the water, prelates visiting their dependencies and attending meetings at the mother-house, and scholars seeking knowledge in the schools. A renewed interest in civility and courtesy at this time, coupled with a concern to codify and set down in writing existing practices, led to the proliferation of works on conduct. Nicholas Orme has justifiably described the twelfth century as 'a new era in the history of manners'. It gave rise to the first comprehensive etiquette texts and the earliest courtesy book compiled c. 1140 by Petrus Alfonsi.[5] The first in England, the *Urbanus* or *Liber Urbani* ('Book of the Civilised Man'), was produced some fifty years later by Daniel of Beccles who is thought to have been a member of Henry II's court, writing c. 1180.[6] His poem, which consists of some 3000 lines of Latin, was and remains the most extensive in any language.[7] These same concerns nurtured the compilation of prescriptive texts in the religious houses, primarily, customaries and guides for novices. This means that there is now a large corpus of evidence to enable us access to the ideals and practices of religious life at the time. The Victorines of Paris made a particularly notable contribution producing a detailed customary, the *Liber Ordinis*, c. 1116, and Hugh of St Victor's *Institutione Novitiorum* which is thought to date from the early 1120s. The latter was highly influential and has been described by C. S. Jaeger as the 'best documentation in ethical training', for it is especially concerned with manners and gestures.[8]

    in the anthropology of the Mediterranean (Cambridge, 1977); 'Honour and social status', *Honour and Shame*, ed. J. Péristiany (London, 1966).

5   N. Orme, *From Childhood to Chivalry: the education of the English kings and aristocracy 1066–1530* (London, 1984), pp. 136–41.

6   *Urbanus Magnus Danielis Becclesiensis*, ed. J. Gilbart Smyly (Dublin, 1939). For details of Daniel and his work see R. Bartlett, *England Under the Norman and Angevin Kings, 1075–1225* (Oxford, 2000), pp. 582–8 and J. Gillingham, 'From *civilitas* to civility: codes of manners in medieval and early modern England', *TRHS* 6: 12 (2002), pp. 267–89. Beccles' work should not be confused with the *Urbanus Paruus*, also known as *Facetus*, see A. Rigg, *A History of Anglo-Latin Literature, 1066–1421* (Cambridge, 1992), p. 127.

7   J. Nicholls, *The Matter of Courtesy: Medieval Courtesy Books and the Gawain Poet* (Cambridge, 1985), pp. 179–90 (p. 185).

8   C. S. Jaeger, 'Humanism and ethics in the School of St Victor in the early twelfth century', *Mediaeval Studies* 55 (1993), pp. 51–79 (pp. 53–4). For the number of surviving manuscripts, which indicate its popularity, see p. 54. The potential impact that Victorine humanism had on the importance and practice of monastic hospitality in England is considered below, pp. 6–8.

Monastic hospitality

The subject of this book is monastic hospitality in England over a long twelfth century, extending from c. 1070 until c. 1250. It is chiefly concerned with Benedictine hospitality, particularly the large southern houses of Abingdon, Bury St Edmunds, Christ Church, Canterbury and St Albans for which there is a relatively rich and varied body of surviving evidence. As royal foundations that were situated in the towns they inevitably faced considerable demands and were frequently called upon to entertain royalty and ecclesiastics, and to host important state gatherings. Moreover they might expect a number of pilgrims to visit their shrines. Accordingly their experience of hospitality and the nature of their provision for guests may have differed considerably from Benedictines living in smaller and more remote communities. Future research may shed light on these less well documented houses and offer a wider perspective of Benedictine hospitality. To set the Benedictine material in context other orders are considered, especially the Cistercian monks who settled in secluded sites rather than urban centres.

Hospitality was of particular significance in the Benedictine monastery and from the outset monks were charged with a special role *vis à vis* the reception of guests. The *Rule of St Benedict* addresses the reception of guests in chapter 53 and these precepts remained the backbone of monastic practice throughout the Middle Ages. Given that monks had, in theory, retreated from the world it may seem incongruous that hospitality should be accorded such importance, yet there were Biblical precedents, and the care of guests was closely associated with charity.[9] In twelfth-century England some houses were established specifically to provide hospitality, for example, Henry I's foundation at Reading. Morville Priory was converted from a minster to a cell of Shrewsbury Abbey in 1138 on the understanding that the abbey sent monks to take over the church at Morville and provide hospitality there.[10] While hospitality was integral to monastic life the admittance of guests and their entertainment within the precinct had to be carefully organised lest it impeded rather than fulfilled monastic ideals, and drained the community's resources.[11]

Developments in the administration of the Benedictine monastery during the twelfth and thirteenth centuries had an impact on the organisation and execution of monastic hospitality, chiefly, the abbot's growing withdrawal

[9]   Chapter 36 of the thirteenth-century *Rule* of Grandmont presents charity as the motive, hospitality as the action, 'For the sake of charity you will show hospitality', see C. A. Hutchinson, *The Hermit Monks of Grandmont* (Kalamazoo, 1989), p. 85.

[10] Bishop Robert de Bethune of Hereford granted Morville to Shrewsbury in 1138 on this understanding, *The Cartulary of Shrewsbury Abbey*, ed. U. Rees, 2 vols (Aberystwyth, 1975), 2, no. 334 (pp. 303–4); 1210 x 1219 Morville was given the chapel of Astley by Hugh of Hereford, to improve upon hospitality at the priory, no. 347 (p. 313); see also M. Heale, *The Dependent Priories of Medieval English Monasteries*, Studies in the History of Medieval Religion 22 (Woodbridge, 2004), p. 58 n. 151.

[11] This is discussed in chapters 2 and 6.

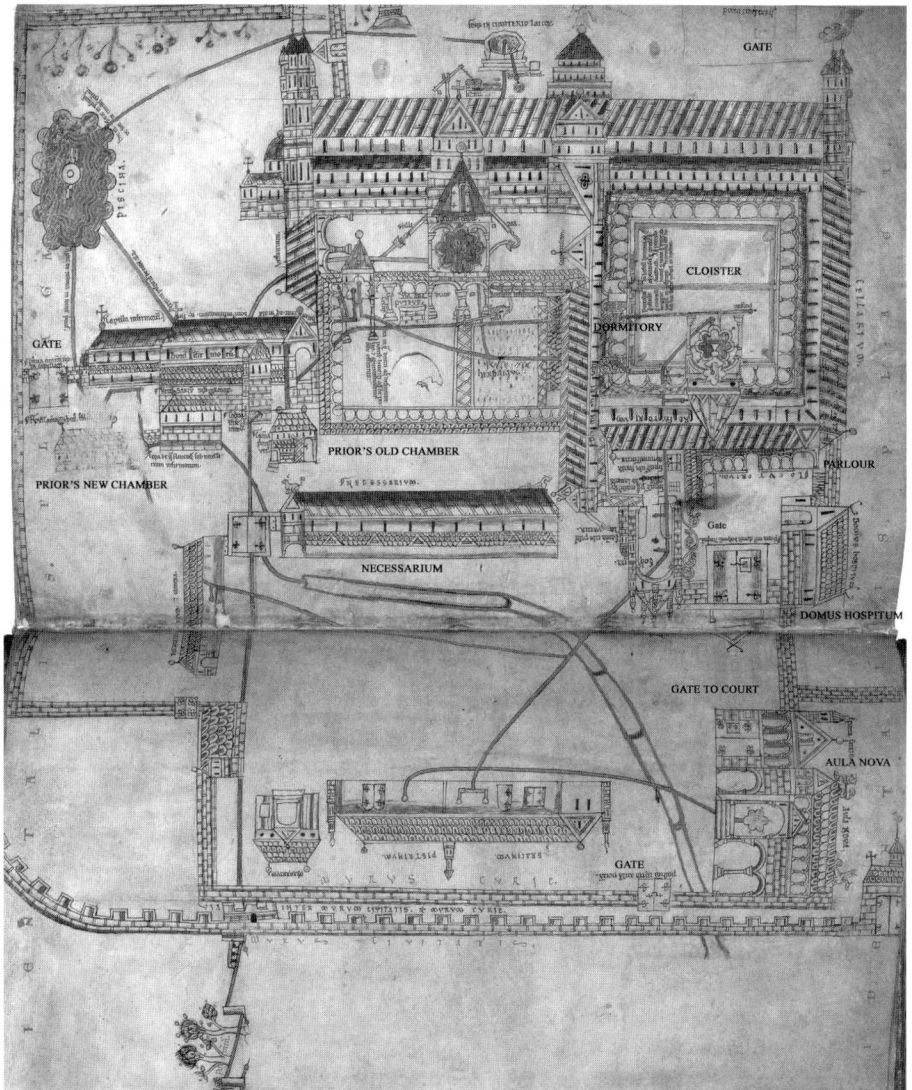

Figure 1 Waterworks Plan, Christ Church, Canterbury, Eadwine Psalter, Trinity College Cambridge, MS R.17.1, fols 284v–285r (c. 1165).

from communal life and his establishment of private quarters, the division of revenues between the prelate and convent and the distribution of resources amongst the various monastic offices. In a number of houses this led to the division of guests between the abbot and convent, and meant that there might now be several officials associated with the administration of hospitality and various places within and outside the precinct where guests were entertained.[12]

---

[12] See in particular chapters 2 and 4.

It is useful to consider the arrangements at Christ Church, Canterbury whose buildings are shown in a mid-twelfth-century plan known as the Waterworks Plan. This depicts the monastery's hydraulic system, which was central to Prior Wibert's building programme of 1155–67, and is the only known plan of a western monastery prior to the sixteenth century.[13] The plan shows various lodgings at Christ Church associated with hospitality, namely, the prior's lodgings to the NE of the church, the *domus hospitum* that stood to the NW of the cloister, and the *aula nova*, in the NW corner of the precinct. It reveals little about the interior layout of these buildings or their use but it is likely that the prior received more distinguished visitors in his lodgings, while the cellarer and guestmaster entertained middling guests in the *domus hospitum* and guests arriving on foot were shown to the *aula nova*.[14] As the seat of the primate and a popular pilgrim site, even before the martyrdom of 1170, Christ Church is not, perhaps, representative of other houses but most monasteries at this time would have had several lodgings for guests within the precinct.

The growing burden of monastic hospitality

At that time monks did not yet feel the press of a tumult of strangers crowding upon them.[15]

Various developments may have heightened the importance of monastic hospitality throughout Europe in the twelfth century, not least of all an increased number of people on the roads travelling by horse and on foot. Communities certainly felt that they were now more greatly burdened by guests than their predecessors. Both Peter the Venerable, abbot of Cluny (d. 1156), and Hildegard of Bingen (d. 1178) cited this as a reason for modifying Benedict's precepts and curtailing hospitality. The Cluniac in Idung of Prüfening's 'Dialogue' (c. 1155) claimed that if they were to follow the *Rule of St Benedict* and welcome all guests who flocked to the house, they would not themselves have enough to survive.[16] Pilgrimage, the Crusades and urban renewal meant there was potentially a vast and wide range of people requiring refreshment, accommodation or provisions along the way. The monastery's role in providing provisions for travellers to purchase *en route* is

---

13   Trinity College Cambridge, MS R171.1 (987), fols 284v–285r (large diagram), fol. 286r (smaller sketch). F. Woodman, 'The Waterworks drawing of the Eadwine Psalter', *The Eadwine Psalter: Text, Image and Monastic Culture in Twelfth-Century Canterbury*, ed. M. Gibson, T. A. Heslop, R. W. Pfaff (London, 1992), pp. 168–77 (p. 172). See below, appendix 2.

14   These buildings are discussed in greater detail in appendix 2.

15   *Hildegard of Bingen, Explanation of the Rule of St Benedict*, trans. with intro., notes and commentary by H. Feiss, Peregrina Translation Series (Toronto, 1998), ch. 26, 'On hospitality', p. 32.

16   *Hildegard, Explanation of the Rule*, ch. 26, 'On hospitality', p. 32; *The Letters of Peter the Venerable*, ed. G. Constable, 2 vols (Cambridge, MA, 1967), 1, ep. 28, clause 9 (pp. 71–2 at p. 72); Idung, *Dialogue*, III: 54 (p. 139).

an aspect of their care that merits closer analysis.[17] The monastery was not the only recourse for travellers, particularly in the towns where alternative lodgings could be secured with locals or in a hospice. Visitors attending the consecration of the church at Ely in 1252 were accommodated in the monks' buildings, the bishop's lodgings and also with the townsfolk.[18] Eastbridge Hospital in Canterbury was established for pilgrims travelling to the shrine of Thomas Becket, and the miracle stories suggest it was common for pilgrims to stay with locals.[19] A number of nobles had houses in urban centres such as London and Winchester, but it is difficult to gauge how many visitors to the monastery would have expected to secure independent lodgings and how extensive this provision was.[20] Still, the monastery remained an important source of hospitality, particularly in remote areas where there were was little other provision for travellers. Several Cistercian houses claimed this as the reason for an influx of guests. In 1336 the abbot of Margam complained that as the abbey was on the high road and far from other places of refuge it was 'continuously overrun by rich and poor strangers'.[21] The Cistercians, or the White Monks as they were also known, were perhaps more susceptible since they chose sites 'far from the haunts of men'.

Hospitality and humanism

Advances in scholasticism and humanism may have enhanced the importance of monastic hospitality in England, and more specifically, how it was practised. The humanism propounded by the School of St Victor, Paris, linked manners with the 'congruence of inner world and outer appearance'.[22] Accordingly, it placed great import on gestures, speech, gait and manners, which were regarded not simply as an outer manifestation of inner harmony, but a means of achieving this. Rigorous training in decorum and control of one's actions were thus seen as ways to attain beauty within. For Jaeger, the founders and early teachers of St Victor's took from Cicero an 'ethic of refined bearing' which they superimposed 'onto the ideals of the apostolic life, equality of

---

[17] For brief reference to this in the later Middle Ages, see J. Kerr, 'Cistercian hospitality in the later Middle Ages', in *Monasteries and Society in the later Middle Ages*, ed. J. Burton and K. Stöber (forthcoming, Woodbridge, 2008).

[18] *Chronica Majora* 4, p. 322.

[19] Eastbridge Hospital is discussed below, p. 207 n. 18.

[20] According to William Fitzstephen's late-twelfth-century description of London almost every bishop, magnate and abbot in England had a 'lordly habitation' here where he stayed in splendour when summoned to the city, either to attend a council or assembly, or simply to conduct personal affairs, *Materials for Becket* 3, p. 8. For the London houses of the abbots of Reading, Bury and Abingdon, and the bishop of Lincoln, see *RAC* 1, p. 469; *Feudal Documents from the Abbey of Bury St Edmunds*, ed. D. C. Douglas, Records of the Social and Economic History of England and Wales, 8 (London, 1932), nos 176–7; *History of Abingdon* 2, pp. 18–19; *Magna Vita Sancti Hugonis*, ed. and trans. D. Douie and D. H. Farmer, 2 vols, OMT (Oxford, 1961–62), 2, p. 184.

[21] In 1384 reference was made to its 'great hospitality', as it was on the public route, D. H. Williams, *The Welsh Cistercians* (Leominster, 2001), p. 144.

[22] Jaeger, 'Humanism and ethics', p. 62.

manners and renunciation of possessions'.[23] This would clearly have had important consequences for hospitality since the reception of guests offered an opportunity to exhibit and develop courtesy, and was subsequently an effective way to attain this. Not least of all, it provided an audience to witness this laudable conduct and would undoubtedly have helped to curry good favour and enhance the community's reputation. Indeed the Cistercian monk, Caesarius of Heisterbach (c. 1180–c. 1240), paid tribute to the Victorines' willingness to help outsiders and the promptness with which they acted. He recounts how one student who arrived at the house wracked with guilt asked for the prior to hear his confession. The prior came immediately to meet him since he, like all the brethren there, 'was always ready for that duty'. The prior evidently conducted himself with the utmost courtesy, for after delivering the customary exhortation he remained silent, allowing the student to make his confession.[24]

The Victorine brand of humanism would most probably have made other communities more conscious of how they received their guests and perhaps also heightened the expectations of their visitors. It may help to explain why the *Constitutions* compiled by Archbishop Lanfranc in the late eleventh century is a rather 'dry and practical' text that does not discuss the reception of guests, yet subsequent customaries compiled in England set out the procedure for their welcome and also the qualities required of the guestmaster and other officials responsible for visitors. Examples include the *De Obedientiariis* of Abingdon which was probably compiled c. 1220, and the customary of Eynsham Abbey which is later, but thought to stem from the same source.[25] In fact, the Eynsham customary in places cites the *Liber Ordinis* of St Victor's verbatim. This change in the content of the customaries can perhaps be attributed to the widespread influence of Victorine humanism and the dissemination of their ideas and texts in England. It is unfortunate that so little is now known of the library holdings at Eynsham and Abingdon, and also of their neighbouring canons at Osney for it may have been through Osney that the text was transmitted. The houses were relatively close, Osney being some six miles from Eynsham which was nine miles from Abingdon.[26] The communities may even have been connected through the D'Oilly family, who held the constableship of Oxford. Robert D'Oilly I (d. c. 1093) and his wife were buried in the chapter-house of Abingdon. Robert II who founded the Augustinian house at Osney in 1129 was a benefactor of Eynsham, where he was buried in 1142. The foundation charter of Osney reveals that it was witnessed by two monks of Abingdon.[27]

23   Jaeger, 'Humanism and ethics', p. 53.
24   Caesarius, *Dialogue on Miracles* 1, bk II: 10, pp. 82–4.
25   The customaries are discussed below, pp. 13–18.
26   It is perhaps significant that the canons of Osney, like those of St Frideswide, were to be more fully integrated than other canons whenever they dined in the refectory at Eynsham; this implies that there were ties of sorts, *Eynsham Customary*, ch. 19: 2 (506), p. 200 lines 11–17.
27   E. Amt, *Oxford DNB* 41, p. 644; *History of Abingdon* 2, pp. lvii n, 32–5, 330–1; see also pp. 2–3, 10–11, 18–19, 326–31.

Not everyone subscribed to the Victorines' humanism, and it was rejected by Peter Abelard (c. 1079–1132). Another opponent was the Cistercian, Bernard of Clairvaux (c. 1090–1153), who held that fine manners were innate and could not be learned; he thus regarded Christ as the true master of *mores*.[28] Whilst this obviously undermined the need for training in decorum, which was fundamental to the canons, it was nonetheless an acknowledgement of the link between inner harmony and outer behaviour.

The guests

A vast and diverse number of people availed themselves of monastic hospitality throughout the Middle Ages, whether they travelled on horse or on foot. The late-thirteenth-century account book of the Cistercian abbey of Beaulieu incorporates a comprehensive list of would-be guests. This includes royalty, barons, church dignitaries, monastic officials, clerics, relatives, messengers, mariners and grooms.[29] How they were received and where they were entertained invariably depended upon their standing and relationship with the community. At Beaulieu, visitors were carefully graded at the door and provided for accordingly.[30] This would not have included women who were prohibited from entering the Cistercian precincts as guests. This ban extended to royalty as much as lay women, and in 1246 the prior and cellarer of Beaulieu were deposed for having permitted the queen to stay in their infirmary for almost three weeks, to tend the young prince, Edward.[31] The Benedictine stance is less easy to determine, and whilst there may not at this time have been an official policy, the order was evidently less exclusive. Abbot Geoffrey of St Albans (1119–46), for example, built a chamber especially for the use of the queen and her attendants.[32]

Not everyone who entered the monastery precinct was received as a guest but the division between visitors and guests is rather hazy. Moreover, it is often unclear when charity should be distinguished from hospitality, since the lines of distinction are not absolute. Thus, while the administration of alms at the gate hardly constituted hospitality, the poor were at times received as guests, for example, on Maundy Thursday they were refreshed within the monastery gates.[33] The presence of corrodians living within the precincts is

---

28   Jaeger, *Envy of the Angels*, p. 272.

29   *The Account Book of Beaulieu Abbey*, ed. S. F. Hockey, CS, 4th ser. 16 (London, 1975).

30   *Account Book of Beaulieu Abbey*, p. 33.

31   *Annales Monastici*, ed. H. R. Luard, 5 vols, RS 36 (London, 1864–69), 2, p. 337. See also below, p. 82.

32   The reception of women is discussed below, pp. 82–3, 139, 176.

33   For contemporary discussions of charity, see Hugh of St Victor's *De Sacramentis, On the Sacraments of the Christian Faith*, ed. and trans. R. J. Deferrai (Cambridge, MA, 1951), e.g. pp. 378–9, 381, 393; Aelred of Rievaulx's letter of advice to his sister describes charity as love of God and love of one's neighbour, 'De Institutione Inclusarum', *Aelredi Rievallensis, Opera Omnia 1: Opera Ascetic*, ed. A. Hoste and C. H. Talbot, CCCM 1, pp. 635–82 (p. 659). A stimulating discussion of charity is R. H. Bremner's *Giving: charity and philanthropy in history* (New Brunswick and London, 1996).

also problematic, but as they were effectively members of the wider community who resided in the monastery on a fixed basis, they are not included as recipients of hospitality in this analysis.[34] In contrast, troops billeted at the house stayed at the monastery on a temporary basis and are perhaps best regarded as an example of hospitality functioning within lordship. Similarly, ecclesiastical dignitaries who arrived to conduct visitation and were refreshed and accommodated by the community are included as a type of guest, although they were clearly more than guests and the implications of receiving them might have significant consequences.[35]

A group commonly associated with monastic hospitality is that of pilgrims (*peregrini*). Yet most would not have stayed within the monastery precinct but in the vill, or perhaps in a hospice built especially for their use at the abbey gates, such as those constructed by abbots Odo of Battle (1175–1200) and Hugh II of Reading (1186–99). The account of the dedication of Bec in 1077 explains that visitors refreshed at the abbey were lodged in nearby houses and remote villages.[36] Pilgrims seeking relief at the saint's shrine may have spent the night in vigil in the church or simply returned home; analysis of the miracle collections suggests that a number of these pilgrims lived in the locality.[37] Access for these visitors might be restricted to prevent undue disruption. The sick who flocked to Dunfermline Abbey seeking miraculous relief from St Margaret were accustomed to visit on Saturdays and the vigils of feasts, and were monitored by a clerk stationed at the door of the church.[38] The crowds that visited to celebrate a dedication or translation would have likely been entertained to a fine celebratory feast within the precinct.[39] The term *peregrinus* could, of course, be used for a high-ranking individual, including the

---

[34] The type of corrody awarded could vary greatly, and range from the allocation of basic supplies to men and women living outside the precinct, to board and lodging within the confines of the monastery. The latter, the full corrody, was more common in the later Middle Ages. For discussion of corrodies and corrodians, see B. Harvey, *Living and Dying in England 1100–1540: The Monastic Experience* (Oxford, 1993), pp. 179–209; for a list of corrodians at Westminster, 1100–1540, see pp. 239–51. For corrodians in Cistercian houses in the later Middle Ages, see D. H. Williams, 'Layfolk within Cistercian precincts', *Monastic Studies* 2, ed. J. Loades (Bangor, 1991), pp. 87–117 (pp. 101–4).

[35] This is discussed in chapter 3.

[36] *Vita Domni Herluini Abbatis Beccensis Liber Domni Gisleberti Abbatis de Simoniacis*, ed. J. A. Robinson, *Gilbert Crispin, Abbot of Westminster: A Study of the Abbey Under Norman Rule* (Cambridge, 1911), pp. 87–110 (p. 107). Hospices outside the abbey gates are discussed further in chapters 1 and 2.

[37] E.g. L. Milis, *Angelic Monks and Earthly Men: Monasticism and its Meaning to Mediaeval Society* (Woodbridge, 1992), p. 83, explains that from analysis of shrines in England and France it emerges that half of the devotees returned home the same day that they left; three-quarters came from a thirty-seven-mile radius. Others would have kept vigil at the shrine, and clearly would not have required lodging, see B. Ward, *Miracles and the Mediaeval Mind: theory, record and event, 1000–1215* (London, 1982), e.g. pp. 73, 94.

[38] 'The miracles of St Margaret', *The Miracles of Saint Aebbe of Coldingham and Saint Margaret of Scotland*, ed. and trans. R. Bartlett, OMT (Oxford, 2003), no 1 (pp. 74–7).

[39] See below, p. 11–12, 160–1.

king, and pilgrims of this ilk would inevitably have been warmly received by the community. But, certainly in the twelfth century the term *peregrini* seems to have defined a group of visitors distinct from guests (*hospites*), for the two are often set in apposition. For example, Geoffrey of Burton's *Life* of the fifth-century saint, Modwena, describes how she divided her monastery's revenues in three, setting aside one portion for the poor, another for guests and pilgrims, and a third for the building of churches and for the salvation of souls.[40] Hugh of Coventry (February 1188 x March 1198) conceded that the profits of the church of Baschurch should be used to support guests, pilgrims and the poor at Shrewsbury Abbey upon the deaths of the present incumbents. Archbishop Thurstan stipulated that the monks of Fountains Abbey should only spend the revenues and tithes of their churches on guests, pilgrims and the poor.[41] The term *supervenientes* may have similarly been used to distinguish visitors who actually stayed at the house (*hospites*) from those who simply passed through, for again, the terms often appear together. It is perhaps significant that the customary of Eynsham Abbey describes how the hosteller need only celebrate Compline with those staying in the dormitory.[42]

If monastic hospitality is most frequently associated with pilgrims and patrons, it is rarely thought of in terms of visiting monks who might be required to travel to conduct business or undertake research, to deliver messages or to visit their families. Yet, as the following analysis will seek to show, they constituted a significant proportion of the community's guests and, certainly by the end of our period, were often assigned their own hosteller and separate quarters. This was not a twelfth-century development. St Benedict refers specifically to visiting monks in chapter 53 of his *Rule*, and the idealised plan of St Gall (c. 820) allocates them separate accommodation so that they might continue their observances unimpeded.[43] This remained an important concern and in the set of injunctions he issued to Christ Church, Canterbury, in December 1298, Archbishop Winchelsey complained of the inadequate provision for visiting monks who were forced to seek inappropriate lodgings with laymen.[44] An anecdote recounted by the German Cistercian, Caesarius of Heisterbach, underlines the risk this posed, and from even the most well meaning of hosts. Caesarius describes one occasion when Ensfrid, dean of Cologne, generously offered hospitality to some religious guests only to find that he had no convent food. He therefore asked his steward to make a hash

[40] *Geoffrey of Burton: Life and Miracles of St Modwena*, ed. and trans. R. Bartlett, OMT (Oxford, 2002), p. 63. Geoffrey was writing in the early twelfth century.

[41] *Cartulary of Shrewsbury* 1, no. 71 (pp. 70–1); 'Narratio de fundatione Fontanis monasterii', *Memorials of the Abbey of St Mary of Fountains* 1, ed. J. R. Walbran, SS 42 (Durham, 1862), pp. 1–129 (p. 21). The Cistercians prohibited their abbeys from receiving tithes unless this was to support the poor, guests and pilgrims, see clause 9 of the *Institutes of the General Chapter*, ed. and trans. C. Waddell, NLT, p. 460.

[42] See chapter 5.

[43] An accessible analysis of the plan is L. Price, *The Plan of St Gall in Brief* (University of California, Berkeley, CA, and London, 1982).

[44] *Registrum Roberti Winchelsey* 2, transcribed and ed. R. Graham, Canterbury and York Society 52 (London, 1956), pp. 813–27 (pp. 822–3), cited in D. Webb, *Pilgrimage in Medieval England* (London, 2000), p. 225.

from the meat and serve it as turbot. The meal passed harmoniously until one of the guests found a pig's ear on his plate; unperturbed, Ensfrid simply declared that turbot had ears.[45]

To prevent mishaps of this kind the community might secure independent urban lodgings or obtain a hospice along a well-trodden route. Abbot William of St Albans (1214–35) purchased a house in London so that he, the brethren and his successors would find appropriate and private lodgings when visiting the city; Faritius of Abingdon (1101–17) secured a hospice for his monks *en route* to London.[46] The monks might, of course, break their journey at a manor, grange or a cell of their house. When the legate, Nicholas of Tusculum, left Bury St Edmunds in 1213, he was accompanied by various members of the community, including the prior, the abbot-elect and the sacrist of Bury; the party stayed overnight at a manor belonging to the house.[47] Matthew Paris praised Abbot John of St Albans (1195–1214) for the 'pious statute' he issued in the first year of his abbacy whereby any brother of the house making a journey might stop off at one of their manors if he was tired and night was approaching, and there find refreshment for himself, his companions and horses.[48]

The monastery as a venue

The size, grandeur and often the location of monasteries meant they were frequently regarded as an ideal venue for a national or international gathering. This might be a ceremonial occasion, such as a coronation, crown-wearing or dubbing, or an important state or ecclesiastical council. The monastery might also be used as a military base. Following the Conquest of 1066, English rebels stayed at Ely for a year. In 1143, during the civil war of Stephen's reign, the king took over the town of Wilton and lodged within the abbey precinct; unfortunately for the nuns this resulted in the burning of their abbey.[49] The threat of civil war in November 1263 prompted Henry III and his whole army to stay at Abingdon, where they remained for three days 'with banners flying'.[50]

---

45 Caesarius, *Dialogue on Miracles* 1, bk VI: 10 (pp. 397–401).
46 GASA 1, p. 289; *History of Abingdon* 2, pp. 142–5; see below, p. 46. It was common for the nobility to secure urban lodgings, see above n. 20.
47 *The Chronicle of the Election of Hugh, Abbot of Bury St Edmunds and Later Bishop of Ely*, ed. and trans. R. M. Thomson (Oxford, 1974), p. 34.
48 GASA 1, p. 234; trans. R. Vaughan, *Chronicles of Matthew Paris: Monastic life in the thirteenth century* (Gloucester, 1984) p. 25.
49 *Liber Eliensis*, pp. 179–81, esp. p. 181; Dugdale, *Monasticon* 2, pp. 316–17. The fate of the Cistercian monks of Rievaulx who had sheltered Edward II in 1322 and were raided by the Scots is vividly recounted in the *The Chronicle of Lanercost, 1201–1346* (Glasgow, 1913; Llanerch facsimile, Felinfach, 2001), p. 240.
50 M. Cox, *The Story of Abingdon: Part 2, medieval Abingdon, 1186–1556* (Abingdon, 1996), p. 41. Edward I and his troops used a number of monasteries as their military headquarters during the campaigns against the Welsh and the Scots, for example, he stayed at Aberconwy, Cymmer, Melrose, Strata Florida – see Kerr, 'Cistercian hospitality', forthcoming.

The great royal abbeys of Reading and Westminster were popular venues for meetings of state which would have often been held in the chapter-house; indeed, Reading had one of the finest chapter-houses in the country.[51] At Westminster Abbey, the infirmary chapel of St Catherine's was sometimes used, and 'parliament' gathered here at Easter 1229; amongst those who attended were archbishops, bishops, the king, priors, Templars, Hospitallers, earls and barons.[52] On these occasions the monastery essentially functioned as a venue, and whilst the community would no doubt have suffered disruption and was probably drained of resources, it did not, strictly speaking, administer hospitality. Moreover delegates did not necessarily stay at the monastery. When Henry II held a council at Eynsham Abbey in 1186 to discuss matters of state with the bishops and nobles of the kingdom, Archbishop Baldwin and his suffragans lodged freely at the abbey and the king stayed at the royal hunting lodge at Woodstock, commuting daily to the abbey.[53] Henry III stayed at Woodstock when he visited Abingdon Abbey in August 1255. The royal entourage arrived at the abbey after supper. This was an impressive line-up for the king and queen were accompanied by their daughter, Margaret, her husband, Alexander III of Scotland, and their son, Prince Edward with his child wife, Eleanor of Castile.[54]

The staging of a council or another important event at the monastery would invariably have affected the entire town or neighbourhood, and locals would often have been called upon to provide lodgings and provisions. The *Life of Godric of Finchale* describes a crown-wearing at Bury St Edmunds in Henry II's reign, and explains that the town was overwhelmed by the number of visitors who stayed there; this included the royal retainers.[55] The pressure that events of this kind must have put on the town is aptly illustrated in a later example relating to Abingdon, where Henry VIII arrived unexpectedly in 1518, to escape the sweating sickness in London. The town was hard pressed to accommodate the royal entourage that encamped here for almost three weeks, prompting the king's secretary, Richard Pace, to complain to Wolsey of the lack of accommodation in the town. He recommended that great persons should be forewarned of this and the lack of fodder, and advised to travel with a small retinue.[56]

51   J. B. Hurry, *Reading Abbey* (London, 1901), pp. 31–3.
52   *Chronica Majora* 3, p. 186. Additional parliaments held at Westminster in the first half of the thirteenth century include those of 1231, October 1233, February and April 1234, *Chronica Majora* 3, pp. 200, 251, 268, 278.
53   *Magna Vita* 1, p. 92.
54   Cox, *The Story of Abingdon*, pt 2, p. 39.
55   *De Vita et Miraculis S. Godrici, Hermitae de Finchale Auctore Reginalso Monacho Dunelmensis*, ed. J. Stevenson, SS 20 (Durham, 1847), pp. 178–9 (p. 178). While the text refers to this as a 'coronation' it was probably Henry II's crown-wearing at Pentecost, 1157 for *coronandus* could either refer to a coronation or a crown-wearing, H. G. Richardson, 'The coronation in medieval England', *Traditio* 16 (1960), pp. 111–202 (p. 127).
56   *L/P Henry VIII*: 2 pt 2, no. 4043 (p. 1249).

The sources

This study of monastic hospitality is based on the analysis of a large body of wide-ranging evidence, for every source potentially offers an insight to the ideals and practices of hospitality at this time. Whereas injunctions, statutes and customaries shed light on the prescriptive, chronicles, letters and miracle collections may offer a glimpse of the reality by describing a particular case. Charters might mention buildings and officials associated with guests and resources assigned to support hospitality, while archaeological research and standing remains can contribute to our understanding of the facilities provided for visitors. An analysis of this kind, which depends on surveying a large and varied corpus of evidence, has been greatly helped in recent years with the publication of new and also revised editions of primary sources. It has similarly benefited from a readiness to work with and learn from other disciplines, notably, archaeological and architectural research, and anthropological studies.

Whilst there is a vast array of sources surviving for this period, evidence is widely scattered. The process of gathering evidence is a piecemeal one, particularly for the nunneries since there are few explicit examples prior to the mid–late thirteenth century and no consuetudinary source survives.[57] The earliest explicit directives in England are the injunctions issued to Marrick Priory in 1252.[58] Furthermore, whereas the Cistercians compiled a detailed customary to be observed in all abbeys pertaining to the Order, the Benedictines at this time were less concerned with implementing uniformity of practice and produced no such blueprint. Practices therefore differed from house to house and the picture that emerges of Benedictine hospitality is rather fragmented. For this reason a number of case studies are included. Most of these relate to the great royal foundations of Bury St Edmunds and Abingdon Abbey, for which a relatively large and diverse body of material survives. However, as noted above this gives a rather limited perspective of Benedictine hospitality.

The monastic customaries and other prescriptive texts

The monastic customaries are central to analysis. They have previously been rather under-used as a source, yet can reveal much about the routine life of

---

[57]   There is perhaps more information relating to Continental Benedictine nunneries, for example, the statutes compiled for the nuns of the Paraclete and Hildegard of Bingen's exposition of the *Rule of St Benedict*, C. Waddell, *The Paraclete Statutes: Institutiones Nostrae* (Trappist, Kentucky, 1987); ep. 8, *Petri Abelardi, Epistolae*, PL 178. 113–379 (255–326); *Hildegard, Explanation of the Rule*; and also for other orders, such as the double foundation of Fontevrault and the Institutes of the Gilbertine Order, *Rule of Fontevrault (Fontis Ebraldi)*, PL 162. 1079–82, *The Gilbertine Institutiones*, Dugdale, *Monasticon* 6: 2, pp. xxix–lviii.

[58]   J. Tillotson, *Marrick Priory: a nunnery in late medieval Yorkshire*, Borthwick Papers 75 (York, 1989).

the monks and the administrative structure of the monastery. Customaries that discuss the material organisation of the convent, or a section of the customary that deals with this,[59] generally include instructions for receiving guests and may shed considerable light on the officials appointed to care for visitors, the resources assigned to support hospitality and the buildings where guests were entertained. Customaries were intended to regularise internal life, either to codify or formalise past and present practice or to introduce new guidelines and effect reform.[60] They might also be regarded as a way of preserving the community's customs from external reform. Thomas of Marlborough, a monk of Evesham who compiled the early-thirteenth-century chronicle of the abbey, explains that on returning from the Papal *Curia* c. 1206 he advised that the customs and revenues of his house be written down, since this was taught in the *Curia* and done at many abbeys elsewhere. Thomas recommended that they be confirmed with the seal of the abbot, convent, legate, and even the Pope, to prevent future controversy.[61] An earlier Continental example is equally instructive. In the mid-eleventh century, Bernard of Cluny compiled a customary for his house as uncertainty and confusion as to what was custom had arisen when the older monks passed away, and had led to disputes amongst the community. Bernard thus sought to establish the truth from written documents so that he might leave a record for his successors and, no doubt, prevent further bickering.[62] Giles Constable explains that oral customs were written down in periods of change and growth, for instance, if old ways were threatened or if these customs were to be introduced to another house.[63]

It is often difficult to know if the customary was intended to reform and implement the new, or if it records customs that were observed at that time, for this is rarely stated. Moreover, it is likely that when circumstance demanded they were adapted to suit the needs of the time.[64] The incorporation of passages copied verbatim from other customaries may lead us to conclude that these were stylised and not used as working manuals. Whilst some sections may well have been formulaic, there is evidence nonetheless that these were living

---

[59]   For example, the thirteenth-century customary of Westminster Abbey was originally in four parts and the Norwich customary of c. 1260 in two, *Westminster Customary*, pp. vi–vii; *The Customary of the Cathedral Priory Church of Norwich*, ed. J. B. L. Tolhurst, HBS 82 (London, 1948), p. xiv. Accordingly, it is often difficult to know whether the surviving customary is actually part of a larger work.

[60]   D. Iogna-Prat, 'Coutumes et statuts Clunisiens comme sources historiques c. 990–c. 1200', *Revue Mabillon* 64 (1992), pp. 23–48 (pp. 31–4); A. Gransden, 'The separation of the portions between the abbot and convent at Bury St Edmunds: the decisive years, 1278–1281', EHR 109 (2004), pp. 373–406 (p. 386).

[61]   Thomas Marlborough, *History of Evesham*, ch. 518 (pp. 484–7).

[62]   R. Graham, 'The relation of Cluny to some other movements of monastic reform', *Journal of Theological Studies* 15 (1914), pp. 179–95 (p. 182). For Bernard of Cluny's customs see M. Herrgott, *Vetus Disciplina Monastica* (Paris, 1726), pp. 133–374. A new edition by K. Hallinger is under way and will be published in the *Corpus Consuetudinum Monasticarum* series.

[63]   G. Constable, *Cluniac Studies* (London, 1980), essay 1, p. 152.

[64]   I am grateful to Miss Barbara Harvey for her helpful comments regarding consuetudinary sources.

texts that were modified and updated to suit the community's needs. The Bury customary, for example, describes the different opinions held by members of the community regarding the reception and care of bishops and the discussion this generated. It compares practices at Bury with those observed elsewhere; other customaries mention observances that were now obsolete.[65] Both the *De Obedientiariis* of Abingdon and the Bury customary refer to buildings and officials that were peculiar to the house, such as the curtar of Abingdon and the green door at Bury.[66]

The earliest post-Conquest customary is Lanfranc's *Constitutions*, compiled by the archbishop c. 1077 for the monks of Christ Church, Canterbury.[67] Lanfranc assembled his *Constitutions* from a number of known customaries, including those of Cluny and his former house at Bec.[68] The first part of the work is primarily concerned with liturgical arrangements, the second with the organisation and discipline of the community. Whereas Knowles regarded this as a 'methodical' work that is 'reasonable and practical', it is for Jaeger rather 'dry and practical'.[69] Significantly, at least in the context of the present analysis, Lanfranc barely pays lip service to the administration of hospitality. Regardless of whether or not Lanfranc had intended that the *Constitutions* be circulated, they were adopted by a number of communities. These included St Albans, where his nephew, Paul, was elevated to the abbacy in 1077, and Battle, where Prior Henry of Christ Church was appointed abbot in 1096.[70] Transmission of the text may have been rather slow during Lanfranc's lifetime, perhaps owing to a lack of expert scribes at Christ Church, but by the mid-twelfth century the *Constitutions* had been accepted in a number of houses. They included Westminster, Durham and Evesham.[71] It is difficult to know just

---

65   *Bury Customary*, p. 5. Examples of customs that were no longer practised include, *Westminster Customary*, pp. 112–13; *Eynsham Customary*, ch. 19: 3 (508), p. 201 lines 19–27.

66   *Bury Customary*, p. 12 line 29; *De Obedientiariis*, pp. 352–3. For references to the chapel of St Dunstan at Westminster and the Tobie gate at St Mary's, York, see *Westminster Customary*, p. 112 lines 31–2, *St Mary's Customary*, p. 95.

67   In his introduction to Knowles' edition of the *Constitutions*, Brooke argues for a date of c. 1077 and certainly no later than 1096, p. xxx.

68   Brooke argues that Lanfranc was less reliant on Bernard of Cluny's customs than previously thought, but there is nonetheless 'a great deal of Cluny in the Constitutions', *Constitutions*, p. xlii.

69   Lanfranc, *Constitutions*, p. xvi; Jaeger, 'Humanism and ethics', p. 76, n. 85.

70   Lanfranc, *Constitutions*, pp. xxviii–xxxiii; for its use at St Albans, see GASA 1, pp. 52, 58, 61. The St Albans copy is in Lanfranc's hand, M. Gibson, *Lanfranc of Bec* (Oxford, 1978), p. 156, n. 3.

71   Brooke, Lanfranc, *Constitutions*, pp. xxx–xxxi. Brooke's modification of Klukas's fifteen houses where the *Constitutions* were accepted includes Westminster Abbey, where Gilbert Crispin of Bec brought the text c. 1085, and Evesham, where they were brought in 1077; there were copies also at Rochester Cathedral Priory, St Martin's Priory, Dover, Eynsham Abbey and Durham, where the copy still survives. It seems they were adopted at Worcester and perhaps also at Salisbury, E. Mason, *St Wulfstan of Worcester c. 1008–1095* (Oxford, 1990), p. 221; Brooke, *Constitutions*, pp. xxxi–ii; A. Klukas, 'The architectural implications of the *Decreta* of Lanfranc', *AN Studies* 6 (Woodbridge, 1984), pp. 136–71 (pp. 143–4).

how widely the text was disseminated, but surviving library catalogues show that copies were owned by various houses in the late twelfth and thirteenth centuries.[72]

The *De Obedientiariis Abbatiae Abbendonensis* survives in BL Cotton MS B vi and is printed in Stevenson's edition of the *History*.[73] The manuscript has recently been dated to c. 1230 which makes the *De Obedientariis* one of the earliest known customaries in England post-Lanfranc. Its compilation must surely be connected with the disagreements between the abbot and convent at this time, and the episcopal visitation of 1219.[74] The *De Obedientiariis* follows the *History* of the house in the Cotton manuscript. Its position here is rather curious, but is no doubt responsible for the preservation of the text. The Abingdon customary offers a unique insight into the internal organisation of the abbey in the late twelfth and early thirteenth centuries, or at least to the prescribed arrangements for the administration of the convent. It sets out the various duties pertaining to each of the monastic officials, from the abbot to the gardener, discussing their conduct and participation in claustral affairs and any concessions permitted on account of their work. The section on the hosteller and the reception of guests is fairly substantial and occupies just over five pages in Stevenson's edition.[75] However, the text is rather obscure in places and does not provide a comprehensive or even coherent picture of hospitality at the house. Notably, it is not clear if the hosteller received all guests who visited the abbey or simply those for whom the convent was liable since the abbot by this time had his own quarters, revenues and responsibilities.[76]

Antonia Gransden has remarked on the similarities between the *De Obedientiariis* and the later customary of Eynsham, which was compiled by John of Wood Eaton at some time between January 1228–9 and the early fourteenth century, and the customary of St Mary's, York, which has been dated loosely to the thirteenth or fourteenth century. She argues that they are probably citing a common source and are cousins, rather than directly related.[77] It is not clear what text they were using or, indeed, how this may

---

[72]   For example, Lanfranc's *Constitutions* appears in the library catalogue of Rochester, 1122/3, and the late-twelfth-century library catalogues of Bury St Edmunds, *Corpus of Mediaeval Library Catalogues 4: English Benedictine Libraries: The Shorter Catalogues*, ed. R. Sharpe, J. P. Carley, R. M. Thomson, A. G. Watson (London, 1996), no. B77: 71 (p. 487); no. B13: 246 (p. 86).

[73]   *De Obedientiariis*, pp. 335–417.

[74]   I am indebted to Professor John Hudson for advice on the date of the manuscript and text. Gabrielle Lambrick had previously dated the treatise to the late twelfth century, *Two Cartularies of Abingdon Abbey*, G. Lambrick and C. Slade, 2 vols, Oxford Historical Society 32, 33 (Oxford, 1990–91), 2, p. xlv.

[75]   *De Obedientiariis*, pp. 411–16.

[76]   See below, pp. 68–72.

[77]   Gransden, *Eynsham Customary*, p. 17. For similarities between the two customaries, see p. 18. As neighbouring religious news of any deaths in one community were to be announced at the other, see for example, *De Obedientiariis*, p. 405. Neither Abingdon nor Eynsham is listed in the twelfth-century confraternity list of St Mary's, see J. Burton, 'A confraternity list from St Mary's Abbey, York', *Revue Bénédictine* 89 (1979), pp. 325–33. Bury St Edmunds appears on the list, p. 327.

have been disseminated but as noted earlier there may be a link with the canons of Osney and the *Liber Ordinis* of St Victor's, Paris, a source that is cited verbatim in the Eynsham customary and whose influence is evident also in the other works.[78] These later customaries are more detailed than the *De Obedientiariis* and are occasionally included in this analysis where they may help shed light on earlier practice.

The Bury customary, which was compiled between 1234 and 1256, has been edited by Antonia Gransden. She argues that the 'proliferation of new customs and the need to clarify old ones' may largely explain why it was recorded at this time, but the visitation of the papal delegates in July 1234 is likely to have prompted the work.[79] The Bury customary is largely concerned with the monastery's finances and resources. It discusses the obedientiaries' supplies rather than their conduct, and reveals little about the manner in which guests were received. Nevertheless, it is an exceptional source for the nature of division of guests at this time, and describes how they were allocated to either the abbot or the community, and the debate this generated within the convent.[80] The Bury treatise is chiefly concerned with the administration of conventual affairs, and it would thus seem that the guests referred to are essentially those for whom the convent, rather than the abbot, was liable. It is perhaps for this reason that the abbot and his household of St Mary's, York are mentioned in the 1206 injunctions but are not referred to in the thirteenth- or fourteenth-century customary of the house.

Although the Benedictines of twelfth-century England did not produce a handbook of customs to be observed in their houses, other orders were more concerned with uniformity of practice and compiled official blueprints for their communities. These now provide us with a clear and coherent idea of how hospitality was to be administered in their respective houses and help to set the Benedictine material in its wider context. Not least of all, they are of interest for the influence they may have had on Benedictine practice. The customs of Cluny were owned by, and presumably observed at, Cluniac dependencies and affiliated houses such as Reading, Lewes and Bermondsey.[81] The Benedictine libraries at Durham, St Albans and Westminster had copies of Bernard of Cluny's customs.[82] Cluniac monks who were raised to a Benedictine abbacy may have introduced the practices of their former house to their new

---

78   *De Obedientiariis*, p. 405.
79   *Bury Customary*, p. xxxiii; R. Thomson, 'The Obedientiaries of St Edmund's Abbey', *Proceedings of the Suffolk Institute of Archaeology and History* 35 (1983), pp. 91–103 (p. 91).
80   This is discussed in chapter 2.
81   Gibson, *Lanfranc*, p. 174. The library catalogue for Reading, c. 1192, refers to Cluny customs in one volume, *Corpus of Library Catalogues 4: English Benedictine Libraries*, no. B71: 150 (p. 443). For a copy listed at Bermondsey in the fourteenth century (1310 x 1328), see no. B10: 11 (pp. 24).
82   Entries in the library catalogues generally refer to 'Cluny's customs', and it is not clear whether this refers to Bernard's mid-eleventh-century customs, Udalicus' late-eleventh-century customs or a compendium of the two. For example, the 1247 catalogue for Glastonbury *Corpus of Library Catalogues 4: English Benedictine Libraries*, no. B39: 212 (p. 193). The catalogue also refers to the customs of 'Cadomus', which may refer to the

community. This was perhaps the case at Evesham and Ramsey where Adam of Bermondsey and William of St-Martin-des-Champs were elevated to the abbacies in 1161, and at Abingdon where Roger of Bermondsey was appointed abbot in 1175.[83] Other important and influential customaries include the twelfth-century *Liber Ordinis* of the Victorines of Paris, which has already been discussed, and the Cistercian *Ecclesiastica Officia* ('Usages').[84] The Cistercians were driven by concerns of unity and uniformity of practice, and to implement this compiled an extensive customary that was to be owned and followed by all abbeys of the Order.

The customaries are not the only prescriptive texts available. Also revealing are statutes drawn up between the abbot and convent, injunctions formulated by the order and issued to houses following visitation and, from 1215, statutes promulgated by the Benedictine general chapters.[85] Statutes and injunctions were often intended to implement reform and can thus contribute to our understanding of what constituted ideal practice, and provide evidence of misdemeanours.[86] Clauses may, however, have been intended to prevent rather than to correct abuse, and might even have been emphatic.[87] The statutes promulgated by the early Benedictine chapters say little about hospitality other than to remind communities that this ought to be observed in accordance with their resources.[88] Injunctions issued to specific houses are more revealing. The statutes of St Mary's, York, c. 1206, are probably the earliest known for

customs of Caen brought over by Thurstan or Lanfranc's *Constitutions*, ibid., no. B39: 208b. (p. 193).

83   J. Warrilow, 'Cluny: *silentia claustri*', *Benedict's Disciples*, ed. D. H. Farmer (Leominster, 1980), pp. 118–38 (p. 132).

84   For an edition of the *Liber Usus* based on a twelfth-century manuscript, see *Les Ecclesiastica Officia Cisterciens du xiième siècle*, ed. D. Choisselet and P. Vernet (Reiningue, 1989). Guadalupe Translations has published an English translation, *The Ancient Usages of the Cistercian Order* (Lafayette, 1998); a critical edition with Latin text and an English translation is currently under way by Chrysogonus Waddell.

85   *Documents Illustrating the Activities of the General and Provincial Chapters of the English Black Monks 1215–1500*, ed. W. A. Pantin, 3 vols, CS, 3rd ser. 45, 47, 54 (London, 1931–37).

86   Knowles discusses visitation records as a source and the lack of evidence before c. 1270 in his *The Religious Orders in England*, 3 vols (Cambridge, 1948–59), 1, pp. 83–6.

87   For the fourteenth-century register of Bishop Simon of Worcester Haines see R. M. Haines, 'Some visitation injunctions for Worcester Cathedral priory appended to the register of Bishop Simon de Montacute', *Revue Bénédictine* 106 (1996), pp. 332–55 (p. 336).

88   For the statutes issued by the Canterbury Chapter in 1225, see Dugdale, *Monasticon* 1, pp. xlvi–li. These statutes, and the Fourth Lateran Council which promulgated them, are discussed in C. Butler, *Benedictine Monachism: Studies in Benedictine Life and Rule* (London, 1919), pp. 220–2, 239–41, and by A. Morey, 'Chapters of the English Black monks', *Downside Review* 49 (1931), pp. 420–9. For episcopal visitation in general, see C. Cheney, *Episcopal Visitation of the Monasteries in the Thirteenth Century*, 2nd edn (Manchester, 1982), Knowles, *Religious Orders* 1, pp. 9–12, Knowles, 'Essays in monastic history 4: the growth of exemption', *Downside Review* 50 (1932), pp. 201–31, 396–436; Pantin, *Chapters* 1, e.g. 10, 39, 234.

an English monastery and have been edited by Christopher Cheney.[89] He explains that they were intended to inaugurate change and issue prohibitions, whereas the later customary of the abbey 'embalmed customs and rights'.[90] This highlights the importance of analysing a wide range of sources, since each may shed light on a different aspect of hospitality. The statutes issued to Bury St Edmunds and Westminster Abbey following the visitations of 1234 are equally incisive, and closely resemble the injunctions promulgated by the General Chapter at Northampton in 1225.[91] The Bury statutes are more extensive than Westminster's which may imply that its monks were less scrupulous in their observance or that the visitors here, Henry of Waltham, Thomas of Sempringham and Richard of Holy Trinity, London, were more rigorous in their enquiry.[92] Several clauses appear in both sets of statutes and may indicate that these particular injunctions were preventative rather than corrective; they include the enjoinder to increase hospitality according to the community's resources.[93]

As evidence relating to the ideals and, more specifically, to the practice of hospitality is widely scattered it is important to analyse a large corpus of material. A number of charters and chronicles survive for this period, but yield relatively little information. Still, they are an important part of the jigsaw, and contribute to our overall understanding of hospitality at this time. One chronicle stands out. This is Jocelin of Brakelond's chronicle of Bury St Edmunds, which he compiled c. 1201–2.[94] Jocelin was guestmaster of the house and some have argued that he was, in fact, the cellarer, Jocellus, whom he mentions in his chronicle.[95]

Jocelin provides a wealth of information regarding the administration of hospitality at Bury. Notably, he describes the customary reception of guests and explains how visitors were allocated to either the abbot or convent, and the antagonism that this raised. He also discusses financial problems that resulted from maladministration of the guesthouse, and the conflict that

---

89 C. R. Cheney, 'The papal legate and English monasteries in 1206', *EHR* 46 (1931), pp. 443–52 (p. 448).

90 Cheney, 'The papal legate', p. 449.

91 For an introduction to and transcription of these statutes, see R. Graham, 'A papal visitation of Bury St Edmunds and Westminster in 1234', *EHR* 27 (1912), pp. 728–39; Graham compares these with the statutes issued at Northampton, p. 729.

92 The bishop and prior of Ely and Prior Ralph of Norwich were sent to Westminster on 25 January 1234. These visitations were the result of Gregory IX's prescriptions in 1232 that all houses in the province of Canterbury which were exempt from episcopal visitation should be visited, following reports of misconduct. For the severity of the first visitation which was to St Augustine's, Canterbury, and the furore that followed see Graham, 'A papal visitation', p. 728, Gransden, *Bury*, p. xxviii, and Matthew Paris, *Chronica Majora* 3, pp. 235 ff., esp. p. 239; see, too, E. Bishop, 'The method and degree of fasting and abstinence of the Black monks in England before the Reformation', *Downside Review* 43 (1925), pp. 184–237 (pp. 195–200).

93 'A papal visitation', pp. 733, 738.

94 *The Chronicle of Jocelin of Brakelond*, ed. and trans. H. E. Butler (Edinburgh, 1949); trans. D. Greenway and J. Sayers, *Chronicle of the Abbey of Bury St Edmunds* (Oxford, 1989).

95 For discussion of this debate, see appendix 1.

erupted between the abbot and the convent over reforms. In addition, he alludes to various buildings and officials involved in the reception of guests, thereby furnishing us with important evidence regarding the layout of the monastery and personnel at this time. Jocelin's chronicle, in conjunction with the customary of Bury and charters, agreements and miracle collections relating to the house, means that our understanding of the administration of hospitality at Bury is more comprehensive than for any other abbey at this time. Still, it is difficult to reach an understanding of the guest's experience from the surviving evidence.

Historiography

Hospitality in medieval England, and more specifically in its monasteries, attracted the attention of historians writing in the nineteenth and early twentieth centuries, who were interested more generally in domestic and social life.[96] However, they tended to skirt over inconsistencies and oversimplify the evidence to construct an artificially coherent picture of hospitality. Furthermore, their accounts were invariably assembled from sources spanning the entire Middle Ages; they disregarded the possibility of change over time, and potential differences between the laity and religious, and amongst the various orders.[97] Hospitality in medieval England has since been considered only indirectly, for example, in the context of courtesy and civility,[98] patronage and gift-giving, and for the monasteries, also in relation to pilgrimage and fraternity.[99] The

---

[96] For example, T. D. Fosbroke, *British Monachism or Manners and Customs of Monks and Nuns of England* (London, 1817); T. Wright, *A History of Domestic Manners in England During the Middle Ages* (London, 1862); F. Gasquet, *English Monastic Life* (London, 1904).

[97] Gasquet, for example, synthesises references to the canons, Cistercians and Benedictines from the eleventh to the sixteenth centuries; much of his argument is based on the late-sixteenth-century *Rites of Durham*.

[98] For example, C. S. Jaeger, *The Origins of Courtliness: Civilising trends and the formation of courtly ideals, 939–1200* (Philadelphia, 1985); Nicholls, *Matter of Courtesy*; Bartlett, *England Under the Norman and Angevin Kings*, pp. 582–8; Gillingham, 'From *civilitas* to civility'.

[99] For example, D. Birch, *Pilgrimage in Medieval England* (London, 2000); E. Cownie, *Religious Patronage in Anglo-Norman England* (Woodbridge, 1998); E. Jamroziak, *Rievaulx Abbey and its Social Context, 1132–1300: Memory, Locality and Network* (Turnholt, 2005); H. Tsurushima, 'The fraternity of Rochester Cathedral priory, c. 1100', *AN Studies* 14 (Woodbridge, 1992), pp. 313–37; H. Tsurushima, 'Forging unity between monks and laity in Anglo-Norman England: the fraternity of Ramsey Abbey', *Negotiating Secular and Ecclesiastical Power: Western Europe in the Central Middle Ages*, ed. A. A. Bijsterveld, H. Teunis and A. Wareham (Brepols, 1999), pp. 133–46; Webb, *Pilgrimage in Medieval England*. Hospitality has been looked at briefly in the context of travel and feasting, see for example, N. Ohler, *The Mediaeval Traveller*, trans. C. Hillier (Woodbridge, 1989); P. W. Hammond, *Food and Feast in Mediaeval Society* (Stroud, 1993); B. A. Henisch, *Fast and Food: food in mediaeval society* (London, 1976); M. Carlin and J. T. Rosenthal, *Food and Eating in Mediaeval Europe* (London, 1998).

subject has been better served for other periods and countries, notably, Felicity Heal's work on hospitality in Early Modern England and Steve Reece's analysis of Homeric hospitality.[100] A welcome addition is Catherine O'Sullivan's study of hospitality in medieval Ireland.[101] In a specifically monastic context, Jutta Berger has examined hospitality in the Cistercian abbeys of Germany in the High Middle Ages,[102] and monastic scholars have maintained an interest in the importance of hospitality to the Benedictine life.[103] Yet, there remains no comprehensive study of hospitality in medieval England, let alone in its monasteries. The most extensive account is still Knowles' overview in his *Monastic Order in England*. A possible explanation for this neglect is that research has been directed on the monastery's activities and associations beyond the precinct, chiefly, the acquisition and consolidation of monastic estates and the wheeling and dealing this involved; of the links communities forged with the laity and other religious, and of the monastery's role in the political and economic landscape.[104] But, interest seems to be turning once more to the internal organisation of the monastery and life within the precinct, in an attempt to understand the monastery as a living institution and in its entirety. Notably, Barbara Harvey has examined the diet and health of the monks of Westminster Abbey; Roberta Gilchrist, Valerie Flint, and Meggan-Cassidy Welch have contributed to the resurgence of interest in the

---

100 F. Heal, *Hospitality in Early Modern England* (Oxford, 1990); S. Reece, *The Stranger's Welcome: oral theory and the aesthetics of the Homeric hospitality scene* (Kalamazoo, 1993).

101 C. O'Sullivan, *Hospitality in Medieval Ireland, 900–1500* (Dublin, 2004).

102 J. M. Berger, *Die Geschichte der Gastfreundschaft im hochmittelalterlichen Münchtun* (Berlin, 1999).

103 For example, Kevin Seasoltz, 'Monastic hospitality', *American Benedictine Review* 25 (1975), pp. 427–59; Donald Winzen, 'Conference on the reception of guests', *Monastic Studies* 10 (1974), pp. 55–63; more recently, John Fortin, 'The reaffirmation of monastic hospitality', *Downside Review* 121:423 (2003), pp. 105–18, outlines Benedict's prescriptions in his *Rule* and reflects on the importance of monastic hospitality today.

104 Important contributions include Barbara Harvey's analysis of *Westminster Abbey and its Estates* (Oxford, 1977), which considers how the community built up and consolidated its landed holdings and the impact of its actions on the abbey tenants, and Janet Burton's detailed analysis of Rievaulx's estates, 'The estates and economy of Rievaulx Abbey', *Cîteaux* 49 (1998), pp. 29–93, and her *The Monastic Order in Yorkshire, 1069–1215* (Cambridge, 1999), which includes sections on the monasteries and the landscape and their management of economic resources; Barbara Rosenwin's study of the significance of Cluny's property, B. H. Rosenwein, *To be the Neighbor of St Peter: the social meaning of Cluny's property, 909–1049* (Ithaca and London, 1989); Steve White's analysis of gifts and counter-gifts, *Custom, Kinship and Gifts to Saints: the Laudatio Parentum in Western France, 1050–1150* (Chapel Hill, London, 1988), and the recent collection of essays relating to the Durham *Liber Vitae*, *The Durham Liber Vitae and its Context*, ed. D. Rollason, A. Piper, M. Harvey and L. Rollason (Woodbridge, 2004). Additional examples include, S. Vaughn, *The Abbey of Bec and the Anglo-Norman State, 1034–1136* (Woodbridge, 1981); Cownie, *Religious Patronage*; J. Bond, *Monastic Landscapes* (Stroud, 2004); R. Donkin, *The Cistercians: studies in the geography of medieval England and Wales* (Toronto, 1978).

use of space and its significance within the monastery.[105] Additional aspects of monastic life that are currently being explored include leadership of the community, medicine, education and attitudes to death.[106] There has been a similar shift of focus in archaeology, which is now exploring the courts and ancillary buildings, to understand the monastery as a site rather than a set of buildings, and to appreciate the totality of monastic life.[107] There is much to be learned, but it is hoped that this study of monastic hospitality will offer an insight into its place in the Benedictine monastery and the landscape of medieval England, and that it may contribute to a clearer understanding of the organisation and structure of the monastery, and of monastic life in general.

[105]   Harvey, *Living and Dying*; R. Gilchrist, *Norwich Cathedral Close: the evolution of the cathedral landscape* (Woodbridge, 2005); Gilchrist, *Gender and Material Culture: the archaeology of religious women* (London, 1994), p. 52; V. I. J. Flint, 'Space and discipline in early medieval Europe', *Medieval Practices of Space*, ed. Barbara A. Hanawalt and Michal Kobialka (Minneapolis and London, 2000), pp. 149–66; M. Cassidy-Welch, *Monastic Spaces and their Meanings: thirteenth-century English monasteries* (Turnhout, 2001).

[106]   For example, V. Spear, *Leadership in Medieval English Nunneries* (Woodbridge, 2005); M. Stil, *The Abbot and the Rule: religious life at St Albans, 1290–1349* (Aldershot, 2002); C. Rawcliffe, '"On the threshold of eternity": care for the sick in East Anglian monasteries', *East Anglia's History: studies in honour of Norman Scarfe*, ed. C. Harper-Bill, C. Rawcliffe, R. G. Wilson (Woodbridge, 2002), pp. 41–72; *Medieval Monastic Education*, ed. G. Ferzoco and C. Muessig (London, 2002). More recently, interest has been fuelled in gardens and animals within the monastery precinct.

[107]   S. Bonde and C. Maines, 'The archaeology of monasticism: a summary of recent work in France, 1970–87', *Speculum* 63 (1988), pp. 794–825. For an overview of archaeological research, the relative neglect of buildings outside the claustral area, and a 'resurgence of interest' in monastic archaeology in the 1990s, see R. Gilchrist and H. Mytum, *Advances in Monastic Archaeology*, ed. R. Gilchrist and H. Mytum, BAR British Series 227 (Oxford, 1993), p. 1; L. Butler, 'The archaeology of rural monasteries in England and Wales', *The Archaeology of Rural Monasteries*, ed. R. Gilchrist and H. Mytum, BAR British Series 203 (Oxford, 1989), pp. 1–28, esp. pp. 8–14; and S. Moorhouse, 'Monastic estates: their composition and development', *The Archaeology of Rural Monasteries*, pp. 29–81 (pp. 9–43).

1

The impulse:
what prompted monastic hospitality?

Remember too how I always used to gain friends for the church of Bec: following this example, hasten to gain friends for yourselves from all sides by exercising the good deed of hospitality, dispensing generosity to all men, and when you do not have the opportunity of doing good works, by according at least the gift of a kind word.[1]

The monastic community that extended a warm welcome to guests stood to enhance its reputation and might also reap financial benefits. Shortly after his consecration to the See of Canterbury in 1093, Anselm wrote a letter of advice to his former community at Bec in which he encouraged the monks to use hospitality to secure the goodwill and support of others. Anselm was not alone in realising the potential benefits of extending a warm welcome to guests. Following his visitation of Abingdon Abbey in 1245, Robert de Carevill instructed the monks to receive ecclesiastical and lay visitors according to their nobility, importance, rank and dignity, since this would increase charity, project the honour of the church, and secure advantage in a diversity of things and places.[2] The episcopal injunctions issued to Prior Walter of Ely (occ. 1241–59) stipulated that for the sake of the church's reputation guests be shown humility. The importance of this enjoinder is suggested by its appearance second on the list of his ordinances.[3] These were clearly not empty words of advice, for Osbert de Clare maintained that it was the warm welcome he had received at Lewes Priory which sparked off his close friendship with its prior, Hugh. The Norman poet, Garnier, was so grateful for the liberal hospitality

[1] Anselm, archbishop of Canterbury, to the community of Bec, 1093, *The Letters of Anselm of Canterbury*, trans. and annotated W. Fröhlich, 3 vols (Kalamazoo, 1990–94), 2, ep. 165. St Évroul's admonition to his community in the seventh century to observe hospitality is recorded by Orderic Vitalis, *Orderic*, 3, pp. 298–301.

[2] *Two Cartularies of Abingdon* 2, C. 7 (p. 23). Robert visited the abbey on behalf of the bishop of Salisbury who had received complaints from the monks regarding Abbot John's behaviour.

[3] 'Ely ordinances and visitation records: 1241–1515', ed. S. Evans, *Camden Miscellany XVII*, CS, 3rd ser. 64 (London, 1940), pp. 1–74 (p. 1), 1241/54: 2. For dates of his rule, see *The Heads of Religious Houses in England and Wales 2, 1216–1377*, ed. D. M. Smith and V. C. M. London (Cambridge, 2001), p. 40.

he had received at Barking Abbey, that he promised to sing the praises of the abbess and her nuns to everyone he met.[4]

Concern for salvation

> Then the King will say to those on his right, 'Come you who are blessed and take your inheritance ... For I was hungry and you gave me something to eat, thirsty and you gave me something to drink, I was a stranger and you took me in' ... Then the righteous will answer him, 'Lord, when did we see you hungry and feed you or thirsty and give you something to drink? When did we see you a stranger and invite you in? ... The King will reply, 'I tell you the truth, whatever you did for one of the least of these my brothers, you did for me.' (Matthew 25: 34–40)

The main incentive behind hospitality, or that purported to be the underlying concern, was the promise of heavenly reward and accordingly, the fear of damnation. This was informed largely by biblical passages such as Matthew 25: 34–40, which describes how Christ will separate the blessed from the damned on the Day of Judgement. Their fate will be based partly upon their reception of the outsider who, in verse 35, is equated with Christ Himself ('I was a stranger and you took me in'). Whereas those who welcomed the stranger will be rewarded with eternal life and a place at the heavenly table, those who withheld their hospitality and therefore denied Christ will be punished accordingly. This passage had a profound impact on the understanding of hospitality in the Middle Ages. It is often presented as the rationale for monastic hospitality in twelfth-century texts and also in earlier works of authority that exerted a strong influence throughout the period, for example, the writings of Jerome and Augustine,[5] and the *Rule of St Benedict*. Benedict cites this passage on two occasions. In chapter 31 of his *Rule*, which discusses

---

4   *Osbert de Clare, The Letters of Osbert of Clare, Prior of Westminster*, ed. E. W. Williamson (Oxford, 1929), ep. 1 (pp. 40–1); *La Vie de Sainte Thomas le Martyr, par Guernes de Pont-Sainte-Maxence*, ed. E. Walberg (Lund, 1922), appendix 1, p. 211 line 7; trans. J. Shirley, *Garnier's Becket* (Llanerch Publications, Felinfach, 1975), 'Postscript', p. 165. Garnier had visited the community to obtain information for his life of Thomas Becket; the abbess of Barking was none other than Becket's sister. See below, p. 166.

5   For example, see Jerome's apology to Rufinus, *Hieronymus Stridonensis: S. Eusebii Hieronymi Stridonensis Presbyteri Apologia Aduersus Libros Rufini, Missa ad Pammachium et Marcellam, Liber Tertius, uel Ultima Responsio S. Hieronymi Aduersus Scripta Rufini*, PL 23. 415–514 (491) and St Augustine's 'City of God', *Concerning the City of God against the Pagans*, trans. H. Bettenson (Harmondsworth, 1984), pp. 902–3. Both works were extremely popular in the twelfth century and copies would have been owned by a number of monasteries; William of Malmesbury cites Jerome's work in his *Polyhistor Deflorationum*, ed. H. Testroet Ouellette (Binghamton, 1982), pp. 120–1; twelfth-century library catalogues reveal that copies of Augustine's *City of God* were owned by Abingdon, Bury St Edmunds, Reading and the Cistercian abbey of Rievaulx, *Corpus of Library Catalogues 4: English Benedictine Libraries*, nos B2: 1, B13: 182, B71: 40; *The British Academy Corpus of British Medieval Library Catalogues volume 3: The Library of*

reward and punishment, Benedict warns that the cellarer of the monastery should take care of the sick, children, guests and the poor, since he will have to render account for his actions on the Day of Judgement.[6] Chapter 53, on the reception of guests, evokes the image of Christ as the outsider in Matthew 25: 35 to reinforce the importance of administering hospitality, but also to provide guidance on how visitors should be received: 'Let all guests that come be received as Christ Himself, for He will say, "I was a stranger and you took me in".'[7] The twelfth- and early-thirteenth-century sources that present Matthew 25 as the cornerstone of monastic hospitality are wide ranging and include a late-twelfth-century grant to the monks of Glastonbury Abbey and an early-thirteenth-century confirmation to Reading Abbey, in Berkshire.[8] The former records an agreement between Abbot Henry de Sully (1189–93) and the monks of Glastonbury. This explains that as the revenues assigned to visiting religious were inadequate for their honourable reception, the community should henceforth receive an annual pension of two marks of silver from the church of Bassaleg in Monmouthshire to boost these resources. Abbot Henry cites Matthew 25: 35 as justification for this.[9] Bishop Silvester of Worcester's confirmation of various appropriations his predecessor had made to Reading Abbey evokes the community's great works of charity. Silvester quotes Matthew 25: 35 to underline the importance of their achievement and describes hospitality as 'the mother and mistress' of all pious acts. This echoes of chapter 64 of the *Rule of St Benedict* which describes 'discretion as the mother of all virtues'.[10] Interestingly, the twelfth-century romancer, Chrétien de Troyes, refers to *largesse* as 'the queen who brightens all virtues'.[11]

For those in the monastery, hospitality was both a Christian duty and a monastic obligation, given that it was prescribed in both the Bible and the *Rule of St Benedict*. But hospitality was not simply an act of obedience, and its significance was heightened through Christ's identification with the stranger. This may, in fact, have assumed greater significance during the twelfth century, with the growing popularity of the humanising of Christ and also the Virgin.[12] The correlation between Christ and the outsider meant that whoever refused the stranger effectively refused Christ and risked damnation; conversely, those who opened their doors engaged in a heavenly relationship and would be

the Cistercians, Gilbertines and Premonstratensians, ed. D. N. Bell (London, 1992), no. Z19: 5.

6   *Rule of St Benedict*, ch. 31 (p. 90).

7   Benedict's prescriptions for the reception of guests are discussed in chapter 3.

8   It is rather unusual, as here, for charters to specify the rationale behind such grants.

9   *The Great Cartulary of Glastonbury*, ed. A. Watkins, 3 vols, Somerset Rec. Soc. 59, 63, 64 (Frome, 1947–56), 3 no. 1305 (p. 705).

10 *RAC* 1, no. 630 (p. 467). The charter is dated 3 July 1216 x 16 July 1218.

11 *Les Romans de Chrétien de Troyes 2: Cliges*, ed. A. Micha, CFMA 84 (Paris, 1957), lines 188–90.

12 See, for example, G. Constable, 'The ideal of the imitation of Christ', in his *Three Studies in Medieval Religious and Social Thought* (Cambridge, 1995), pp. 143–248 esp. 179–93, and his *The Reformation of the Twelfth Century* (Cambridge, 1996), pp. 153–6, 278–95; R. Southern, 'Aspects of medieval humanism', in his *Medieval Humanism and other Studies* (Oxford, 1970), pp. 29–60 (pp. 35–7).

rewarded with a place at the celestial table. This particular image and thus the language of hospitality, was sometimes evoked by contemporaries to describe the state of optimum bliss. The chronicler, Roger of Howden, concluded his account of the brutal murder of Thomas Becket in 1170 by describing how the archbishop had been made a worthy guest at the heavenly table; in other words, Thomas had taken his place amongst the saints.[13] Eadmer's biography of Anselm of Bec recounts how the dying archbishop anticipated his imminent beatitude by reciting the words from the mass for that day 'that you may eat and drink at My table in My kingdom, and sit on thrones judging the twelve tribes of Israel' (Luke 22: 30).[14]

The poor outsider

> Show particular care to the poor and pilgrims, in whom Christ is more truly received.[15]

Christ's association with the outsider was central to the monastic understanding of hospitality and it was upon this basis that communities, and also individuals, were judged. Writing at St Évroul in the early twelfth century, Orderic Vitalis praised the monks of Bec whose door was open to all travellers and whose bread was available to everyone who asked in the name of Christ. The German Cistercian, Idung of Prüfung, criticised Cluniac abbots for he maintained that they did not honour their guests as Christ.[16] This identification of Christ with the outsider was an incentive also to those living outside the cloister. During the rift between Henry II and his archbishop, Thomas Becket, Pope Alexander III wrote urging the king to receive Thomas for the sake of his salvation, and reminding him of the words of Matthew 10:40, 'He that receives you receives me, and he that receives me receives Him who sent me'.[17]

Although Christ was associated with the outsider in general, He was identified in particular with the poor and needy. Notably, Archbishop Kilwardby urged the monks of Abingdon to exercise hospitality and charity with 'virtuous assiduity' on behalf of Christ since 'the name of the pauper is humble before God'.[18] This relationship between Christ and the poor was in keeping with the tenor of chapter 53 of the *Rule of St Benedict*, which was itself influenced by Biblical passages such as Matthew 18:5 and Matthew 25: 40, 45. Bishop Wulfstan of Worcester, who was a former monk of the cathedral

---

[13]   *Chronica Rogeri de Houedene*, ed. W. Stubbs, 4 vols, RS 51 (London, 1868–71), 2, p. 16.

[14]   *Vita Anselmi*, pp. 142–3. This was the Wednesday before Lent. Also note John of Salisbury's letter to Henry, bishop of Winchester, *The Letters of John of Salisbury*, ed. W. J. Millor and C. N. L. Brooke, 2 vols, OMT (Oxford, 1979), 2, ep. 260, pp. 524–8 (p. 526).

[15]   *Rule of St Benedict*, ch. 53 (p. 134).

[16]   *Orderic* 2, pp. 296–7; Idung, *Dialogue*, II: 20 (pp. 73–4).

[17]   Ralph of Diceto, *Opera Historica*, ed. W. Stubbs, 2 vols, RS 86 (London, 1876), 1, pp. 334–5 (p. 334).

[18]   *Two Chartularies of Abingdon* 2, C5, Chatsworth (p. 7).

priory, was so concerned to uphold this mandate that he insisted the noble boys training in his household observe Christ's teaching and serve the poor with reverence, for in doing so they revered Him who said, 'Inasmuch as you have done (it) unto one of the least of these my brethren, you have done (it) unto me.' (Matthew 25: 40).[19] Wulfstan took this a step further on Easter Day 1094 when, to the horror of his household, he invited a crowd of poor men to his episcopal banquet.[20] Gilbert of Sempringham (d. 1189), founder of the English Order of Sempringham, named his almsdish 'Lord Jesus dish', so that Christ's connection with the poor and the need to care for them would be remembered at mealtimes.[21] The importance of welcoming the poor as guests was influenced also by Biblical passages. For example, Psalm 41:1 ('Blessed is he that considers the poor and needy: the Lord will deliver him in time of trouble') and Luke 16:9 ('Make to yourselves friends of the mammon of unrighteousness; that when you fail, they may receive you into everlasting habitations'), fostered the belief that whoever received the needy would be rewarded by Christ, who reciprocated on behalf of those too poor to do so for themselves.[22]

Christ's association with the poor made it more important – and perhaps more appealing – to extend a personal welcome to them. But inevitably this was not always practised. Abbot Hugh II of Reading (1186–99) expressed his concern that although rich and powerful visitors to Reading were warmly and honourably entertained, pilgrims and the poor received a less reverent welcome than was appropriate and that was quite different to the intentions of their royal founder, Henry I (1100–35). Hugh's determination to get his abbey back on track led to the construction of a new hospice outside the abbey gates to provide for the poor and also pilgrims who were not admitted to the 'upper hospice'; this presumably refers to travellers of lesser means who arrived on foot and were not shown to the guesthouse within the abbey precinct.[23] Thomas of Marlborough, a monk of Evesham Abbey, complained to the papal legate that the tyranny inflicted on the monks by Abbot Norreys (1190–1213) had led to their neglect of the poor. Hospitality had been all but abandoned and, contrary to the *Rule of St Benedict*, only the rich were now received.[24] Reading and Evesham were not exceptional. Injunctions issued in 1206 to the Benedictine abbey of St Mary's, York, stipulated that the poor should

---

19 *The Vita Wulfstani of William of Malmesbury*, ed. R. R. Darlington, CS, 3rd ser. 40 (London, 1928), p. 50.
20 *Vita Wulfstani*, p. 59.
21 *The Book of St Gilbert*, ed. R. Foreville and G. Keir (Oxford, 1987), p. 62.
22 The former is cited in *Orderic* 3, pp. 274–5. For the latter see Peter the Venerable, *Letters* 1, ep. 53 (pp. 153–73 at p. 160); John of Salisbury, *Letters* 2, ep. 260 (p. 525). Walter Map's account of Conan the Fearless provides a revealing parallel. Map relates that Conan was reluctant to rob a Welsh knight who had received another in the name of charity since he had God for a guest; as any conflict with God was unequal Conan reasoned that he should leave the knight alone, Walter Map, *De Nugis Curialium*, ed. and trans. M. R. James, rev. C. N. L. Brooke and R. A. B. Mynors, OMT (Oxford, 1983), p. 196. See, too, *Liber Eliensis*, p. 279, *Book of St Gilbert*, p. 120.
23 *RAC* 1, no. 224 (p. 185). This hospice is discussed further in chapter 2.
24 Thomas Marlborough, *History of Evesham*, ch. 467 (p. 444).

not lack essentials while superfluities were squandered on the rich.[25] This particular issue was raised by the scholastic theologian, Alexander of Neckam (1157–1217), in a sermon addressed to monks. Alexander expressed concern that whilst monasteries were swift to welcome anyone who sought hospitality in the name of the king and served these visitors the finest of foods, they extended a rather frosty welcome to the man who had no lord save Christ, and might even refuse him entry.[26] There are many similar complaints, notably Peter Abelard's colourful account of his experience at the Cistercian abbey of Clairvaux where he was received with the poor when he arrived alone and poorly clad, but entered their chapter when more appropriately attired.[27] Admittedly, the community would often have had little choice but to open its doors to distinguished visitors and, having entertained the noble party would have had little remaining for the reception of others.[28]

That monasteries might be forced to discriminate in favour of the rich and powerful is implied by Robert Grosseteste (1235–54). He rather caustically remarked that although Henry III was sometimes invited to the monasteries where he stayed, this was motivated by fear rather than love.[29] Whatever the reason, preferring the rich to the poor in this way ran counter to the monastic ideal and might therefore obstruct the path to salvation. This was not simply a worry for those within the cloister. It was of particular concern to Gerald of Wales' brother, Philip de Barri, who lived between two seaports and was consequently inundated with passers-by seeking hospitality. Faced with these numbers, Philip had been forced to discriminate; he chose to favour the more distinguished of these visitors, turning away those from the lower ranks. Philip's actions caused him great anxiety for he worried that offering hospitality to the rich was less effective than that to the poor in earning him a heavenly crown. He vowed that should this be so, he would move to a different region and leave the castle to his heir. Philip's fears prompted him to seek counsel from the Roman Curia. He was reassured by the cardinal of St

---

25   Cheney, 'Papal legate', p. 450.

26   Sermon 16, cited in R. W. Hunt, The Life and Writings of Alexander Nequam (1157–1217), rev. M. Gibson (Oxford, 1984), pp. 91–2 (p. 92, n. 40). This was probably written c. 1200, when Alexander was teaching at Oxford. Alexander later presided over the Augustinian Canons of Cirencester. Note, however, that in the fourteenth century the monks of Battle attempted to appropriate one of their advowsons to sustain the considerable number of rich and poor who flocked to the abbey, maintaining that without this help they would be unable to exercise indiscriminate hospitality, Accounts of the Cellarers of Battle Abbey, 1275–1513, ed. E. Searle and B. Ross (Sydney, 1967), p. 25.

27   'It is said that P. Abelard, wishing to see the order of the monks of Clairvaux, entered alone in cheap clothing and was very poorly received with the poor. The following day, however, having put on different clothing, he entered their chapter and at once explained, "If there shall come a man with a golden ring [James 2:2]." And from then on they hated him', cited in Constable, Reformation, p. 99. Also note Gerald of Wales' complaint about the canons of Llanthony Secunda, 'Itinerarium Kambriae', Giraldi Cambrensis Opera 6, ed. J. F. Dimock, RS 21 (London, 1868), pp. 2–152 (p. 39).

28   Financial repercussions are discussed further in chapter 6.

29   Grievances formerly stated by Grosseteste in the 'Annales of Burton', see Annales Monnastici 1, p. 424.

Priscia, John of St Paul, who urged him not to alter his ways since God would judge on the spirit of the welcome rather than the person received.[30]

The significance of the Maundy

> If I then, your Lord and Master, have washed your feet, you also should wash one another's feet. For I have given you an example, that you should do as I have done to you. (John 13: 14–15)

The identification of Christ with the poor is most vividly seen in the celebration of the Maundy, when the abbot and community gathered in the cloister to perform the ritual washing of the feet of the poor, whom they received as guests.[31] The arrangements for the daily Maundy are set out in the tenth-century Anglo-Saxon monastic customary, the *Regularis Concordia*. This states that the community should admit three poor men every day and receive Christ in them.[32] In effect, hospitality was wedded to charity. This practice may not have been universally observed in post-Conquest England, but it was certainly upheld at a number of houses including Abingdon and also Evesham, where Abbot Aethelwig (1059–77) provided for twelve Maundy men, some of whom were lepers. When one died he was replaced by another. These men were evidently regarded as part of the wider community. They had literally to pray for their supper and were obliged to attend Matins, the two masses and all the offices; on the main feasts they spent the whole night in the church.[33] Maundy Thursday was another occasion when a number of poor folk were admitted to the monastery cloister for the ritual washing of feet. According to Archbishop Lanfranc's *Constitutions* of c. 1077, the brothers should genuflect at the abbot's command and bow to adore Christ in the poor. This evokes Luke 7: 38, which describes how a woman washed and anointed Christ's feet as he was seated at the table.[34] The recipient of the Maundy essentially offered a bridge to eternal life, for by adoring Christ in him the community helped secure its salvation. Yet there were two levels of symbolism, for although Christ was identified with the recipient of the Maundy, the act of washing the feet was itself after the example of Christ washing the disciples' feet in John 13: 14–15. Similarly, while hospitality to the poor was inspired and nurtured by Christ's association with the outsider, it was also in imitation of His mingling

---

30   'Invectiones', *Giraldi Cambrensis Opera* 1, ed. J. S. Brewer, RS 21 (London, 1861), pp. 123–96 (pp. 188–9). This section is included in *The Autobiography of Gerald of Wales*, ed. and trans. H. E. Butler, intro. C. H. Williams (Woodbridge, 2005), pp. 201–2.

31   The Maundy is discussed further in chapter 3.

32   *Regularis Concordia Anglicae Nationis Monachorum et Sanctimonialium*, ed. and trans. T. Symons (Edinburgh, 1953), ch. 10, pp. 61–2; the *Rule of St Benedict* only describes the Maundy in relation to guests, ch. 53. According to Chibnall, *World of Orderic*, p. 66, there is no trace of the tenth-century *Concordia* in Lanfranc's *Constitutions*, although some of it was observed at Norwich Cathedral Priory, alongside the customs of Fécamp.

33   *De Obedientiariis*, p. 405; Thomas of Marlborough, *History of Evesham*, ch. 160 (pp. 168–9).

34   Lanfranc, *Constitutions*, ch. 32 (pp. 48–53).

with the poor and marginals. For this very reason it was considered particularly praiseworthy to entertain the lower ranks.

It was equally important for royalty, laity and ecclesiastics to mingle with the poor in this way. On Maundy Thursdays Wulfstan of Worcester often dined with the penitents whose feet he had washed; when Thomas Becket stayed at Northampton with the canons regular of St Andrews, he insisted that the poor before the gate joined him and his men in the refectory and were refreshed amply in the name of Jesus Christ.[35] The satirist, Walter Map (d. c. 1209), commended Luke of Hungary who took his meals in the company of poor men, that they would seem invited guests rather than beggars of food. William of Malmesbury maintained that Stephen, count of Mortain, endeared himself to the English and secured their loyalty in his bid for the kingdom as he sat, jested and even ate in the company of the humblest.[36] The poor were present at guild feasts in the twelfth and thirteenth centuries, and at fraternity feasts in the later Middle Ages.[37] This kind of openness was perhaps less practicable in an institution like the monastery, where resources were limited and it was important to prevent disruption. Hospitality of this sort was more commonly symbolic, with a token number of poor folk entertained on certain fixed occasions. For example, in the late eleventh / early twelfth century it was customary at Glastonbury Abbey to entertain thirteen poor folk in the refectory, as if it were a festival, on the anniversaries of kings, bishops, abbots and ealdormen who had helped to build the church.[38] Later sources are more explicit. According to the customary of St Mary's, York, if any poor pilgrims or monks arrived on foot at dinner, the almoner was to send one to dine in the 'poor place' in the refectory.[39] The late-thirteenth-century account book of King John's Cistercian foundation, Beaulieu Abbey, states that every night the porter should receive thirteen poor men, and lodge them in the hospice if they arrived after dinner. On special occasions such as Christmas and Maundy Thursday, and also whenever a sermon was preached in the chapter-house, there were fewer restrictions and all the poor were refreshed in Beaulieu's hospice.[40]

35   *Vita Wulfstani*, p. 58; Howden, *Chronicle* 1, p. 229. This was just after Becket's flight from Northampton. *Materials for Becket* 4, p. 52, trans. *The Lives of Thomas Becket*, selected, trans. and annotated M. Staunton (Manchester, 2001), p. 116.

36   Walter Map, *De Nugis*, p. 142; William of Malmesbury, *Historia Novella*, ed. E. King, trans. K. R. Potter, OMT (Oxford, 1998), bk 1: 17 (p. 32). John of Salisbury criticised the Roman prelates who rarely, if ever, invited a poor man to dine; when they did, 'it is their vainglory which brings him thither, rather than the spirit of Christ', *Policraticus*, ed. C. Webb, 2 vols (Oxford, 1909), 2, p. 67.

37   E. Clark, 'Social welfare and mutual aid in the countryside', *Journal of British Studies* 33 (1994), pp. 381–406 (pp. 404–5), G. Rosser, 'Going to the fraternity feast: commensality and social relations in late medieval England', *Journal of British Studies* 33, pp. 430–46, esp. pp. 435, 437.

38   *The Early History of Glastonbury by William of Malmesbury, De Antiquitate Glastoniae Ecclesiae*, ed. and trans. J. Scott (Woodbridge, 1981), p. 162.

39   *St Mary's Customary*, pp. 96–7.

40   *Account Book of Beaulieu*, 'Table for the guest house', ch. 72 (p. 272). For a summary of the account book, see C. Talbot, 'The account book of Beaulieu Abbey', *Cîteaux in de*

Figure 2 Christ washing the disciples' feet, St Albans Psalter, Hildesheim, St Godehard, p. 38 (1119 x 1155).

Ritualised hospitality of this kind should perhaps be placed in the context of the growing trend during the thirteenth century to exercise discriminating charity.[41] With fewer resources available it was not always prudent, or indeed possible, to distribute alms freely and entertain everyone who arrived at the gate. Of course, this was true of any period of political or social upheaval, from the anarchic years of Stephen's reign (1135–54) to times of famine in the late twelfth century. Communities might also restrict hospitality if resources were urgently needed for restoration or repair work, for example, after a fire. However, this measured approach to hospitality and charity is perhaps more a reflection of a change in record-keeping, for there was at this time a growing concern to categorise, calculate and define, and commit this to writing.

The idea of the sacred stranger

Chapter 61 of the *Rule of St Benedict* states that if any visiting monk (*monachus peregrinus*) should arrive from distant parts and wish to dwell in the house as a guest (*hospes*), he ought to be received for as long as he wishes, providing that he follows the customs and is content with all that he finds there; if the visitor should humbly and reasonably point out what is amiss, the abbot ought to mark his words, 'in case God perchance hath sent him for this very end'.[42] Whilst the outsider was identified with Christ, he was also associated more generally with the Divine, and seen as a heavenly agent sent to carry out God's work. It was thus prudent to receive strangers with respect and heed any advice they might offer. This perception of the outsider is vividly expressed in an anecdote recounted in the early thirteenth century by a Cistercian monk, Caesarius of Heisterbach. Caesarius describes a particular monastery whose greedy abbot had 'put an end to hospitality' and, under the guise of prudence, withdrawn accustomed benefits from the poor. The community was duly visited by a venerable old man, whom Caesarius concludes must have been an 'angelic person, by whose agency the Lord desired to recall the Brethren to their former Charity'.[43] Such a mysterious stranger appears in several sources, including Jocelin of Furness' early-thirteenth-century *Life of St Waldef*, the Cistercian abbot of Melrose.[44] Jocelin describes how three travellers seeking lodging at Melrose were appropriately received by the community and taken

Nederlanden (1958), pp. 189–210.

41 For a comprehensive discussion of this see Harvey, *Living and Dying*, pp. 7–23. While Rubin sees c. 1200 as the turning point, Harvey points out that from the second half of the twelfth century the decretists addressed the matter of discrimination in almsgiving, and that inadequate resources would inevitably affect the definition of alms, *Living and Dying*, pp. 8–9.

42 *Rule of St Benedict*, ch. 53 (p. 154).

43 *Caesarius, Dialogue on Miracles* 1, bk IV: 68 (pp. 268–70). For additional examples of the angelic stranger who offers guidance see Chibnall, *World of Orderic*, pp. 103–4 and *Reginaldi Monachi Dunelmensis Libellus de Admirandis Beati Cuthberti*, ed. J. Raine, SS 1 (Durham, 1835), ch. 106 (pp. 236–9).

44 'An edition and translation of the *Life of Waldef*, Abbot of Melrose, by Jocelin of Furness', ed. and trans. G. J. Mcfadden, D.Phil. thesis, University of Columbia (1952), pp. 138–40.

to eat. Just as they were about to be seated, it was noted that one of the three men had disappeared. The visitors insisted they had only ever been two, but the monastic officials were adamant that they had received three men and had not seen anyone leave the precinct. The mystery was resolved the following night when the lay guestmaster (*hospitarius*), Brother Walter, had a vision in which a splendid figure appeared to him. This was none other than the third stranger, who announced that God had appointed him guardian of the abbey and reassured Walter that the community's alms and prayers for the departed had ascended heavenwards.[45] The inexplicable disappearance of strangers recurs in a variety of narratives, including the chronicle of the Cistercian abbot, Ralph of Coggeshall, who recounts how several Templar visitors vanished mysteriously from his abbey.[46] The *Life* of the female recluse, Christina of Markyate, describes how she and her nuns were visited by a holy pilgrim who disappeared without a trace; her biographer concludes that this must have been an angel or Christ.[47] Christopher Holdsworth describes this as Christina's 'Emmaus experience' and considers the probable influence of Luke 24: 13–35, which records Christ's appearance to two of the disciples on the road to Emmaus and his subsequent disappearance into the sky during their meal together.[48] Interestingly, and perhaps significantly, these scenes are depicted in the St Albans Psalter, which was probably brought together for Christina (see over).[49]

Luke 24 is cited by Osbert de Clare, prior of Westminster Abbey, in his thank you note to Adelidis, the abbess of Barking, who had shown him kindness during his recent visit to the abbey. Osbert's letter includes a brief exposition on the virtues of hospitality and cites a number of biblical references relating to hospitality.[50] Perhaps the most influential Biblical passage to nurture the link between the outsider and the Divine was Genesis 18: 1–15.[51] This recounts Abraham's warm reception of strangers who, unbeknown to him were angels. Abraham was accordingly presented as the model host: whoever followed his example would, like him, be rewarded for his kindness,

---

[45] McFadden notes that Walter, the *conuersus*, was in 'an unmatched position for gossip and story-telling' and is a principal source of the miraculous tales, *Life of Waldef*, p. 272, n. 57, 1.

[46] See below, pp. 86, 125.

[47] *The Life of Christina of Markyate: A Twelfth-Century Recluse*, ed. and trans. C. H. Talbot, rev. (Oxford, 1987), pp. 182–8. For discussion of this episode, see C. J. Holdsworth, 'Christina of Markyate', *Medieval Women*, ed. D. Baker (Oxford, 1978), pp. 185–204 (p. 192). See also John of Ford's account of the venerable looking pilgrim who requested a relic of the holy Wulfric, and was believed to be an angel, *Wulfric of Haselbury by John, Abbot of Ford*, ed. M. Bell, Somerset Rec. Soc. 47 (Frome and London, 1933), pp. 130–1.

[48] Holdsworth, 'Christina', p. 192.

[49] Holdsworth, 'Christina', p. 185.

[50] *The St Albans Psalter*, ed. F. Wormald (London, 1960), p. 5; for Wormald's discussion of their significance in the Psalter, see pp. 69–71. Osbert de Clare, *Letters*, ep. 42 (pp. 154, 170–2); this letter is translated by V. Morton in *Guidance for Women in Twelfth-Century Convents* (Cambridge, 2003), pp. 15–49 (p. 41). See also below, pp. 106–7.

[51] Genesis 19: 1–29 describes Lot's entertainment of the angels.

Figure 3 Christ on the road to Emmaus, St Albans Psalter, Hildesheim, St Godehard, p. 69 (1119 x 1155).

whereas those who neglected to do so would suffer a similar plight to the men of Sodom who withheld their hospitality. The epitaph of Abbess Euphemia of Wherwell, Hampshire (d. 1257), records that she was 'zealous in works of charity, gladly and freely exercising hospitality, so that she and her daughters might find favour with One whom Lot and Abraham and others have pleased by the grace of hospitality'.[52] Abraham's example was evoked also to berate anyone guilty of withholding hospitality or extending a tepid welcome to the outsider. In a letter complaining of his rude reception at Wallingford Priory in Berkshire, Peter of Blois underlined the gravity of the monks' offence by contrasting them with Abraham.[53] Abraham's encounter with his holy visitors may also have informed descriptions of distinguished guests received as angels. Accounts of Thomas Becket's arrival at Christ Church, Canterbury, shortly before the martyrdom of 1170, describe how he was welcomed with great weeping and joy, as if he were an angel. Abbot Odo of Battle (1175–1200) evidently received a similar reception when he visited his old community at Christ Church and was welcomed with as much ceremony 'as if he had been an angel sent by the Lord' ('ac si adesse nuntiaretur celestis angelus').[54] Hugh of Lincoln's biographer describes how the bishop was rapturously received by the community of St Domninus who welcomed him 'like an angel of the Lord' ('uelud angelum Domini').[55] Whilst these accounts, and others like them, may be read simply as *topoi* which were intended to demonstrate the high regard in which these venerable figures were held, contemporaries would nonetheless have drawn the analogy between the host communities and Abraham, and presumably have been duly impressed by the monks' conduct.

Mysterious visitors were not confined to the cloister and might appear to even the humblest of men. Turkhill, a simple rustic, from Stisted, was reputedly visited by St Julian the Hospitaller, the patron of travellers and innkeepers, who was honoured in the area. This occurred just after Vespers on 27 October 1206, when Turkhill was draining his fields.[56] The account of Turkhill's experiences is thought to have been written by the Cistercian abbot, Ralph of

52 Cited in *VCH Hants.* 2, ed. H. A. Doubleday and W. Page (Westminster, 1903), p. 133. *Policraticus* 2, p. 323, refers to Genesis 18:2 and Hebrews 13:2. See also the twelfth-century *Libellus de Diuersus Ordinibus et Professionibus qui sunt in Aecclesia*, ed. and trans. G. Constable and B. Smith, OMT (Oxford, 1972), p. 66.

53 *Petrus Blesensis Bathoniensis Archdiaconi, Opera Omnia*, ed. I. A. Giles, 4 vols (Oxford, 1846–47), 1, ep. 29.

54 Howden, *Chronicle* 2, p. 12, *Materials for Becket* 3, pp. 478–9; *The Chronicle of Battle Abbey*, ed. and trans. E. Searle, OMT (Oxford, 1980), pp. 308–9. Odo's reception is discussed further below, p. 113.

55 *Magna Vita* 2, p. 171. William of Malmesbury described Thorney Abbey as a place where women were regarded as monsters, but where their husbands were received as angels, *Willelmi Malmesbiriensis Monachi Gesta Pontificum Anglorum*, ed. N. E. S. A. Hamilton, RS 52 (London, 1870), p. 327.

56 Stisted was some six miles from Colchester. I am indebted to Professor Robert Bartlett for drawing my attention to this example. For the most recent Latin version, see P. G. Schmidt, *Visio Thurkilli: Relatore et Idetur, Radulpho de Coggeshall* (Leipzig, 1978). For discussion of the text, see G. G. King, 'The Vision of Thurkill and St James of Compostella', *The Romanic Review* 10 (1919), pp. 38–47; P. G. Schmidt, 'The Vision of Turkhill', *Journal of Warburg and Courtauld Institute* 41 (1978), pp. 50–64. For an

Coggeshall, and may therefore be reflective of monastic rather than lay ideals. Turkhill is described as an assiduous host and indeed he immediately offered lodgings to the stranger, alias St Julian, even though his wife had already received two women at home. Turkhill was duly rewarded for his kindness for that night he was roused by the saint who led him to the shrine of St James of Compostella.[57] The visitor's association with the Divine was not straightforward and there remained a possibility that he instead represented the devil. This is explicit in the *Rule of St Benedict* which warns that 'on account of the delusions of the devil' ('propter illusiones diabolicas') the kiss of peace should be extended to guests only after they had prayed. The prayer was, in part at least, a precautionary measure to protect the abbey from external evils.[58] The devil's appearance in the guise of a guest emerges as a common motif. Caesarius of Heisterbach recounts one occasion when Bernard of Clairvaux was visited by the devil disguised as an honourable guest, while he was humbly polishing his shoes. Bernard realised that this was 'a spirit unclean' and duly ignored the devil who subsequently disappeared into the air.[59]

The stranger essentially represented the unknown, and introduced an element of uncertainty, as well as an air of mystery, that linked him either to the divine or the demonic. Associations of this kind are by no means peculiar to the Christian West in the Middle Ages and are common to other cultures and periods. Nomadic societies believe that the stranger is under divine protection, and in Homer's *Odyssey* the Greek God, Zeus, is portrayed as a friend and protector of strangers.[60] Nevertheless, biblical passages such as Abraham's encounter of the angels, the disciples' experience on the road to Emmaus and Matthew 10: 41–42 [61] would have nurtured these links and given a profound significance to the perception of the stranger and, indeed, to the understanding of hospitality in the medieval West. It is rather surprising that none of the sources considered evokes the analogy of Mary and Martha but this is perhaps more prevalent in sermons. Indeed, Giles Constable discusses

---

earlier translation and summary see H. L. D. Ward, 'The Vision of Thurkhill, probably by Ralph of Coggeshall', *British Archaeological Journal* 31 (1875), pp. 420–59.

57   Schmidt, 'Vision', p. 57. For details of this 'mythical saint' and the legends surrounding him, see *The Oxford Dictionary of Saints*, ed. D. H. Farmer, 3rd edn (Oxford, 1992), pp. 273–4.

58   *Rule of St Benedict* ch. 34 (p. 134).

59   Caesarius, *Dialogue on Miracles* 1, bk IV: 7 (pp. 202–3). Caesarius also relates how a knight was visited by the devil in the guise of a pilgrim, *Dialogue on Miracles* 2, bk VIII: 59 (pp. 61–3).

60   See A. J. Malherbe's entry on hospitality in *The Oxford Companion to the Bible*, ed. B. M. Metzger and M. D. Coogan (New York and Oxford, 1993), pp. 292–3. Marcel Mauss' anthropological analysis of the gift exchange reveals that in Indian saga the God of Totem appears as a beggar, and that the Hausa tribe of Sudan believe that the only way to avoid the spread of fever when the Guinea corn is ripe is to make presents of the corn to the poor, Mauss, *Gift*, p. 120, n. 176; p. 17.

61   'He that receives a prophet in the name of a prophet shall receive a prophet's reward, and he that receives a righteous man in the name of a righteous man shall receive a righteous man's reward. And whoever shall give to drink unto one of these little ones a cup of cold water only in the name of a disciple, verily I say unto you, he shall in no wise lose his reward.'

the Mary / Martha imagery in Germanic sermons and explains that it featured in a number of polemical works, advocating various religious lives.[62] It is interesting to note that in Ireland saints, particularly female saints, were held up as model hosts; they are frequently founders of hospices or portrayed as ideal guesthouse-keepers, and might even remind communities of their duties to guests. Examples include Saint Attracta, who reputedly offered indiscriminate hospitality at Glendalough, and Saint Columba, who alerted the monks of Iona to the imminent arrival of a visiting crane.[63] It is perhaps significant that Geoffrey of Burton's *Life of St Modwena*, an early-twelfth-century reworking of Conchbranus' Irish life, depicts her as a generous and willing hostess.[64]

The worldly incentive

For whosoever hath, to him shall be given, and he shall have more in abundance: but whosoever hath not, from him shall be taken away even that he hath. (Matthew 13:12.)

Hospitality was associated with worldly gain, as well as spiritual advantage. The Cistercian, Caesarius of Heisterbach, cites Matthew 13: 12 to argue that whoever welcomes guests with kindness and joy will receive up to a hundred-fold in this world and that to come, but whoever neglects hospitality and alms, or does so grudgingly, will 'by God's just decree' lose his temporal wealth.[65] To the medieval and, more specifically, monastic eye, temporal and spiritual concerns were clearly not incompatible or, at least, not necessarily so for hospitality could offer a way to secure one's salvation and worldly position. Monastic hospitality was therefore driven by the community's concern for its reputation, by its hopes of material gain and of securing goodwill.

Hospitality and reputation: a matter of honour

The number of references praising communities and their prelates who warmly extended hospitality, and criticising those who neglected their guests, underlines how hospitality was acknowledged as a valid means of evaluating a monastery or individual. William of Malmesbury (c. 1080–1143), who officiated as precentor of the abbey, warmly commended the Benedictine communities at Reading, Lewes and St Swithun's, Winchester. He described the monks of Reading as an example of holiness, remarking on their tireless administration of hospitality, and noted that the monks of St Swithun's had limitless resources for guests, which meant that visitors by land and sea might stay for as long

62 Constable, *Three Studies*, p. 84.
63 See O'Sullivan, *Hospitality in Medieval Ireland*, esp. pp. 143–6.
64 For example, as abbess of Killeuy, her second foundation, Modwena willingly received visitors, gave them lodging and refreshed them with words of salvation, *Life and Miracles of St Modwena*, p. 63.
65 Caesarius, *Dialogue on Miracles* 1, bk IV: 70 (p. 271).

as they wished.[66] The Abingdon chronicler records that his abbey flourished under Faritius (1100–17) and could thus support the constant tide of prelates and leading men of the kingdom who came with their households and often stayed for many days.[67] The Cistercians were renowned for choosing desolate sites yet they considered hospitality an important part of monastic life. The General Chapter of Cîteaux, like that of the Cluniacs, issued statutes instructing its abbeys to welcome guests appropriately and punishing those who withheld hospitality or received visitors inadequately.[68] In 1188, for example, the General Chapter of Cîteaux stipulated that its abbeys should show fitting hospitality.[69] Visitation records from the later Middle Ages invariably addressed the same matter.[70] Praise was similarly lavished upon Cistercian houses and abbots who extended a warm welcome to guests. The foundation history of Fountains Abbey, for example, commends abbots Robert of Pipewell (1170–80) and John of York (1203–11) for their reception of guests and for participating with visitors.[71] Even Gerald of Wales, a rather acerbic commentator on the Cistercians, acknowledged that they were liberal hosts, excelling all others, and paid tribute to the monks of Margam Abbey. His praise was, however, rather back-handed for Gerald reasoned that as this need to provide so generously for guests fuelled the Cistercians' greed for land they should rather temper their liberality and so 'rid themselves of the damnable stigma of ambition'.[72]

Whereas monasteries that extended hospitality and warmly welcomed visitors were commended and stood to enhance their reputations, those

---

[66] *William of Malmesbury, Gesta Regum Anglorum*, ed. and trans. R. A. B. Mynors, R. M. Thomson and M. Winterbottom, 2 vols, OMT (Oxford, 1998–99), 1, pp. 746–7, 794–5; *Gesta Pontificum*, p. 207. For additional examples see *Liber Eliensis*, ed. E. O. Blake, CS, 3rd ser. 92 (London, 1962), p. 131, *Chronicon Abbatiae Ramensiensis*, ed. W. D. Macray, RS 83 (London, 1886), p. 336. Also note *Orderic* 2, pp. 296–7.

[67] *History of Abingdon* 2, pp. 70–3. A similar description is given of Abbot Laurence of Westminster's abbacy (1158–73) in John Flete's fifteenth-century history of the abbey, *Notes and Documents relative to Westminster Abbey no. 2: Flete's History of Westminster Abbey*, ed. J. A. Robinson (Cambridge, 1909), p. 92.

[68] For example, in 1205–6 the General Chapter of Cluny set out what punishment should be meted out to the prior if he was present and hospitality was refused, and who should be punished in his absence, *Statuts, Chapitres Généraux et Visites de L'Ordre de Cluny*, ed. G. Charvin, 9 vols (Paris, 1965–), 1, 1205–6: 4 (p. 56).

[69] *Twelfth-Century Statutes from the Cistercian General Chapter, Latin text with English notes and commentary*, ed. C. Waddell (Brecht, 2002), 1188: 1 (p. 147); complaints of inhospitality include 1196: 2, 3, 17 (pp. 352, 353, 358); 1199: 45 (p. 436).

[70] Examples include Abbot William of Hailes's visitation of Buckfast in 1422 and Archbishop Winchelsey's admonishment of the monks of Christ Church in 1296, C. Harper-Bill, 'Cistercian visitation in the late Middle Ages: the case of Hailes Abbey', *Bulletin of Historical Research* 53 (1980), pp. 103–14 (p. 106), B. Dobson, 'The monks of Canterbury in the later Middle Ages', *A History of Canterbury Cathedral*, ed. P. Collinson, N. Ramsey and M. Sparks (Oxford, 1995), pp. 69–157 (p. 83).

[71] *Memorials of Fountains* 1, pp. 114, 125–6. See, too, Jocelin of Furness praise of Waldef, prior of the Augustinian community at Kirkham and later abbot of Melrose, *Life of Waldef*, p. 108.

[72] 'Speculum Ecclesiae', *Giraldi Opera* 4, ed. J. S. Brewer, RS 21 (London, 1873), pp. 3–354 (p. 120); 'Itinerarium Kambriae', pp. 43–4, 67–8. I am grateful to Professor Janet Burton for reminding me of Gerald's tribute to Margam.

that neglected guests were likely to incur reproach. It was noted earlier that Thomas of Marlborough's complaint to the legate of Abbot Norreys' tyranny in 1213 cited the abandonment of hospitality at Evesham as one reprehensible consequence of the abbot's misdeeds, and a testimony to the poor state of monastic life at his house.[73] Of course, it was not always possible to receive guests freely and this was excused in times of adversity, for example, during warfare, famine or oppression. The anarchy of Stephen's reign meant that Walter of Battle (1139–71) was unable to devote much to the hospitality of the house in the early days of his abbacy. Once Walter was in a better position and had recovered abbey land and customs, he made sure that nobody was refused entry.[74] Excuses were not always needed and those who provided for their guests when faced with adversity were commended all the more. Martin of Bec (1133–55) successfully sustained his monks of Peterborough Abbey and their guests, despite the troubles of his abbacy and the dearth caused by the anarchy.[75] Matthew Paris commended the achievements of Abbot John of Hertford (1235–55) who 'patiently suffered the worst persecutions, losses and insults' of his enemies yet managed to accord distinguished guests due honour and provide for the community and its guests.[76] Gervase of Canterbury, a monk of Christ Church Cathedral Priory, maintained that hospitality here suffered from the monks' oppression by archbishops Theobald (1139–61) and Baldwin (1180–90). He claimed that during Theobald's rule the monks were almost starved and guests excluded from the court; Archbishop Baldwin, he claimed, seized gifts customarily given to the cellars of the guests and infirm of the priory, thereby depriving them and the monks of food.[77]

The extent to which hospitality might affect one's reputation is vividly illustrated by William of Malmesbury's account of Herluin of Glastonbury. Herluin succeeded to the abbacy in 1101 and was known for his parsimony.[78] William, however, stresses that this was not a reflection of the abbot's meanness, but rather a custom in his native land.[79] Nevertheless, Herluin was 'filled with shame' and determined to reverse his reputation for frugality. Accordingly, he completely removed the doors of his courtyard which had hitherto prevented anyone from reaching him, thereby ensuring that there would no longer be

---

73 Thomas Marlborough, *History of Evesham*, ch. 467 (p. 444). See above, p. 27 and below, pp. 99 n. 30, 194.

74 *Battle Chronicle*, p. 260; see below, p. 194.

75 *The Chronicle of Hugh Candidus, a Monk of Peterborough*, ed. W. T. Mellows, OMT (Oxford, 1949), pp. 105, 122. Boso of Bec provided for the monks and guests, in spite of illness, *Chronica Roberti de Torigneio, Abbatis Monasterii Sancti Michaelis in Periculo Maris*, ed. R. Howlett, *Chronicles and Memorials of Stephen, Henry II and Richard I*, 4, p. 110.

76 GASA 1, p. 320; Vaughan, *Chronicles of Matthew Paris*, p. 77.

77 Gervase, *Chronicle* 1, pp. 46, 54, 144, and 2, pp. 387, 403.

78 William of Malmesbury, *De Antiquitate*, pp. 158–60.

79 This may have been Normandy for the fourteenth-century chronicle of John of Glastonbury states that Herluin was a monk of Caen, *The Chronicle of Glastonbury Abbey: An Edition, Translation and Study of John of Glastonbury's Cronica Siue Antiquitates Glastoniensis Ecclesie*, ed. J. P. Carley, trans. D. Townsend (Woodbridge, 1985), p. 162.

any difficulty in seeing him during the night or day. As an added precaution Herluin summoned his officials and threatened the doorkeeper with the loss of his property, or even his ear, should he shut anyone out. Unfortunately, the abbot's efforts were in vain, for he was now accused of extravagance. Herluin was not the only one to be censured for his overly liberal hospitality. Goscelin of St Bertin's *Life of St Edith of Wilton* notes that shortly after the Norman Conquest of England in 1066, Saint Edith appeared to one of the nuns of the abbey to ask that the community pray for the last remaining sin of their former abbess, Aelfgifu, who had recently passed away; significantly the nuns thought this must relate to her excessive hospitality.[80]

While there was clearly a concept of over-generous hospitality, it was important, nonetheless, to be seen as a warm and welcoming host. Prior Robert, who presided over Bury St Edmunds for the two years preceding Samson's appointment to the abbacy in 1182, was chiefly concerned to maintain peace and preserve Bury's honour in the entertainment of guests.[81] When Samson succeeded as abbot he was anxious to avoid any accusations of meanness whilst new in office, and warned his household to take care and provide fittingly for the hospitality of his house.[82] Samson was evidently less concerned with his image as a warm and welcoming host in later years. According to Jocelin of Brakelond, who was the guestmaster of the house, while Samson continued to ply visitors with food and drink, he lost their goodwill on account of his 'stern face' (*rigidus uultus*). Jocelin also implies that Samson's increasing withdrawal to his manors was less a matter of economy than an attempt to escape what he considered the tedious business of hospitality.[83] Samson, of course, may not be the most representative of his contemporaries, and indeed the abbot emerges as rather an exceptional individual in Jocelin's account. But his example is nonetheless a testimony to the impact that hospitality might have on one's reputation.

Hospitality could therefore act as a stabilising force to prevent dishonour or, as Herluin hoped, to inaugurate change and transform one's reputation for the better. The generous host could advertise his liberality or, at the very least, stave off reproach for meanness, and the successful host was one who struck the balance between liberality and profligacy, frugality and meanness.

---

80   Goscelin of Canterbury, 'La Légende de Sainte Edith en prose et vers par le moine Goscelin', ed A. Wilmart, *Analecta Bollandiana* 56 (Brussels/Paris, 1938), pp. 1–101 and pp. 265–307, ch. 20 (pp. 296–7). For a recent translation and discussion see *Writing the Wilton Women: Goscelin's Legend of Edith and Liber Confortatorius*, ed. S. Hollis *et al.*, Medieval Women: Texts and Contexts 9 (Turnhout, 2004). Also referred to as Algive/Alveva/Alfyne, she died in 1067 after an abbacy of over thirty years and was remembered for keeping an open house for rich and poor alike, providing meat and drink for all who visited, see J. Nightingale in *Memorials of Wilton and Other Papers*, ed. E. Kite (Devizes, 1906), p. 17 and S. Millinger, 'Humility and power: Anglo-Saxon nuns in Anglo-Norman hagiography', *Medieval Religious Women 1, Distant Echoes*, ed. J. A. Nichols and L. T. Shank (Kalamazoo, 1984), pp. 115–29 (p. 120).
81   *Jocelin*, pp. 8–9.
82   *Jocelin*, p. 26. Of course this is an account by the guestmaster of the house and accordingly reflects his interests and knowledge.
83   *Jocelin*, p. 35; for further discussion see below, p. 57.

This applied also to non-monastic hosts. Gilbert of Sempringham's biographer claimed that the holy man's expenses were 'neither of a prodigal nor a miser' and John of Salisbury paid tribute to Bishop Hugh of Winchester since he did not squander his money on wasters to spread his fame but gave wisely.[84] Yet, although there was considerable discussion as to what constituted ideal practice, this remained a rather ill-defined and even contentious area. William of Malmesbury discussed the various types of givers, distinguishing liberality and prodigality; the *Corrogationes novi Promethei*, thought to have been written by Alexander of Neckam, considers the correct measure of hospitality.[85] What was approved or even commended by one might be criticised by another. Thus, while Robert, count of Meulan and earl of Leicester (d. 1118), maintained that his recent decision to eat only once a day was informed by his 'fear of surfeit or indigestion' and after the practice of Alexis, emperor of Constantinople, these new dining arrangements were interpreted by his critics as 'want of liberality'. William of Malmesbury, however, accepted Robert's explanation, given his reputation for generosity, lavish entertainments and self restraint.[86]

Not everyone was concerned to enhance or safeguard their reputation through the administration of hospitality. The Carthusian monks, who were founded in 1084 by St Bruno and fused eremitic and coenobitic living, made no attempt to promote themselves as active hosts and made no apology for their rather reserved hospitality. As far as they were concerned, or at least according to Prior Guiges' customs of 1127, they had withdrawn to lead the monastic life for the benefit of their own souls rather than the bodily comfort of others; whilst they would not deny the little bread that they had to the poor, they would rarely receive guests, sending them instead to the vill.[87] The Carthusian rationale swam against the current of contemporary thought, and can be attributed to the eremitic nature of the order and its emphasis on solitary contemplation. Indeed, Aelred of Rievaulx's 'Rule for the recluse' expresses a similar sentiment. Aelred warns the recluse that she should not be inundated by beggars, orphans and widows, but 'guard against assuming the obligations of hospitality', since she should not have the means to give to others; nor should she be distracted by the outside world. Aelred notes that

---

84   *Book of St Gilbert*, p. 62, John of Salisbury, *Letters* 2, ep. 260 (p. 526). Lay examples include Eadmer's account of Anselm's father, *Vita Anselmi*, pp. 3–4.

85   *Gesta Regum* 1, esp. pp. 556–63; *Corrogationes novi Promethei*, lines 379–448, see Hunt, *The Schools and the Cloister*, pp. 58–61. According to the Paris theologian, Raoul Ardent (c. 1191–1215), parsimony without largesse was avarice, largesse without parsimony prodigality, and parsimony with largesse was good, cited in J. W. Baldwin, *Aristocratic Life in Medieval France: the Romances of Jean Renart and Gerbert de Montreuil 1190–1230* (Baltimore, 2000), p. 107.

86   *Gesta Regum* 1, pp. 736–7.

87   Clause 20 ('De pauperibus et eleemosynis'), Guigues, 'Consuetudines', *PL* 153. 631–760 (673–4), 'Pauperibus saeculi panem uel aliud aliquid, quod uel facultas offert uel uoluntas suggerit damus, raro tecto suscipimus, sed ad uillam alienorum temporalem curam corporum, sed pro nostrarum sempiterna salute animarum in hujus eremi secessus anfugimus. Et ideo mirandum non est si plus familiaritatis et solatii his qui pro animabus quam qui pro suis huc corporibus ueniunt, exhibemus.'

although this behaviour might at first scandalise her neighbours, nobody would condemn her once they had witnessed her resolve.[88]

Whereas the Benedictines pursued salvation through the communal life and perceived hospitality as a means to facilitate their spiritual passage, the Carthusians, like the recluse, sought salvation through isolation and contemplation within their individual cells which were the focus of Carthusian life. Each monk ate, slept, prayed and worked in his cell. Hospitality was not so much a way of fulfilling the Carthusian ideal as an impediment to it and, as Guigues feared, might lead the monks into mendicancy.[89] Richard of Devizes, a Benedictine monk of St Swithun's, Winchester, was evidently taken aback by his rather tepid reception by the Carthusians of Witham, Lincolnshire in the late twelfth century, and by what he perceived as the peculiar organisation of the house. Richard was particularly puzzled that although the doors to the brothers' cells were open, no one was permitted to enter, and that while they had perfect charity to each other they 'cut' their charity to visitors, giving them a blessing but not a meal.[90] The Winchester party had clearly not received the kind of welcome that they had anticipated or would have extended to guests at St Swithun's, an abbey that was singled out for praise by William of Malmesbury.[91] However, it is important to note that Richard harboured some hostility towards the Carthusians before he visited Witham, for his own prior and sacrist had left Winchester to join the community at Witham. Accordingly, Richard is perhaps not the most impartial commentator on the Carthusians or their hospitality, but his comments cannot simply be attributed to ill-will since their moderate hospitality was noted by others, including Gerald of Wales, and Guigues specifically states this as Carthusian policy in the twelfth-century customs.[92] Still, not everyone was struck by the Carthusians' cool reception of guests. Nigel Wireker, a monk of Christ Church, Canterbury, includes a favourable report of their hospitality in his satirical allegory on the religious orders, A Mirror for Fools (Speculum Stultorum), composed c. 1179/80. Nigel, like Richard, must have based his observations on the Witham community, since the Carthusians' second house at Hinton was not founded until 1222,[93] and he implies that the Carthusians were willing, if not lavish, hosts:

---

[88] Aelred, De Institutione Inclusarum, ch. 28 (pp. 660–2). Aelred compiled this text for his sister.

[89] Guigues, Consuetudines, cols 671–4; 753–4.

[90] Chronicon Richardi Diuisiensis De Tempore Regis Richardi Primi, ed. and trans. J. Appleby (London, 1963), pp. 1–2. E. M. Thompson, The Carthusian Order in England (London, 1930), pp. 77–8, claims that Richard's tone was one of sarcasm and hostility, and describes his remarks on Carthusian hospitality as 'a little caustic'.

[91] See above, p. 37–8.

[92] Speculum Ecclesiae, pp. 246–7.

[93] Medieval Religious Houses, England and Wales, ed. D. Knowles and R. N. Hadcock, 2nd edn (Harlow, 1971), pp. 122–3.

When'er a guest arrives, with change of food
They welcome him, and what they have impart
With cheerfulness of voice and hand and heart.[94]

Material benefits

The community that extended a warm welcome to guests did not simply stand to secure goodwill and favourable reports, but might benefit by receiving gifts, grants or concessions, or even a body for burial. Thomas Becket allegedly prophesised that his saintly successor, exiled for the same reason as himself (Edmund of Abingdon), would be entombed at Pontigny in return for the kind hospitality they had shown to him during his exile.[95] When the abbot of Rebaix visited the monks of Bury in the late eleventh century, he presented them with some antiphons and the accompanying music.[96] While there are relatively few explicit references to gifts received from guests, this must have been fairly commonplace and indeed expected of visiting dignitaries, especially royalty. There are a number of examples of gifts sent to religious houses following a royal visit, particularly from the thirteenth century. In 1256 Henry III sent two fallow deer to Abbess Euphemia of Wherwell Abbey, in thanks for her hospitality when he stopped off at the abbey *en route* to Winchester.[97] One of the few twelfth-century examples is Jocelin of Brakelond's account of King John's visit to Bury St Edmunds in 1199, shortly after his coronation. The monks evidently anticipated a handsome reward in return for their generous hospitality but, as Jocelin explains, they were to be sorely disappointed,

> We indeed believed that he would make some great oblation but he offered nothing save a single silken cloth which his servants had borrowed from our sacrist – and they have not yet paid the price. And yet he received the hospitality of St Edmund at great cost to the abbey, and when he departed he gave nothing at all to the honour or advantage of the saint save twelve pence sterling which he offered at his mass on the day that he left us.[98]

Jocelin passes no such comment on Henry II, who visited the abbey in 1188, and we can probably conclude that on this occasion the monks benefited

94 J. H. Mozley's translation in *A Mirror for Fools: the book of Burnel the Ass*, by Nigel Longchamp (Oxford, 1961), p. 65 lines 2255–6 ('Hospitis aduentu gaudent mutantque diaetam dant quod habent hilari pectore, uoce, manu').

95 A. Duggan, 'The cult of St Thomas Becket in the thirteenth century', *St Thomas Cantilupe, Bishop of Hereford: essays in his honour*, ed. M. Jancey (Hereford, 1982), pp. 21–44 (p. 43).

96 'De miraculis sancti Eadmundi by Hermannus the archdeacon', *Memorials of St Edmund's Abbey* 1, pp. 69–70 (p. 70); cited by D. Knowles, 'Essays in monastic history 3: The Norman Monasticism', *The Downside Review* 50 (1932), pp. 33–48 (p. 42).

97 D. Coldicott, *The Hampshire Nunneries* (Sussex, 1989), p. 77 (citing *Cal. Close Rolls* 1256–59, p. 17).

98 *Jocelin*, pp. 116–17. See Dugdale, *Monasticon* 3, p. 105 n. d for details of Harl. MS 447 ('Rex adiit Northumbriam ubi magnam adquisiuit pecuniam. Inde rediens Sabbato Palmarum adiit Sanctum Aedmundum Samson abbas exhibuit eum cum omni sequda sua honorifice eo die et in crastino. Inde recedens adiit Cantuariam').

from their visitor's largesse.[99] Indeed, the chronicles are perhaps more likely to record instances when expectations were not met, at least those compiled in England. The Norman chronicles are more explicit but presumably reflect the situation in England and deserve brief mention.[100] Orderic Vitalis records a number of gifts that his community of St Évroul received from distinguished visitors. Queen Matilda, who visited the abbey in 1084, donated a chasuble adorned with gold and pearls and a fine cantor's cope; she also placed a gold mark on the altar for prayers and left instructions for a stone refectory where the brethren could dine together.[101] When Henry I and his magnates spent Candlemas at the abbey in 1113, the king requested admission to the monks' fraternity, confirmed earlier benefactions, and donated sixty salted hogs and ten measures of wheat.[102] The hogs were presumably intended for the sick and infirm, as well as guests and perhaps servants.[103] Orderic's account of Geoffrey, a Breton living in Corbonnais, is especially revealing and indicates what communities might expect to receive from visitors who arrived on feast days – or thought they ought to receive on these occasions. Orderic explains that Geoffrey, who had once lived by thieving and brigandage, had 'by God's grace' turned away from his former wickedness and joined the fraternity of St Évroul. He was now 'mindful of the precepts of the law' and according to the chronicler, never visited the abbey on a major feast day without a gift.[104] This would surely have encouraged others to come similarly prepared when visiting the abbey.

That the prospect of material gain might act as a stimulus to monastic hospitality is clearly shown by two twelfth-century accounts of Earl Brihtnoth's bequest to the monks of Ely in the tenth century, recorded by the chroniclers of Ely and Ramsey.[105] The accounts are not without their problems and various inconsistencies have been noted.[106] For the purpose of this analysis,

---

99   Of the charters Henry II issued for Bury, only one was issued there and is a confirmation rather than a grant (1155 x 1158), see *Feudal Documents of Bury*, no. 85 (p. 96).

100 This is perhaps reflective of their respective interests; Gervase of Canterbury, for example, is concerned with national affairs and arbitration between Baldwin and the community.

101 *Orderic* 3, pp. 240–1.

102 *Orderic* 6, pp. 174–7.

103 According to the late-twelfth-century Abingdon customs, whenever the carpenter did work at court he was to receive a corrody *in curia* and a pig at Christmas, *De Obedientiariis*, p. 366. See also *Two Cartularies of Abingdon* 1, L. 167 (p. 110), and *Materials for Becket* 1, p. 464.

104 *Orderic* 3, pp. 342–3.

105 *Liber Eliensis*, pp. 135–6; *Chronicon Ramesiensis*, pp. 116–17. For a summary of the Ely account, see M. Ashdown, *English and Norse Documents Relating to the Reign of Ethelred the Unready* (Cambridge, 1930), pp. 276–7, and W. D. Sweeting, *The Cathedral Church of Ely* (London, 1924), pp. 103–4. For discussion of this passage see J. Pope, 'Monks and nobles in the Anglo-Saxon monastic reform', *AN Studies* 17 (1995), pp. 165–80, esp. p. 171, n. 33, p. 177, p. 180.

106 For example, Wulfsey's abbacy (1006–16), actually post-dates Brihtnoth's death; the earl had existing ties with Ely prior to his visit, which makes it unlikely that his gift was simply in response to the monks' liberal hospitality. Macray argues that the

the accuracy of the narrative is less important than the fact that two twelfth-century writers used the episode, and even contorted the facts, to warn their respective communities of the advantages to be gained through extending a warm welcome to guests, and of what might be forfeited through withholding hospitality.

Both chroniclers describe how Earl Brihtnoth stopped off with his men at Ramsey Abbey on his way to fight the Danish invaders, seeking shelter and provisions. Their stay here was brief, since the abbot, Wulfsey, claimed he could only provide for the earl and six of his men, and not the entire troop. The party thus moved on to Ely, where the men received a rapturous welcome and were royally entertained by the monks there. Brihtnoth expressed his gratitude to the brethren by granting Ely a number of manors for their immediate possession, and promising certain others if he died in battle and they buried him in their church. Brihtnoth was subsequently slain on the battlefield and the monks ensured that his body was brought to Ely for burial. The community duly received the extra lands Brihtnoth had promised them, lands which the Ramsey chronicler maintained had originally been intended for his own community but had been lost through Wulfsey's lack of hospitality. He claimed that Brihtnoth's favour for Ramsey returned just after the earl received his fatal wound, and that he bequeathed them a hide of land at Doddington. Ashdown, however, has convincingly argued that this statement is difficult to reconcile with the description of his death in the *Historia Eliensis*.[107] Wulfsey's behaviour had indeed cost the abbey dearly, for Ramsey also lost out on future benefactions that the community might have secured from Brihtnoth's heirs. The Ramsey chronicler clearly intended that his community should learn from this and ensure that history did not repeat itself. Interestingly, the Ramsey chronicler records that during Walter's abbacy (1133–c. 1160) the monastery flourished and the abbey shone externally with the honour of hospitality.[108] The monks of Ely who warmly received the earl and his men in the tenth century may not have entertained any hopes of reward, but the prospect of gain was certainly foremost in the minds of the later chroniclers and was the lesson to be learned by their twelfth-century successors.

An interesting parallel to the Brihtnoth account is Samson of Bury's judicial dealings with two knights of Risby in the twelfth century, Norman and William. According to Jocelin of Brakelond's version of events, both men were amerced in Abbot Samson's court and charged with twenty shillings. Samson decided to waive William's debt, for he recalled an occasion when he was a

Ramsey account is 'quite irreconcilable' with the chronology of Brihtnoth's life; Pope maintains that Brihtnoth already had ties with the monks of Ely, which suggests that the earl's munificence was not simply a mark of gratitude, *Chronicon Ramensiensis*, pp. 117, n. 4. 171, n. 33.

107 *Chronicon Ramensiensis*, p. 117; Ashdown, *English and Norse Documents*, p. 277.

108 *Chronicon Ramensiensis*, p. 336. Ely apparently sustained its reputation for hospitality throughout the twelfth century for Osbert de Clare, prior of Westminster, stayed with the community during his period of exile (pre-1123) and praised the kindness of his reception there, Osbert de Clare, *Letters*, ep. 42 (p. 157).

claustral monk returning from Durham and William had honourably lodged him. On that same occasion, Norman had refused to accommodate him and Samson now demanded the full payment from him.[109] It was clearly prudent that hosts erred on the side of caution and welcomed all strangers warmly, lest there were repercussions. The importance of receiving strangers with honour, lest they were of noble birth, is a recurring motif in the romance literature. For example, in the 'Romance of Horn', King Gudreche of Ireland advises his son to honour the stranger, whom he suspects is well born – 'The honour you show him will be turned to good account.'[110] Walter Map's account of how Godwine, the lowly son of a cowherd, became earl of Gloucester is equally revealing and has obvious parallels with Abraham's reception of the angels. Map explains that when Godwine was visited by King Aethelred (978–1016), he eagerly attended his guest and supplied him with all that was needed, even though he was unaware of his visitor's true identity. Godwine was well recompensed for his efforts. He was later taken into the king's chambers and given the earldom of Gloucester.[111]

It has been argued that hospitality was 'a political performance' that was employed as a 'diplomatic tool' and might yield gifts and foster good relations.[112] This may certainly have been true at times and communities, no doubt, often saw the arrival of a distinguished person as an opportunity to negotiate a favour. On other occasions, however, hospitality was less calculated; for example, when the guest made an impromptu visit. Nevertheless, the quick-thinking abbot might seize the opportunity to make a request. This may have been the case at Abingdon in the early twelfth century when Henry I's queen, Matilda, was passing through Abingdon and made a detour to the abbey to celebrate the feast of the Assumption.[113] It is not clear if Abbot Faritius (1100–17) had advance warning of the queen's arrival, but he seized this chance to request a favour and asked that she grant his monks a suitable lodging place to stay on their arduous journey to London. Matilda responded favourably and granted the community an appropriate spot some fifteen miles from London, which was near to woods, meadows and markets.[114] Abbot Robert (1151–66) of St Albans was equally prudent when King Stephen (1135–54) visited his abbey and used the occasion to raise an issue that had been agitating his community for some time. Robert extended a warm welcome to his regal guest, presenting him with fitting gifts, and threw himself at the king's feet after Mass to make an emotive plea. Robert complained that so-called royal

---

109 *Jocelin*, pp. 44–5.
110 *The Romance of Horn*, ed. M. K. Pope, 2 vols, ANTS, 9–10, 12–13 (Oxford, 1955–64), 1, lines 2379–81. For further discussion of this motif see Kerr, 'The open door', pp. 326–7. This is a common theme elsewhere – one need only think of the example of Odysseus.
111 Map, *De Nugis*, pp. 412–14.
112 Cownie, *Religious Patronage*, p. 138.
113 This was probably 1104, see *History of Abingdon* 2, p. 143, n. 341.
114 *History of Abingdon* 2, pp. 142–4. Matilda granted the community a certain Robert, who lived in the neighbourhood of the causeway of Colnbrook, together with all his land, for their long and laborious passage to London.

retainers, who claimed to be guardians of the peace and faithful servants to the king, had taken up residence in the ruins of Kingsbury Castle where they were disrupting the peace and the country. They had seemingly built a small tower of sorts amongst the ruins as a dwelling and a refuge. Robert pleaded with Stephen to put an end to this disturbance, and his request was evidently heeded, for the remains were duly levelled to the ground and the land was ploughed.[115] While the opportunity to engage in a spot of royal lobbying may not have been a primary incentive behind hospitality, especially when visits were unexpected, it would nonetheless have offered the monks some consolation for their efforts.

Gifts might be given by guests and also, as the previous example shows, to guests, but there were other advantages to be gained from visitors. The community might receive advice in spiritual or worldly matters – and the guest may, of course, have come specifically to offer counsel or to arbitrate.[116] It was likely expected that venerable guests would share their wisdom with the monks, evocative of Christ who, as a guest, shared his teachings with those gathered around Him.[117] When Hugh of Lincoln recovered his rights as patron of Eynsham Abbey, Oxfordshire, he visited the monastery for eight days and edified the brethren 'by the wine of his good humour and the excellent fare of his kindliness.'[118] During his visit to England in the late eleventh century, Anselm of Bec stopped off at Christ Church, Canterbury, where he was honourably welcomed by the monks of the cathedral priory and received into their fraternity. Anselm stayed for several days with the community and demonstrated his humility by taking his place with the monks and speaking with them in the chapter-house and cloister. Of course, the very fact that Anselm was permitted to mingle with the community was also a mark of his authority.[119] On his journey to Rome, c. 1140, Malachy, bishop of Down, reputedly 'gladdened his hosts with his presence and deeds, advice and miracles'.[120] The host community did not simply benefit from wisdom and guidance imparted by their guests; the fact that a venerable figure had visited the community and mingled with the monks would have invariably reflected well on the monastery and enhanced its reputation. It is thus significant that during the bid for Edmund of Abingdon's canonisation, c. 1241, both the monks of Reading and the canons of Merton claimed to have

---

115 GASA 1, pp. 121–2. See 3, pp. xxiii–xxiv, for Riley's translation of the episode. He dates this to the end of Stephen's reign.

116 Henry II and various prelates visited Christ Church, Canterbury, during the controversy between Baldwin and the monks, see Gervase, *Chronicle* 1, pp. 348–9, pp. 353–4, pp. 394–5. See pp. 428–9, for the proposed visit by the bishop of Ostia.

117 See Mark 1: 29–34 and Luke 7: 36–50.

118 *Magna Vita* 2, p. 42.

119 *Vita Anselmi*, pp. 48–50; see below, p. 164. Anselm made this journey to England to visit Bec's possessions in 1079, shortly after his consecration to the abbacy of Bec.

120 Jocelin of Furness, *Life of Waldef*, bk 1 ch. 8 (27), p. 112 (tr. p. 232). For similar examples see Archbishop Lanfranc's participation at Bec in 1077, *Vita Herluini*, p. 105, and Thomas Becket's participation with the brethren of Christ Church, Canterbury, *Materials for Becket* 3, p. 39.

entertained the holy man.[121] The guest / host relationship could be mutually advantageous, and visitors might benefit from their spiritual exchanges with the host community. When Hugh of Lincoln visited the Carthusians at La Grande Chartreuse in 1200, he stayed in the lower house for several days so that the lay brethren might enjoy his discourse and he, in turn, might feast on their disciplined conduct and conversation 'as if it were the anteroom of the kingdom of God'.[122]

The venerable visitor might offer help of a more practical nature, this being a testimony to his humility and industry. Whenever Gilbert of Sempringham stopped off at a religious house to break up a long and hard journey, he did not, reputedly, 'eat the bread of idleness' (Proverbs, 31:27) but gave advice and assistance on important business. Gilbert also worked during his stay and either copied books, constructed household articles or helped with the building work.[123] Bishop Hugh of Lincoln was perhaps the most industrious guest, and according to his biographer Hugh loved nothing better than to help with the washing up whenever he visited his old house at Witham.[124]

Hospitality was clearly integral to monastic life and society at large. But the admission of guests within the precinct required caution lest this impeded, rather than fulfilled, monastic observance. This discussion suggests that monastic hospitality was motivated by both spiritual and worldly concerns, and that the two were not mutually exclusive. Moreover, many of the ideals that inspired Benedictine hospitality were shared by other orders and also non-monastic hosts. These conclusions are based largely on ecclesiastical and monastic sources, and as such reflect the monks' perceptions. It is interesting, however, to consider what others identified as the impetus behind monastic hospitality. There is ample evidence to suggest that contemporaries deemed it both right and proper that monasteries should exercise hospitality. For example, in a charter to the Cistercians of Aberconwy in 1199, Prince Llewelyn of Wales stated that it behoved the monks to give food and lodging to travellers and guests.[125] However, there is little explicit evidence of what they thought motivated monastic hospitality. Two men who did voice an opinion on the matter were Walter Map and Gerald of Wales. Whereas Walter thought that the monks were motivated by greed, Gerald believed that they were driven by hopes of salvation; both men expressed these views in their characteristically caustic and colourful tones.[126] According to Walter, the monks were avaricious and discriminating hosts who preyed on their guests 'as the hawk spies on the frightened lark'. He complained that knights who had wasted their patrimony and those whom the monks feared or intended to fleece, were urged to come inside the monastery and be lavishly entertained, yet others, including the

121   See the introduction to the 'Vision of the monk of Eynsham', *Eynsham Cartulary*, ed. H. E. Salter, 2 vols, Oxford Historical Society 49, 51 (Oxford, 1906–8) 2, p. 270.
122   *Magna Vita* 2, pp. 165–6.
123   *Book of St Gilbert*, p. 58. Chapter 48 of the *Rule* discusses the daily manual labour, and claims 'idleness is an enemy of the soul', *Rule of St Benedict*, ch. 48 (p. 122).
124   *Magna Vita* 2, p. 50.
125   D. H. Williams, *The Cistercians in the Early Middle Ages* (Leominster, 1998), p. 124.
126   Walter makes no distinction between Cistercians and Benedictines.

secular clergy, received an altogether cooler reception.[127] Walter is hardly the most impartial commentator on the monastic orders, and there are plenty of examples of secular clerics enjoying the monks' hospitality, amongst them, Gerald of Wales who in 1179 dined with the monks of Christ Church, Canterbury, to celebrate the feast of Holy Trinity.[128] Still, Walter's complaints were not wholly unfounded and the later customaries, including that of Bury St Edmunds, are a testimony to this distinction and separation of guests.[129] Gerald of Wales's invective against the Cistercian Order criticised their untoward methods of financing hospitality and argued that their exploitative policies undermined any hopes of salvation. Gerald evoked the scene at Judgement Day to illustrate this point, and in so doing identified Matthew 25, albeit inadvertently, as the primary impetus behind monastic hospitality,

> What shall they answer who seize other men's goods, and have then given it away in alms? They will say: 'O, Lord, in thy name we have done charitable deeds, we have fed the poor, we have clothed the naked, we have fed and received the stranger at the gate. The Lord will answer: 'You speak of what you have given away, but you do not mention the fact that you have stolen it in the first place. You are mindful of those whom you have fed, but you have forgotten those whom you have destroyed.[130]

---

[127] Map, *De Nugis*, p. 84. However, greed is something of a personal crusade for Walter; see *De Nugis*, p. 68, for his criticism of the Hospitallers.
[128] *Speculum Ecclesiae*, pp. 39–41.
[129] This is discussed in chapter 4.
[130] 'Itinerarium Kambriae', p. 44; Thorpe's translation, *Journey through Wales*, p. 104.

2

The Administrative Structure

Let the care of the guesthouse be entrusted to a brother whose soul is possessed with the fear of God: let there be sufficient beds prepared there and let the house of God be governed by prudent men.[1]

The twelfth century saw significant changes to the administrative and social organisation of the monastery. The growing withdrawal of the abbot from communal life meant that he might have his own quarters and household, and was frequently absent from the monastery leaving the prior in command. Related to this was the division of revenues between the abbot and convent, a lengthy process that began in a number of houses from the mid-twelfth century. There was an increase also in the number of monastic officials appointed who might now be assigned independent revenues and delegate much of their work to lay assistants. These developments had significant implications for the administration of hospitality and Benedict's prescriptions in his *Rule* were adapted to suit contemporary needs. This was not a contravention of the *Rule* for Benedict had envisaged that this should be a beginning, a framework that communities could modify according to their needs and circumstances.

These changes to monastic organisation meant that from the twelfth century the abbot and convent might each be made responsible for a specific group or groups of visitors, whom they were to receive, accommodate and finance during their stay. These developments would have affected guests as much as their hosts, shaping the manner and course of their visit from their arrival until their departure. They determined where they were entertained, whom they encountered and what they were served at table. The precise arrangements are not always easy to fathom for the sources are often ambiguous and there are few standing remains. It is thus particularly difficult to identify where exactly the guest lodgings stood. The complexities of these arrangements are discussed later in the chapter but it is useful here to outline the basic procedure at Bury St Edmunds and the divisions implemented. A Benedictine monk visiting Bury in the early/mid-thirteenth century would have been received at the gate of the abbey and escorted to the inner court and claustral area where he was probably met in the parlour by the intern hosteller or his assistant. During his stay he would have dined either with the brethren in the refectory or in

---

1   *Rule of St Benedict*, ch. 53 (p. 136).

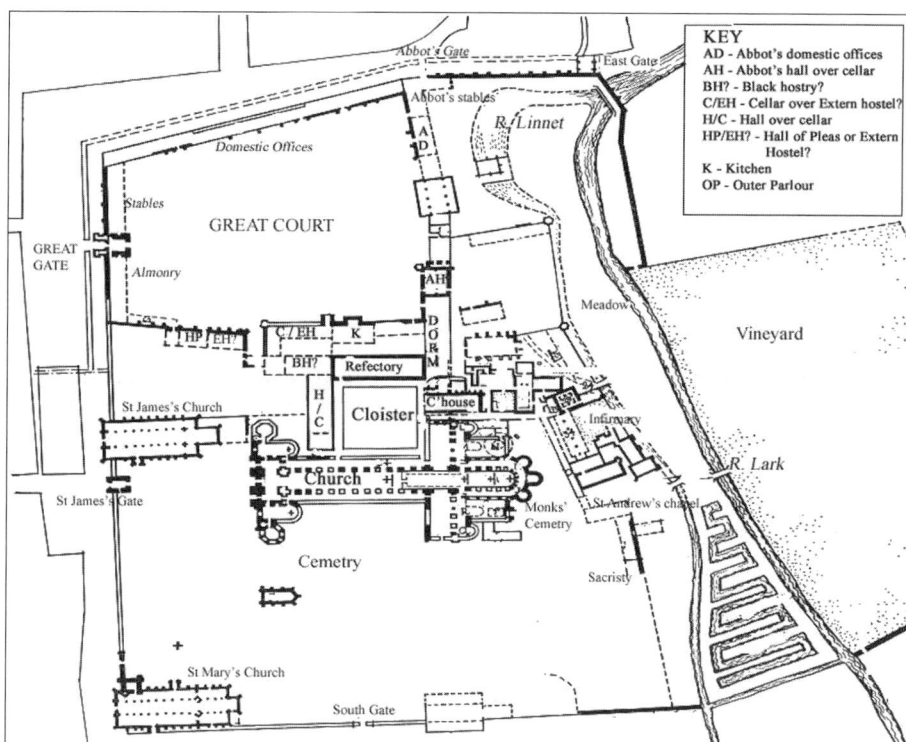

KEY
AD - Abbot's domestic offices
AH - Abbot's hall over cellar
BH? - Black hostry?
C/EH - Cellar over Extern hostel?
H/C? - Hall over cellar
HP/EH? - Hall of Pleas or Extern Hostel?
K - Kitchen
OP - Outer Parlour

Figure 4 Conjectural plan of the abbey precinct, Bury St Edmunds.

an adjacent chamber, and slept in the Black hostelry which would have been in or around the claustral area; a conjectural location is shown on the plan. A Benedictine prelate, such as a visiting abbot or episcopal prior, would have been directed to the abbot's court and received by members of his household who would have organised accommodation and refreshment in this area of the precinct. A Cistercian monk or Augustinian canon who visited the abbey at this time would have been entertained outside the claustral area in the extern hosteller's hall. It is not known where this hall was situated but two possible locations are marked on the plan.[2]

To understand the impact that these developments had on the administration of hospitality, it is helpful to consider briefly the division of revenues and the emergence of what is known as the obedientiary system.[3] The mid-twelfth century marked the first true division of the monastery's resources

---

[2] These arrangements are discussed in more detail later in the chapter and in subsequent chapters.

[3] The 'obedientiary system' is described by Knowles as 'the manner in which the revenues of the house were allotted to departmental officials and administered by them, and which resulted in a vast scheme of devolution', D. Knowles, *The Monastic Order in England: a history of its development from the times of St Dunstan to the Fourth Lateran Council, 940–1216*, 2nd edn (Cambridge, 1963), p. 431.

between the abbot and the monks, and the subsequent distribution of the community's share amongst the obedientiaries of the house. This was a long and gradual process that was preceded by the division of revenues between the bishop and chapter.[4] The origins of division remain unclear but are here of less consequence than its impact on the administration of hospitality.[5] Division was not absolute. The brethren's portion might, for example, be used to feed the abbot; certainly, he was provided for from the community's revenues whenever he dined in the refectory.[6]

The mid-twelfth century heralded the formal distinction between the abbot's and convent's revenues, although piecemeal allocations had previously been assigned to specific causes. The first rumblings of division at Peterborough Abbey, for example, can be traced to a charter of 1107 x 15, whereby the knights of the abbey were to give two thirds of their tithes to the sacristy.[7] The division of revenues between the abbot and convent at Abingdon probably occurred in the early twelfth century when the obedientiary system was introduced.[8] The Abingdon chronicle records that Faritius (1100–17) made grants to the monks' chamber and refectory, and earmarked revenues for alms, as well as for parchment to renew books in the church and for a fire to warm the sick and bloodlet in the house of the infirm.[9] Barbara Harvey's comprehensive analysis of the division of revenues at Westminster Abbey reveals a similar pattern. Here, signs of division can be traced to Gilbert Crispin's abbacy (1085–1117/18), when the abbot allocated seventy pounds annually to the monks' chamber to clothe eighty brothers. A grant of almost sixty pounds was later assigned for alms, the monks' pittances and fuel, to support their servants and also for the Maundy; from this time 'an obedientiary system

4   The division of revenues has been the subject of considerable interest and discussion; see, for example Knowles, *Monastic Order*, pp. 404–6, 434–7, 612–15, 625–6; G. Lambrick, 'Abingdon abbey administration', *JEH* 17 (1966), pp. 159–83 (pp. 165–8). For discussion of this division in relation to vacancies, see E. John, 'The division of the *mensa* in early English monasteries', *JEH* 6 (1955), pp. 143–55; M. Howell, *Regalian Rights in England* (London, 1962); M. Howell, 'Abbatial vacancies and the divided *mensa* in medieval England', *JEH* 33 (1982), pp. 173–92; L. H. Jared, 'English ecclesiastical vacancies during the reigns of William II and Henry I', *JEH* 42 (1991), pp. 362–93.

5   Knowles, *Monastic Order*, p. 757. For a useful historiographical summary of this debate, see E. U. Crosby, *Bishop and Chapter in Twelfth-Century England: a study of the Mensa Episcopalis* (Cambridge, 1994), pp. 1–9. Crosby acknowledges that the origins of episcopal separation can be traced to the Anglo-Saxon period, but questions what exactly is meant by 'essential separation' and 'vital change', and concludes that the 'sufficient disagreement' over the nature and origins of the division of the *mensa* 'warrants another look', Crosby, *Bishop and Chapter*, pp. 6–7.

6   Howell, 'Abbatial vacancies, p. 175.

7   E. King, *Peterborough Abbey, 1086–1310: a study in the land market* (Cambridge, 1973), p. 88. He cites a grant of 1117 as more direct evidence for this division, as it assigned revenues 'ad opus monasterii' and 'ad opus abbatis'.

8   *Two Cartularies of Abingdon* 2, pp. xliii, xlv.

9   *History of Abingdon* 2, pp. 216–19. For additional references, see Howell, 'Abbatial vacancies', p. 174, n. 5; see below, p. 56, for division at Bury.

began to take shape'.[10] It was not, however, until William de Humez (1214–22) made a perpetual grant of c. £150 to the community, that there was a 'true division' of revenues. The importance of William's grant was clearly not lost on the monks, who cited this in their main chartularies, where relevant.[11] The division of revenues between the abbot and convent occurred at different times in different places, and whilst widespread was not universal. For example, there was no distinction of this kind at either Battle Abbey, in Sussex, Reading Abbey in Berkshire or the nunneries of Barking, Shaftesbury and Wilton.[12] Nor was there a division of this sort in Cistercian houses. At Beaulieu Abbey, Hampshire, in the late thirteenth century, distinguished visitors were provided for from the common fund rather than the hosteller's although it was the guestmaster who tended them.[13]

The obedientiary system had its origins in the domestic posts named in the *Rule of St Benedict*, namely, the cellarer, the guestmaster, the brothers responsible for the iron, tools, clothes and other property belonging to the house, and the brother appointed to care for the sick.[14] Benedict named relatively few fixed posts for he envisaged that most duties would be rotated on a weekly basis, such as serving in the kitchen and reading in the refectory.[15] This would not only ensure that each monk pulled his weight, but was intended to suppress jealousies. The growing complexity of monastic administration, and the increased burden this placed on each official, led to the creation of additional posts including the almoner, precentor and kitchener.[16] It also meant that officials might be assigned the help of deputies and lay assistants, while they themselves assumed a more managerial role. Accordingly, the obedientiaries were no longer responsible simply for domestic duties, but contributed more directly to the management of the house. In post-Conquest

---

10   Harvey, *Westminster Abbey*, pp. 85–91, esp. p. 85. See, too, *Westminster Customary*, p. 149, and Robinson, *Gilbert Crispin*, p. 30.

11   Harvey, *Westminster Abbey*, p. 86. Division was taken further in the agreement of 1225.

12   Howell, 'Abbatial vacancies', pp. 180–1; *Accounts of Cellarers of Battle*, p. 8; B. Harvey, 'The aristocratic consumer in England in the long thirteenth century', *Thirteenth-Century England* 6, ed. M. Prestwich, R. H. Britnell and R. Frame (Woodbridge, 1997), pp. 13–37 (p. 20); *RAC* 1, no. 1 (pp. 33–6). Crosby explains that at Reading 'the case was argued for an integrated administration which was closer to the ideal of the eleventh-century reform program than the development that took place in most of the religious houses', Crosby, *Bishop and Chapter*, p. 28.

13   *Account Book of Beaulieu*, ch. 72 (p. 276).

14   *Rule of St Benedict*, ch. 31, 32, 36 (pp. 90–2, 94, 100–2). Benedict also refers to deans and the prior, although the latter was not essential to his schema and was only to be appointed if necessary, see ch. 21 (p. 76), ch. 65 (pp. 166–70). The porter is mentioned in chapter 66 (pp. 170–3) and is discussed below, pp. 78–9.

15   *Rule of St Benedict*, ch. 35 (pp. 98–100), ch. 38 (pp. 104–6).

16   Whereas Knowles suggested that Lanfranc introduced the offices of precentor, sacrist, chamberlain and almoner, Greatrex has since argued that there were precentors at Winchester in Aethelwold's day (963–984), and that the origins of the English obedientiary system remain uncertain, J. Greatrex, 'St Swithun's Priory in the later Middle Ages', *Winchester Cathedral 900 Years: 1093–1993*, ed. J. Crook (Guildford, 1993), pp. 139–66 (p. 144).

England this process was gradual but, as Knowles explains, it was 'almost universal' and had been 'firmly established' in all major houses by the second half of the twelfth century.[17] Still, it was not uniform, and arrangements were modified according to the particular needs of each community. The number of obedientiaries, their relative importance and the precise nature of their work might vary from house to house.[18] Whereas the sacrist and cellarer held the greatest sway at Bury, the sacrist and almoner were the weightiest officials at Peterborough and the cellarer's share was 'by far the largest' at early-thirteenth-century Rochester.[19] Whilst the office of kitchener was well established in many houses by the thirteenth century, this post was only introduced to Christ Church, Canterbury in 1216–17, and was short-lived for the kitchener was dismissed the following year and the cellarer resumed his function.[20]

The increased number of monastic officials led to a distinction between major and minor obedientiaries, whose duties, status and financial standing could vary considerably. At Peterborough, some of the 'new officials' were, like the sub-almoner, essentially 'juniors to major obedientiaries', whereas others, like the sub-sacrist and master of works, were effectively independent officials with their own revenues and specific duties.[21] At Bury St Edmunds the minor obedientiaries had fewer financial responsibilities than the greater monastic officials. Accordingly, they had only to render account twice rather than four times a year and were expected to attend all regular hours unless engaged in duties pertaining to their obedience.[22] The division of the almoner's office at Glastonbury Abbey in the fourteenth century is incisive, for it shows how partitions of this kind might be effected. In 1340, it was decided that the office hitherto belonging to the almoner should now be known as the external almoner, and that the monk who had formerly collected leftovers from the monks' table should be accorded the status of obedientiary and the title,

[17] Knowles, *Monastic Order*, pp. 757, 437.

[18] D. Knowles, *Christian Monasticism* (Hampshire, 1969), p. 109. See, too, G. Rosser, *Medieval Westminster, 1200–1540* (Oxford, 1989), p. 4, n. 5, and Brooke, *The Book of William Morton, Almoner of Peterborough, 1448–1467*, ed. P. I. King, trans. W. T. Mellows, intro. C. N. L. Brooke, Northamptonshire Record Society 16 (Oxford, 1954), p. xix. Smith's discussion of financial receivership at Christ Church, Canterbury explains the tendency for each house to 'develop on individual lines', R. A. L. Smith, 'The central financing system of Christ Church, Canterbury, 1186–1512', *EHR* 50 (1940), pp. 353–69 (p. 362); also see R. A. L. Smith, 'The financial system of Rochester Cathedral Priory', *EHR* 56 (1941), pp. 586–95.

[19] *Election of Abbot Hugh*, p. xxxv, King, *Peterborough Abbey*, pp. 89–91, C. Flight, *The Bishops and Monks of Rochester, 1076–1214* (Maidstone, 1997), p. 199. The cellarer of Bury was a major obedientiary but not the major obedientiary that he often was in other houses, Thomson, 'Obedientiaries', p. 91.

[20] Smith, *Canterbury*, p. 21; for the office of kitchener at Abingdon see *De Obedientiariis*, pp. 391–5.

[21] Brooke, *William Morton*, p. xxiii. This, too, would have varied from house to house and over time.

[22] Graham, 'A papal visitation', p. 735. A similar distinction between lesser and greater obedientiaries is made in the late-thirteenth-century customary of Westminster Abbey, e.g. *Westminster Customary*, pp. 93–7.

intern almoner.[23] That the intern almoner was assigned an office in the extern almoner's yard is of interest in relation to the physical layout of the monastery and notions of shared space. It suggests that intern and extern officials might operate from the same area of the precinct, and that these terms might relate to the nature of their work rather than their location in the precinct.

In 1954 Brooke wrote that the obedientiary system lacked an historian.[24] Little has changed over the last fifty years and Knowles' survey remains the chief point of reference.[25] While the subject has been addressed briefly in recent monastic histories, and those editing account rolls have produced useful studies of specific houses, there remains no comprehensive analysis of the emergence, growth and nature of the obedientiary system that discusses changes over time and variations amongst the Benedictine houses, as well as between orders.[26] As a result, the obedientiary system is rather poorly understood and, indeed, misunderstood. Even the term 'obedientiary' is used inconsistently. It is sometimes applied to all officials who ministered within the abbey, and not simply to those of monastic standing. Furthermore, it is unclear if having independent revenues was a defining feature of the obedientiary.[27] It is here posited that the obedientiary was a monastic official who administered a conventual department. Accordingly, this excludes non-monks who officiated in the convent, and also members of the abbot's household, regardless of whether or not they were of monastic standing.[28] While obedientiaries often held an endowed office, and with the growing complexity of monastic administration were increasingly likely to have independent resources of a kind, this was not a defining characteristic of the twelfth-century obedientiary.[29]

---

[23] *Chartulary of Glastonbury* 3, no. 1335 (pp. 727–8), p. ccxxiv.

[24] Brooke, *William Morton*, p. xxv.

[25] Knowles, *Monastic Order*, pp. 427–39. Barbara Harvey's edition of the obedientiary rolls of Westminster Abbey in the later Middle Ages includes an extremely useful overview of the obedientiary system from its inception, *The Obedientiaries of Westminster Abbey and their Financial Records c. 1275–1500*, ed. B. Harvey, Westminster Abbey Record Series 3 (Woodbridge, 2002), pp. xiii–xvii.

[26] Useful analyses of the system at specific houses, in particular by those editing later account rolls, include *Obedientiaries of Westminster Abbey*, ed. Harvey; *The Account Rolls of the Obedientiaries of Peterborough*, ed. J. Greatrex, Northamptonshire Rec. Soc. 33 (Northampton, 1984); *Accounts of the Obedientiars of Abingdon Abbey*, ed. R. E. G. Kirk, CS, new ser. 51 (London, 1892); *The Compotus Rolls of the Obedientiaries of St Swithun's, Winchester*, ed. G. W. Kitchin (Winchester, 1892); Thomson, 'Obedientiaries'; *Two Cartularies of Abingdon* 2, pp. xlii ff; A. Léotaud 'Monastic officials in the Middle Ages', *Downside Review* 56 (1938), pp. 391–409, discusses the situation at Worcester in the fifteenth and sixteenth centuries.

[27] For example, whereas Kitchin, *Compotus Rolls*, pp. 30–3, and Fosbroke, *British Monachism*, e.g. pp. 184–5, include non-monastic officials as obedientiaries, Kirk, *Obedientiars*, p. xi, and C. H. Lawrence, *Medieval Monasticism*, 2nd edn (London, 1989), p. 298, define him as a monastic official. The latter is implied in Gasquet, *English Monastic Life*, p. 58, and R. H. Moorman, *Church Life in England in the Thirteenth Century* (Cambridge, 1945), p. 280.

[28] Indeed, Kirk, *Obedientiars*, p. xi, maintains that lay servants should never be defined as obedientiaries, regardless of their standing.

[29] As Rosser explains, it was an evolutionary process, Rosser, *Medieval Westminster*, p. 4, n. 5. Lawrence, *Medieval Monasticism*, p. 298, defines the obedientiary in relation to

The example of Bury

Division

The precise nature of the division of revenues and its impact on the administration of hospitality varied from house to house, and is examined here through a case study of Bury St Edmunds, the 'citadel of division'.[30] The separation of revenues was advanced here at an early stage. The first steps were taken during Baldwin's abbacy (1065–97), when the abbot granted the manors of Hinderclay and Newton Suffolk, along with two pools and the fishery of 'Sydolvesmaere', to contribute to the brethren's clothing.[31] It was not until Robert II's abbacy (1102–7) that Bury's revenues were actually split between the abbot and the community, and the convent's portion shared amongst the various offices.[32] This comparatively early division was ostensibly confirmed by Henry I in a charter of June 1108 x February 1114; or so it seems, for the authenticity of this document has recently been questioned.[33] Crosby suggests that division should instead be attributed to Abbot Hugh (c. 1157–80).[34]

The customary reception of guests

No other house provides as detailed and comprehensive a record of the distinction of guests in the twelfth and early thirteenth centuries as Bury St Edmunds, and three important accounts offer an insight into the procedure at this time. They are Jocelin of Brakelond's chronicle of the abbey written c. 1201/2,[35] the statutes between the abbot and convent compiled at the beginning of the thirteenth century,[36] and the customs of Bury dated 1234 x 56, but which may, of course, reflect earlier practice.[37] These reveal that the care of guests was divided between the abbot and convent. Each was made responsible for receiving and providing for a certain group or groups of visitors.

---

his task rather than his economic standing.

30   Howell, 'Abbatial vacancies', p. 189.
31   *Feudal Documents from Bury*, no. 105 (p. 108). See, too, p. cxxxviii.
32   Jocelin, p. 90, celebrates this as Robert's great deed. See, too, Howell, 'Abbatial vacancies', pp. 177–8.
33   *Feudal Documents from Bury*, no. 35 (p. 69). Professor Richard Sharpe's forthcoming remarks on this charter in the Acta Henry I Project, Oxford, offers various reasons to suggest this is a forgery; I am grateful to Dr Mark Hagger for providing me with this information.
34   Crosby, *Bishop and Chapter*, pp. 26–8. According to recent analysis of the division of abbatial and conventual revenues this first received adequate legal protection in November 1281, Gransden, 'Separation of portions', p. 373.
35   Jocelin, p. 39.
36   'De Consuetudiunibus statutes inter Abbatem et conventum Sancti Edmundi', which appears as appendix 5 in *Bury Customary*, pp. 100–7 (pp. 104–6). This dates from late in Samson's abbacy (1182–1211) or early in Hugh of Northwold's abbacy (1213–29), ibid., p. xxxix.
37   *Bury Customary*, pp. 5–7.

The community was essentially liable for visiting regulars and the abbot for all other guests, although it fell on the monks to provide for some of the abbot's visitors in his absence. This obligation to cover for the abbot stirred up considerable debate for by this time the abbot was often away, either on business or at his manors. The community therefore sought to thrash out an arrangement that was feasible and fair, that did not lay the convent open to exploitation and, moreover, jeopardise its revenues during a vacancy when the king assumed control of the abbot's portion.[38]

Jocelin of Brakelond, the guestmaster of the house, offers a personal insight into the workings of Bury in the late twelfth and early thirteenth centuries. He explains that whenever the abbot was at home he was to receive all guests, whatever their circumstance, that is, whether they arrived on horse or by foot. The abbot was not liable for religious men, secular priests and their retainers, who pertained to the convent, but might choose to honour religious men and receive them in his hall; presumably they were otherwise entertained in the convent's quarters.[39] If the abbot was not residing at Bury it was the community and more specifically, the cellarer, who provided for any of his guests who arrived with thirteen or fewer horses. The abbot's household remained liable for visitors with fourteen or more horses, whom they received at the abbot's expense either in the court or 'outside', which likely refers to the vill. Inevitably customs were not always observed, but during Hugh's abbacy (1157–80), disregard for the rules prompted Denis, the cellarer, to threaten his resignation. This occurred when three knights and their squires were shown to the community's guesthouse even though the abbot was present and they ought to have been entertained in his hall. As it was the cellarer's duty to supply the guesthouse, the onus fell on Denis, who was incensed that his office should be unjustly burdened in this way. He therefore confronted Hugh in the abbot's hall and threatened to resign. His words did not, evidently, fall on deaf ears for Jocelin notes that from then on Abbot Hugh was careful to observe the customary division of guests.[40]

The community's obligation to cover for the abbot when he was away could saddle the monks with a number of extra guests and additional expenses. This could be particularly onerous if the abbot was frequently absent. Jocelin explains that Samson of Bury's regular withdrawal to his manors was the cause of contention, since some of the monks believed he was deliberately trying to conserve his resources by off-loading guests on to the community. Jocelin did not himself hold this opinion and thought that Samson was simply happier on his manors, where he was free from the quibbles of visitors.[41] Whatever the reason it is significant that the community or, at least some of the monks,

---

[38] For further discussion, see Gransden, 'Separation of portions', esp. pp. 374–5.

[39] *Jocelin*, p. 39. Carville's ordinances of December 1245 suggest there was a similar arrangement at Abingdon in the mid-thirteenth century, see *Two Chartularies of Abingdon* 2, C7 (p. 23).

[40] *Jocelin*, pp. 6, 55–6.

[41] *Jocelin*, p. 35.

saw this as a weighty and unnecessary burden on their own resources and a contributing cause of the convent's financial difficulties.

Both the early-thirteenth-century statutes and the customary of the house indicate that these grievances were acted upon or, in any case discussed, and steps were taken towards defining and refining the extent of the community's obligations. To reduce the burden on the monastery's resources, the statutes sought to reduce the abbot's absenteeism and thus enjoined him to remain with the community. When present, he was to receive all guests, whether they arrived on horse or on foot, except for religious men and their followers who remained the convent's responsibility.[42] This clause suggests that the community was no longer liable for secular priests, and may represent a move towards releasing the convent of any responsibility for secular guests. In the abbot's absence, the monks were to receive guests of his who arrived on foot or with up to thirteen horses; those with fourteen or more remained the abbot's responsibility and were to be received warmly by his deputy, the custodian of the abbot's houses and granary.[43] This distinction was not absolute, for the community might choose to receive certain of the abbot's guests who had more than thirteen horses, such as regular bishops, and also visitors who had been specially invited by the prior or had come to be of service specifically to the convent.[44] Significantly, the abbot's kitchen only received fuel from the convent's wood pile if he was himself at home and was not supplied if guests resided there in his absence.[45]

Whereas the early-thirteenth-century agreement implies that at this time the community received all Benedictine bishops with fewer than fourteen horses, regardless of whether or not the abbot was in residence, the later and more detailed customs of the house reveal that liability for visiting bishops was now a source of debate. It is certainly possible that this discussion and diversity of opinions had been generated by the earlier agreement. It was argued by some that the abbot should receive all bishops, whether secular or regular. Others believed that the community was responsible for Benedictine bishops, but were divided as to whether this should apply only to those with under fourteen horses or if it should extend to all Benedictine bishops, regardless of how many horses they had and whether or not the abbot was present.[46] Whilst it was agreed that the abbot should entertain secular bishops if he was present, it was less clear what should be done in his absence. Various scenarios were discussed. For example, should the prior admit a secular bishop with fewer than

---

42   *De Consuetudinibus statutes*, p. 104 lines 15–18.

43   *De Consuetudinibus statutes*, p. 104 lines 17–28.

44   *Bury Customary*, pp. 5, 6.

45   *Bury Customary*, p. 31; *De Consuetudinibus statutes*, p. 105 line 27 – p. 106 line 4. These guests are described as *extraneus nobilis* and *hospites extranei* and were presumably those who were tended by the abbot's household and not the convent, when the abbot was absent. Similar arrangements are detailed in an earlier agreement between the abbot and convent of Bury, *De Consuetudinibus statutes*, pp. 105–6.

46   *Bury Customary*, p. 6 lines 16–19. Given that the bishop of Hereford travelled with at least thirty-five horses in the late thirteenth century, an open policy of this kind was potentially costly, see Harvey, 'Aristocratic consumer', p. 20.

fourteen horses if he requested food or lodging out of charity or, should the convent receive everyone equally and indiscriminately for the sake of Christ? The compiler of the customs was himself of the opinion that the convent should only ever receive seculars who had fewer than fourteen horses or who had been invited specially by the prior.[47]

The Bury customs therefore offer a rare insight into a community at work, and show the discussion and debate that helped shape future practice regarding the abbot's and convent's respective responsibilities to guests. It was clearly important to implement a policy that was fair and proper, so that visitors would be received appropriately and neither the abbot nor convent would be unjustly burdened. This particular concern is vividly expressed in a passage relating to the custodian of the abbot's houses and granary. He was responsible for receiving the abbot's guests when the prelate was away and was urged to be vigilant lest the doorkeepers of the abbey, or even any visitors who were familiar with the customary distinction of guests at Bury, manipulated the system and wrongly burdened either the abbot or convent. Evidently the doorkeepers and the guests themselves had been accustomed to join forces and either grouped their horses to ensure that they were received as the abbot's guests or, conversely, distributed their horses to present themselves as the community's guests. The abbot's deputy was warned to be on guard and ensure that neither party was unfairly hampered by trickery of this kind.[48]

These three accounts show how the separation of abbatial and conventual revenues had a considerable impact on the administration of hospitality at Bury, and led to the careful, if at times controversial, distribution of guests between the abbot and convent, and to the thrashing out of a policy that was just and practical. Both the abbot and the monks were to contribute fairly to the entertainment of guests and neither party was to be overwhelmed. Boundaries were set up and areas of responsibility mapped out, yet there was room for manoeuvre and all importantly, for discretion. Inevitably discussions of this kind and failure to observe the rules could lead to tensions and exacerbate divisions between the abbot and convent, such as the clash between Denis, the cellarer of Bury, and Abbot Hugh of Bury. Disregard of the rules led to a similar rift at Abingdon in 1241 when visiting abbots were lodged with the guestmaster and not in the abbot's house.[49]

The detail of the arrangements at Bury is exceptional, and there is unfortunately little comparative evidence to indicate how guests were distinguished at other houses in the late twelfth and early thirteenth centuries.[50] A few isolated

---

[47] *Bury Customary*, pp. 5, 6.

[48] *Bury Customary*, p. 6 lines 19–23.

[49] Cox, *The Story of Abingdon*, pt II, p. 31.

[50] A Continental example is instructive: the early-thirteenth-century ordinal of Fécamp sets out in detail which guests pertained to the abbot and which to the cellarer; whereas the abbot was to provide for kings, archbishops, earls and bishops, the cellarer and also the kitchener were to provide for all guests, monks, canons, knights, barons, clerics, their clients, nuns (who ought to stay in the vill) and other pilgrims, *The Ordinal of the Holy Trinity, Fécamp* (pts 1, 2, 3), ed. D. Chadd, HBS 112 (London, 2002), pp. 379–885, 'De procuratione domus Fiscanni', ch. 286 (p. 693).

examples are instructive. The bishop of Salisbury's prescriptions for Abingdon Abbey in 1219 suggest that the convent here was essentially responsible for visiting Benedictines, who were received in a chamber within the claustral area (*receptaculum*); the abbot received all other guests in his court, but, as at Bury, he might choose to honour distinguished Benedictine visitors and invite them to his chamber.[51] An agreement between Abbot Richard de Berking and the monks of Westminster Abbey, dated 11 November 1225, offers an insight into the arrangements here in the early thirteenth century. This states that the custodian of hospitality (*custos hospitalitatis*) should receive all guests, regardless of their order, station or origin, and provide for them honourably in accordance with the funds at his disposal.[52] It fell on the abbot of Westminster to receive kings, legates, and papal messengers who arrived with twelve or more horsemen, and those whom he had personally invited to feast or lodge. The abbot was also to provision the horses of anyone sent to lodge at the house.[53] The distribution of guests between the abbot and the convent is explicit in a passage relating to the refectory arrangements at Westminster Abbey. It was agreed that the convent would refresh the abbot and up to four of his guests (*persona*)[54] dining with the community in the refectory, but it fell on the abbot to provide for any additional visitors he might bring.[55] There was a similar arrangement at Abingdon Abbey in the mid-thirteenth century.[56] This presumably refers to special occasions when the abbot joined the brethren for by this time he would generally have dined apart with his household or on his manors.[57]

Injunctions issued following the visitation of Westminster in 1234 shed further light on the division of guests. They indicate that the monks were responsible for visiting regulars, and that the abbot shouldered the cost of entertaining all other guests. They also reveal that hospitality at Westminster had been inadequate and was in need of reform, for the visitors instructed

---

51   *Two Chartularies of Abingdon* 1, L167 (p. 112). In contrast, the later customary of St Mary's, York suggests there was no financial distinction between regulars and seculars who visited the abbey; the cellarer supplied all guests with twelve horses or less from his kitchen, the abbot provided for those with thirteen or more, and the almoner sustained monks on foot and poor pilgrims, *St Mary's Customary*, pp. 93, 96–7. According to the injunctions for Ely in 1304, the monk-seneschal of the prior's hospice received magnates with fourteen or more horses, 'Ely ordinances', 1304: 11 (p. 27).

52   *Walter de Wenlok*, pp. 217–22 (p. 219).

53   *Walter de Wenlok*, p. 219. At the Cistercian abbey of Beaulieu, c. 1270, where there was no division between abbatial and conventual revenues; distinguished guests, such as cardinals, royalty and their people, bishops and earls were financed from the common fund and not the hosteller's office, although it was the guestmaster who tended them, *Account Book of Beaulieu*, ch. 72 (p. 276). There was presumably a similar arrangement at Benedictine houses where the abbot did not have independent revenues, such as Battle and Reading.

54   The term *persona* used here presumably refers to distinguished guests, see below, pp. 111 n. 92, 112 n. 94, for further discussion of this term. The same clause is found in the late-thirteenth-century customary of the house, *Westminster Customary*, p. 103.

55   *Walter de Wenlok*, p. 222.

56   *Two Cartularies of Abingdon* 2, no. C. 405 (p. 328).

57   See below, pp. 125, 135, 143.

the abbot to procure for guests and also servants of religious men through his cellarer more generously than before. Furthermore, he was enjoined to restore permanently the vaults where he had previously stored his own wine, so that visiting monks, whether Benedictine or Cistercian, could be received more honourably.[58] Other rulings concern the monks' relatives and friends who were to be provided for from the abbot's table, through his cellarer, regardless of whether they stayed in the abbey's hospice or in the town.[59] The Evesham customs of c. 1206 offer another insight into the nature of the distinction of guests at the turn of the thirteenth century. These state that the cellarer should provide for (all) guests according to the resources of the house, and that he should minister to visiting religious in matters pertaining to his office as he did for the other brethren; this would have meant supplying their bread, ale, corn for pottage and pancakes, oats for gruel, beans, salt and kindling. The cellarer was liable only for visiting abbots and their chaplains on fast days, when they dined with the community.[60] Similarly, the kitchener of Evesham was to provide for visiting religious from his office and according to later versions of the customs, should only supply abbots and their chaplains when they dined in the refectory, as, for example, on the eves of festivals.[61] Visiting religious are singled out for mention in Abbot Randulf of Evesham's (1214–29) grant to the community of the chapel of Littleton. This was intended to provide fodder for the horses of religious men with under seven horses who were lodged at the monastery; they had previously been supplied from the abbot's granary.[62]

The saga of the cellarer's debt at Bury

> The knights wondered and the people wondered at the things that were done; and one of the common fold said, "It is a wonder that the monks, being so many and with such knowledge of letters, suffer their property and revenues to be confounded and mingled with the property of the abbot; for these things used always to be distinguished and kept apart."[63]

Jocelin of Brakelond's detailed account of the ongoing financial problems suffered by the cellarer in the late twelfth century reveals much about the nature and extent of division between the abbot and convent of Bury, of the abbot's rather autocratic measures to remedy the situation and of the feistiness of the monks who objected loudly to these reforms. Notably, it sheds light on the pivotal role the cellarer had in supporting the administration of

58   Graham, 'A papal visitation', p. 738.
59   Graham, 'A papal visitation', p. 739. The term *mensa* seems here a general reference to the abbot's supplies.
60   Thomas of Marlborough, *History of Evesham*, appendix II A (pp. 516–32).
61   *Chronicon Abbatiae de Evesham adannum 1418*, ed. W. D. Macray, RS 29 (London, 1863), p. 263, n. 2, inserted Harl. 3763 (fourteenth century); see also below, p. 143.
62   Thomas of Marlborough, *History of Evesham*, ch. 421 (pp. 402–3); appendix II B, pp. 556–7.
63   *Jocelin*, p. 89.

hospitality and of the close working relationship between these two offices, and subsequently, how a careless guestmaster might jeopardise the financial well-being of the cellar.[64]

Abbot Samson sought to make good the cellarer's debts and granted the office extra revenue. When this proved inadequate he resorted to more extreme measures, and assigned a clerk from his own table to advise and witness the administration of the cellar. This enraged various members of the community who argued that by placing a clerk over a monk Samson had made them a laughing stock. But Samson had his supporters, and Jocelin explains that one wise monk claimed the abbot had acted sensibly, given that it was ultimately his responsibility, as Father of the monastery, to remedy the convent's debts.[65] Whether Samson acted for right or for wrong, the cellar remained in debt and it was rumoured that mismanagement and extravagance in the prior's lodging and guesthouse were to blame for the over-expenditure; in other words, the financial mess was attributed to the cellarer's and guestmaster's maladministration of hospitality. Samson now embarked on a more drastic course of action. He himself assumed management of the cellar and expenses for guests, and paid off the community's debts from the abbatial funds. Furthermore, he deposed both the cellarer and hosteller, appointing two new monks to replace them as sub-cellarer and hosteller, and set them under a clerk from his own table, Master G., who had supreme authority for all purchases and receipts. These reforms provoked a new wave of hostility against the abbot, and presumably also fears for the implications this might have during a vacancy, when the king was entitled to take over the abbot's portion. The laity were reputedly just as astonished by Samson's actions, and wondered that the monks had allowed their abbot to 'confound and mingle' their property with his own. Samson's new system of administering the cellar was evidently effective, for Jocelin acknowledges that unnecessary expenses were cut and that guests and monks were adequately provided for. Nevertheless, 'venomous hissings' continued against him and even the autocratic Samson was forced to yield and reconsider arrangements. A compromise was reached whereby the sub-cellarer was promoted to the cellar and a new sub-cellarer appointed; both were to remain under the supervision of the abbot's clerk.[66]

Jocelin's account suggests that whilst the distinction between abbatial and conventual resources was deeply entrenched in the minds of the monks

---

[64]   The cellarer's responsibility for guests at Bury is explicit in the arrangements made upon Hugh of Northwold's succession to the abbacy in 1215, and in the list of injunctions issued following the visitation of Bury in 1234. The former divided the cellarer's office amongst four monks; two were in charge of external business (adminis-tering the cellar's manors) and two presided over internal affairs (provisioning the monks and guests), *Election of Abbot Hugh*, pp. 164–6. The injunctions suggest that a quadripartite division still functioned at this time, for the cellarer was to divide his revenues into four and was warned that neither the sub-cellarer, hosteller, nor any other, save for the abbot or prior, should presume to take that which belonged to him, Graham, 'A papal visitation', p. 734.

[65]   *Jocelin*, pp. 79, 81.

[66]   This episode is recounted *Jocelin*, pp. 88–90; see also Gransden, 'Separation of portions', p. 374.

and also their neighbours, interaction continued but what was seen by some as an intrusion was regarded by others as a necessary rescue operation.[67] Interaction of this kind might be mutually supportive, and benefit the abbot as much as the convent. In 1231 Hugh of Wells enjoined the obedientiaries of Peterborough Abbey to support their abbot should he require help.[68] In the late eleventh century the archbishop of Canterbury and the monks of Christ Church Cathedral Priory were joined in a reciprocal arrangement through which they were bound to help each other financially, should this be required.[69] The customs of Evesham Abbey stipulated that if any office should suffer a shortfall, it ought to be helped by another obedience which had money remaining; where no office could meet this deficit, the abbot was to make good this loss with funds from the external cellarer.[70]

The guestmaster

> Hospitality should always be given with charity and cheer. In accordance with the *Rule*, a mannerly and kind monk should be appointed to ensure that this is done.[71]

The increasing withdrawal of the abbot from communal life and the division of revenues between the abbot and convent meant that, in the larger houses at least, the administration of hospitality was rather complex. It was no longer the case that one monk officiated in the guesthouse on behalf of the community.[72] As previously noted, the abbot and convent might each have responsibility for specific guests. While the abbot's household was largely responsible for visitors assigned to his care, the monks' guests were tended by their hosteller(s), in conjunction with various obedientiaries and lay assistants. The precise nature of the guestmaster's duties varied from house to house and over time, and in some communities the office was split amongst two or more obedientiaries. Moreover, much of his work might now be delegated to lay assistants. Yet the complexity of these arrangements has been largely overlooked. Previous

---

67 *Jocelin*, p. 89
68 King, *Peterborough Abbey*, pp. 94–5. King explains that departmental autonomy, rather than abbatial autocracy seems to have been the main problem at Peterborough. Knowles, *Religious Orders* 1, p. 275, discusses this intermingling of duties and support, whereby the abbots and monks might finance one another.
69 M. Gibson, 'Normans and Angevins, 1070–1220', *A History of Canterbury Cathedral*, ed. P. Collinson, N. Ramsey and M. Sparks (Oxford, 1995), pp. 38–68 (p. 56).
70 If any office had a surplus of money, the abbot was to consult with the chapter or a majority of the brethren of wiser counsel as to how they might spend this to benefit the church, Thomas of Marlborough, *History of Evesham*, appendix II (1206 customs), pp. 518–19. This is repeated in two later versions, Thomas of Marlborough, *History*, pp. 388–90, appendix IIB, pp. 536–7.
71 The Benedictine Statutes of 1238 issued by the Benedictine province of Canterbury, cited in the *Chronica Majora* (3, p. 502).
72 See the *Rule of St Benedict*, ch. 53 (p. 136).

discussions of the guestmaster's office have tended to ignore inconsistencies and form an understanding of the post from evidence relating to a specific house at a particular time. For example, Kitchin's description of the guestmaster of St Swithun's, Winchester, and, indeed, of the office in general, is informed by his analysis of the late medieval obedientiary rolls. These provide only a partial insight into the office and led him erroneously to suggest that the office was held by a layman.[73] Furthermore, in the absence of evidence for the guestmaster of St Swithun's duties, Kitchin simply imposes Lanfranc's late-eleventh-century ordinances and ignores the possibility of variation and change.[74] Kitchin's method is not untypical and highlights the general confusion regarding the guestmaster's status and the nature of his duties. The following section looks more closely at this office in the twelfth and early thirteenth centuries to explore the guestmaster's status, the nature of his duties and the other personnel involved in the reception of guests.

The guestmaster's status

> This said he (Abbot Samson) deposed the cellarer and guestmaster, setting in their places two other monks, entitled sub-cellarer and guestmaster.[75]

The guestmaster, also referred to as the master of guests (*magister hospitum*), the custodian of guests (*custos hospitum*) but, more frequently, as the hosteller (*hostilarius/hospitarius*), was an obedientiary and was accordingly of monastic standing. These terms seem to be used indiscriminately and while *hostellarius* is most often found in the customaries the terms seem to be neither date nor source specific. However, a more exhaustive analysis of the terminology might prove otherwise.[76] The guestmaster's status as a monk is explicit in the *Rule of St Benedict*, in Lanfranc's *Constitutions*, and also in a number of twelfth- and thirteenth-century sources pertaining to the Benedictines in England. Jocelin of Brakelond's account of the financial plight at Bury in the late twelfth century directly mentions the guestmaster's monastic standing, for he

---

73   Kitchin divides the obedientiaries into four groups and assigns the guestmaster to the fourth, a small group concerned with external affairs whose members, he argues, included lay stewards and seneschals, and were generally not a part of the 'conventual body', Kitchin, *Compotus Rolls*, pp. 31–3.
74   Kitchin, *Compotus Rolls*, pp. 80–1. Moreover, Kitchin equates the *hostillarius* with the doorkeeper (*hostiarius*).
75   *Jocelin*, p. 89.
76   For example, the term *magister hospitum* appears in both the 1206 customs of Evesham and Jocelin's chronicle of Bury, Thomas of Marlborough, *History of Evesham*, appendix IIA, p. 516, *Jocelin*, p. 7. The *hospitarius* appears in the inquisition of Glastonbury's manors in 1189, in Jocelin's chronicle of Bury St Edmunds and the later customary of St Mary's, York, *Inquisition of the Manors of Glastonbury*, ed. J. Jackson (London, 1882), p. 8; *Jocelin*, p. 129; *St Mary's Customary*, pp. 94–6. The *hostilarius* is mentioned in the late-twelfth-century *De Obedientiariis* of Abingdon, the Bury customary of c. 1234 and the later customaries of Eynsham and Westminster, *De Obedientiariis*, pp. 411–14, *Bury Customary*, pp. 25–6, *Eynsham Customary*, ch. 19: 1 (505), p. 198, *Westminster Customary*, pp. 79 ff.

explains that Abbot Samson (1182–1211) deposed the guestmaster and cellarer of Bury, and replaced them with two monks as sub-cellarer and guestmaster (*hospitiarius*).[77] Abbot Samson was at one time guestmaster of Bury (*magister hospitum*) and Jocelin himself held this post.[78] The Benedictine Statutes of 1238 for the province of Canterbury state that the guestmaster ought to be a kind and gentle monk.[79]

If, then, the evidence for the guestmaster's monastic standing is unequivocal, why is he often accorded lay status by historians? It seems that this confusion can be attributed, in part, to the increasing complexity of the administration of hospitality. This meant that the management of the hospice was no longer in the hands of one man. The monk hosteller might well have lay deputies and servants to assist him. They are often described as pertaining to the hospice, and this has evidently led some to infer that the guestmaster was himself a layman. Another potential cause of confusion – and the one that seemingly clouds Kitchin's perception – relates more specifically to the division of hospitality between the abbot and convent, and the tendency for the abbot to appoint within his household a layman to look after guests for whom he was responsible; but this official should be distinguished from the monastic hosteller who received the convent's guests. Thomson states that the office of guestmaster at Bury St Edmunds was divided into three – the intern, who cared for visiting monks, the extern who cared for the laity, and the abbot's.[80] This is to oversimplify matters for the administration of hospitality at Bury was in the hands of at least four officials. The almoner was responsible for less notable guests, the extern hosteller might entertain monks and other regulars who did not belong to the Benedictine order, and the intern largely cared for visiting Benedictines; the brother assigned the care of the court tended the abbot's guests. Moreover these were only guidelines, for the specific arrangements depended on who was staying at the house and whether or not the abbot was in residence.[81]

The nature of the guestmaster's duties

The Benedictine guestmaster was essentially responsible for receiving and tending the convent's guests but the precise nature of his duties varied depending

---

[77] *Jocelin*, p. 89.

[78] *Jocelin*, p. 7. For additional examples of monk hostellers, see *Election of Abbot Hugh*, p. 188, and Thomson, 'Obedientiaries', p. 98.

[79] '*monachus benignus et mansuetus*'. These statutes are cited in the *Chronica Majora* (3, p. 502). The clause reappears in the statutes issued by the Canterbury Province in 1249, Pantin, *Chapters* 1, p. 39 (clause 14).

[80] Thomson maintains that the three types of guestmaster at Bury – the abbot's, the intern and extern – are not distinguished in the records, apart from on one occasion when John of Northwold is named as the intern guestmaster, Thomson, 'Obedientiaries', pp. 91, 98. Presumably the abbot's guestmaster is to be identified with the brother assigned the care of the abbot's court.

[81] This is discussed further above, pp. 56–9, and below, pp. 131–8, 142.

on the community's needs and resources at the time.[82] He was not simply responsible for visitors and was potentially involved with anyone who was in some way removed from claustral life. This might include visiting regulars and clerics, members of the convent who had returned from a journey or undergone bloodletting, novices who were about to make their first profession or laymen who sought fraternity and were to be introduced to the chapter.[83] The hosteller's task was in many ways a difficult one, for he was to promote the abbey and endeavour to satisfy guests, yet ensure that the monks were not unduly disrupted by the presence of outsiders. His post therefore married service with supervision. The duality of his role is highlighted in Lanfranc's *Constitutions* which state that should any guest wish to see the monastery buildings, he ought to be escorted by the hosteller;[84] moreover, if any cleric was to dine with the community, it was the guestmaster's duty to brief him on how he should behave in the refectory.[85] 'The brother assigned to administer the guesthouse' in the *Rule of St Benedict* and the *Constitutions* of Lanfranc is not associated with the initial reception of visitors. Guests were welcomed by the porter and then met by the prior or another member of the community who prayed with them and exchanged the Kiss of Peace. It was only after this that the visitor was introduced to the guestmaster.[86] By the late twelfth century this had changed and the new arrangement would have made the process more efficient. It was now the hosteller's task to meet guests and lead them to pray, to extend the Kiss of Peace and offer edificatory words, or to ensure that another did so in his stead. Similar procedures are set down in the twelfth-century customary of the Victorines (*Liber Ordinis*), but not in the Cistercian customary (*Ecclesiastica Officia*) which follows St Benedict to the letter.[87]

The nature of the guestmaster's office can be considered more closely through two case studies, offering different perspectives on his role. The *De Obedientiariis* of Abingdon, probably compiled c. 1220, focuses on the guestmaster's deeds and sheds light on the nature of his duties and the extent of his responsibilities. The customary of Bury St Edmunds is more concerned

---

[82]   Knowles, *Monastic Order*, p. 431, includes veterinary treatment and the shoeing of the monks' and pilgrims' horses amongst the guestmaster's duties, but this does not seem to have been universally imposed, particularly veterinary treatment, and indeed Knowles cites no examples to substantiate this.

[83]   See for example *Westminster Customary*, p. 87 lines 14–20 (bloodletting); Lanfranc, *Constitutions*, ch. 90 (pp. 128–33) and *Udalrici Cluniacensis Consuetudines*, PL 149.765 (novices and fraternity). Chapter 9 of Bernard of Cluny's eleventh-century customs make the guestmaster responsible for bringing letters to the chapter meeting and also for closing the cloister doors, 'Ordo Cluniacensis per Bernardum Saeculi XI Scriptorem', ed. M. Herrgott, *Vetus Disciplina Monastica* (Paris, 1726), pp. 133–374 (p. 153).

[84]   Lanfranc, *Constitutions*, ch. 90 (p. 88). See below, p. 167.

[85]   Lanfranc, *Constitutions*, ch. 90 (pp. 130–1). See below, pp. 139–40, 143.

[86]   *Rule of St Benedict*, ch. 53 (p. 136); Lanfranc, *Constitutions*, ch. 90 (pp. 128–31).

[87]   According to the twelfth-century customary of the Victorines of Paris, the hosteller took his place with the community until notified by the sub-hosteller that the guest had been received and his horses stabled; once summoned the guestmaster led the visitor to pray, extended the kiss and attended to his needs, *Liber Ordinis, S. Victoris Parisiensis*, ed. L. Jocqu and L. Mills, CCCM 61 (Turnholdt, 1984), ch. 17, pp. 60–1 lines 12ff. See below, pp. 107–10 for the procedure at Cistercian abbeys.

with practicalities, a legacy, perhaps, of the abbey's financial problems in the late twelfth century; it clarifies how the hosteller should be resourced and who precisely should benefit. While the customaries provide a useful survey of the nature and scope of the guestmaster's duties they reveal little of his personal dealings with visitors and assistants. Moreover, it is difficult to know the extent to which these precepts were acted upon and it is likely that practices were often adapted to meet current needs.[88]

Case study 1: Abingdon Abbey

> The hosteller ought to be of great honour and courteously hospitable. He ought not to be a gossip or fickle, but eloquent, discreet, of clear reason and learned talk.[89]

It was vital that the guestmaster conducted himself appropriately and received guests courteously, since he was instrumental in promoting a positive image of the house.[90] The opening section on the hosteller in the *De Obedientiariis* therefore lists the personal qualities required of this monk. The guestmaster was to blend the duties of his office with those of his broader monastic vocation. He was expected to participate in communal activities and, just like the other monks of Abingdon, was assigned tasks on the weekly rota and was obliged to celebrate Mass and the Hours when he was not busy tending guests.[91] If the hosteller had to sing Matins with a guest who was unable to join the community, he was to return to the choir as soon as he had done so, particularly on feasts celebrated in copes, when his presence in the choir was particularly important.[92] The hosteller was to welcome guests who arrived at Abingdon, and then see to their physical and spiritual needs. He was not self-sufficient and relied on a number of obedientiaries for resources. He procured food and drink from the cellarer, candles from the sacrist and lanterns from the chamberlain.[93] The hosteller was to control access to the claustral area and supervise those who entered so that the monks would not be unduly disrupted by their presence.[94] He also mediated on the guest's behalf and in so dong helped preserve decorum within the abbey. If, for example, the visitor wished to be bloodlet, to speak with another member of the house or with his own servants, the guestmaster notified the relevant authority and

---

88 See above, pp. 13–18, for further discussion.
89 *De Obedientiariis*, p. 411.
90 *De Obedientiariis*, p. 411.
91 *De Obedientiariis*, p. 411. For similar rulings, see *Eynsham Customary*, ch. 19: 5 (505), p. 198 lines 20–2; *Westminster Customary*, pp. 84, 93 lines 18–29; *St Augustine's Customary* (fourteenth-century), p. 140 lines 2–6. All obedientiaries at Bury St Edmunds were required to attend Matins, Vespers and great masses, unless necessarily detained; lesser obedientiaries (*minores obedientiarii*) were to attend all regular hours unless engaged in the administration of their duties, Graham, 'A papal visitation', p. 730. This injunction was issued following visitation of the house in 1234.
92 *De Obedientiariis*, p. 412.
93 *De Obedientiariis*, pp. 412, 415.
94 See below, pp. 102, 167, 175.

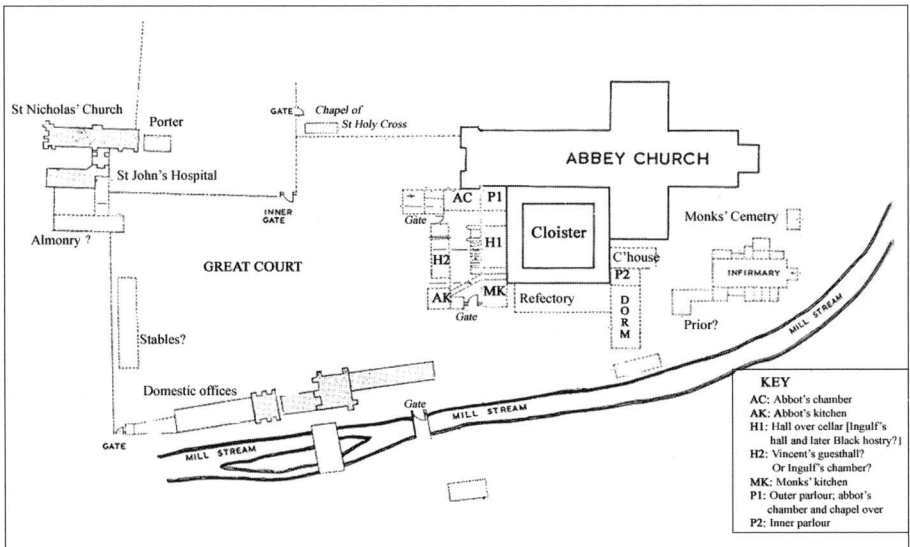

St Nicholas' Church
Porter
GATE Chapel of
St Holy Cross

St John's Hospital

ABBEY CHURCH

INNER
GATE

Gate

AC P1

Almonry ?

Cloister

Monks' Cemetry

GREAT COURT

H1

H2

C'house

INFIRMARY

P2

Stables?

AK MK

Gate

Refectory

D
O
R
M

Prior?

MILL STREAM

Domestic offices

Gate

MILL STREAM

GATE

MILL STREAM

MILL STREAM

KEY
AC: Abbot's chamber
AK: Abbot's kitchen
H1: Hall over cellar [Ingulf's
hall and later Black hostry?]
H2: Vincent's guesthall?
Or Ingulf's chamber?
MK: Monks' kitchen
P1: Outer parlour; abbot's
chamber and chapel over
P2: Inner parlour

Figure 5 Conjectural plan of the abbey precinct, Abingdon.

made the appropriate arrangements.[95] Whilst the monks sought to please guests and meet their requirements, they did not tolerate misbehaviour and any visitor who committed an offence was reported by the hosteller to the prior who dealt with him accordingly. A similar policy is set down in the later customaries.[96]

It is striking that the *De Obedientiariis* does not refer to the hosteller's work in the hospice – or even mention the hospice – for this is pivotal to the guestmaster's office in both the *Rule of St Benedict* and Lanfranc's *Constitutions*.[97] Abingdon would certainly have had a guesthouse at this time. The *History* records that Abbot Vincent (1121–30) constructed a guest-hall with a chamber in the court along with other buildings there, and presumably this, or a revamped version, was still serving the community in the early thirteenth century, when the *De Obedientiariis* was compiled.[98] How then can we explain the hosteller's seeming lack of responsibility for the guesthouse at

95   See below, pp. 152, 162.
96   *De Obedientiariis*, p. 414. *Eynsham Customary*, ch. 19: 4 (515), p. 202 lines 27–33; *Westminster Customary*, p. 82 lines 12–21; *St Augustine's Customary* (fourteenth-century), p. 138 lines 27–36.
97   *Rule of St Benedict*, ch. 53 (p. 136); Lanfranc, *Constitutions*, ch. 90 (pp. 128–31). Knowles' summary of the guestmaster's duties states that in addition to the 'social side of his activities', the guestmaster was 'to furnish the guest-rooms', Knowles, *Monastic Order*, p. 431.
98   *History of Abingdon* 2, appendix I (from MS B), pp. 340–1. The other buildings that he constructed in the court were a brewery, granary and bakehouse, a double stable, and an almonry with three towers. This accommodation is discussed further in chapter 4, pp. 141–2.

Abingdon? It is possible that his association with the hospice was dealt with in another text or, indeed, that his duties here were discussed orally and not committed to writing. A more likely explanation is that the guest-hall and chamber were staffed by the abbot's household who entertained visitors for whom he – rather than the community – was responsible. In other words, the guestmaster of the *De Obedientiariis* may only have been liable for the convent's guests who were refreshed and accommodated within the claustral area. It is not made explicit who these guests were, but it is likely they were visiting regulars and perhaps simply Benedictines, who would have slept and dined either in the monks' dormitory and refectory or in an adjacent chamber, such as the 'receptaculum monachorum' that is mentioned in Robert of Carville's ordinances of 17 December 1245.[99]

There are further indications that the hosteller of the Abingdon customary was not directly involved in the management of the guesthouse but was based in the claustral area. The arrangements for the early departure of guests state that if anyone wished to leave before daybreak, when the door of the outer parlour was officially opened, the hosteller should fetch the keys of the parlour from the prior's 'couch' and send guests forth according to their dignity.[100] Given that the door of the outer parlour stood on the western range, where it connected the cloister to the court, it seems that these were guests staying in the claustral area, rather than the court. This is also implicit in the late-thirteenth-century customary of Westminster Abbey, which stipulates that in accordance with old custom, the parlour door should be shut each day after Compline and remain closed until after chapter the following day unless guests were to enter or leave, or brothers were to embark on or return from a journey; it reveals that guests accommodated within the claustral area were visiting Benedictines.[101] Another important, though rather ambiguous, passage in the *De Obedientiariis* discusses visiting canons. It seems that any canons wishing to visit the abbey church were escorted there by the hosteller and then returned to the abbot's doorkeeper (*janitor*), who ministered to their needs; it is not clear if the doorkeeper himself provided their refreshments or ensured that they were aptly tended by the appropriate officials.[102] The passage suggests that the hosteller's involvement with canons began and ended with their visit to the church and this is implied also in Robert of Carville's ordinances for the abbey in 1245. These state that any ecclesiastics and lay visitors who happened to arrive at Abingdon should be received through the abbot, and then fittingly

---

[99]   *Two Cartularies of Abingdon* 2, no. C.7 (pp. 12–25 at p. 23). The accommodation of visiting Benedictines is discussed further below, pp. 83–4, 131–2, 142.

[100] *De Obedientiariis*, p. 412. For similar arrangements see *Eynsham Customary*, ch. 19: 5 (519), p. 203 lines 18–21.

[101] *Westminster Customary*, p. 158 line 36 – p. 159 line 4.

[102] *De Obedientiariis*, p. 415. Comparison with other passages in the treatise (*Chronicon Monasterii de Abingdon*, ed. J. Stevenson, 2 vols, RS 2 (London, 1858), 2, pp. 338, 339, 349, 352, 363, 365), and indeed with other sources (*St Mary's Customary*, p. 91), suggests that this rather ambiguous phrase 'pro uoto eorum' should be interpreted 'according to their wish', rather than 'to make their offering'. I am grateful to Dr Michael Staunton for his advice on this matter.

collected and tended according to their rank.[103] The fact that the hosteller was to return to choir rather than the guesthouse after he had received guests, and that the hospice is not mentioned in a memorandum of 1219 that discusses the obedientiaries' servants, also suggest that the guestmaster of Abingdon may not have been directly involved in the management of the hospice.[104]

The question of who precisely was responsible for the guest-hall might be easier to resolve if its location could be established with certainty. Unfortunately the *History* does not state where in the court Vincent built his hall and chamber or, indeed, for whom it was intended. Various suggestions have been made. A location near to the main abbey gates has been posited, on account of its proximity to the stables and almonry that were built around the same time.[105] A more convincing suggestion is that the complex formed part of the quadrangular enclosure that constituted the abbot's court and was, accordingly, under the management of his household. In the absence of specific evidence, we can only speculate, and ultimately the site and indeed the number of halls at Abingdon, remains unclear.[106] The guesthouse complex is discussed more fully below.

It thus seems that by the mid-thirteenth century, if not earlier, the division of guests at Abingdon was such that the abbot's household ministered to his guests in either the court or the vill, while the hosteller tended the convent's guests in the claustral area. This arrangement is similar to that at Bury St Edmunds, which is so vividly recorded by Jocelin of Brakelond. Although the administration of hospitality was split between the abbot and convent, boundaries were not absolute and the hosteller evidently accepted responsibility for the abbot's guests whenever they entered the claustral area. In fact, the hosteller may have welcomed all visitors who arrived at the abbey regardless of whether they were the abbot's or convent's responsibility, and before he escorted them to the relevant authority for refreshment led them to pray, extended the Kiss of Peace, bestowed the blessing and delivered a few edificatory words.

The administration of hospitality was clearly not a one-man show performed by the hosteller, and involved a number of officials and ministers. A particularly significant contribution was made by the abbot's household, whose input at this time has been somewhat overlooked. This merits a brief discussion of the chief dispensers of the abbot's hospitality at Abingdon, namely the curtar (*curiarius*) and the abbot's doorkeeper (*janitor*). As members of the abbatial household they were not conventual obedientiaries. Whereas the curtar was a monk, the doorkeeper seemingly was not professed and there is no mention of

103 *Two Cartularies of Abingdon 2*, C. 7 (p. 23).
104 *De Obedientiariis*, p. 413; *Two Cartularies of Abingdon 1*, no. L. 167 (pp. 107–13).
105 Both Knowles and Lambrick suggest that Vincent's hall may have been beside St John's Hospital, at the gate of the abbey, Lambrick, 'Early history', p. 53.
106 Lambrick, 'Early history', p. 52. However, as Lambrick underlines, it is particularly difficult to establish just how many halls there were at a given time and where they were situated, pp. 53, 54.

his attending services.[107] Significantly, a papal letter of c. 1187 describes the two doorkeepers of Christ Church, Canterbury as *seruientes*, and the *janitor* of the twelfth-century Victorine Customary (*Liber Ordinis*) is styled *conversus*.[108] The doorkeeper should not, it seems, simply be identified with the porter; indeed, the porter of the great gate was usually a prestigious post.[109]

Whenever guests arrived at Abingdon, the *janitor* notified the curtar, who then provided for visitors according to their person.[110] Lambrick explains that the curtar received all supplies in kind, and had the larder, granary and brewery at his disposal. It is not clear if the curtar simply provided for the abbot's visitors, such as the passing guests, knights and men of the province who were ministered to from the court when they visited to celebrate the Nativity of St Mary, and the monks' relatives whom he was warned to receive with respect, or, if he supplied all guests who arrived at the abbey and allocated the convent's share to the cellarer, who then distributed this to the various obediences.[111] The guestmaster certainly received his provisions directly from the cellarer.

The *curiarius*, or curtar as he was later known, was appointed by the abbot and had custody of the entire court. He held the keys of the larder and granary. The butler, dispenser, larderer and other ministers of the court were under his custody and were to render daily account to him. At the abbot's discretion the curtar was assigned the help of a cleric or layman, who could cover for him in his absence; he was thus to be 'wise, skilled and affable'.[112] The curtar was expected to celebrate the Office with the brethren whenever he was free, especially on feasts celebrated in copes or albs. He was excused from attending Compline if he was busy distributing prebends.[113] Gabrielle Lambrick explains that the curtar at Abingdon fulfilled the function of cellarer and was part of the unique administrative arrangements at Abingdon.[114] This requires some refinement, for although the title of curtar is unique his job was similar to that of the extern cellarers at Evesham and St Albans, and to the brother assigned care of the court at Bury.[115] The extern cellarer of St Albans, who is described

107 *De Obedientiariis*, p. 351; Lambrick, 'Abingdon abbey', pp. 167, 174, and Kirk, *Obedientiars*, p. xliii n.a.

108 This is from Urban III's letter to the prior and convent of Christ Church in 1187, *Papsturkunden in England*, ed. W. Holtzmann, 3 vols (Berlin and Göttingham, 1930–52), 2, no. 251 (pp. 447–8); *Liber Ordinis*, ch. 15 pp. 55–7, esp. p. 57.

109 His office is discussed below, pp. 78–9.

110 *De Obedientiariis*, p. 415, see below, pp. 97–9.

111 These visitors are mentioned in the customs relating to the obedientiaries, c. 1185, *Chronicon de Abingdon* 2, p. 313; *Two Cartularies of Abingdon* 1, no. L. 167 (p. 112).

112 *Two Cartularies of Abingdon* 1, no. L. 167 (p. 112).

113 *De Obedientiariis*, p. 352.

114 Lambrick, 'Early history', p. 53.

115 E.g. Thomas of Marlborough, *History of Evesham*, appendix II A, pp. 520–1; GASA 1, p. 119; *Bury Customary*, p. 6 lines 14–23. Reginald of Durham's miracle collection of St Cuthbert describes the cellarer at Durham as the procurator; the sub-cellarer was evidently akin to an intern cellarer, *Reginaldi Monachi Dunmelensis*, ch. 106 (p. 237).

also as the cellarer of the court, was responsible for the guests' cellar.[116] Extern cellarers often served as general receivers of the house. Whereas obedientiaries were generally chosen by the abbot and chapter, these monk officials were often appointed by the abbot.[117] The extern cellarer of Evesham received all revenues that had not been specifically allocated to another office. Should any obedientiary require financial aid, the abbot provided assistance via the extern cellarer. According to the 1206 customs of Evesham, the extern cellarer was to supply the community with bread, ale, two *pulmenta* (dishes of vegetables and cereals),[118] light and salt, and to provide for all visitors according to the resources of the house.[119] The offices of cellarer and curtar were therefore closely linked and might even be combined.[120]

Less is known about the doorkeeper (*janitor*) who is described as 'acting for the abbot', and would have been one of several doorkeepers. In the late twelfth century a certain Walter had custody of the gate in front of the abbot's chamber ('ante cameram abbatis').[121] The doorkeeper helped preserve decorum by controlling access within the precinct and by disseminating information within and beyond the court. Upon the arrival of guests, the doorkeeper notified the curtar so that he might provide for them aptly; he liaised with the sub-chamberlain and sacrist if candles were needed for visiting regulars.[122] Whilst the doorkeeper was essentially concerned with the abbot's guests, and the guestmaster chiefly for the convent's, the two might interact. It was noted earlier that if any canons wished to enter the abbey church, the *janitor* passed these visitors to the guestmaster who showed them to the church and then escorted them back to the doorkeeper to receive refreshments.

[116] GASA 1, p. 119; see also pp. 74–5. The duties of the intern and extern cellarers at Westminster Abbey are set out in the late-thirteenth-century customary of the abbey. The former had care of all manors and possessions, and provided ale and bread for the monks, passing monks, stranger monks and their households; the latter was responsible for supplying the convent with essentials such as bread, ale and vessels, *Westminster Customary*, pp. 69–73.

[117] For example, Thomas of Marlborough, *History of Evesham*, appendix II A, pp. 520–1.

[118] *Pulmenta* supplemented or replaced pittances and also 'generals', which were the two dishes permitted in the *Rule of St Benedict*, see Harvey, *Living and Dying*, pp. 11–12.

[119] Thomas of Marlborough, *History of Evesham*, appendix II A, pp. 520–1; see also the later versions, ch. 405 (pp. 390–1); appendix II B, pp. 538–9.

[120] This was evidently the case at St Swithun's, Winchester, from the fourteenth century Kitchin, *Compotus Rolls*, p. 32. The cellarer of St Augustine's, Canterbury, seems to have fulfilled a similar role to the Abingdon curtar, and the sub-cellarer of St Augustine's to the cellarer of Abingdon, *St Augustine's Customary* (fourteenth-century), pp. 122–3, p. 134.

[121] For example, see above p. 59 for the warning to the abbot's deputy to be vigilant lest any of the doorkeepers or even the guests wrongly encumbered either the abbot or convent with visitors. Lambrick, 'Early history', p. 52.

[122] The sub-chamberlain provided light to direct an abbot, prior or canon; the sacrist provided candles for Benedictine abbots and other notable figures of the Order, *De Obedientiariis*, p. 415.

Case study 2: Bury St Edmunds, c. 1234

The thirteenth-century customs of Bury St Edmunds reveal little about the actual reception of visitors, but they are, as we have already seen, an exceptional source for the division of guests between the abbot and convent and shed much light on how the offices were provisioned. The customs suggest that at this time the administration of hospitality was split. An intern hosteller was mainly responsible for visiting Benedictines, an extern hosteller for other monks and secular guests pertaining to the convent, including the households of visiting Benedictines.[123] Clerics and priests on foot were ministered to by the almoner if they arrived before Compline, for no secular guests were admitted after this time unless they were special friends of the church or convent.[124] The abbot's visitors were received by his clerks and a brother appointed by him. There were exceptions. For example, the almoner, and not the intern hosteller, cared for Benedictines who arrived alone and on foot; this was evidently a precautionary measure lest they were truant monks or deserters. As noted earlier, the community had extra responsibilities when the abbot was absent.[125]

It was not unusual for the hosteller's office to be shared between two officials. Nor was this an invention of the thirteenth century. Two guestmasters are named in the sixth-century *Rule of the Master* but are distinguished according to their function and not, as at Bury, according to whom they received. One guestmaster greeted guests, while the other remained in the guesthouse to guard against thieving visitors.[126] The number of guestmasters appointed at Westminster Abbey in the thirteenth century was reasonably flexible. According to an agreement in 1225, the abbot might appoint one or two brothers as custodians of hospitality; he was to make this appointment in chapter and with the common agreement of the community. In 1252 it was agreed that the abbot of Westminster should choose two of four brothers named by the prior and convent to administer hospitality.[127] The late-thirteenth-century customary of the abbey mentions an extern and intern

---

[123] *Bury Customary*, p. 25. Gransden equates the *hostillarius exterior* with the *hostel-larius forensic*, p. 130; it is, however, possible that the latter functioned as an outside receiver.

[124] *Bury Customary*, p. 26 lines 3–8. As noted above n. 80, Thomson seems to over-simplify this.

[125] *Bury Customary*, p. 26 lines 1–3. *Westminster Customary*, p. 72 lines 34–8; *St Augustine's Customary* (fourteenth-century), p. 141 lines 30–6; *Eynsham Customary*, 19: 5 (520), p. 203 lines 22–36.

[126] *La Règle du Maître*, ed. H. Vanderhoven, F. Masai, P. B. Corbett (Brussels and Paris, 1953), ch. 79 (p. 277). It is interesting to note that at Monte Cassino in the ninth century there were twenty-four posts, which included the porter of the guest block, the hosteller of regulars and the hosteller of the poor, W. Braunfels, *Monasteries of Western Europe: The Architecture of the Orders*, trans. A. Laing (London, 1972), p. 36.

[127] For the agreement of 11 November 1225, see *Walter de Wenlok*, pp. 218–19; for that of 1252, see p. 228. In 1300 there were two guestmasters at the Cistercian abbey of Salem, Germany: one tended 'decent folk', the other ministered to 'lower guests', Williams, *Cistercians in the Early Middle Ages*, p. 127.

hosteller, and an extern and intern hospice.[128] The extern hosteller seemingly had greater financial responsibilities than the intern hosteller, and supplied the guesthouse with bedding, straw and similar necessities.

The customs of Bury stipulate that guests should be received joyfully and honourably, and provided for diligently in accordance with the customs of the abbey.[129] The intern hosteller was assigned houses where he entertained visiting Benedictines, and these were probably situated in the claustral area. Benedictine prelates would have been accommodated in a private chamber.[130] The extern hosteller, who was essentially responsible for non-Benedictine regulars, had a hall with a chamber and kitchen.[131] This complex was probably in the court and it may have been here that Jocelin sat in 1201 to contemplate the recent election of Prior Herbert; he explains that as guestmaster of Bury he sat at the porch of the *aula hospitum*.[132] The intern hosteller was helped by an honest-living clerk who was familiar with the customs of the monastery, and could thus minister to visitors.[133] The intern hosteller does not seem to have had independent resources and relied on provisions from other officials. For example, he received food and straw from the cellarer, fuel from the infirmary, light and wax from the sacrist, and candles from the vestry.[134] His reliance on other obediences is highlighted in a late-twelfth-century grant of land in Whitefield, Kentford, to John of Trotsan, who gave the cellarer of Bury an annual sum of five shillings for hospitality; presumably this was intended for the guests' food and drink.[135]

The extern hosteller, in contrast, was largely self-sufficient and had to provide his own fuel.[136] He was responsible for non-Benedictine regulars who lodged and dined at the abbey, and for laity and clergy who might eat in the hall but generally stayed in the vill.[137] These guests would have been less well integrated with the community than visiting Benedictines, and would not, for example, have joined the monks in the refectory on a regular basis.

---

[128]   E.g. *Westminster Customary*, pp. 79 ff.

[129]   *Bury Customary*, p. 25 lines 22–7.

[130]   See below, p. 133.

[131]   *Bury Customary*, pp. 25–7. See above p. 51 and below pp. 131, 134.

[132]   *Jocelin*, p. 129. For the date of Herbert's appointment see Greenway and Sayers, *Jocelin*, p. 110.

[133]   *Bury Customary*, p. 26 lines 10–29. The customs discuss the corrody of this clerk in great detail, but say little regarding his tasks.

[134]   *Bury Customary*, p. 25 line 18 – p. 26 line 9. For arrangements at Westminster Abbey in the late thirteenth century see *Westminster Customary*, pp. 79–80, 81, 85–6. The hosteller of Fécamp Abbey was evidently more independent than his counterpart at Bury, and whilst the chamberlain provided light for the guest chamber and passed on the sheets of dead monks for visitors, the hosteller himself was to provide horseshoes for all visiting monks, canons regular and other religious men, as well as towels, fuel, vessels, spoons and beds. He was also liable for repairing the guesthouse and associated buildings, *Ordinal of Fécamp*, ch. 288 'De camerario Fiscanni quid debeat facere' (p. 697) and ch. 291, 'Quid facere debet hospitalarius de hospicii' (p. 700).

[135]   R. H. C. Davis, *The Kalendar of Abbot Samson of Bury St Edmunds and Related Documents*, CS, 3rd ser. 84 (London, 1954), charter no. 102 (p. 134).

[136]   *Bury Customary*, p. 25 line 29 – p. 26 line 1.

[137]   See above, p. 134.

It was therefore essential that the extern hosteller had a team of servants to assist him. They included a principal servant, similar to a seneschal, a clerk devoted to the altar of St Lawrence, an honest household manager to procure the guests' food and drink from the cellar and kitchen, a vice-cook to place the food on the dishes and ensure that they were cleared away, and five cooks in the hall's kitchen.[138] The cellarer and hosteller together appointed and financed these servants who ate in the chamber of the hall, either before or after the guests' dinner. This chamber was allocated to Cistercians visiting Bury whenever their diet differed from that of other guests.[139] The seneschal and chief cook were chosen and financed by the convent. The seneschal dined either in his own house or with his companions in the great kitchen, but not in the chamber with the other servants. Similarly, the chief servant only ate in the hall if instructed to do so by the guestmaster or a noble guest, such as a bishop. This may imply that bishops and other distinguished guests occasionally dined in the hall, although they could simply have issued this order and dined elsewhere.

Clearly, the nature of the guestmaster's duties, his relative standing and also how the office was split varied from house to house. The growing complexity of monastic administration and subsequently of hospitality also wrought changes over time. Yet, in spite of these differences the Benedictine hosteller essentially remained responsible for satisfying guests and ensuring that their presence did not impede monastic life. He was not merely a manager of the hospice, but was actively involved with the reception of visitors and, when appropriate, escorted them within the conventual area.

The wider nexus of involvement

The administration of hospitality was not the preserve of the guestmaster. He was supported by other obedientiaries, such as the cellarer, and was invariably assigned the help of assistants. The chamberlain of Abingdon received the sheets and blankets of dead monks, which he then distributed for the use of guests; presumably he passed these items on to the hosteller.[140] The intern hosteller of Bury received fuel from the infirmary, light and wax from the sacrist, candles from the vestry, and food and straw from the cellarer.[141]

---

[138] *Bury Customary*, p. 26 line 30 – p. 27 line 21. A list of servants assigned to the various obediences at Abingdon, which dates from Edward I's reign (1272–1307), shows that twenty-two served in the kitchens; one of the five principal cooks served from the kitchen in the guest-hall, another served in the chamber and to guests whenever they were in the inside hostel, the chamber and other places, Dugdale, *Monasticon* 3, no. xxvi (p. 159).

[139] *Bury Customary*, p. 27 lines 13–18.

[140] *De Obedientiariis*, p. 388. For a similar arrangement at Fécamp in the early thirteenth century, see *Ordinal of Fécamp*, ch. 288 'De camerario Fiscanni quid debeat facere' (p. 697).

[141] *Bury Customary*, p. 25 line 27 – p. 26 line 1.

The actual amount he received depended on the guest's standing, and was calculated with considerable precision. If, for example, an abbot or conventual prior visited, the hosteller received seven candle stumps of ten thumb measures for the grease lamp but was given three or four stumps for other religious guests.[142]

Other monastic officials worked alongside the guestmaster or communicated with him. The refectorer and hosteller of Abingdon together ministered to visitors dining in the refectory.[143] The hosteller communicated also with the abbot and prior if a guest wished to prolong his visit, speak with a member of the community, undergo bloodletting or dine in the refectory. As previously mentioned it was the prior who dealt with any guest who committed an offence.[144] Secular members of the community might also contribute to the administration of hospitality and increasingly so, with the growing devolution of the guestmaster's duties to lay assistants. Henry de Sully's inquisition of Glastonbury's manors in 1189 is particularly interesting, for it lists the abbey's possessions, officials and household at this time and reveals that Henry's predecessor, Robert (1173–80), had assigned the guestmaster (*hospitarius*) a servant for the guesthouse. He was to hold a lifetime corrody of one household loaf,[145] a measure of good ale, a measure of inferior ale, a dish of cooked food, and a wage of five shillings.[146] Other non-monastic positions that were in some way involved with the guestmaster include the custodian of the parlour. He monitored access to the cloister from the outer parlour on the western range and was therefore integral to the preservation of decorum within the conventual area.[147] The custodian of the parlour at Abingdon was one of the almoner's servants, and it was his responsibility to make sure that the custodian received guests honourably from early morning until after Compline.[148] Whilst the Abingdon customary reveals little else about this assistant's duties, his role is more extensively discussed in the later customary of Eynsham Abbey, which is thought to have been compiled from the same source as the *De Obedientiariis*

---

142   *Bury Customary*, p. 58 lines 10–18. The treasurer of Bury provided lamps for any visiting Benedictine abbot as long as he sat in the outside house, but once he moved to his chamber, the hosteller was largely responsible, *Bury Customary*, pp. 59–60. This was perhaps for financial rather than symbolic reasons. For similar arrangements see *St Mary's Customary*, p. 91.

143   *De Obedientiariis*, p. 398. See below, p. 144.

144   E.g. *De Obedientiariis*, p. 414, *Eynsham Customary*, ch. 19: 4 (515), p. 202 lines 27–30.

145   For the various types of bread see Harvey, *Living and Dying*, pp. 171, 239.

146   *Inquisition of Glastonbury*, p. 8. The guestmaster was to receive one mark from the church of Winfrod and five pounds of candles. For the corrodies and stipends of servants at Bury's hospice in 1234, see Graham, 'A papal visitation', p. 736.

147   *De Obedientiariis*, pp. 405–6. In his description of Bury St Edmunds, G. Hills, 'The antiquities of Bury St Edmunds', *Journal of the British Archaeological Association* 21 (1865), pp. 32–56, 104–40 (pp. 21, 130), makes the unlikely suggestion that the custodian of the parlour was attached to the monks' parlour in the eastern range. For later references to this custodian, see, for example, *Westminster Customary*, p. 170 lines 8–9, and *Eynsham Customary*, ch. 19: 12 (541–6), pp. 211–12. The porter of the cloister described in the twelfth-century customary of the Victorines, Paris, seemingly occupied a similar role, *Liber Ordinis*, ch. 16 pp. 58–9.

148   *De Obedientiariis*, pp. 405–6.

and thus merits consideration. The custodian of the parlour at Eynsham was to make sure that no strangers entered or even looked into the cloister, and that they did not leave their stirrups near the door. Ecclesiastical dignitaries were allowed to mingle with the monks in the cloister, but any other visitor wishing to speak with a member of the community was to wait in the parlour while the custodian attracted the monks' attention by making a sound with the iron ring on the cloister door. If nobody was in sight, the custodian might enter the cloister to convey this information.[149] The relationship between the hosteller and custodian of the parlour at Abingdon is alluded to in a rather obscure passage in the *De Obedientiariis*. The Latin is ambiguous but it seems that if a guest wished to speak with his servants who were accommodated 'within the gates of the court', the hosteller should send for them through the custodian of the parlour. If, however, the servants were staying outside the court, the same was done by the *janitor*'s administration.[150]

The guestmaster might also have dealings with the stabler, and Alexander of Neckam recommended that he should be faithful.[151] The customary of Westminster Abbey suggests that it had been the intern hosteller's job to appoint a stabler to minister to those staying in the hostel of the court but from Richard de Crokeley's abbacy (1246–58) the abbot made this appointment.[152] There are few explicit references in the sources to the stabler's involvement with hospitality, but this was surely commonplace given that the maintenance of guests' horses was a basic component of hospitality. Indeed, a number of grants were made specifically to provide fodder and horseshoes for visitors, and stables were often situated near the hospice.[153]

Some members of the community who had few, if any, dealings with the hosteller were also involved with guests. The significance of the abbot's household has already been discussed, in particular, the posts of curtar (*curiarius*) and doorkeeper (*janitor*) at Abingdon, and of the brother assigned the care of the court at Bury. The almoner, a monastic official of considerable standing within the Benedictine community, made a significant contribution to hospitality. The almoner of Bury St Edmunds received the convent's guests who were of moderate means. This essentially meant Benedictines who arrived alone and on foot, and also secular priests and clerics on foot if they arrived before Compline, for no seculars were permitted to enter the house after this time unless they were considered a 'special friend'.[154] Conversely, it was the

---

149 *Eynsham Customary*, ch. 19: 12 (542–3), p. 210 line 26 – p. 211 line 3.
150 *De Obedientiariis*, p. 414. See below, pp. 98–9.
151 Alexander of Neckam, 'De Sacerdos ad altare', ed. T. Hunt, *Teaching and Learning Latin in Thirteenth-century England* 1 (Cambridge, 1991), pp. 250–73 (p. 265).
152 *Westminster Customary*, p. 72 lines 18–23. This presumably refers to the hosteller of the court.
153 See below, pp. 150–1.
154 *Bury Customary*, p. 26 lines 3–8. The almoner of St Mary's, York, sustained monks on foot and poor pilgrims, *St Mary's Customary*, pp. 93, 96–7. The early-thirteenth-century ordinal of Fécamp Abbey records that the almoner managed a house, the xenodochium, where he received pilgrims and the poor; if there was no room they stayed instead in the vill, *Ordinal of Fécamp*, ch. 290, 'Quid facere debeat Elemosinarius' (p. 698). Bernard's and Udalricus of Cluny's eleventh-century customs for the abbey

extern hosteller of Westminster who was responsible for monks on foot.[155] Other monastic officials who had contact with guests include the sacrist and cellarer of Bury St Edmunds, who distributed gifts to certain visitors staying at the house or residing in the town.[156] Visitors might encounter the sacrist in the church where he, or an assistant, collected their offerings and maintained security; the sacrist might also tell them about relics, jewels and miracles. Alexander IV's confirmation of Bury's customs in August 1256 reveals that two monks of the abbey guarded St Edmund's body, on account of the great crowd of pilgrims.[157] During Edmund Rich's archiepiscopate (1233–40), four monks of Christ Church, Canterbury, were appointed to receive pilgrims in the cathedral.[158] Who precisely was involved with the administration of hospitality, and in what capacity, would have varied depending on the community's needs at a particular time. In the late twelfth century, the hayward of Abingdon Abbey provided a box of fruit for guests in the refectory. This, it seems, was to be shared with members of the community recovering from bloodletting.[159] The almoner of Abingdon kept a jug of ale in reserve for any of the monks' friends who happened to arrive, and whilst the brethren were permitted to have a drink or two from this instead of the Collations drink, only pilgrims, poor clerks, sick laity and particularly travellers were allowed three fills.[160]

One official whom we might expect to be extensively involved in the administration of hospitality, and who has not yet been mentioned, is the porter. The porter's office is defined in the *Rule of St Benedict*, which states that he ought to be a mature old man who will guard the gate and welcome visitors courteously. Whilst Benedict does not state that he should be of monastic standing, this was no doubt assumed.[161] Yet, despite his prominence in the *Rule of St Benedict* and, indeed, in the twelfth-century Cistercian customary, the porter is omitted from Lanfranc's *Constitutions* and the *De Obedientiariis* of Abingdon. Furthermore, he does not appear with the obedientiaries in Bernard of Cluny's list of signs, c. 1068, and is not mentioned in the customaries of Bury St Edmunds, Evesham or

accord the almoner responsibility for visitors arriving on foot, although messengers and visitors on horseback were tended by the custodian of the hospice, *Ordo Cluniacensis per Bernardum*, ch. 9 (p. 153); *Udalrici Consuetudines*, cols 765–6.

155   *Westminster Customary*, p. 86 lines 32–3.
156   See below, pp. 147, 180.
157   'Confirmation of the customs of Bury St Edmunds by Alexander IV', printed as appendix I in *Bury Customary*, pp. 63–7 (p. 63 lines 21–3). The treasurer of St Augustine's, Canterbury, was also the keeper of the abbey's relics and he, along with another monk, slept in the church to guard the community's treasures, *St Augustine's Customary* (fourteenth-century), p. 108.
158   Finucane, *Miracles and Pilgrims*, pp. 137–8. For arrangements at Cluny, see Evans, *Monastic Life at Cluny*, p. 75; the practice at Westminster c. 1270, is discussed below, p. 168.
159   *De Obedientiariis*, p. 416.
160   *Two Cartularies of Abingdon* 1, no. L. 167 (pp. 107–8).
161   *Rule of St Benedict*, ch. 66 (p. 170). Peter the Venerable's exchange with Bernard discusses the porter's age but does not mention his status, Peter the Venerable, *Letters* 1, ep. 28 (clause 14, pp. 75–6).

Westminster.[162] In fact, the porter is not cited as an obedientiary in any Benedictine source. An explanation for this apparent omission relates to his status, for the Benedictine porter was a layman and does not, therefore, feature in records relating to obedientiaries. The Cistercian porter, in contrast, was an obedientiary of considerable standing and, as such, is included in Cistercian lists of signs.[163] The portership of the gate of a great Benedictine house was evidently a significant and potentially valuable office. The porter of the great gate at Christ Church, Canterbury, was generally appointed by the archbishop, but might be chosen by the king during a vacancy.[164] Peter the porter's corrody at Abingdon reveals that he and the *dapifer* were the only servants to receive ale from the abbot's store.[165] The fact that in 1202 Andrew de Scaccario secured the keepership of the gate for life indicates that this was a post worth having.[166] The keeper of the gate was often of considerable standing and the post might be hereditary. Thomas Marlborough records that at Evesham, Abbot Adam (1161–89) was the first to confirm the office of porter for Henry 'by a charter of the church', and also for a woman 'who claimed it by hereditary right'.[167] In the early thirteenth century, Adam the Chamberlain, was granted the portership of the great gate at the court of Bury St Edmunds, to be held as Ralph the porter had held it before his death; Ralph was evidently a man of great wealth and position.[168]

---

[162]   Whereas the customary of Westminster simply states that all visitors except Benedictine monks should be taken through the gate to the hostel, the porter is mentioned specifically in the later customary of Eynsham where he is a member of the *famuli* and not an obedientiary, *Westminster Customary*, p. 88; *Eynsham Customary*, ch. 19: 10 (532–6), pp. 209–10. Gransden remarks that this particular section of the Eynsham work is largely copied from the customary of St Victor's, Paris; significantly, the Victorine porter of the court was a lay-brother who, like the lay sub-hosteller, served under the guestmaster, *Liber Ordinis*, ch. 16 pp. 55–7, ch. 17 p. 69 lines 238–40. The porter is discussed below, pp. 95, 99–100.

[163]   His role is discussed more fully in the following chapter, p. 108.

[164]   S. M. Wood, *English Monasteries and their Patrons in the Thirteenth Century* (Oxford, 1955), p. 89.

[165]   Peter's corrody comprised of a measure of ale from the abbot's store and one from the cellarer's hall, *History of Abingdon 2*, pp. 358–9.

[166]   See the editor's note following no. C. 247, *Two Cartularies of Abingdon 2* (p. 216). For reference to Andrew, see N. Denholm Young, *Collected Papers of N. Denholm-Young* (Cardiff, 1969), pp. 201–3.

[167]   Thomas of Marlborough, *History of Evesham*, p. 189 (183). P. Vinogradoff, *Villainage in England: essays in English medieval history*, rev. edn (Oxford, 1927), p. 324, remarks that the first cook and gatekeeper of celebrated abbeys were often 'real magnates', who held this office by hereditary succession, 'and were enfeoffed with considerable estates'. A later example is the keepership of the gate of Burton Abbey, Staffs., which was inherited by Matilda, daughter of Nicholas de Shobnall from her late husband, Walter, who had been granted this as an hereditary office in 1247. In 1295, Matilda yielded the guardianship of the gate with all pertaining to it, to the abbot and monks of Burton, in return for a corrody for herself and her son, *Collections for a History of Staffordshire: Burton Abbey*, ed. I. H. Jeayers, preface, M. Deanesly, Staffordshire Rec. Soc. (Kendal, 1937), no. 104 (pp. 43–4), no. 275 (p. 89).

[168]   This is dated 1200 x 1211, *Kalendar of Abbot Samson*, charter no. 28 (pp. 90–1); and n. 2.

The guest complex at St Albans

> He [Abbot John of Hertford] built a most noble hall for the use of guests, with several buildings adjoining it. This was superbly decorated, with rooms and a fireplace, an entrance hall and an undercroft, and, because it was two-storeyed and with an undercroft, it could be called a royal palace.[169]

Whereas Benedict had envisaged that all visitors would be received in a hospice and refreshed from the abbot's kitchen, twelfth-century arrangements were more complex and have been considered briefly in relation to Abingdon, Bury St Edmunds and Christ Church, Canterbury. The nature of provision would have varied depending on the size and needs of each community, but most houses at this time would have had various lodgings for guests within and outside the precinct. The facilities at St Albans in the mid-thirteenth century included a guest-hall, the queen's chamber (*thalamus*), a Black hostelry for visiting Benedictines, and a hospice for friars.[170] There may, of course, have been additional guest chambers and no doubt other lodgings were made available to visitors if required.

The *Gesta Abbatum* records that Abbot Geoffrey (1119–46) erected a large and noble hall with two roofs for the honourable reception of guests.[171] This was hardly the first (or indeed, only) provision for visitors and those who attended the dedication of the church in 1115 were refreshed in the 'palace' in the court.[172] The *Gesta Abbatum* reveals that Geoffrey's guest-hall adjoined the 'Queen's chamber' (*thalamus reginae*) and was replaced in the mid-thirteenth century by a splendid hall comparable to a royal palace (*aula regia*). This suggests that distinguished visitors were accommodated here or at least in part of this hall. It is possible that both Stephen (1135–54) and Henry II (1154–89) stayed in Geoffrey's hall on their respective visits to St Albans, although Henry may have instead lodged in the abbot's chamber that was built during Radulf's abbacy (c. 1146–51).[173] Geoffrey's guest-hall was probably situated to the west of the cloister, at right angles to the abbot's chambers, and may be the hall described in the *Gesta Abbatum* as 'ugly and gloomy'. This

---

169 Vaughan's translation of the *Gesta Abbatum*, GASA 1, p. 314, in *Chronicles of Matthew Paris*, p. 73.

170 For a description and plan of the monastic buildings see *VCH Herts*. 2, ed. W. Page (Westminster, 1908), pp. 507–10. A slightly different arrangement of the precinct is in C. Brooke, 'St Albans: the great abbey', *Cathedral and City: St Albans ancient and modern*, ed. R. Runcie (London, 1977), pp. 43–70 (p. 47).

171 GASA 1, p. 79.

172 GASA 1, p. 71. Thompson explains that in the twelfth century the term 'palace' was particularly associated with chamberblocks, M. Thompson, *Mediaeval Bishops' Houses in England and Wales* (Aldershot, 1998), p. 5.

173 GASA 1, p. 107. Prior to this the abbot may have had independent lodgings of sorts in another part of the monastery. The abbot's chamber is mentioned in relation to the death of William of Trumpington in 1235, Vaughan, *Chronicles of Matthew Paris*, pp. 63, 71. These chambers were rebuilt under Abbot Roger (1260–90), GASA 1, p. 482.

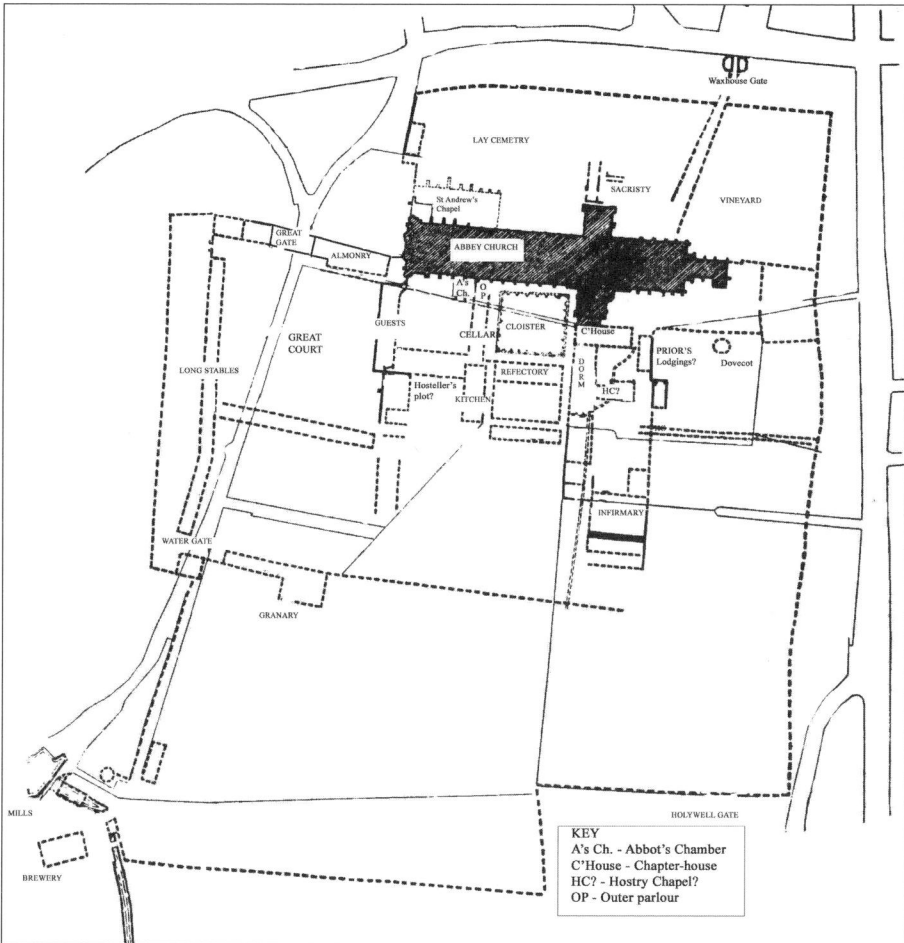

Figure 6 Conjectural plan of the abbey precinct, St Albans.

was evidently in a poor state of repair by John of Hertford's abbacy (1235–60) when the walls were crumbling, and the exterior patched and covered with tiles and shingles. Abbot John thus built an impressive new hall on the same site. The *Gesta Abbatum* includes an unusually explicit description of this magnificent building which was two-storeyed and thus comparable to a royal palace. The hall had bedrooms adjoining it, as well as an entrance hall and undercroft, and chapels and fireplaces; it was clearly well appointed and would have afforded comfortable lodgings to more distinguished guests. The complex was roofed in lead and 'superbly painted and delightfully decorated' by one of the monks, Brother Richard, who was a talented craftsman.[174] It may have

[174] GASA 1, p. 314. For translations of this section, see Vaughan, *Chronicles of Matthew Paris*, p. 73, and L. F. Salzman, *Building in England Down to 1540: A Documentary*

been here that Geoffrey de Lusignan stayed when he arrived at the abbey in 1252; the fine lodgings he secured are described as the royal palace reserved for the king and his kin.[175]

Abbot Geoffrey constructed a chamber for the queen (*thalamus reginae*) adjacent to his guest-hall. She was the only female permitted to stay within the convent (*in hoc coenobio*).[176] The Cistercians, in contrast, made no allowances for any women at this time, not even by the mid-thirteenth century when the prior and cellarer of Beaulieu Abbey were deposed for permitting Queen Eleanor to stay in their infirmary for three weeks to tend the sickly Prince Edward, who had fallen ill at the dedication ceremony in 1246.[177] Queen Eleanor had received permission from the pope in April 1244 to enter the oratories and cloisters of Cistercian and other religious houses for prayers, notwithstanding other customs, but was evidently not permitted to stay the night.[178] The terms *thalamus* and *camera* are often equated, and the queen's lodgings at St Albans probably consisted of a series of chambers rather than a room.[179] It is not known if Geoffrey built these lodgings for Henry I's queen, Adelaide, or Stephen's queen, Matilda, but it was likely upon her instruction or with her input that work was undertaken. This suggests she may have had a special relationship with St Albans or its abbot. This reference to the queen's chamber is exceptional and St Albans was perhaps the only house in England at this time – or one of the few – to construct accommodation specifically for royal or distinguished women. The cathedral priory at Ely certainly had a queen's chamber by the mid-thirteenth century which was built at the instigation of Henry III's queen, Eleanor of Provence (d. 1291).[180] Other Benedictine houses in the twelfth century would have lodged royal and noble women, even if they did not build a chamber especially for their use.[181] Gervase of

History (Oxford, 1952), p. 381. This must have been similar to the two-storey guest complex constructed by Abbot Roger of Bec (d. 1179), for the reception of guests and persons of importance, Torigni, *Chronicle*, p. 286.

175   *Chronica Majora* 5, pp. 344–5.

176   GASA 1, p. 79. The reception of women is discussed also below, pp. 107, 139.

177   *Annales Monastici* 2, p. 337; see above, p. 8. For further discussion of this see Kerr, 'Cistercian hospitality', forthcoming. By the fourteenth century concessions were made to certain worthy females, Harper-Bill, 'Cistercian visitation', p. 111.

178   Canivez, *Statutes* 2, 1250: 23 (TNA SC 7/20/15). See also below, n. 186.

179   Blair discusses these terms that were often interchangeable, but distinguishes the hall (*aula*) from the chamber (*thalamus / camera*), P. Blair, 'Hall and chamber: English domestic planning 1000–1250', *Manorial Domestic Buildings in England and N. France*, ed. G. Meirion-Jones and M. Jones (London, 1993), pp. 1–21.

180   A. Holton-Krayenbuhl, 'The prior's lodgings at Ely', *Archaeological Journal* 156 (1999), pp. 294–341 (p. 344). In 1257 the prior was ordered to repair the queen's chamber; the Queen's Hall, which stands today, dates from the fourteenth century, p. 335.

181   There was certainly a Continental precedence for the accommodation of noble women. The eleventh-century great guesthouse at Cluny, which stood in the outer court, had a wing for forty noble men and another for thirty noble women, J. Evans, *Monastic Life at Cluny 910–1157* (London, 1931), p. 92; R. Graham, *English Ecclesiastical Studies, Being Some Essays in Mediaeval History* (London, 1929), p. 36. The twelfth-century Victorines of Paris were less open and ruled that women should not be lodged within the precincts but accommodated in the vill, *Liber Ordinis*, ch. 17, p. 68 lines 210–16.

Canterbury implies that Stephen's queen, Matilda, stayed at St Augustine's, Canterbury in 1148–9, when the royal foundation at Faversham was under construction.[182] It has been suggested that she may have been accommodated in the new infirmary and chapel here. Regardless of whether the queen actually lodged at St Augustine's, she certainly observed her devotions here but it was monks from Christ Church who sang the services to her here since there was at this time an Interdict and St Augustine's was bound by silence.[183] It is not clear why the queen did not simply stay at Christ Church, but it has been suggested that St Augustine's would have been a more obvious choice, politically, given the special relationship between the Empress and Archbishop Theobald.[184] It is unlikely that the castle at Canterbury functioned as a royal residence at this time. The keep was probably used by royalty soon after its completion in c. 1120, but probably fell out of use thereafter.[185] While there were attempts in the thirteenth century to prohibit or restrict the accommodation of women within the monastic precinct this evidently continued.[186] A particularly interesting example relates to the Cluniac priory of Lenton where Nicholas de Cauntlow's wife gave birth in 1263.[187]

Benedictines visiting St Albans would have stayed in the Black Hostelry which is mentioned in relation to the three-sided cloister built by Abbot William (1214–35). This must have been one of the earliest of its kind in the country. It is certainly one of the first that is known, and is a testimony to the number of Benedictines travelling at this time and seeking accommodation at St Albans.[188] The passage referring to the Black Hostelry is rather ambiguous and it is not clear where exactly this was situated or when it was built. It may originally have stood to the west of the cloister, adjacent to the abbot's chamber and Abbot Geoffrey's guest-hall. The account reveals that one of the three cloister passages was assigned to the hosteller, and that this

[182] Gervase, *Chronicle* 1, p. 139 ('Solebat his diebus regina regis Stephani curiam Sancti Augustini frequentare'). The Latin is rather unclear, but has been interpreted as meaning that the queen actually lodged at the monastery, A. Saltman, *Theobald, Archbishop of Canterbury* (London, 1956), p. 71. Stubbs and Eales state simply that the queen stayed at Canterbury and do not mention St Augustine's specifically, Gervase, *Chronicle* 2, p. 523; R. Eales, 'Local loyalties in Norman England: Kent in Stephen's reign', *AN Studies* 8 (1986), pp. 88–108 (p. 105).

[183] Gervase, *Chronicle* 1, p. 139.

[184] I am indebted to Miss Lorna Walker for this suggestion. Dr Marjorie Chibnall (personal communication) thinks that the royal party would have been more likely to stay in St Augustine's than Christ Church.

[185] I am grateful to Tim Tatton-Brown for this suggestion. He suggests that the keep at Rochester must have been frequently used by distinguished visitors in the late twelfth century.

[186] For example, in 1221 the Benedictine Chapter of York ruled that nuns and other women should not spend the night within the confines of the monastery, lest any suspicions arise, Pantin, *Chapters* 1, p. 234. Fear of scandal was evidently as great a concern as fear of misconduct. The Canterbury Statutes of 1277 forbade women from staying the night or dining within the monastery precinct ('infra fores monasterii'), but made allowances for noble women, Pantin, *Chapters* 1, p. 72.

[187] Moorman, *Church Life*, p. 355.

[188] GASA 1, p. 290.

stretched from the entrance of the cloister to the hospice 'that used to be the guesthouse for Benedictine monks' ('usque ad ostium Hospitii, quod ulterius solet esse Hospitium Nigri Ordinis').[189] This suggests that there was a Black Hostelry at St Albans prior to William's abbacy, and that this had been situated to the west of the cloister.[190] Or, so it would seem for the meaning is unclear and could be read as 'the hospice that was also a black hostelry'.[191] Regardless, we can at least be certain that St Albans had a Black hostelry by William's abbacy (1214–35). The *Gesta Abbatum* also reveals that there was a little garden or perhaps a shrubbery within this three-sided cloister, and that this too was assigned to the guestmaster. Presumably, it was intended as a quiet area for visitors to walk and refresh themselves, and indeed the abbot erected a wattle-work wall to avoid free access to the garden.[192] The Black Hostelry at Ely, which stands to the south of the infirmary complex, dates from the mid/late thirteenth century. It is now a canon's residence.[193] There was a long tradition of accommodating visiting monks apart from other guests. In 817 the Synod of Aachen prescribed that monastic visitors should be lodged near the church, next to the oratory, so that they might observe the regular hours undisturbed by the other guests. Similar arrangements are detailed in Hildemar's commentary on the *Rule of St Benedict*, c. 850.[194] However, the emergence of the Black Hostelry, a lodging place specifically for Benedictines and not for other regulars, is seemingly a development of the late twelfth / early thirteenth centuries and a response to the arrival of the new religious orders.

On account of the large number of Franciscans and Dominicans who visited St Albans on a regular basis, a hospice was built for their use shortly before 1247. This was inside the gate of the new court. Not all friars who visited St Albans stayed here and Matthew Paris explains that the two Franciscans sent to extort papal procurations in 1247 asked instead to be received in a superior hospice ('in hospitio sollempniori'), where bishops and eminent men stayed.[195] The construction of a hospice especially for mendicants visiting St Albans reiterates how provision for guests was affected by developments in

---

189 GASA 1, p. 290.
190 The new location may have been east of the cloister, near the monks' dormitory and infirmary for it has been suggested that the ground-level chapel of St Cuthbert, adjoining the eastern side of the dormitory probably served the Black Hostelry, Peers and Page, *VCH Herts.* 2, p. 508.
191 The first and more likely translation is Vaughan's, the second, Salzman's, Vaughan, *Chronicles of Matthew Paris*, p. 54; Salzman, *Building*, p. 380. I am grateful to Dr Peter Maxwell-Stuart for his advice on this passage.
192 GASA 1, p. 290; see below, p. 169.
193 The Black Hostelry is discussed in Holton-Krayenbuhl's detailed account of the infirmary complex, A. Holton-Krayenbuhl, 'The infirmary complex at Ely', *Archaeological Journal* 154 (1997), pp. 118–73, esp. pp. 138, 141–3, 160. For an overview, see P. Dixon, 'The monastic buildings', *A History of Ely Cathedral*, ed. P. Meadows and N. Ramsay (Woodbridge, 2003), pp. 143–56 esp. pp. 150–2.
194 Braunfels, *Monasteries*, pp. 40, 238.
195 *Chronica Majora* 4, p. 600. For a translation of this passage, see Vaughan, *Chronicles of Matthew Paris*, pp. 88–9.

the religious life as well as by individual pressures on each house. Thus, with the arrival of the Cistercians in the twelfth century, Benedictine communities might differentiate White Monks from visitors of their own order and provide for them accordingly; the appearance of the mendicants in the thirteenth century brought further distinctions and might lead to the construction of additional lodgings.

The guest facilities at St Albans in the twelfth and thirteenth centuries were well developed and perhaps more advanced than at other houses. Certainly as a royal foundation, an important pilgrim site and a convenient stopping-off point for travellers, the abbey would have attracted a number and variety of visitors. Still, the arrangements here are likely indicative of developments that were taking place gradually elsewhere, albeit on a smaller scale.

The administration of Cistercian hospitality: the guestmaster and hospice

A new abbot is not to be sent to a new place without at least twelve monks ... and without having first constructed an oratory, refectory, guest quarters and a gatehouse, that they might straightaway serve God there and live in keeping with the *Rule*.[196]

To set the Benedictine material in its wider context, it is instructive briefly to consider the administration of hospitality in Cistercian houses. The Cistercians' concern for unity and uniformity of practice led them to produce a detailed customary, the *Ecclesiastica Officia*, which covered all aspects of liturgical and daily life in the monastery. This sets out precisely how guests should be received from the moment they knocked at the door; accordingly, we now have a clear understanding of the guestmaster's office and of the process of hospitality, at least, in its prescriptive form. As there was no division between abbatial and conventual revenues in Cistercian houses there was no formal distinction between the abbot's and convent's guests or, at least, financial responsibility for visitors was not split. In theory hospitality was conducted within a single framework and the Cistercian guestmaster, therefore, acted on behalf of the community as a whole; in practice, the abbot might extend a personal and warmer welcome to distinguished guests The procedure set down in the *Ecclesiastica Officia* may reflect a simpler process that was also implemented in Benedictine houses where the abbot did not have independent resources, such as Reading and Battle, and may not be a defining feature of Cistercian hospitality.

The Cistercians sought to follow the *Rule of St Benedict* to the letter and, unlike the Benedictine hosteller, the guestmaster of the *Ecclesiastica Officia* was not involved with the initial reception of visitors.[197] This was entrusted to two monks rotated on a weekly basis. The Cistercian hosteller

---

[196] Capitula 9, 'Of the building of abbeys', *NLT*, p. 408.
[197] *Ecclesiastica Officia*, ch. 87 (p. 248). See below, pp. 108–9.

first encountered guests after they had been formally welcomed and were shown to the guest complex. This might include a hall and houses and was invariably situated outside the western range, on the fringes of monastic life. A good surviving example is Fountains Abbey, Yorkshire, where substantial remains of the two guesthouses can be seen and the outline of an adjacent guest-hall is known from geophysical survey of the site. The complex here is discussed in more detail later in the chapter. While the Cistercians made no distinction between the abbot's and convent's guests, visitors were nonetheless distinguished and tended according to their standing, their relationship with the community and perhaps also the occasion. It was the guestmaster who decided where each visitor should be accommodated and how he should be served.[198] At Fountains Abbey, noteworthy guests would have been entertained in relative comfort in one of the two guesthouses, while less distinguished visitors were more frugally provided for in the hall. These could evidently be rather rough places. An 'untoward event' occurred in the guest-hall refectory of Margam Abbey in 1180 when a young man was found dead on the very spot where he had struck another visitor the previous day.[199] The Cistercian abbey at Boyle, Roscommon, had a 'great stone house' for guests by 1202, almost twenty years before the church was completed. The Empress Mathilda gave two large guesthouses to Mortemer, Rouen, so that the poor, mercenaries, rich and religious could be accommodated separately.[200]

In the early days, the guestmaster probably waited upon visitors in person, and, William of Malmesbury remarked that the guestmaster and cellarer of the Cistercian mother-house, Cîteaux, tended visitors after Compline in the strictest silence.[201] It is likely that the guestmaster later assumed a more managerial role and delegated much of this work to his lay servant or deputy.[202] This is implied by both Ralph of Coggeshall and Jocelin of Furness in their accounts of mysterious visitors to Coggeshall and Melrose respectively. In Ralph's description of the reception of three Templars at Coggeshall, it is Brother Robert, the lay-brother in charge of the guest-hall, who greets the visitors and decides how they ought to be entertained.[203] Brother Walter, the

---

[198] See, for example, *Account Book of Beaulieu Abbey*, p. 33.

[199] Gerald of Wales, *Journey through Wales*, trans. Thorpe, p. 127. In 1246 a brawl in the abbot's stables at Furness resulted in the death of the baker (Henry the Pestur) who was stabbed by a visiting groom, *Annales Furnesiensis*, ed. T. Beck (London, 1844), p. 207.

[200] R. Stalley, *The Cistercian Monasteries of Ireland: an account of the history and architecture of the White Monks in Ireland from 1142 to 1540* (London, New Haven, 1987), p. 173; 'Le Recit de la Fondation de Mortemer', ed. J. Bouvet, *Collectanea Ordinis Cisterciensium Reformatorum* 22 (1960), pp. 149–68 (p. 159).

[201] *Gesta Regum* 1, p. 582. It was their observation of silence after Compline that impressed William. Not surprisingly there are less edificatory examples, notably, the abbot of Tintern who in 1217 was reprimanded for speaking and even drinking with monks and bishops after Compline, Canivez, *Statutes* 1, 1217: 30 (p. 472).

[202] *Ecclesiastica Officia*, ch. 109: 7 (p. 310).

[203] Coggeshall, *Chronicle*, pp. 134–5. Fergusson, *Architecture of Solitude: Cistercian Abbeys in Twelfth-Century England* (Princeton, 1984), p. 120, translates the Coggeshall helper as the 'assistant hosteller'.

lay-hosteller of Melrose Abbey, plays an equally prominent role.[204] It is possible that in both cases the lay-helpers were deputising for their monk hostellers, but their involvement more likely reflects the greater responsibility they now had or that might be accorded to them.[205] The late-thirteenth-century accounts of Beaulieu Abbey state that the hosteller should be assisted by two lay-brothers (*conuersi*) and two servants (*famuli*).[206]

The Cistercian guestmaster was not simply responsible for refreshing and accommodating visitors. He was expected to prepare the maundy of the guests or to ensure that another did so in his stead. Members of the community were assigned to help him on a weekly rota.[207] The guestmaster was also involved with the arrangements for Maundy Thursday, when he helped lead the poor into the cloister for the ceremonial washing of their feet, and made sure that afterwards they were well tended in the cell of the guesthouse (*cella hospitum*).[208] In contrast to his Benedictine counterpart, the Cistercian guestmaster did not seemingly escort visitors on tours around the abbey or liaise with other officials on their behalf. This is probably a reflection of the Cistercians' concern to keep outsiders well away from the brethren, and indeed the White Monks were renowned for their more exclusive attitude to outsiders, including monks of other orders. The hosteller was, however, to notify the prior of any guest who was close to death, so that he could arrange for a priest to celebrate communion.[209]

In recognition of his involvement with guests, the Cistercian hosteller was exempted from various claustral activities. He might, for example, be excused from work after chapter and the blessing at Collations; as one who prepared the Maundy, he was permitted to leave the dormitory after Compline.[210] If the guestmaster was busy with his duties and missed the post-Vespers drink, he did not have to atone for this in chapter; the cellarer, infirmarer and porter were

---

204   *Life of Waldef*, p. 139. Note also 'frater Willelmus, conuersus hospitalis de Forda', who was a trusted and respected friend to Wulfric and a major source for John's work, John of Ford's *Life of Wulfric*, pp. 24, 28, 99. Bell describes him as the 'junior guestmaster' and, citing Jubainville, explains that the monk guestmaster was helped by a *conversus hospitalis*, p. 148.

205   Williams, *Cistercians in the Early Middle Ages*, p. 125, argues that sometimes the *conuersi* took charge, as was the case at Coggeshall in c. 1180 and Barbeaux in 1220. Caesarius of Heisterbach recounts how a knight possessed by the devil and shown to a Cistercian hostel on the Continent received the prayers of the monk guestmaster, Walter Birbech, while the lay-brother tended him, *Caesarius, Dialogue on Miracles* 2, bk VIII: 38 (p. 514).

206   *Account Book of Beaulieu*, p. 18. The sub-hosteller of St Victor's, Paris, was a *conuersus* who manned the guesthouse and notified the guestmaster when visitors arrived, *Liber Ordinis*, ch. 15, p. 56 lines 28–39; for a similar arrangement at the Augustinian priory of Barnwell in the late thirteenth century, see *Observances in Use at St Giles and St Andrew at Barnwell*, p. 194.

207   *Ecclesiastica Officia*, ch. 106: 1 (p. 304). See below, p. 105–9.

208   *Ecclesiastica Officia*, ch. 21: 21 (p. 102). The guestmaster helped the lay *conuersus* and other lay-brothers appointed by the cellarer, *Ecclesiastica Officia*, ch. 21: 9 (p. 102).

209   *Ecclesiastica Officia*, ch. 100: 1 (p. 292).

210   *Ecclesiastica Officia*, ch. 74: 10, 80: 8, 82: 7 (pp. 218, 234, 236).

similarly excused.[211] The hosteller was granted certain concessions relating to the observance of silence and might speak with anyone who ate or slept in the guesthouse. Still, there were limits and he was not permitted to talk to guests or to the lay hosteller (*conuersus hospitalis*) outside the gate.[212]

An important distinction between Benedictine and Cistercian hostellers was that the latter seemingly had no contact with visiting members of the Order, other than the care of their horses. As part of the wider family, visiting Cistercians were considered fellow brethren, rather than guests, and took their place with the community in the choir, the refectory and the dormitory.[213] An exception was made on the first day of their visit when they were entitled to an extra pittance in the refectory but this was perhaps more an acknowledgement of the journey they had made than recognition of their status as guest.[214]

The Cistercian guesthouse complex

Fountains Abbey, in Yorkshire, is one of the most important and greatly visited monastic sites in the country and is now a World Heritage Site.[215] The remains of the guest complex shed light on the differing accommodation provided for guests visiting the abbey and, accordingly, of the distinction of guests. The Cistercians sought to establish self-sufficient communities and therefore required large precincts to house the necessary barns, outhouses and workshops. The entire precinct at Fountains covered about seventy acres, and was therefore much larger than most Benedictine precincts. Abingdon, for example, was around eighteen acres and Battle, twenty acres; Reading and St Augustine's, Canterbury, were some thirty acres and Westminster forty.[216] Access to the monastery precinct was regulated. Visitors were first admitted through an outer gate that stood to the west of the abbey. Nothing now remains of this West Gate but surviving documents reveal that by the sixteenth

---

211   *Ecclesiastica Officia*, ch. 80: 7 (p. 232).
212   *Ecclesiastica Officia*, ch. 119: 1 (p. 332).
213   Cistercian bishops and Cistercians on foot were evidently received in Beaulieu's hospice, c. 1270, *Account Book of Beaulieu*, ch. 72 'Table of the guest house', pp. 271, 273.
214   *Ecclesiastica Officia*, ch. 117: 5 (p. 330). *Twelfth-Century Statutes from the Cistercian General Chapter* ed. and commentary, C. Waddell (Brecht, 2002), 1157: 50 (p. 598); see also Waddell's note following 1195: 9 (pp. 311–12).
215   For discussion of the precincts, see G. Coppack, *Fountains Abbey: the Cistercians in northern England* (Stroud, 2003), pp. 79–81; G. Coppack, 'The interface between estate and monastery', *L'Espace Cistercien*, ed. L. Pressouyre (Paris, 1994), pp. 415–25. For the archaeology of the site, see R. Gilyard-Beer, 'Fountains abbey: the early buildings, 1132–50', *Archaeological Journal* 125 (1968), pp. 313–19; a plan is on p. 316; G. Coppack and R. Gilyard-Beer, *Fountains Abbey* (London, 1995); G. Coppack and R. Gilyard-Beer, 'Excavations at Fountains Abbey in N. Yorkshire, 1979–80: the early development of the church', *Archaeologia* 108 (1986), pp. 147–88.
216   *VCH Sussex* 9, ed. L. F. Salzman (Westminster, 1937), p. 102; J. Hurry, 'Reading Abbey church', *Archaeologia* 108 (1986), pp. 147–88; J. Robuck, *St Augustine's Abbey, Canterbury* (London, 1997), p. 3; B. Philp, *Excavations at Faversham, 1965: the royal abbey, Roman villa and Belgic farmstead* (Bromley, 1968), p. 30.

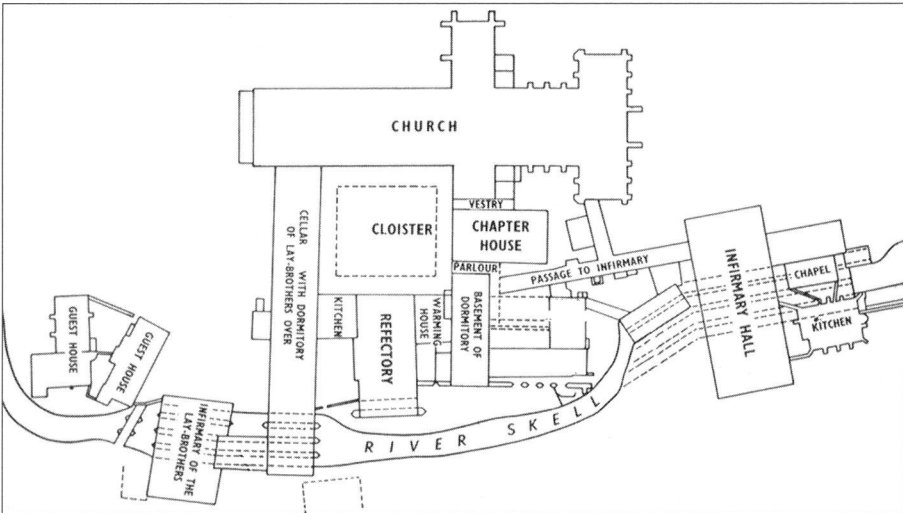

Figure 7 Plan of the abbey precinct, Fountains.

century it was leased to lay keepers, the Dawsons and the Johnsons.[217] Visitors proceeded through the gate to an inner gatehouse (the great gatehouse), which was also known as Kirk Garth Gate. It dates from the 1170s and, whilst heavily ruined, there is enough surviving to show that this was vaulted. It must have been similar to the twelfth-century Cistercian gatehouses at Roche Abbey, near Maltby, and Kirkstall Abbey in Leeds.[218] The monk porter received guests and administered alms at the great gatehouse each day, from Lauds until Compline. He had a room which gave access to the porch and also the gate hall.[219] In the later Middle Ages corrodians might receive their allowances here. Thomas Wel, who received a corrody from Fountains in the sixteenth century, was entitled to six loads of wood each year that was delivered to him at the inner gate (Kirk Garth Gate). The abbey tenants and keepers attended an annual audit at the gate, but it is not clear whether this was the outer gate

[217] These married couples rented a dwelling house at the West Gate and managed some kind of hospice here with stables for visitors, see below p. 91. Both husband and wife had duties in return for their allowances of food, drink and fuel. While the husband acted as porter of the West Gate and was to ensure that the gate was closed at night, his wife was to launder and repair linen belonging to the abbot's chamber, the hospice and buttery, *The Fountains Abbey Lease Book*, ed. D. J. H. Michelmore, YAS Rec. Ser. 140 (Leeds, 1981), p. 250. For the agreement between Fountains and Robert and Ellen Dawson in 1512, see no. 276 (pp. 291–3); for their successors as keepers, John and Margaret Johnson, see no. 237 (pp. 248–51).

[218] G. Coppack and R. Gilyard-Beer, *Fountains Abbey, Yorkshire*, English Heritage Guide (London, 1993), pp. 61–2.

[219] For the Cistercian gatehouse, see P. Fergusson, 'Porta patens esto. Notes on early Cistercian gatehouses in the north of England', *Mediaeval Architecture and its Intellectual Context: studies in honour of Peter Kidson*, ed. E. Fernie and P. Crossley (London, 1990), pp. 47–60. The gatehouse was also used for administrative purposes.

(West Gate) or inner gate (Kirk Garth).[220] From the inner gate visitors were directed either to the inner court where the guest complex stood, or to the outer court where the outhouses and workshops were located.

Upon entering the inner gate, guests would have had an impressive view of the narthex (galilee) and west end of the abbey church. The guest complex stood to the west of the lay-brothers' range, on the edge of monastic life. Hospitality was therefore confined to one area of the precinct, and would have caused minimal disruption to claustral life. The complex at Fountains comprised of a hall and two houses, and had its own drainage system to flush the latrines. Whereas more distinguished visitors would have stayed in one of the houses, other guests would have been shown to the hall. As previously noted, visiting Cistercians were welcomed as part of the extended family and would have joined their hosts in the claustral area.

The guesthouses were built in the 1160s and the remains, which are substantial, are amongst the finest in the country. Both were two-storey structures and vaulted, providing four suites for distinguished visitors and their households. Superior accommodation would have been located on the upper levels. The eastern house was the larger of the two and the lower storey comprised of six bays, divided into two rooms. The upper storey was accessed via an external timber staircase; this was later replaced by a stone staircase. The western guesthouse is less well preserved but was evidently similar, though smaller, in layout and design, having four bays. The two houses were well equipped and designed for comfort, with fireplaces, latrines and even rose windows. Both guesthouses were renovated in the fourteenth century, the western house more radically so and a new two-storey hall was built to its north; the former guesthouse served as the chamberblock to this hall.[221]

Geophysical survey has revealed that a large aisled guest-hall lay to the north of the guesthouses. This was probably intended as a public hall for less notable visitors or, as Gerald of Wales remarks, for 'the common folk'.[222] They would have slept and also eaten here. In the early days the abbot of Fountains would have presided as host in the hall, but later entertained distinguished visitors in a private chamber. The hall was built c. 1170 by Robert of Pipewell, who was renowned for his hospitality and is praised for showing fitting honour to guests.[223] All that remains from the guest-hall is a table leg. The hall originally comprised of seven bays and would have been heated; it was probably entered via a porch at the southern end.[224]

Fountains may also have had guest accommodation of sorts outside the abbey gates, perhaps for women who were not permitted to be received within the precinct. There certainly seems to have been a hospice here that was affiliated to the abbey in the sixteenth century, for the keepers of the West

[220]   *Fountains Abbey Lease Book*, no. 240 (pp. 254–5).
[221]   G. Coppack, *Fountains Abbey: the Cistercians in northern England* (Stroud, 2003), pp. 59–60; Coppack and Gilyard-Beer, *Fountains Abbey, Yorkshire*, pp. 59–61.
[222]   Gerald of Wales, 'De Iure et statu Menuensis ecclesiae', *Giraldi Cambrensis Opera* 3, ed. J. S. Brewer, RS 21 (London, 1863), pp. 99–373 (pp. 201–2).
[223]   *Memorials of Fountains* 1, pp. 125–6, 114.
[224]   Coppack and Gilyard-Beer, *Fountains Abbey, Yorkshire*, p. 60.

Gates, Robert and Ellen Dawson, were obliged to build stables by their house or the hospice for their own horses and those of their guests,

> the which guests Robert agrees by these presents to receive and care for diligently and humanely in everything, both in word and deed, and to treat them courteously and kindly in the accounts of their expenses as far as he is able, without damage to the monastery or of himself.[225]

Fountains probably also had lodgings for visiting Cistercian abbots, and these may have been located to the east of the cloister, near the infirmary area. A hall in a similar position at Clairvaux Abbey was known as the '*hospitium regis*'.[226] From his excavations at Waverley Abbey, Brakspear suggested that the visiting abbot's lodgings here comprised of two chambers.[227] Knowles identified a set of chambers linking the infirmary at Kirkstall Abbey to what is thought to have been the abbots's lodgings as the most likely quarters for visiting abbots.[228]

Whilst it is difficult to now identify these lodgings amongst the ruins it is likely that most, if not all houses, had provision of this kind to accommodate the abbot of their mother-house, who was known as the Father Immediate, on his annual visitation. This accommodation may also have been used by abbots stopping off *en route* to the General Chapter. Walter Daniel's account of a miraculous occurrence at Dundrennan Abbey, during Aelred of Rievaulx's visitation of the house, c. 1164–65, suggests that even more modest houses may have had separate accommodation for visiting abbots, though perhaps of a rather rudimentary nature. Walter explains that when Aelred visited Dundrennan as Father Immediate, he and his attendant brothers were accommodated in a small dwelling and served attentively during the six or seven days that they stayed. Aelred's bedclothes were spread in a corner of the dwelling and miraculously remained dry, despite the leaky roof. The dwelling here referred to was probably a temporary lodging, for Walter reveals that the regular offices were incomplete at this time.[229] If a relatively modest house like Dundrennan set aside lodgings for its Father Immediate in the mid-twelfth century, it is likely that from an early date Fountains made provision for visiting abbots. It did not, however, follow that these prelates were guaranteed a warm welcome and Abbot Ralph Haget (1190–1203) was reprimanded by the General Chapter on two occasions. In 1199 he was punished for showing

---

[225] *Fountains Abbey Lease Book*, no. 270 (p. 293). The lease was drawn up in 1512.

[226] H. Brakspear, *Waverley Abbey* (Guildford, 1905), pp. 65–6 (p. 66). Brakspear discusses the likelihood of such halls at Waverley, Fountains, Jervaulx and Whalley.

[227] Brakspear, *Waverley*, pp. 65–6.

[228] D. Knowles, *The Historian and Character, and Other Essays*, ed. C. N. L. Brooke and G. Constable (Cambridge, 1963), p. 204.

[229] This is mentioned in Aelred's *Epistola ad Mauricium*, an *apologia* for his *Life of Aelred*, and follows Powicke's edition of the *Life of Aelred*, pp. 66–81 (p. 74). Dundrennan was established by Rievaulx c. 1142. Visiting abbots were not necessarily assigned separate lodgings: when Abbot Guelerannus, abbot of Ursicampus, visited Mortemer in 1137 to establish their acceptance into the Cistercian Order, he dined and slept with the brethren, *Fondation de Mortemer*, p. 155.

'unequal hospitality' to Cistercian abbots staying at Fountains on their way to the General Chapter at Cîteaux; these were presumably abbots from the Cistercian houses in Scotland. The following year Ralph was reproached for receiving his Father Immediate, Abbot Guy of Clairvaux, less reverently than was deemed appropriate.[230]

Concluding remarks

With the development of monastic offices and the growing separation of the abbot from the convent, the administration of hospitality in Benedictine houses became increasingly complex from the mid- / late twelfth century. This was particularly true of houses whose revenues had been divided between the abbot and convent, for each was now accorded a body of guests and responsibilities. Subsequently there were more places within and outside the precinct where guests might be entertained, and a greater number of people were now involved with the administration of hospitality. While most houses would have had several lodgings for guests others would have been made available if required and, indeed, the community might use the guest chambers when they were not needed for visitors. In 1215, for example, the monks of Bury St Edmunds assembled in the abbey guest-house to discuss the disputed election to the abbacy.[231]

The nature of the evidence makes it difficult for us now to understand how precisely the process of hospitality operated. This is largely attributable to the obscurity and ambiguity of the surviving sources, but is a consequence also of there being no uniformity of practice amongst the Benedictines at this time. Procedures therefore varied from house to house and over time, and there was a tendency for each monastery to develop along individual lines.[232] Arrangements were discussed and debated, and might, as at Bury St Edmunds and Abingdon, cause rivalries and tensions and worsen relations between abbot and convent. It is rather paradoxical that while hospitality was prescribed in the *Rule of St Benedict* and was therefore a fundamental component of Benedictine life, the need to provide for guests visiting the monastery contributed to and perhaps triggered the separation of the abbot from the community, since it was his responsibility to entertain guests apart from the brethren. But later developments within the organisational structure of the monastery, largely the division of revenues between abbot and convent, the growth of the abbot's household and the obedientiary system, in turn affected the way in which hospitality was administered and perceived, and perhaps

---

[230] *Twelfth-Century Statutes from the General Chapter*, 1199: 45 (p. 436); 1200: 23 (p. 462).

[231] *Election of Abbot Hugh*, p. 108. In the late fourteenth century, the Cistercians of Meaux Abbey, Yorkshire, met in their guesthouse to resolve the dispute over Thomas Burton's election to the abbacy, *Monastic Chancery Proceedings*, ed. J. S. Purvis, YAS Rec. Ser. 88 (Wakefield, 1934), no. 80 (pp. 87–8).

[232] Smith, 'The central financing system of Christ Church', p. 362.

meant that guests now received a more impersonal reception than previously. They were likely to be met by a lay representative of the abbot or convent and tended in one of several lodgings administered by the abbot's household or the monk hosteller and his team. Given that by the late twelfth century the abbot of a great Benedictine house such as Bury St Edmunds, Abingdon or St Albans was often away from his community and when present dined with select guests, it is unlikely that many visitors now received the personal hospitality of the abbot, as envisaged by St Benedict in his *Rule*.

3

The reception of guests

It is our custom that those who wish to be entertained ask for hospitality as a kindness and do not demand it as a right, for this is a house of charity.[1]

How were guests welcomed upon their arrival at the monastery and just how important was the manner of their reception? The monastic community that received its guests warmly and courteously stood to enhance its reputation and might thereby secure goodwill and material benefits.[2] Therefore, the way in which guests were welcomed was potentially of practical and symbolic importance. The *Rule of St Benedict* sets down basic guidelines and states that everyone should be welcomed as Christ but an especially warm reception extended to pilgrims and monks. Whilst the *Rule* remained the basic point of reference throughout the Middle Ages, practices tended to vary from house to house. It is thus useful to analyse the procedure through a case study of Abingdon Abbey, as set out in the thirteenth-century customary of the house, the *De Obedientiariis*. This is a complex, ambiguous but important text, and is perhaps the earliest surviving discussion of the welcome procedure in a post-Conquest Benedictine customary.[3] The Abingdon material is set in context through an introductory analysis of Benedict's prescriptions; a final section discusses the reception of distinguished visitors.

---

[1]   The porter of St Albans, 1252, to Geoffrey de Lusignan's marshal, *Chronica Majora* 5, p. 344

[2]   See above, pp. 37–47.

[3]   Lanfranc, rather surprisingly, does not address this in his Constitutions of c. 1077, although he discusses the ceremonial reception of notable visitors, who were met by the entire community with a procession; see below.

Benedict's precepts

Let all guests that come be received like Christ Himself for He will say 'I was a stranger and you took Me in'. And let fitting honour be shown to all, especially to such as are of the household of the faith and to pilgrims.[4]

Chapter 53 of the *Rule* of St Benedict sets out broad guidelines for the reception of guests and states that all visitors should be warmly (and appropriately) welcomed as Christ Himself, and that particular care ought to be shown to fellow religious and pilgrims. This particular section of the *Rule* does not mention the porter, but his involvement is implied and indeed a later chapter (66) states that whenever a visitor knocks at the door, the porter should welcome him with the customary greeting (*Deo gratias*).[5] It is not clear from the *Rule* if it was the porter's job to notify the community of the guest's arrival, but given Benedict's recommendation that the porter should be an 'old and wise man' who would act efficiently and with humility to ensure that the gate was always manned, it is perhaps more likely that an assistant informed the abbot or prior. It is, of course, perfectly feasible that there was no hard and fast rule, and that Benedict intended this to be a matter for the community to decide according to its resources, facilities and the number of guests expected.

Once the visitor's arrival had been announced he was met either by the Superior or one of the monks – '*Ut ergo nuntiatus fuerit hospes, occuratur ei a Priore vel a fratribus cum omni officio caritatis*'. The use of *uel* here is, however, ambiguous since it can mean either 'and' or 'or', and has led some to interpret the welcome of guests as 'a community ritual', whereby the abbot and all the monks greeted the visitor.[6] To extend a welcome of this kind to all guests as a matter of course would have severely disrupted communal life, and it is more likely that visitors were usually met by a representative of the monastic body, and that a community turn-out was reserved for distinguished visitors.[7] In fact, Peter the Venerable, abbot of Cluny, makes this very point when discussing the washing of guests' feet.[8] Benedict sets out fairly detailed instructions for a guest's initial reception. The monk should bow before the visitor both upon his arrival and at his departure, in a show of humility, and greet him as if he were Christ. The monk (or monks) assigned to the task prayed with the guest, thereby associating with him in peace, and then

---

4   *Rule of St Benedict*, ch. 53 (p. 132).
5   *Rule of St Benedict*, ch. 66 (pp. 170–2). Note Abbot Peter the Venerable of Cluny's response to Bernard of Clairvaux on the minutiae of this passage, Peter the Venerable, *Letters* 1, ep. 28, clause 14.
6   See, for example, L. Coffin, 'Hospitality: an orientation to Benedictine spirituality', *American Benedictine Review* 39 (1988), pp. 50–71 (p. 63).
7   See below p. 109.
8   Peter the Venerable, *Letters* 1, ep. 28, clause 9 (p. 72).

extended the kiss.[9] For 'fear of delusions of the devil', it was vital not to reverse this order, and this concern was expressed also by the Fathers of the East in the fourth and fifth centuries, who saw prayer as a way to neutralise diabolical influence.[10] It has been suggested that by including the kiss in the reception procedure Benedict intended that the guest should become a part of the community.[11] This is not entirely convincing, for although the outsider became associated with the brethren, he was not fully integrated. The kiss was simply a stage in the reception process; it was part of the ceremonial reception by which the visitor was prepared for his entrance and it was an expression of unity in Christ.[12]

Following this initial reception the guest was led to pray and thereafter either the Superior or one of the monks edified him with a reading from the Divine Law, to prepare him spiritually for his stay at the monastery.[13] Once the soul had been refreshed in this way 'all kindness was shown'; presumably this refers to refreshment of a more earthly kind such as the 'friendly and companionable conversation and (tending of) every bodily need', that Hildegard of Bingen (d. 1178) mentions in her twelfth-century commentary on the *Rule*.[14] The Maundy of the guests was then carried out, when the abbot washed the visitors' hands and he, as much as the others, washed their feet.[15] This probably took place in the cloister. Once the visitor had been fully and formally welcomed he was shown to the guesthouse (*cella hospitum*) and cared for by the guestmaster who alone was permitted to speak with visitors. If one of the other monks happened to meet a guest he was not to dally or indulge in chit chat, but humbly excuse himself and explain that they were not permitted

---

9   This was the ancient form of greeting amongst Christians. St Paul argued that Christians should 'salute one another with a holy kiss' (e.g. Romans 16:16; I Corinthians 16:20); Rufinus discussed the fraternal kiss of monks and guests, see Winzen, 'Conference', p. 59. Although the kiss was associated with receiving and greeting it was, of course, a component of other ceremonials. St Augustine describes the kiss as 'a great sacrament'; the kiss of peace was often used in the liturgy of the early Church, usually at the start and finish of ceremonies, see Constable, *Culture and Spirituality*, essay 7, p. 795, n. 93. For the symbolism of the kiss, see J. Le Goff, *Time, Work and Culture in the Middle Ages*, trans. A. Goldhammer (Chicago, London, 1977), pp. 242–4, 256.

10   P. Delatte, *Commentary on the Rule of St Benedict*, trans. J. McCann (London, 1959), p. 334. The later medieval customary of Eynsham suggests that this clause was less concerned with 'safety' than with ensuring that the guest prayed on his arrival, for it states that monks in particular, whether Benedictines or Cistercians, should not receive the kiss until after they had prayed, *Eynsham Customary*, ch. 19: 2 (506), p. 199 lines 13–17.

11   Delatte, *Commentary*, p. 334.

12   Note Aelred of Rievaulx's description of the kiss to guests as a sign of Catholic unity, which underlines that this gesture was symbolic of their present state (i.e. unity in Christ) and was not intended to augment change by making the outsider one of the community, see 'De Spiritali Amicitia' in *Aelredi, Opera Omnia* 1, pp. 279–350 (p. 307).

13   Delatte, *Commentary*, p. 335, explains that a passage from the Holy Scriptures or a Catholic author was read; a collection of short exhortations from Gregory was used at Monte Cassino.

14   *Hildegard, Explanation of the Rule*, ch. 26, 'On hospitality' (p. 32).

15   *Rule of St Benedict*, ch. 53 (p. 134).

to talk with visitors.[16] The monks were to act with courtesy at all times, but were not to compromise their ideals.

Neither the components nor the sequence of this welcome procedure are peculiar to the reception of guests and recur in other rituals such as the installation of abbots,[17] the profession of novices[18] and the celebration of the Eucharist.[19] On these occasions also prayer is followed by a kiss and then by food and drink, either on a symbolic level, like the bread and wine of the Mass, or as a source of physical nourishment. In each case the components – or symbols – take on a different meaning within the sequence, but together are an acknowledgement of fellowship and linked to the process of conversion.[20]

The example of Abingdon

Benedict intended that his 'little rule for beginners' should be a starting point, offering basic guidelines for daily life in the cloister which could then be modified to suit the community's needs and abilities. An early, if not the earliest, known post-Conquest customary to address the reception of guests is the *De Obedientiariis* of Abingdon Abbey, which was probably compiled c. 1220. Its laconic style presents problems for the modern reader and it is therefore useful, at times, to refer to later and more explicit customaries, particularly those of Eynsham and St Mary's, York which are thought to share the same source.[21]

Stage one: the initial reception

It is not clear from the *De Obedientiariis* how precisely guests were welcomed when they first arrived at the gate of the abbey, for the customary does not set out the porter's duties, presumably as he was a layman and this was intended as a manual for monastic officials.[22] However, the section dealing with the abbot and his household mentions the abbot's doorkeeper (*janitor*), who would have been one of several doorkeepers operating within the precinct.[23] While he was unlikely the first member of Abingdon to greet visitors, details of his duties shed some light on certain aspects of the welcome procedure. The

---

16 *Rule of St Benedict*, ch. 53 (p. 136).
17 E.g. *Jocelin*, p. 25.
18 E.g. Lanfranc, *Constitutions*, ch. 102–4 (pp. 155–63).
19 See A. Heron, *Table and Tradition: towards an ecumenical understanding of the Eucharist* (Edinburgh, 1983), pp. 59–60, for a detailed account of Justin the Martyr's description of the Eucharist in his 'First Apology', c. 150 AD, which is the oldest reasonably detailed description of the Eucharist and how it was celebrated.
20 See below, p. 112.
21 See above, p. 16–17.
22 In Cistercian abbeys and, indeed, the nunneries, a member of the religious community held this post, see below, p. 108.
23 The abbot's role is dealt with in *De Obedientiariis*, pp. 336–55.

De Obedientiariis does not state how the abbot's doorkeeper should respond to guests, but the curtar or another abbey official may have instructed him on how to greet them courteously to project a positive image of Abingdon to the outside world.[24] The importance of welcoming guests warmly is addressed in Alexander of Neckam's 'programme for clerical study', the *De Sacerdos ad altare*, which he seemingly compiled in the early thirteenth century, as a canon of Cirencester. This states that the porter should be polite, courteous, honest and educated from boyhood, and ought to extend a cheerful welcome to guests.[25] Visitors who were arrogant might meet with frostiness rather than humility. When Geoffrey de Lusignan's marshal arrived at St Albans in 1252 to announce the imminent arrival of his lord, he did not greet the doorkeeper but asked him rather brusquely where Geoffrey would be accommodated. When told simply wherever he wished, the marshal secured the best the abbey could offer, namely, the royal palace that was reserved for the king and his kin. The doorkeeper tersely replied that those requesting accommodation should not make demands, but ask for this charitably.[26] The pilgrims and travellers who arrived at Lewes Priory in 1200 no doubt anticipated a warm welcome from a community renowned for its hospitality, but were in for a shock when they were met instead by armed guards who had been stationed there by the earl of Warenne. This was connected with a dispute between the earl and the abbot of Cluny regarding the election of a new prior. As the pope favoured the abbot of Cluny's candidate over the earl of Warenne's, the earl had everyone who arrived at the priory searched, lest they were carrying letters from the abbot of Cluny.[27]

To return to the procedure at Abingdon, once the abbot's doorkeeper had welcomed the visitor he notified the curtar who could then ensure that the guest was adequately and appropriately provided for throughout his stay. The customary implies that the monks and not the doorkeeper notified the curtar of the arrival of their own relatives, but it is difficult to envisage just how this would have worked. The hosteller of Abingdon was not involved in the initial reception of guests, but was notified of their arrival once they had been admitted to the precinct. He would have met visitors in the outer parlour, also known as the guest parlour, which was on the western range.[28] The guestmaster was probably informed of the visitor's arrival by either the custodian of the

---

[24] For the porter's and portress's role in conveying a positive impression of the house to outsiders see, *Liber Ordinis*, ch. 15 (pp. 55–6 lines 13–22), Abelard, *Epistolae*, ep. 8, col. 280.

[25] J. Goering, 'Neckam, Alexander (1157–1217)', *Oxford Dictionary of National Biography* (Oxford, 2004).

[26] *Chronica Majora* 5, p. 344.

[27] The various documents relating to this dispute are discussed and edited by G. F. Duckett in his *Charters and Records Illustrative of the Ancient Abbey of Cluni, from 1077 to 1534*, 8 vols (Lewes, 1888), 1, pp. 86–101; see in particular Hubert Walter's charter of 1200, no. 284 (pp. 88–9).

[28] For the description of this as the guest parlour, see the account of the prior's post-Compline rounds, *De Obedientiariis*, p. 364.

outer parlour or the doorkeeper; certainly, it was the doorkeeper who notified him of any canons wishing to enter the monastery.[29]

This rather sketchy outline of the initial reception of guests prompts a number of questions. For example, how precisely were visitors greeted when they knocked at the abbey gate and where did they wait while the porter notified the curtar of their arrival? Did the porter receive all guests in the same manner or were different procedures implemented depending on whether the visitor was a regular or secular, and on his standing? Moreover, did the hosteller meet everyone who visited the abbey, irrespective of whether the guest was to be entertained by the community or the abbot? Or did he simply receive those who were the monks' responsibility and leave the abbot's household to tend his guests, as is suggested by the rather obscure passage relating to canons? Did he, like the intern hosteller of Westminster Abbey, send visiting monks the long-sleeved monastic garment (*froccus*), which was to be worn by monks in church, and then meet them in the parlour?[30]

To explore these questions more fully it is helpful to refer to the later and more explicit customary of Eynsham Abbey, which is thought to have been compiled from the same source as the *De Obedientiariis*. The Eynsham customary sets out the porter's duties in considerable detail and in places it cites the twelfth-century customary of the Victorine Canons (*Liber Ordinis*) almost verbatim.[31] It stresses the porter's role as an ambassador of the abbey, for he was after all the guest's first encounter with the monastery which might have a considerable impact on his subsequent assessment of monastic

---

[29] *De Obedientiariis*, p. 415; for the arrangements at Eynsham, see *Eynsham Customary*, ch. 19: 10 (532–40), pp. 210–11. At Westminster Abbey the hosteller was notified by the servant of the parlour, *Westminster Customary*, p. 80 lines 2–8.

[30] *Westminster Customary*, p. 80 lines 2–8, p. 83 lines 3–6. For similar instructions, see *St Augustine's Customary* (fourteenth-century), p. 136 line 35 – p. 137 line 3, and *St Mary's Customary*, p. 95. The hosteller of Westminster did not meet any visiting monk who had been professed at Westminster but simply sent the *froccus* via his servant. Various rulings regarding the wearing of this garment include the 1221 statutes issued by the York General Chapter, clause 45 and the 1249 statutes issued by the province of Canterbury, clause 30, Pantin, *Chapters* 1, p. 242, p. 42; *Eynsham Customary* ch. 19: 20 (230), p. 123. Bernard of Cluny's eleventh-century customs for the monastery stipulated that the guestmaster should keep 'cappas et superpellicia' for any guests dining in the refectory, although laity were not permitted to eat there, *Ordo Cluniacensis per Bernardum*, ch. 9 (p. 154). During Norrey's tyrannical abbacy at Evesham, c. 1213, the brethren were obliged to remain in the infirmary through want of the *froccus* and *cuculla*, since by custom they could only follow the convent if wearing these, Thomas of Marlborough, *History of Evesham*, ch. 464 (pp. 442–3).

[31] *Liber Ordinis*, ch. 15, pp. 55–6. The porter of the court and the sub-hosteller, both *conversi*, were responsible for the initial reception of guests. The porter welcomed guests cheerily and notified the sub-hosteller who greeted guests with a bow and gave them keys to the stables, and also to the chambers where servants stayed. He then took their horses and asked them to wait while he notified the guestmaster (*hospitarius maior*), who was a canon, and thus remained in the claustral area. The guestmaster immediately came to welcome guests as soon as he learned of their arrival, even if the Hours were in progress. He led them to the church to pray, exchanged the kiss and edified them with a brief sermon.

life within.[32] It was thus vital that the porter should act with courtesy and respect at all times, particularly to anyone who was visiting for the first time or whom he had to turn away, lest they were offended by the rebuff.[33] The porter greeted regular guests cheerfully and took the stirrups and reins of the one whom he considered to be the superior, welcoming him with the words 'Bene veniatis domini' ('May your lords be welcome'). Thereafter he led them to wait in the parlour or another appropriate place while the guestmaster was notified by the custodian of the parlour. The porter was instructed to greet secular visitors and those of humble means (*ignoti*) with kindness and humility, and to establish who they were and what they wanted so that he could deal with them accordingly.[34] Distinguished visitors were presumably greeted personally by the abbot or prior, and perhaps even a group of the leading monastic officials. A late-twelfth-century depiction of Cuthbert's reception by Abbot Boisil of Old Melrose shows the abbot warmly embracing his visitor at the threshold of the monastery (opposite). Although this meeting occurred in the seventh century it likely reflects practices at the time of composition, c. 1180.[35] The entire community might turn out to welcome a noteworthy person. When Abbot William (1214–35) of St Albans visited Tynemouth, a cell of the house, he was met not only by the community but by hordes of the leading men of the neighbourhood; such was the crowd that had turned out to greet him that it seemed as though an army had gathered.[36]

Stage two: reception in the church

> The brothers pray to God so that they will not violate their order with the guests; the guests, that they will be better for seeing their way of life.[37]

The second stage of the guest's reception took place in the church or oratory, where the visitor prayed for sins committed on the journey. The Abingdon customary elaborates on the procedure set out in the *Rule of St Benedict*, but is more succinct than later customaries and is accordingly rather ambiguous in places. The hosteller led visitors to the door of the church where they made a little bow and, upon rising at the entrance, sprinkled themselves with holy

---

32   *Eynsham Customary*, ch. 19: 10 (535), p. 210 lines 7–13, citing *Liber Ordinis*, ch. 15, p. 56 lines 18–22.

33   *Eynsham Customary*, ch. 19: 10 (535), p. 210 lines 2–6. If the Victorine porter had to turn anyone away he was to avoid offending them by asking their pardon, *Liber Ordinis*, ch. 15, p. 55 lines 14–18.

34   The Victorine porter welcomed guests cheerily and with a bow, and led religious guests to the parlour where they awaited the arrival of the sub-hosteller; he seemingly asked secular guests to remain in his lodge while the sub-hosteller was notified, *Liber Ordinis*, ch. 15, p. 56 lines 25–33. I am grateful to Miss Barbara Harvey for her advice on the term 'ignoti'.

35   BL Yates Thompson MS 26, fol. 16. This is discussed by D. Marner, St *Cuthbert: His Life and Cult in Medieval Durham* (Toronto, 2000), p. 44.

36   GASA 1, p. 271; Vaughan, *Chronicles of Matthew Paris*, pp. 41–2. See below, p. 109, for Aelred's reception at the Cistercian abbey of Rievaulx.

37   *Hildegard, Explanation of the Rule*, ch. 26, 'On hospitality' (p. 32).

Figure 8 St Cuthbert greeted by Abbot Boisil of Melrose, Bede's *Life of St Cuthbert*, BL Yates Thompson 26, fol. 16 (late twelfth century).

water.[38] In some houses this was done by the hosteller, although he showed deference to abbots, cathedral priors and other dignitaries.[39] It was clearly important that the arrival of guests should cause the minimum of disruption to monastic observance and the guestmaster of Abingdon was only to lead visitors into the church to pray if the community was not in the choir, but in the cloister or somewhere elsewhere outside the church. Otherwise, guests were brought to pray at the altar in the vestry. There were other factors that had a bearing on how the visitor prayed. If it was a feast day and the benches (forma)[40] in the choir were cleared from this area, the guest bowed (inclinando) to make his prayer. On days when the monks lay over their benches to pray, the guest made a low bow (venia)[41] as he prayed. Similar instructions are set out in the later customaries of Eynsham, Westminster and St Mary's, York.[42]

Stage three: reception in the parlour

After they had prayed guests were led to the parlour which stood on the eastern range, next to the chapter-house; this is sometimes referred to as the

---

[38]   De Obedientiariis, p. 411. The precise meaning of expeditus here is unclear, and can mean either physically able or free to do so; thus, for example, the hosteller of Abingdon was to attend all hours and Masses when 'free' of guests, De Obedientiariis, p. 411.

[39]   For example, see Eynsham Customary, ch. 10: 2 (506), p. 198 line 32 – p. 199 line 1; St Mary's Customary, p. 95, St Augustine's Customary (fourteenth-century), p. 137. The Eynsham customary specifically mentions the priors of Rochester and Canterbury; the customary of St Mary's states that he should show deference to any bishop, abbot, prior or another great prior 'de stallo'.

[40]   Brooke explains that these forma were portable benches or desks placed in the middle of the choir, and were used before the community had permanent choir stalls. The term supra forma refers to their kneeling at the benches rather than sitting on them; by prostrating themselves supra forma they prostrated themselves out between the benches, Lanfranc, Constitutions, p. 18 n. 52. According to the thirteenth-century instructions for novices at Christ Church to lie on the bench was 'when one kneeling bows over the desk with his breast upon it', Instructio Novicorum, pp. 206–7.

[41]   The terms used in the De Obedientiariis to denote the alternative positions of prayer are consistent with other sources. They suggest that, in general, a venia was made when there were desks in the choir area, but a bow (inclinando) on major feast days when the space was cleared. The Eynsham customary describes this as a long bow (longam veniam) made in the choir; the customary of St Mary's, York, states that on a fast day the guest should prostrate his whole body to pray; according to the late-thirteenth-century customary of Westminster Abbey, the visitor should make a low bow (curta venia) if the convent was on that day at their benches, Eynsham Customary, ch. 19: 1 (506), p. 199 lines 2–4; St Mary's Customary, p. 95; Westminster Customary, p. 80 lines 11–16. Novices at Christ Church, Canterbury, were informed that on feasts of twelve lessons they should not lie over their desks and should omit the low bow (curta venia) at the altar, Instructio Novicorum, pp. 206–7.

[42]   Guests visiting Eynsham on a feast day bowed to pray (inclinabit); visitors at Westminster bowed to pray (inclinando) if the convent was not that day at their benches, and guests at St Mary's, York, on a feast day bowed to pray in the space cleared, Eynsham Customary, ch. 19: 2 (506), p. 199 lines 2–6, Westminster Customary, p. 80 lines 2–14, St Mary's Customary, p. 95.

inner or regular parlour.[43] Here the Kiss of Peace and Love was extended and the hosteller of Abingdon offered 'words of consolation'.[44] It is not clear if this should be equated with the formal reading that Benedict prescribed, or if it refers to a more informal address that had replaced this. Certainly, Abingdon would not have been alone in either abandoning or modifying Benedict's precepts. At the turn of the thirteenth century Hugh of Lincoln's biographer, Adam of Eynsham, complained that monasteries now rarely observed this custom and he lavishly praised the monks of Cluny since they had read to Bishop Hugh from Gregory's *Pastoral Care* on his recent visit to the community.[45] The practice of delivering a formal reading to visitors had been abandoned by some communities, but the custom was not obsolete. Whereas the later customaries of Eynsham and St Mary's, York make no mention of a formal reading or even simple words of comfort that ought to be extended to the guest, the late-thirteenth-century customary of Westminster Abbey and the early-fourteenth-century customary of St Augustine's, Canterbury, both state that the hosteller should offer visitors some words from the Divine Page.[46] Whilst it is clear that practices varied from house to house, it is less certain if these 'words of consolation' show Abingdon upholding a custom that was on the wane or contributing to its demise.[47]

After the hosteller had edified the visitor he turned his attention to more practical matters and established the reason for the guest's visit. At this point he presumably made inquiries about the guest's identity, for he was to inform the refectorer of anyone who had arrived before dinner and wished to dine, so that he could make the suitable preparations to serve them according to their standing.[48] The grading of guests in this way might seem rather incongruous to the monastic spirit and, indeed, to the spirit of hospitality itself. However, this was acceptable for the time and did not mean that lesser guests should be neglected, but that those of note should be suitably honoured. Thus Abbot Walter of Battle was commended for welcoming all comers and showing good manners to each according to his rank or station; similarly, Abbot Robert of

---

43   *De Obedientiariis*, p. 411. The Eynsham and Westminster customaries also describe this as the 'regular parlour', see for example, *Eynsham Customary*, ch. 19: 2 (506), pp. 198–9; *Westminster Customary*, p. 80 line 14.

44   According to the late-thirteenth-century customary of St Mary's, York, this was carried out in the hospice, *St Mary's Customary*, p. 95.

45   *Magna Vita* 2, p. 176. The particular passage read might correspond with the guest's identity. A fragment of customs relating to the monastery of Rheinau lists seven categories of guest and includes a passage for each; for example, the reading given to popes, bishops and abbots begins 'You are the salt of the earth', see Herrgot, *Vetus Disciplina Monastica*, pp. 586–7. I am indebted to Professor Robert Bartlett for identifying this monastery.

46   *Westminster Customary*, p. 80 lines 17–19; *St Augustine's Customary* (fourteenth-century), p. 137. The twelfth-century customary of the Victorines mentions a brief sermon, *Liber Ordinis*, ch. 17, p. 60 line 30.

47   It is interesting that this practice is no longer observed today and there is simply a reading in the refectory, Delatte, *Commentary*, p. 335; perhaps what we have in the twelfth century is the start of a custom on the wane.

48   *De Obedientiariis*, p. 415.

Fountains (1170–80) was praised for showing fitting honour to guests.[49] To ensure that visitors were welcomed appropriately and that the community, in turn, preserved its reputation, it was crucial that the hosteller interrogated them early on. This is quite different to the lay sources which stress that hosts should refrain from questioning visitors until after they had been received and refreshed, lest it seemed they were reluctant to extend their hospitality.[50] According to Walter Map, the Welsh were so concerned to be seen as willing hosts that they did not make any inquiries of their guests until the third day of the stay.[51]

Matters of a practical nature become increasingly prominent in the customaries; questions that ought to be posed to guests and information relayed to them now appear alongside, and even in place of, spiritual discourse. This may be related to the growing tendency to consign issues to writing, or was perhaps intended to deal more efficiently with the numbers of guests. The late-thirteenth-century customary of Westminster Abbey, for example, states that the hosteller should question guests in the parlour to establish who they were and where they were from, thereby ensuring that everyone was accorded fitting honour. He was also to check if visitors required refreshments and how many horses they had, so that the extern hosteller could make suitable preparations. The guest was then led to the guest cell (*cella hospitum*) where he was edified with a holy reading and informed of practicalities.[52] A similar arrangement is detailed in the early-fourteenth-century customary of St Augustine's, Canterbury. This states that after the reading any stranger monks should be given a tour around the court and then asked about the number of their grooms and servants, so that they could be provided for appropriately.[53] The customary of Eynsham Abbey is particularly explicit and warns the hosteller that before bringing guests to the parlour he should find out if they required food or other necessities, and also ask if anyone wished to see the dormitory to spare the embarrassment of those needing to use the facilities.[54]

49   *Battle Chronicle*, pp. 260–1, *Memorials of Fountains* 1, pp. 125–6, p. 114.
50   For further discussion, see Kerr, 'The open door', p. 329.
51   Map, *De Nugis*, pp. 182–3.
52   *Westminster Customary*, p. 80 lines 23–9.
53   *St Augustine's Customary* (fourteenth-century), p. 137.
54   *Eynsham Customary*, ch. 19: 3 (506), p. 199 lines 20–30.

The maundy of the guests

When the guests whom blessed Father Benedict received were about to eat he gave them water for their hands; and when they had risen from the table he washed their feet.[55]

One particular component of hospitality prescribed in the *Rule of St Benedict*, and previously mentioned in Chapter 1, is the maundy of the guests. Benedict stipulated that the abbot and community should wash guests' feet while saying the *Suscipimus Deus*, and that the abbot should wash their hands.[56] By the twelfth century this was no longer intrinsic to Benedictine – or Cluniac – hospitality. It was, however, strictly observed by the Cistercians whose customary sets out exactly how this should be conducted. The Cistercians criticised the Benedictines for what they considered a breach of the *Rule*.[57] Peter the Venerable defended the Cluniacs' abandonment of this on practical grounds, reasoning that if the feet of all guests were washed, the community would spend the whole day bowing, prostrating and washing hands and feet, rather than celebrating the Office; either visitors would always be in the cloister and offices or the brethren would always be in the guesthouse. Hildegard of Bingen makes a similar point in her commentary on the *Rule*.[58] Nevertheless, it is likely that some Benedictine communities continued to uphold this practice; a later, twelfth-century illustration of St Cuthbert's reception of an angel shows the saint washing his guest's feet.[59] Nevertheless, the Benedictines, like the Cistercians, continued to observe the Maundy of the poor, and at Abingdon the feet were washed of three poor men admitted each day to the monastery.[60] On Maundy Thursday the chamberlain, almoner and doorkeeper (*janitor*) of Abingdon introduced the poor and indigent to the cloister. The feet of needy relatives were washed first, and thereafter those of clerks and pilgrims; each received 3d before he left.[61]

---

55 Hildegard, 'Commentary on the Rule', ch. 26 (p. 32).

56 *Rule of St Benedict*, ch. 53 (p. 134). Delatte, *Commentary*, p. 337, explains that in ancient times the servant or disciple poured water on the hands of those about to dine; St Martin of Tours made it the act of a monk wishing to honour his guests, and with Benedict it became the rule.

57 *Ecclesiastica Officia*, 107 (p. 304), 119 (p. 332); Idung, *Dialogue*, III: 50–1 (p. 137). For further discussion of the administration of the Maundy at Cistercian houses, see Kerr, 'Cistercian hospitality', forthcoming.

58 Peter the Venerable, *Letters* 1, ep. 28, clause 9 (p. 72); Hildegard, *Commentary on the Rule*, ch. 26, 'On hospitality', pp. 32–3. Hildegard noted that Benedict washed the feet of guests after the example of Christ at the Last Supper but in his time, 'monks did not yet feel the press of a tumult of strangers crowding upon them'. See also Peter Abelard's letter of advice to Heloise and the nuns of the Paraclete, *PL* 178, letter 8, cols 280–1.

59 BL Yates Thompson MS 126, fol. 17v. This is reproduced as plate 8 in Marner, *St Cuthbert: his life and cult*, p. 65.

60 *History of Abingdon* 2, p. 335; *De Obedientiariis*, p. 405. See above p. 29 for further discussion.

61 *De Obedientiariis*, p. 387.

A cheerful reception

> There ought in the monastery to be suitable places where guests can be welcomed respectfully and cheerfully.[62]

It was important to extend a warm welcome to guests. This is explicit in the *Rule of St Benedict* which stipulates that visitors should be received with humility. The *De Obedientiariis* of Abingdon prescribes that guests should be shown all kindness and received diligently.[63] Other sources are more specific and state that visitors should be welcomed joyfully and with cheerful faces. The customary of Bury St Edmunds, for example, instructs the intern hosteller to receive all visiting Benedictines joyfully and show them honour.[64] Anselm of Bec, who is described by his biographer as a cheerful and generous host, evidently hoped others would follow his example, for he urged his successor, William, to receive visitors with joy and tend them cheerfully.[65] The archdeacon, Walter Map, who was hardly an ardent admirer of the monks, maintained that they reserved a cheerful welcome for those whom they feared or intended to fleece, but extended an altogether frostier reception to secular clerks and others whom Walter deemed equally worthy.[66] Accounts recording the reception of distinguished visitors (which are discussed in the final section of this analysis) invariably describe the great joy exhibited by the host communities on these occasions as a testimony to the monasteries' exemplary hospitality, as well as to the guests' worthiness. Matthew Paris records that Henry II and Walter of Lincoln were received with great reverence and joy when they visited his own community at St Albans in 1184.[67]

There were obvious benefits to be gained by extending a cheery welcome to guests. This was a sure way to secure the visitor's favour and hopefully to enhance the reputation of the house, and it was also a way to demonstrate the community's willingness to exercise hospitality. There were biblical associations too, chiefly Abraham's enthusiastic reception of the angels (Genesis 18: 1–15), discussed in Chapter 1, and I Peter 4: 9 ('Be hospitable to each other and do not grudge it'), which was evoked by Osbert de Clare (d. c. 1158) in his letter

62   *De Sacerdos ad altare*, p. 265.
63   *Rule of St Benedict*, ch. 53 (p. 134); *De Obedientiariis*, p. 411.
64   *Bury Customary*, p. 25. Other examples include clause 4 of the statutes issued by the General Chapter of Cluny, 1205–6, *Statuts, Chapitres* 1, p. 55; *Eynsham Customary*, ch. 19: 1 (505), p. 198 line 20, ch. 20: 10 (536), p. 210 lines 14–17; *St Mary's Customary*, p. 88; 'Ely ordinances', pp. 1–74 (p. 40), 1314: 17. The late-thirteenth-century ordinances for the Augustinian priory at Barnwell state that the canons' hosteller should be well-mannered and respectable, and, if he had nothing to offer, should show a cheerful face and agreeable conversation, 'for friends are multiplied by agreeable words', *Ordinances of Barnwell*, p. 192.
65   Eadmer, *Vita Anselmi*, p. 46; Anselm, *Letters* 2, ep. 178 (pp. 93–5).
66   Map, *De Nugis*, pp. 84–5; 98–101.
67   GASA 1, p. 197. *Vita Anselmi*, p. 50, gives a similar account of Archbishop Anselm's visit to Bec in 1103.

thanking the abbess of Barking for her fine entertainment.[68] II Corinthians 9.7 ('Every man according as he purposes in his heart, so let him give not grudgingly, or of necessity: for God loves a cheerful giver') is cited in the *Rule of St Benedict* to warn of the importance of acting with grace and joy, and of the punishment awaiting those who give grudgingly.[69] This was also quoted by Peter of Blois, who wrote to St Albans complaining of his poor reception at their cell of Wallingford Priory.[70] A cheery welcome may have been desirable, but it was clearly not guaranteed.

The Cistercian example

Whereas our understanding of the reception of guests at Benedictine houses is rather fragmented and confused, the detailed and comprehensive customary compiled by the Cistercians means that we now have a clear and coherent idea of how visitors to their abbeys ought to have been received from their arrival at the gate.[71] It is important to note that 'guest' at this time referred to male visitors, for the Cistercians initially refused to admit women within the monastic precinct. The Order was soon obliged to make concessions and agreed that they might visit the abbey church on certain stated occasions. Further concessions were later granted to individual houses.[72] For example, the monks of Meaux Abbey in Yorkshire were permitted, c. 1339, to allow men and women of honest character to enter the abbey church and view the crucifix in the lay-brothers' choir, which was reputedly working miracles. Unfortunately this privilege turned out to be something of a poisoned chalice, for the community was overwhelmed by the hordes of women who flocked to the church not, it was noted, from great devotion, but out of nosiness and to indulge in the hospitality of the house.[73] Perhaps news that this crucifix had been carved from a naked model had enhanced the appeal of a trip to Meaux.

---

68 Osbert de Clare, *Letters*, ep. 42 (p. 171). Aelred of Rievaulx's letter of advice to his sister, a recluse, describes Christ's happy countenance and delight when he comes to meet the one who has renounced the world, Aelred, *De Institutione Inclusarum*, p. 676.

69 *Rule of St Benedict*, ch. 5 (p. 36). For further warnings in the *Rule* against grumbling, see ch. 4 (p. 30); ch. 35 (p. 100). II Corinthians 9: 7 is discussed in chapter 1.

70 Peter of Blois, *Epistolae*, ep. 29. See below, p. 190.

71 For various editions of this text, see above, p. 18 n. 84.

72 See above, pp. 8, 82. For the prohibition of women from the granges and precinct in the twelfth-century Institutes of the General Chapter, see *NLT*, pp. 459–60. In 1154 it was agreed that dignified women could be tended in the vill; in 1157 women were permitted to enter the church on the first nine days of the dedication, although this did not extend to breast-feeding women, Canivez, *Statutes* 1, 1157: 10 (p. 61), 1157: 58 (p. 67); Waddell, *Twelfth-Century Statutes*, Tre-Fontane, c. 1160, 24 (p. 706). For further discussion see Kerr, 'Cistercian hospitality', forthcoming.

73 *Chronica Monasterii de Melsa*, ed. E. A. Bond (3 vols, London 1868–88), 3, pp. 35–6; see also below, p. 178.

The porter of the Cistercian abbey was not a layman but a monastic official of some standing, who officiated as almoner and doorkeeper and acted as a link between the community and its neighbours.[74] Accordingly, the customary addresses his role in considerable detail and provides us with a full account of the reception procedure from start to finish. This, as we have noted, is quite different to contemporary Benedictine customaries which reveal little about the guest's initial welcome. The Cistercian porter had at his disposal a full set of instructions prompting him how to respond when a guest knocked at the abbey gate, and how to vary his answer depending on the identity of the visitor and his time of arrival. Whenever a guest knocked at the door, the porter was to reply 'Deo Gratias', open the door and greet him with the customary 'Benedictus'. At this point, and no doubt to the guest's great relief, the porter addressed him in the vernacular to discover what he wanted. He then bowed to the guest and seated him in his cell while he notified the abbot of the new arrival. The porter was expected to man the gate from early morning until Compline, and was thus excused from attending the Canonical Hours in the church. Nevertheless, he was expected to show reverence at these times and stand at the gate in silence, with his hood drawn up, while the Office was celebrated. If any guest happened to arrive at this time, the porter was to explain that it was not their custom to speak when the Hours were celebrated and that no arrivals could be announced until the brethren had finished singing the Office.[75]

It is clear from the Cistercian customary that the porter or his deputy was to notify the abbot of the guest's arrival. He might enter any of the offices to pass on this message except for the infirmary, where he was to stand at the door and signal to those inside. Upon learning of the guest's arrival, the abbot sent two monks to welcome the visitor formally on behalf of the community, thereby ensuring that monastic life suffered as little disruption as possible.[76] While the monk delegates put on their copes and hoods to greet the guest, the porter returned to his cell and briefed him on how to behave during his stay. The monks exercised humility and prostrated themselves before the visitor, adoring Christ in him. They then led him to the oratory to pray, sprinkling him with Holy Water at the entrance. Following this they gave the blessing and bowed to each visitor in turn before extending the Kiss of Peace. Once the visitor had been rendered safe in this way, he was edified with the Divine Word and an explanation was given if required; a sconce might be lit if needed.[77] The customary does not state where this reading should take place,

---

[74] As noted above, p. 78–9, the porter of the Benedictine monastery was a layman but a monastic almoner officiated; the Cistercian porter, in contrast, acted as almoner.

[75] *Ecclesiastica Officia*, ch. 87 (pp. 246–8), ch. 120 (pp. 334–6). The Victorine hosteller, in contrast, was to leave the choir to greet guests even if the Offices were being sung; provision was also made for the reception of guests after Compline, when the door was officially shut, *Liber Ordinis*, ch. 17, p. 60 lines 14–16; pp. 68–9 lines 225–37.

[76] The reception of guests is dealt with in chapter 87 (pp. 246–8) of the *Ecclesiastica Officia*.

[77] *Ecclesiastica Officia*, ch. 87 (pp. 248–9); Williams, *Cistercians in the Early Middle Ages*, p. 125.

and it may well be that no specific place was set aside. Possible locations are the parlour, the guesthouse or the oratory itself.[78] After the guest had been edified he was fully prepared for his stay and was led to the guest lodgings, where he was introduced to the guestmaster or hosteller (*hospitalis*), as he was also known. The guestmaster decided where each guest should sleep and how he should be served.[79] He also made sure that, in accordance with chapter 53 of the *Rule*, the Maundy was administered and two monks were assigned to help him on the weekly rota.[80] As noted in an earlier chapter, and discussed further in Chapter 5, the Benedictines seem to have largely dispensed with this practice.

Whilst the Cistercian customary provides a blow by blow account of the prescribed procedure for receiving guests, we are less well informed of the extent to which this was implemented. One of the few examples of a specific case is Jocelin of Furness's account of three strangers who visited Melrose, during Waldef's abbacy (1148–59), which was discussed earlier, in Chapter 1.[81] Given that this is cited in a work of hagiography it may be indicative of ideals rather than practice. Jocelin describes how the three men were respectfully received at Melrose, in accordance with the customs of the Order and especially of the house. They were taken to the oratory to pray, as stipulated in the *Rule*, and edified with the word of Divine Law. The visitors were then led to the guesthouse and commended to the lay hosteller (*hospitarius*), Brother Walter, who ensured that their feet were duly washed, according to the rite. Thereafter the guests were seated to eat and at this point they noticed that one of the strangers had mysteriously – and inexplicably – vanished.[82]

Walter Daniel's *Life of Aelred* suggests that noteworthy guests were often met by the abbot or prior, and perhaps even by the entire community. When King David of Scotland's steward, Aelred, was on royal business at York in 1134, he visited the Cistercian community of Rievaulx with its founder, Walter Espec. The distinguished party was greeted upon arrival by the prior, the porter and the guestmaster; Abbot William, who is not mentioned, was presumably away from Rievaulx on this occasion. Walter Daniel maintains that Aelred was so impressed by what he had seen that he returned to the abbey the following day when he was met by the prior, the porter, the guestmaster and a great number of the brethren. Aelred subsequently joined the community and became one of the most distinguished members of the Order.[83]

The initial reception of guests was an act of courtesy; as such it could earn the goodwill of visitors and hopefully enhance the reputation of the

---

78   For the possibility that this might take place in the oratory, see Jocelin of Furness' *Life of Waldef*, pp. 138–9.

79   *Ecclesiastica Officia*, ch. 87 (pp. 248–9).

80   *Rule of St Benedict*, ch. 53 (p. 134).

81   See above, p. 32–3.

82   *Life of Waldef*, pp. 138–9. McFadden argues that Jocelin's step-by-step account of the ideal procedure suggests that he was a newcomer or writing for a general audience, p. 275, n. 2; but, it is more likely that Jocelin was concerned to show a worthy community that adhered strictly to the customs of the Order.

83   *Life of Aelred*, pp. 14, 15.

abbey. It was also of practical importance, for visitors would have required guidance around these unfamiliar surroundings and monitoring lest they strayed into private areas and disrupted monastic life. Not least of all, the welcome procedure was of spiritual importance since it offered a way to adore Christ and also rendered the visitor fit and safe to enter and associate with the community. The format for welcoming guests was based on the *Rule of St Benedict*, but was subsequently modified and might vary from house to house in accordance with the community's facilities and also the number of guests it was accustomed to receive.

The reception of distinguished guests

This final section considers the reception of distinguished guests, who were welcomed by the community with a procession. This procedure was effectively reserved for kings, prelates and, according to late-twelfth-century canon law, for patrons.[84] The *De Obedientiariis* of Abingdon stipulates that the king, queen and their metropolitan or diocesan should be met with a procession after their consecration, and that the latter two might also be received in this way if returning from the papal court.[85] Other monastic orders similarly reserved this ceremonial welcome for select individuals. The Cistercians welcomed the pope, apostolic legates, the archbishop, the king, their own bishop and abbot with a procession on their first visit; the pope, however, was to be ceremoniously greeted whenever he visited.[86] The *Institutiones* of the Gilbertines, also known as the Order of Sempringham, state that only the pope, a king, a legate of the apostolic see, the archbishop, their bishop and their own master should be met with a procession.[87] The Carthusian monks do not seem to have extended a ceremonial reception to any visitors, although they prostrated before certain dignitaries.[88] There are surprisingly few explicit references to the ceremonial reception of patrons, and it is striking that Adam of Eynsham makes no mention of this when describing Bishop Hugh's visit to Eynsham Abbey,

---

[84]   Wood, *English Monasteries*, p. 127, n. 6. Clement III's (1188–91) definition of the patron's position permitted him 'the honour of procession' and canon law stipulated that he should be received with a procession if making a ceremonial visit, for instance, for the dedication of a rebuilt church, the installation of an abbot, or a feast, Wood, *English Monasteries*, p. 104. See, too, *Corpus Iuris Canonici*, ed. A. Friedberg (2 vols, Leipzig, 1878–81), 2, p. 617 (III 38. 25).

[85]   *De Obedientiariis*, pp. 338–9. See below, pp. 116–18, for the controversy at Battle.

[86]   *Ecclesiastica Officia*, ch. 87 (pp. 246–7). Similar arrangements are detailed in the late-thirteenth-century customs for the Augustinians of Barnwell Priory, *Ordinances of Barnwell*, pp. 150–2.

[87]   Dugdale, *Monasticon*, 6: 2, p. xxxvi. The king was the only layman received in this way which, according to Golding, relates to his role as patron. He explains that the Gilbertines, more than any other Order, were under the direct protection of the Crown and argues that 'the King could be regarded as the Order's paramount patron', Golding, *Gilbert*, p. 312.

[88]   Guiges, *Consuetudines*, PL 153. 711–12 (ch. 36).

following the successful reassertion of his rights of patronage there.[89] However, it is likely that on this occasion, and no doubt in many other unrecorded cases, the monks acknowledged their patron's authority by receiving him with great pomp and ceremony. It is interesting, and also important, to consider what precisely was meant by a ceremonial reception. The earliest and most comprehensive account of this procedure in post-Conquest England is set out in Lanfranc's *Constitutions* of c. 1077, and is discussed in the first part of the analysis. Thereafter specific examples are considered. The ceremonial reception of guests was not simply an act of courtesy but an admission of rights and could thus be contentious, particularly if a bishop or archbishop announced his intention to visit an exempt house.[90] A final section considers clashes of this kind and explores the implications of extending a ceremonial welcome to prelates.

The prescribed procedure

Lanfranc's *Constitutions* provide a detailed outline of the ceremonial welcome accorded to distinguished visitors.[91] Whenever a dignitary[92] was to be met with a solemn procession, one of the greater bells was sounded three times to summon the brethren to vest themselves in the church and await the guest's arrival. Meanwhile, the sacrist placed a carpet, covered with a pall, on the step before the High Altar and another before the crucifix in the centre of the church. Two bells sounded when the visitor approached to notify the community to assemble outside the church in readiness for the procession. This was led by the senior monks bearing holy water and whatever else was required; they were followed by the abbot, with the children (oblates) and their masters at the rear. Everyone assembled in rank to receive the visitor who was either sprinkled with holy water or sprinkled himself, depending on his standing. While bells rang and the precentor began a suitable chant, the visitor was offered incense and the Gospel. Thereafter the procession returned to the church, but this time the abbot and guest followed the brethren. Lanfranc

---

89 *Magna Vita* 2, p. 42.
90 See below, pp. 115–16, 118. For a general discussion of episcopal exemption, see D. Knowles, 'Essays in monastic history 4: the growth of exemption', *Downside Review* 50 (1932), pp. 201–31, 396–436.
91 Lanfranc, *Constitutions*, ch. 81 (pp. 104–9). For the reception of distinguished persons at Bec, according to the rites of the *Liber Usuum Beccensium*, see A. A. Porée, *Histoire de L'Abbaye du Bec*, 2 vols (Évreux, 1901), 1, pp. 251–2; the reception of dignitaries is discussed by Bernard of Cluny in chapter 23 of his customs, *Ordo Cluniacensis per Bernardum*, pp. 217–19. For an interesting parallel, see Ohler's description of the 'protocol' in the Carolingian period, N. Ohler, *The Medieval Traveller*, trans. C. Hillier (Woodbridge, 1989), pp. 134–5. For a detailed description of this ceremonial reception of kings by the religious houses at the time of the Dissolution, see Michael Sherbrook, 'The fall of the religious houses', *Tudor Treatises*, ed. A. G. Dickens, YAS Rec. Ser. 125 (Wakefield, 1959), pp. 89–142 (p. 97).
92 The phrase *aliqua persona* seems to refer to bishops, ecclesiastics, and abbots, but may also have included royalty and great laity. The implications of this term are discussed below, n. 94.

describes in full the arrangements inside the church. He sets out the cantor's duties and states when and where the visitor should pray and how the brethren should assemble. The precise format varied depending on who the dignitary was. A visiting bishop, for example, bestowed the blessing and kissed the monks in order after the chant. The brethren remained vested and were not therefore expected to genuflect before the bishop as was customary, but simply make a low bow and kiss him.[93] If the visitor was an ecclesiastical dignitary[94] and the abbot deemed it appropriate, he might permit the monks to unvest and sit as they were wont to do in chapter. Once the proceedings were finished in the church, a visiting ecclesiastic was led to the chapter-house and asked to bestow a blessing. A reading followed and the guest was invited to deliver a sermon. Visiting abbots were to stand at the door of the chapter-house and kiss the brethren as they left; if they did not actually enter the chapter-house, they instead greeted the monks in the cloister, at an appropriate time.[95]

This ceremonial reception of guests embraces components associated with other ceremonies conducted in the church, including the installation of new abbots and the coronation of kings.[96] Jocelin of Brakelond's detailed description of Samson's installation at Bury St Edmunds in 1182 recounts how he was met at the gate with a solemn procession amidst singing, the ringing of bells and the sound of the organ. Samson was led to the altar to pray and then made an offering. Thereafter he gave the Kiss of Peace and everyone retired to the chapter-house for the various addresses and the reading of the king's charters. The ceremony was aptly concluded with a great and joyous feast.[97] The Battle chronicler explains that Abbot Odo (1175–1200) was ceremoniously welcomed by his community, even though he had not actually received the episcopal blessing. Odo was magnificently welcomed with a joyous procession and escorted to the monastery, where he said a prayer and extended the Kiss of Peace to all the brethren. The new abbot was then led to the chapter-house for the appropriate reading from the *Rule of St Benedict*.[98] Abbots might also be received ceremoniously by their communities when returning from overseas, but were not necessarily accorded the full honours. Thus, the Abingdon customary states that if the monks wished they could receive their returning abbot with a procession, but he should not remove his shoes and the community should not sing the *Te Deum*.[99]

[93]   Lanfranc, *Constitutions*, ch. 81 (pp. 104–9).
[94]   The term used is *spiritualis persona* which Knowles translates as 'ecclesiastic' ch. 81 (pp. 106–7).
[95]   For the ceremonial reception of those conducting visitation and the subsequent procedure, see Knowles, *Religious Orders* 1, pp. 81–2.
[96]   See below, pp. 114, 124 n. 14, for Richard I's coronation at St Swithun's.
[97]   *Jocelin*, pp. 24–5.
[98]   *Battle Chronicle*, pp. 300–1. For Odo's reception after he had been blessed, see p. 308. Additional examples include *Candidus*, pp. 120–1, Diceto, *Opera Historica* 2, p. 101.
[99]   *De Obedientiariis*, pp. 336 ff. Upon Archbishop Baldwin's return from overseas in 1189, the community at Christ Church, Canterbury, received him appropriately with a procession, the ringing of bells etc., Gervase, *Chronicle* 1, p. 452.

The detail of Lanfranc's *Constitutions* is neither matched nor surpassed in any twelfth-century Benedictine customary. There are, however, a number of specific accounts of dignitaries who were honourably received in this way as a testimony to their position and authority. When Bishop Hilary of Chichester visited Battle Abbey soon after his consecration in 1147, he was ceremoniously received by the abbot and monks. The bishop entered the chapter-house, where he preached to the community, and then proceeded to the guesthouse where he was 'fittingly loaded with gifts'.[100] In 1198/9 the exempt house of Bury St Edmunds agreed to receive the archbishop and legate, Hubert Walter, with a procession, the ringing of bells and other solemnities, but carefully outlined the limits of his authority and warned that he should not hold scrutiny in their chapter-house.[101] Bury was much more flexible when the cardinal bishop, Nicholas of Tusculum, visited during the interdict of 1213.[102] Nicholas had travelled to England to confirm the king's surrender of England and Ireland, to oversee the filling of vacancies and attend to other matters. He arrived at Bury St Edmunds on 21 December to conduct an official inquiry regarding the disputed abbatial election, and was ceremoniously received with a procession at the door of the church. The precentor of the abbey led the singing of the *Summa Trinitati*[103] and Nicholas offered prayers before the High Altar before retiring to his chamber to prepare for the day's ordinations. The following day he preached a sermon in the chapter-house and addressed the convent about the disputed election. On Christmas Day Nicholas granted the community an indulgence to celebrate Mass, which he himself conducted at the High Altar, and then honoured the monks by joining them in the refectory.[104] By according Nicholas a ceremonious reception of this kind Bury honoured his position as legate and acknowledged his authority to carry out this inquiry.

Other references to this ceremonial reception of prelates are rather less detailed. They include Odo of Battle's rapturous reception at his former house of Christ Church, Canterbury in 1175. On this occasion the entire community turned out to welcome Odo with a solemn procession, and the monks were joined by a crowd of men and women.[105] The monks of Westminster Abbey received the archbishop of Cologne with a solemn and costly procession in

---

100 *Battle Chronicle*, pp. 188–91. Crosby, explains that bishops were to be received with a procession in their own churches, and bells were to be rung, Crosby, *Bishops*, p. 45. For an overview of the reception of a bishop with a solemn procession and hospitality, see C. Bruhl, 'Zur Geschichte der *Procuratio canonica* vornehmlich im 11. und 12. Jahrhundert', *Aus Mittelalter und Diplomatik*, 1 (Hildesheim, Munich and Zurich, 1989), pp. 323–35.

101 *Jocelin*, p. 82. This is discussed below, pp. 115–16.

102 *Election of Abbot Hugh*, pp. 26–35. Nicholas was legate 1204–19, p. 24 n. 1.

103 In the Sarum Rite the *Summe Trinitati* was sung in processions for the reception of a king or queen, *Election of Abbot Hugh*, pp. 26–7 n. 4.

104 *Election of Abbot Hugh*, pp. 32–3. When the papal legate, John of Anagni, visited Christ Church in 1189, during the Baldwin affair, he was met with a solemn procession, Howden, *Chronicle* 3, p. 24.

105 *Battle Chronicle*, pp. 308–9; see above, p. 35.

1184,[106] and the legate, Hubert Walter, was accorded a similar welcome at Winchester in 1186.[107] The papal legate who visited Evesham Abbey in 1213, to help heal the rift between Abbot Norreys and his monks, was fittingly received with a solemn procession. The next day he was accompanied by many of his clerics and abbots to the chapter-house where he delivered a sermon.[108] The sources are often less explicit and simply state that these distinguished visitors were received 'honourably', 'fittingly', 'aptly', or 'with due regard to their dignity'. Thus, the abbot of Cluny was 'fittingly received' at Bury, and 'honourably received' at Peterborough; the legate who visited Christ Church in 1121 was 'magnificently received' and Matilda was warmly welcomed by Abbot Faritius (1100–17) of Abingdon, as befitted such a guest.[109] It is likely that in such cases a ceremonial reception is implied, although the precise format may have varied from house to house and in accordance with the visitor's identity, his or her relationship with the community and reason for visiting.

There are surprisingly few direct references to royalty, magnates or patrons who were met with a procession. Richard I's ceremonial reception at St Swithun's, Winchester, for his second coronation is one of the few examples that we have and is discussed in the following chapter. Other less detailed examples include King John's visit to Worcester Cathedral Priory in September 1207, and the young King Henry's reception by the monks of Christ Church, Canterbury, when he visited the martyr's tomb in 1172.[110] As previously noted, it was customary to accord kings and queens the honour of a ceremonial welcome on at least their first visit to the monastery but there are indications that royalty were received in this way whenever they visited. Garnier's description of Henry II's penance, following the martyrdom of 1170, explains that it was usual to ring a full peal of bells and to gather in a procession to greet a king. However, as a mark of his contrition and a sign of humility, Henry II ordered that all this should be put aside when he visited Christ Church, since he wished to enter the church as a beggar, and not a king.[111] Robert of Torigni describes how Henry II acted with courtesy and liberality when he visited France in September 1158, but disregarded the protestations of Louis and others, and refused to be met with a procession at any of the churches that he visited. The two kings were, however, received with a procession when they visited the Norman houses of Bec and Mont St Michel, which suggests that Henry's

---

[106] Diceto, *Opera Historica* 2, p. 31. The archbishop was received at St Paul's, London, and then at Westminster.

[107] Diceto, *Opera Historica* 2, p. 41. Hubert was similarly received at St Mary's, York, where he entered the chapter-house and deposed the abbot, Howden, *Chronicle* 3, p. 294.

[108] Thomas of Marlborough, *History of Evesham*, chs 459–60 (pp. 438–9).

[109] *Jocelin*, p. 124; *Candidus*, p. 102; *Historia Nouorum*, p. 296; *History of Abingdon* 2, pp. 142–3. Additional examples include Gervase, *Chronicle* 2, pp. 401, 407, *Materials for Becket* 3, p. 122. For Continental examples, see *Orderic* 6, pp. 338–9.

[110] *Annales Monastici* 4, p. 395; *Materials for Becket* 4, p. 179. For additional references, see Matthew Paris, *Historia Anglorum* 2, p. 81, Diceto, *Opera Historica* 2, p. 114. It is interesting and perhaps significant, that a greater number of references are cited by the Norman chroniclers, Orderic Vitalis and Robert of Torigni, e.g. Robert of Torigni, *Chronicle*, p. 198 ('*Continuatio Beccensis*'), p. 322.

[111] *Vie de Sainte Thomas*, lines 5951–5.

former resistance may have been intended as a public expression of humility to Louis, and a sign of their recent concord.[112]

The implications

The ceremonial reception of prelates and other distinguished persons was not simply an act of common courtesy, but a symbolic recognition of their position and authority. This was particularly true of prelates conducting a visitation. Refusal to welcome them with a procession could be seen as an open denial of their rights or, indeed, intended as a deliberate act of defiance by a community defending its liberties.[113] Whilst the manner of one's reception, and the very fact one was admitted, might be of considerable consequence, the precise implications were not always clear, especially if the visitor in question held several offices. This was the problem faced by the monks of Bury St Edmunds when Hubert Walter notified them of his intention to visit the community, for Hubert was archbishop of Canterbury (1193–1205), justiciar to Richard I (1193–98) and, from March 1195 to January 1198, Celestine III's papal legate in England.[114] Bury St Edmunds was an exempt house and was therefore under no obligation to admit the archbishop of Canterbury, but Hubert hoped he would be received in his capacity as the legate of the Apostolic See. Hubert was evidently aware that this was a rather contentious and ill-defined area, for he sent two messengers to Bury to check if the monks would receive him and, perhaps more importantly, how; he was clearly intent to avoid any humiliation that might result from their refusal to welcome him appropriately. The prospect of a visit from the legate – who was also the royal justiciar and the archbishop of Canterbury – threw Bury into disarray, and Abbot Samson took counsel from several of his monks to decide a course of action. It was agreed that should Hubert visit Bury immediately, the community would honour him as legate and welcome him with all due reverence, that is, with a procession, the ringing of bells and other solemnities; should he, however, attempt to hold scrutiny in their chapter-house, which was an infringement of their immunity, they would appeal to Rome.[115] Moreover, if Hubert did not visit Bury immediately, the monks would send a messenger from Bury to Rome for advice. In the event, Hubert had to postpone his visit to East Anglia and a messenger from Bury was duly dispatched to Rome. He returned with the papal pronouncement that no legate had any authority to visit St Edmunds, except the legate *a latere*, who was sent as the pope's personal representative and accorded full papal powers; accordingly, Hubert Walter should not be

112 Robert of Torigni, *Chronicle*, p. 197. Indeed, W. L. Warren, *Henry II* (London, 1973), p. 77, argues that their recent accord was publicly demonstrated through these state visits and Henry's intent to travel modestly.

113 As Cheney, *Episcopal Visitation*, p. 118, writes, 'visitation was a mark of authority'.

114 For a comprehensive analysis of Hubert's work as archbishop, justiciar and legate, see C. R. Young, *Hubert Walter, Lord of Canterbury and Lord of England* (Durham, 1968). Following the death of Richard I, Hubert served as John's chancellor, from 1199 to 1205.

115 *Jocelin*, pp. 82–3.

received. News of the papal verdict reached Hubert's ears and, fearing he should be denied entrance and publicly humiliated, he avoided the abbey and travelled to London via Ely.[116] Significantly, Abbot Samson avoided meeting Hubert when he was in Norwich lest this would seem that he, like others, was willing to come to an agreement regarding Hubert's hospitality at Bury. Whilst Hubert was an old friend of Samson's and, of course, the royal justiciar, Samson could not jeopardise the immunity of his house by receiving him at Bury.

The account of the ongoing controversy between the bishops of Chichester and the monks of Battle Abbey, recorded in the chronicle of the house, is a further testimony to the symbolic significance of according prelates a ceremonial reception, and of the implications this might have on the liberty of the house. According to this version of events, William the Conqueror was so angry at Stigand of Chichester's (1070–87) refusal to bless Abbot Gausbert (1076–95) at Battle that he granted the abbey freedom and ruled that neither the bishop nor his household should claim lodging or food from the community as a customary right.[117] During Ralph of Battle's abbacy (1107–24) the bishop agreed that neither he nor his successors at Chichester should have authority or lordship over Battle, or any claim to its subjection excepting that which was 'courteously expended upon them as a gift of charity'.[118] Liberty evidently meant the freedom to choose whether or not to entertain the bishop. Friction between Battle and the bishop brewed during Warner's abbacy (1125–38) and reached a climax during the abbacy of his successor, Walter de Luci (1139–71). In fact, the struggle was really only concluded with the 'Composition' of 1235 which was drawn up by John de Ferentino, archdeacon of Norwich, Master Gentilis and a canon of Chichester and sealed in the cloister of Westminster Abbey.[119] The early details of the controversy are carefully recorded for the Battle chronicler was concerned that future generations of monks might remember how his community had finally triumphed over the bishop or, as he rather more tactfully puts it, how this long-standing dispute between the convent and the bishop of Chichester 'was brought to harmonious peace and affection'.[120]

The account in the chronicle centres on Bishop Seffrid of Chichester's (1125–45) visit to Battle, at the request of Abbot Warner. His presence

---

[116]   *Jocelin*, p. 84. Gerald of Wales' stand off with the bishop of St Asaph's regarding their respective rights over the church of Kerry, is revealing. The bishop maintained that he was visiting to dedicate the church and carry out episcopal office in his parish whilst Gerald, who was concerned to defend the rights of St David's, claimed that the bishop would be welcomed with all honour as a guest and a neighbour. This provoked a series of antagonisms between the archdeacon and the bishop, 'De rebus a se gestis', *Giraldi Cambrensis Opera* 1, ed. J. S. Brewer, RS 21 (London, 1863), pp. 1–122 (pp. 33–4), and Butler, *Autobiography of Gerald*, pp. 50–1.

[117]   *Battle Chronicle*, pp. 70–3; 194–7. See also pp. 148–51.

[118]   *Battle Chronicle*, pp. 126–9.

[119]   Graham, *English Ecclesiastical Studies*, pp. 200–1. Cheney, *Episcopal Visitation*, pp. 41–2, explains that whilst visitation of Battle was to be undertaken by two Benedictine monks of the diocese, the bishop and a retinue of twenty-five on horseback were entitled to entertainment at the abbey every three years.

[120]   *Battle Chronicle*, pp. 146–7.

at the abbey was thus an act of charity and not a right.[121] What should have been a festive occasion was marred by the misconduct of the bishop and his men. Warner, who was keen to preserve the peace and uphold the words of Matthew 5: 9, 'Blessed are the peacemakers, for they shall be the children of God', initially tolerated the men's provocative behaviour, but was forced to respond when the bishop declared his lordship over Battle. Warner vowed that from thenceforth neither the bishop nor his retinue should receive food that the community normally provided. He remained true to his word, for the next day Seffrid was forced to buy his own provisions at the market; presumably the party had been allowed to lodge at the abbey.[122] Interestingly, when Thomas Becket visited France in 1158 as Henry II's chancellor, he went to considerable lengths to evade Louis' attempts to uphold the custom of the Gallic kings, namely, that the king should provide for the chancellor as long as he stayed in the country. Thomas was so concerned that he should not be indebted to the king of France, that when Louis forbade the Parisians to sell any provisions to the chancellor or his retainers, Becket sent his men to neighbouring markets to purchase their supplies.[123]

A second clash between Battle and the bishop of Chichester was precipitated by Hilary's (1147–69) visit to the abbey soon after his elevation to the see.[124] Hilary was met with a procession and accorded the right to speak to the community in the chapter-house; he was provided with honourable hospitality in the guesthouse and presented with gifts on his departure. The community's kindness on this occasion was to have serious repercussions for Hilary subsequently evoked this to support his claim to diocesan rights over the house. He argued that by receiving him in this way the community had effectively acknowledged his authority over the abbey. Both the king's constable and the royal chancellor, Thomas Becket, dismissed Hilary's claims and maintained that his reception at Battle was honorific rather than symbolic, and was simply indicative of respect and affection. Becket declared that this was common in all churches in England and abroad, that it was 'gratis and

---

[121] *Battle Chronicle*, pp. 138–9. See below p. 108 for the practice at Bury.

[122] *Battle Chronicle*, pp. 138–41.

[123] *Materials for Becket* 3, p. 32. A similar story is told of Duke Robert of Normandy's (son of Duke Richard III) alleged visit to Constantinople, where 'guarding against the disgrace of beggary' the duke refused Michael IV's provisions, which in turn angered the emperor, *The Gesta Normannorum Ducum of William of Jumièges, Orderic Vitalis and Robert of Torigni*, ed. and trans. E. M. C. van Houts, 2 vols, OMT (Oxford, 1992), 2, pp. 82–4. For the likelihood that Robert never visited Constantinople, see E. van Houts, 'Normandy and Byzantium in the eleventh century', *Byzantion* 55 (1985), pp. 544–9. An interesting parallel is Chrétien de Troyes's account of King Evrain in the romance, 'Erec and Enide', lines 5340–4, see Kerr, 'The open door' p. 334.

[124] *Battle Chronicle*, pp. 148 ff., pp. 188–91. Searle explains that Hilary was consecrated in 1147 and not 1148, as the chronicler says, p. 146, n. 1. For discussion of Hilary, see H. Mayr–Harting, 'Hilary, bishop of Chichester, 1147–1169, and Henry II', *EHR* 78 (1963), pp. 209–24.

no precedent for a custom'.[125] The fact that a debate of this nature could arise underlines just how confused and ill-defined an area this was.

There was a similar state of confusion at Evesham Abbey in 1202, when the bishop of Worcester announced his intention to visit the community. A detailed account of the controversy is recorded by Thomas of Marlborough, a monk and eventual abbot of Evesham.[126] Although Evesham was an exempt house, Abbot Norreys (1190–1213) welcomed the news of the bishop's proposed visit, since he assumed this would be a friendly affair. Other members of the community were less enthusiastic, for they were aware of the deeper implications and feared for the liberty of their house. They called upon Thomas of Marlborough, who had legal training, to clarify matters. He confirmed that as the bishop was coming on visitation to receive him would be tantamount to renouncing Evesham's freedom, and he therefore recommended that the bishop should not be admitted. It is interesting, and surely significant, that Thomas of Marlborough, like Hilary of Chichester, interpreted the reception of the prelate as an admission of his authority, and that both were canonists. The bishop of Worcester encountered a hostile reception when he arrived at Evesham in 1202. The doors of the guesthouse and stables were shut, and the monks flagrantly denied his authority by refusing to attend his summons to the chapter-house. He responded by suspending and then excommunicating the monks.[127] An expensive lawsuit followed and there was an enquiry into the liberties of Evesham. The jurisdiction of the house was initially conceded to the bishop, but in 1206 the decision was reversed.[128]

These examples clearly suggest that hospitality was not necessarily a simple case of providing for visitors, but, when related to visitation and lordship in general, became entangled in the larger issues of liberty and power. An interesting example relates to the church of Wymondham, c. 1162, which was a cell of St Albans and had been founded by Earl William d'Aubigny's father. Earl William and the abbot of St Albans came to blows over their respective rights here when the abbot and his entourage arrived at Wymondham to sort out a dispute. William maintained that the abbot was threatening his lordship and instructed him to leave. He argued that by the terms of his father's foundation charter, the abbot was only entitled to two nights' lodging, one going to Binham and one returning, and that his horses should not exceed thirteen. The abbot responded that his rights could not be confined to days or horses; it was his duty to stay until the dispute was healed. While William endeavoured to deny the abbot access, the earl of Leicester intervened and resolved the issue in the abbot's favour.[129] Hospitality might serve to publicly

---

125   *Battle Chronicle*, pp. 198–9.
126   Thomas of Marlborough, *History of Evesham*, from ch. 199 (pp. 206–7).
127   Thomas of Marlborough, *History of Evesham*, chs 207–11 (pp. 214–17). Compare this to the violent reaction to Archbishop Thurstan's arrival at St Mary's, York, in 1132, *Memorials of Fountains* 1, pp. 8–10. For a similar scene at the Cistercian abbey of Mellifont, Ireland, in 1217, see Canivez, *Statutes* 1, 1217: 78 (p. 483).
128   For the first decision, see Thomas of Marlborough, *History of Evesham*, ch. 249 (p. 252); for the second, see ch. 353 (pp. 340–1).
129   GASA 1, pp. 166–75.

proclaim one's loyalties or to vent disapproval. Thus, the monks of Battle Abbey showed their veneration of Odo and their acknowledgement of his authority, by according him a ceremonial reception when he had not received the episcopal blessing.[130] Conversely, in the late eleventh century, the monks of Ely closed their doors to the newly appointed abbot, Simeon, to demonstrate their displeasure that he had received the episcopal blessing without their knowledge.[131] Of course, the entertainment of prelates did not inevitably lead to conflict and was not necessarily a political statement; it could simply serve to honour those whom the monks wished to honour, and contribute to a positive portrayal of the host community.

Open doors

Your gates shall be open continually day and night, they shall not be shut. (Isaiah 60:11)

Unrestricted access to the monastery was clearly not always appropriate or practical, for it imposed a tremendous strain on the monastery's resources and might also cause disruption and upheaval. Yet the idea of the 'open door' was attractive and those who welcomed allcomers were generally deemed praiseworthy. William of Malmesbury noted that at Reading Abbey, which was renowned for its hospitality, guests arrived at all times of the day and consumed as much as the community.[132] The Battle chronicle celebrates Odo's abbacy (1175–1200) as a time when the monastery gates stood open for all passers-by to refresh themselves or to stay the night; given Battle's proximity to the seaports, this would have been no mean feat.[133] Herluin of Glastonbury (1082–1118), who was greatly concerned to reverse his reputation for stinginess, insisted that nobody should be turned away from the abbey; however, as we noted earlier, he was subsequently criticised for his excessive liberality.[134] While the ability to offer open access to allcomers remained an attractive ideal, it was not always a workable reality, particularly by the late twelfth and early thirteenth centuries when the Benedictines were competing for patronage, and had also to contend with famine, warfare and changes in the economy. By

130 *Battle Chronicle*, pp. 300–3. Searle remarks that the monks received Odo as if he had already been blessed, p. 300 n. 1. Furthermore Orderic claimed that Cluny's warm reception of Gregory during the schism in 1134, greatly increased his authority in the West, *Orderic* 4, pp. 418–21.

131 *Liber Eliensis*, pp. 200–2 (p. 202).

132 *Gesta Regum* 1, p. 746; see above, p. 37. In 1205–6, the General Chapter of Cluny issued severe penalties to any priors or their deputies who refused guests, *Statuts, Chapitres* 1, no. 6, clause 4.

133 *Battle Chronicle*, pp. 306–7. Richard of Devizes maintained that the monks of Coventry, unlike the secular canons of the city, always had bread ready for the poor and a door that was open to passers-by at any time, Devizes, *Chronicon*, pp. 70–1. See, too, Orderic Vitalis's praise of Bec, and William of Rouen's epitaph (d. 1110), *Orderic* 6, pp. 172–3.

134 William of Malmesbury, *De Antiquitate*, pp. 158–60; see above, pp. 39–40.

this time, open hospitality probably referred to the spirit of liberality, rather than a twenty-four-hour service. Restrictions were invariably imposed, and the customaries generally state that visitors should be admitted only from Prime until Compline, when the abbey door was to be closed and monastic officials return to the cloister.[135] Concessions were granted to certain individuals or in certain circumstances, and whilst no secular guest was to be admitted at Bury St Edmunds after Compline, an exception was made if he was a special friend of the church; this presumably refers to benefactors, patrons and anyone joined in fraternity.[136] The later customaries of St Augustine's, Canterbury, and Westminster Abbey set out specific guidelines for the admittance of Benedictines who arrived after hours.[137]

In the *Rule of St Benedict*, the procedure for receiving guests is an act of courtesy. It also offers a way to adore Christ who is represented by the stranger, and is an important preventative measure to protect the community from demonic forces entering the abbey. These issues remained integral to the reception process throughout the Middle Ages, but the format of the procedure was modified to suit the growing needs of the monks and their guests. It became more complex and there was a greater preoccupation with practicalities or, at least, it was more important to consign these concerns to writing. Perhaps greater demands on the monks' hospitality made it necessary to address these matters and regulate the procedure. Not least of all, the reception of dignitaries might be harnessed to contemporary issues, such as liberty, allegiance and power. While there is relatively little explicit reference to the reception of patrons, it is likely that they expected to receive a ceremonial welcome when they visited their community and indeed this is stated in twelfth-century canon law. The prospect of being accorded an honour of this kind may have encouraged men and women to offer their patronage and support.

[135] For example, *De Obedientiariis*, pp. 405–6; *Bury Customary*, p. 26; *Ecclesiastica Officia*, ch. 120: 1, 32 (pp. 334–7). Later examples include *Westminster Customary*, pp. 85–6; *Eynsham Customary*, ch. 19: 11 (539), p. 211 lines 1–4. The Victorines made alternative arrangements and latecomers were tended by two *conversi* (the porter and sub-hosteller) and not the master of guests who was a canon and remained in the claustral area after Compline, *Liber Ordinis*, ch. 17, pp. 68–9 lines 225–37.

[136] *Bury Customary*, p. 26 lines 5–8.

[137] *St Augustine's Customary* (fourteenth-century), p. 141 lines 12–29; *Westminster Customary*, p. 85 lines 14–20. The customary of St Mary's, York, implies that while access to the claustral area was restricted after Compline entrance to the precincts was not necessarily prohibited, for the hosteller was to remain in the hospice from Compline each night in case of passing guests, *St Mary's Customary*, p. 96.

4

Provision for guests: body and soul

Offer bread that isn't mouldy, meat that isn't rotten and fish that hasn't been hanging around for more than a day. Remove anything that would offend the eyes of respectable men.[1]

How were guests provided for during their stay, and to what extent did they interact with the monastic community? These questions are not easily answered for whilst the customaries and statutes shed some light on the care of guests, particularly religious guests and prelates who often joined the community in the refectory, they reveal little about how visitors passed their time and the nature of facilities in the guesthouse. Archaeological evidence and standing remains can disclose much about the size and grandeur of the guest lodgings and their location in the precinct, but more personal details are scarce. Alexander of Neckam's recommendations in his treatise, *De Sacerdos ad altare*, which was written c. 1199–1210, offers a rare and sensual insight into the décor of the guest complex. In chapter 4 of this treatise Alexander discusses monastery fittings and a section on guest lodgings underlines the need to create a warm, welcoming and clean environment.[2] Alexander emphasises the importance of showing guests generosity and cheeriness, so that those visiting the monastery might leave with a favourable impression of the house. He advises the monks to offer plenty of fresh, appetising food. As a rule of thumb, they ought to serve nothing that might cause offence to respectable folk. The fourteenth-century customary of St Augustine's, Canterbury, warned the cellarer to provide fresh fish and not offer rotten fish that was two or three days old.[3] It was equally important that the table was fully equipped with spoons, vessels, napkins and the appropriate condiments.[4] Neither was

---

[1] *De Sacerdos ad altare*, p. 267.

[2] *De Sacerdos ad altare*, p. 267. This was written when Alexander was a member of the Augustinian Canons, but before his election to the abbacy of Cirencester in 1215.

[3] *St Augustine's Customary* (fourteenth-century), p. 135 lines 32–5. Note Peter of Blois' complaint about the mouldy bread and muddy wine that was often served at court, the ale that was 'horrid to the taste and abominable to the sight', and fish that were bought when four days old, cited in *Life in the Middle Ages 3: men and manners* (Cambridge, 1929), selected, trans. and annotated G.G. Coulton, pp. 2–5 (p. 2).

[4] For example, see Alexander of Neckam's remarks in his '*De Nominibus utensilium*', in *Teaching and Learning Latin in Thirteenth-century England* I, ed. T. Hunt (Cambridge,

the fire to be neglected, lest smoke caused visitors to cry, rather than smile. Care was also to be given to the guests' sleeping quarters, which were to be clean and quiet. The straw was to be changed regularly, to keep fleas and hence insomnia, at bay.[5] Cleanliness in the guest quarters evidently remained a problem throughout the Middle Ages, and in the late fifteenth century the traveller and antiquary, William of Worcester, complained of the conditions he encountered at St Benet Holme – the filthy linen and stony bedding, the chilly fire in the chimney and dirty stables.[6]

The following two chapters, 4 and 5, explore in greater detail the provision monasteries made for their guests in the twelfth and early thirteenth centuries. The first focuses on physical and spiritual care, chiefly, refreshment, accommodation and religious devotions. The second considers various ways in which guests might be entertained during their stay, and also the nature and extent of their interaction with the community. The section concludes with a brief analysis of the procedure upon the guests' departure. Most information regarding the care of visitors is in the monastic customaries, but whilst these offer considerable detail about the range of facilities and services provided, they reflect the theory more than the practice, and reveal little about individual experiences. Unfortunately, there is hardly any evidence for the care of specific guests. Thus, the agreement in 1109 between the monks of Battle and the knight, Osbern, reveals that in return for securing the community's meadows at Bodiam for fifty shillings, Osbern might eat or stay at the house, but gives no indication of how he was to be cared for during these visits or, indeed, where. Significantly, Osbern's entertainment was to be regarded as an act of charity and not demanded as of right.[7]

Dining and sleeping arrangements

Let the table of the abbot be always with the guests and strangers.

It was appropriate that as head and figurehead of the community the abbot should preside as host at the monastery's guest table. Benedict granted him

1991), pp. 177–90 (p. 183).

5   *De Sacerdos ad altare*, p. 265. The customaries of Westminster Abbey and St Augustine's, Canterbury, recommend that straw in the monks' dormitory be changed once a year, *Westminster Customary*, p. 149 lines 8–15; *St Augustine's Customary* (fourteenth-century), p. 195 lines 24–9. For Aislinge Meich Conglinne's rather unwelcoming stay at a monastery in Cork see *The Vision of MacConglinne: A Middle-Irish Wonder Tale*, ed. and trans. K. Meyer, intro. W. Wellner (Llanerch Press facsimile, Felinfach, 1999), p. 10 lines 20–4. This is thought to have been compiled in the twelfth century.

6   William of Worcester, *Itineraries*, trans. J. H. Harvey (Oxford, 1969), p. 3. William was particularly disappointed with the monks of St Benet's for he felt that they had neglected the memory of his patron, Sir John Falstoff, who had been a generous benefactor and was buried there.

7   Cited in E. Searle, *Lordship and Community: Battle Abbey and its Banlieu, 1066–1538* (Toronto, 1974), p. 145.

certain concessions so that he might fulfil this role without compromising his monastic status. Accordingly, the abbot might break his fast on account of guests if it was not a main fast day, and whilst he was permitted to eat outside the refectory he was to sleep in the dormitory and participate fully in all other aspects of communal life.[8] For practical reasons Benedict ruled that the abbot should have a separate kitchen staffed by two monks, so that the community would not be disturbed by visitors arriving at unaccustomed times and expecting refreshment.[9] This arrangement would also have helped to keep the temptation of fine foods out of the refectory. Benedict's prescriptions may seem clear-cut but his recommendations provoked considerable debate and led to various interpretations and practices. Whereas some held that the abbot should eat outside the refectory with guests, others maintained that he should have a separate table within the refectory where he could entertain visitors; a third group argued for a modification of the *Rule* and claimed that the abbot should take his place with the brethren and delegate the task of host to a steward.

Hildemar, a ninth-century commentator on the *Rule of St Benedict*, remarked on its obscurity on this point, but concluded that the abbot ought to dine in the refectory.[10] This was seemingly the arrangement implemented in Anglo-Saxon houses, for the *Regularis Concordia* states that neither the abbot nor brethren should eat or drink outside the refectory.[11] Knowles suggested that as a consequence of this guests dined in the refectory and not in the hospice, which may explain the presence of certain laymen in the refectory at Ely, shortly after the Norman Conquest of 1066.[12] However, their presence here may instead be attributable to the exceptional times. The *Liber Eliensis* describes how a Norman knight, Deda, imprisoned at Ely during the siege of 1071 dined with the community in the refectory each day, and similarly the English rebels who stayed for a year at the house; their leaders, Hereward and Turkhill, sat beside the abbot in seats of honour.[13] The refectory at St Swithun's, Winchester, was clearly not reserved for the community, for the post-ceremonial feast celebrating Richard I's second coronation in 1194 was held in the monks' refectory. However, and perhaps significantly, the monks

---

8   *Rule of St Benedict*, ch. 53 (p. 134); ch. 56 (p. 142).
9   *Rule of St Benedict*, ch. 53 (p. 134). Whereas the cooks in the abbot's kitchen were rotated on a yearly basis, those in the monks' kitchen were rotated weekly.
10   For discussion of this text, see M. A. Schroll, *Benedictine Monasticism as reflected in the Warnefrid-Hildemar Commentaries on the Rule* (New York, 1941), pp. 33–4 (p. 34). Canon 21 of the Council of Aachen, 817, ruled that no abbot or monk should eat at the monastery gate with guests, see *Cistercians and Cluniacs: the case for Cîteaux*, pp. 202–3, n. 21, 23.
11   *Regularis Concordia*, ch. 10 (p. 62).
12   Knowles, *Monastic Order*, p. 480.
13   *Liber Eliensis*, pp. 179–81, esp. p. 181. The chronicle states that they were refreshed 'in the English way', which Knowles interprets as a reference to the copious feasting of the English, Knowles, *Monastic Order*, p. 463. Deda's account states that a knight always took dinner and supper with the monks, and describes how helmets, shields and lances hung around the walls so they would be near at hand if required. For a recent translation of Deda's account, see *Liber Eliensis*, p. 214.

of St Swithun's may not themselves have been present and on this occasion their refectory was probably used as the venue for this prestigious event.[14] It is interesting that when in 1114 the monks of Crowland Abbey entertained everyone who had helped contribute to the rebuilding of their church, the refectory was seemingly reserved for the community and monastic guests, namely, the abbots of Crowland and Thorney along with some 400 monks. The earls, barons, knights and gentry dined with their wives in the abbot's chamber, the six companies who had raised the pillars were entertained with their wives in the cloister, while the populace dined in the court.[15] This account of events at Crowland is recorded in a fifteenth-century forgery, but may be based on contemporary material.[16]

Lanfranc's *Constitutions* of the late eleventh century assign the abbot a place in the refectory, with the brethren, and not with visitors in the guesthouse.[17] This arrangement was favoured by the Cluniacs, and in the twelfth century both Peter the Venerable (d. 1156) and Peter Abelard (d. 1142) defended their order's deliberate modification of the *Rule*. They argued that the abbot's presence in the refectory was essential to uphold discipline and also to prevent suspicions that he was indulging himself in the guesthouse for, as Abelard warned, a number of abbots and also abbesses used hospitality for their own benefit, rather than that of their guests.[18] Thomas Marlborough, a monk of Evesham Abbey, complained that Abbot Norreys (1190–1213) dined lavishly with guests in his chamber while the brethren starved in the refectory.[19] Indeed, the greedy abbot emerges as something of a caricature in satirical poems of the time. The late-twelfth- /early-thirteenth-century poem *Day in the life of an abbot by Magister Golyas* describes the vast banquet the abbot enjoys which is followed by many toasts and belching, all of which are supported by theological arguments.[20] The Cistercians, in contrast, vehemently argued

---

[14]   A detailed account is given by Roger of Howden, who was himself present at the event, Howden, *Chronicle* 3, pp. 246–9 (p. 248). It is also described by Gervase of Canterbury, although interestingly, he writes that the feast was held in the *palatium*, Gervase, *Chronicle* 1, pp. 524, 526.

[15]   Dugdale, *Monasticon* 3, pp. 100–1.

[16]   I am grateful to Dr Liesbeth Van Houts for her advice on the matter. For recent discussion of the *Historia*, see D. Roffe, 'The Historia Croylandsensis: a plea for reassessment', *EHR* 110 (1995), pp. 93–108.

[17]   Lanfranc, *Constitutions*, ch. 90 (pp. 130–1).

[18]   Peter the Venerable, *Letters* 1, ep. 28, pt 12 (pp. 74–5); Abelard, *Epistolae*, ep. 8; *PL* 178. 273. This is explicit in the late-eleventh-century customs of Cluny and was reissued as clause 1 in the 1205–6 statutes of the General Chapter of Cluny, *Cistercians and Cluniacs: the case for Cîteaux*, p. 203, n. 23; *Statuts, Chapitres* 1, no 6 (p. 53).

[19]   Thomas of Marlborough, *History of Evesham*, ch. 463 (pp. 440–3). The Cistercian abbot, Gervase of Louth Park, 'confessed' that while he dined sumptuously in the guest-hall, the brethren had observed a strict and frugal diet in the refectory, *The Testament of Gervase of Louth Park*, ed. C. H. Talbot, *Analecti Sacri Ordinis Cisterciensis* 7 (Rome, 1951), pp. 32–45 (p. 39).

[20]   A. Rigg, *Anglo-Latin Literature*, p. 144, *The Latin Poems attributed to Walter Mapes* collected and ed. T Wright, CS old ser. 16 (London, 1841), pp. xl–xliv. Additional examples are cited in the Bekynton anthology, compiled c. 1200; see poems 18: 8 and 94: 22, Rigg, *Anglo-Latin Literature*, pp. 152–3.

for a literal interpretation of the *Rule*, and their twelfth-century customary prescribed that the abbot should preside at the guesthouse table. This became a source of contention between the two orders in twelfth-century polemic, and is exemplified in Idung of Prüfening's 'Dialogue between two monks'. Idung, a Cistercian monk, regarded the Cluniacs' decision to dine in the refectory as a breach of the *Rule*, a dishonour to their guests and a slight against Christ,

> Against whom is this violence perpetrated if not against Christ? He is the one who will say at the Last Judgement, 'I was a guest in your house and you robbed me of my dignity.' [21]

The removal of the abbot's table to the refectory meant that he effectively renounced his role as host or, at least, reduced this, for most visitors would have been entertained in the guesthouse by the abbot's steward.[22] On special occasions, however, secular visitors might join the community but would otherwise have eaten in the guest quarters or even in the vill.[23]

From the early twelfth century, there were changes. A number of Benedictine abbots now moved out of the refectory and dined either in a separate chamber with their households and select visitors, or on their manors.[24] Knowles attributes this to the abbot having independent resources and establishing his own household. The Battle chronicle's remark that Abbot Odo (1175–1200) dined with the brethren and only slept apart on account of a long-standing stomach problem seems to confirm Knowles's hypothesis, but a thorough analysis is needed of the arrangements at houses where there was no division of revenues between abbot and convent at this time. Unfortunately there is little explicit evidence.[25] Moreover, there are signs that from the late twelfth century some Cistercian abbots moved out of the guesthouse and entertained more distinguished visitors in a chamber, while less notable visitors dined in the guest-hall.[26] Hence, from this time the difference between the two orders was perhaps less marked, and both abbots were now effectively part-time and partial hosts. Nevertheless, this was not universal. Abelard's letter of guidance to Héloise instructed that the abbess (or abbot) should send a steward to dine with guests while she (or he) remained in the refectory with the community.

---

21 Idung, *Dialogue*, II: 20–2 (pp. 73–6 at 74).
22 This is explicit in Abelard's letter to Heloise, Abelard, *Epistolae*, ep. 8.
23 Lanfranc, *Constitutions*, ch. 90 (pp. 128–31). The hosteller was to procure food from the cellarer, via his servant; but see below, pp. 139–41, for arrangements when clerics and laity dined in the refectory. Bernard of Cluny's eleventh-century customs state that no laity should dine in the refectory but clerics might be permitted to join the community, *Ordo Cluniacensis per Bernardum*, ch. 9 (p. 154).
24 For example, Abbot Norreys (1190–1213) of Evesham entertained the legate's retinue in his chamber (*thalamus*), Thomas Marlborough, *History of Evesham*, ch. 487 (p. 460).
25 Knowles, *Monastic Order*, pp. 405, 480; *Battle Chronicle*, pp. 306–7.
26 For example, Ralph of Coggeshall's account of the three Templars who visited his abbey, above, pp. 33, 86, describes how they refused to dine alone with the abbot as it was not their custom to dine in private chambers, but in the hall with guests, Coggeshall, *Chronicle*, p. 134.

If, however, a pilgrim nun visited she was to be seated at the high table and served by the abbess, who dined afterwards with the servers.[27]

Hospitality at the table

> The lips of many shall bless him that is liberal of his bread, and the testimony of his truth is faithful. Against him that is niggardly of his bread the city will murmur and the testimony of his niggardliness is true. (Ecclesiasticus 31, 28–29)

By the twelfth century, therefore, a number of abbots presided as part-time hosts, dining on occasion with select guests while other visitors were refreshed in the guesthouse or the vill. In houses where the entertainment of guests was divided between the abbot and convent, the community was often made responsible for visiting regulars who were refreshed in the monks' refectory or an adjacent chamber.[28] There is unfortunately little explicit evidence regarding the care of guests who dined in the hospice or elsewhere in the court, that is, guests who were not entertained by the abbot in person or did not join the community in the refectory. As such the sources offer only a partial insight into the refreshment of guests. The following exploration necessarily focuses on the abbot as host and arrangements for guests dining in the refectory, largely distinguished persons and visiting religious.

The abbot as host

Like all good hosts, the abbot aimed to satisfy his guests at the table.[29] He was to be generous and provide an ample spread of appetising foods and was permitted to relax, but not compromise, monastic observance. For example, he might honour visitors by serving fine foods that were not usually associated with the claustral life. Archbishop Peckham stipulated in 1281 that whenever the abbot of Glastonbury dined in his chamber with his household, he should not have more dishes than the monks unless to honour noble guests.[30] When Samson succeeded to the abbacy of Bury in 1182, he was concerned that his household should not be niggardly in administering to guests, lest this would damage his reputation. In later years Samson was less inclined to extend a cheery welcome to his guests, but 'satisfied them in respect of food and drink'. Conversely, Anselm hoped that his cheerful countenance and good-will would compensate for any lack of food in the guesthouse at Bec.[31]

---

27   Abelard, *Epistolae*, ep. 8, *PL* 178. 299.
28   See below, pp. 132, 144–5.
29   For the significance of this to lay hosts, see Kerr, 'The open door', pp. 322–35.
30   *Registrum Epistolarum Fratris Johannis Peckham Archiepiscopi Cantuariensis*, ed. C. T. Martin, 3 vols, RS 77 (London, 1882), 1, no. 212 (p. 261).
31   *Jocelin*, pp. 26, 35; *Vita Anselmi*, pp. 46–8.

Until 1335, the Cistercians officially forbade meat to be served to guests, a practice that John of Salisbury considered 'foreign to all civility, not to say humanity'.[32] The Benedictines, however, were permitted and indeed expected to offer their guests meat or, at least, to provide this on certain occasions. Abbot Samson of Bury made a number of parks that he filled with beasts, huntsmen and hounds, and sometimes when a distinguished guest visited, he would sit with his monks in the glade and watch the hounds hunt deer, and venison was then served at his table; he himself abstained from the meaty feast.[33] The thirteenth-century customs of Bury state that meat should be served to royalty, bishops, magnates, legates or other papal messengers dining with the abbot or prior in their chambers, and that he might break his fast in their presence, in accordance with chapter 53 of the *Rule*.[34] In 1278 Archbishop Kilwardby warned the abbot of Abingdon that he should not serve meat on a regular basis, but might do so occasionally, to honour guests on solemn days.[35] The fact that Samson of Bury did not partake in the meaty feast he served to his guests suggests that it was important for abbots to be overtly abstemious and demonstrate their adherence to the *Rule of St Benedict*. It may also imply that others were less restrained than the abbot of Bury.[36] This could not be said of Waldef, prior of the Augustinian house of Kirkham and later Cistercian abbot of Melrose. His table was set with dishes and other necessities for the benefit of his visitors, yet he himself took so little that guests and servers alike were amazed at how so weak a body, living on such a paltry diet, could carry on in office.[37]

Benedictines who had been raised to the episcopate and consequently occupied a worldlier role than before, might be more discreet than their secular counterparts and mask their abstemious ways. Hence Wulfstan of Worcester appeared to participate in the post-dinner drinking session, but drank water rather than ale or mead. Only Wulfstan's servant knew of this and everyone else assumed that the bishop enjoyed some expensive drink.[38] Anselm similarly sought to maintain a congenial atmosphere and remain true to his ideals.

---

[32] John of Salisbury, *Policraticus* 2, p. 326

[33] *Jocelin*, p. 28.

[34] *Bury Customary*, pp. 49–50.

[35] *Two Chartularies of Abingdon* 2, C5 (Chatsworth), pp. 5–8 (p. 6). Following his visitation of Christ Church, Canterbury, in 1296, Archbishop Winchelsey stipulated that meat should only be eaten in the convent's guesthouses, the prior's chamber, the infirmary and monastic 'deportus' (misericord?), B. Dobson, 'The monks of Canterbury in the later Middle Ages, 1220–1540', *A History of Canterbury Cathedral*, ed. P. Collinson, N. Ramsey and M. Sparks (Oxford, 1995), pp. 69–157 (p. 83).

[36] *Jocelin*, p. 28. Indeed, following the visitation of Cluniac houses in England in 1275, several communities were reprimanded for eating meat in the presence of seculars; offenders included the prior and monks of Monks Horton, a cell of Lewes, *Charters and Records of Cluni* 2, pp. 124–7.

[37] *Life of Waldef*, p. 127. The Cistercian abbot, Stephen of Mortemer (acceded c. 1154), did not abstain from better foods when guests were present; on such occasions he swiftly procured all that was needed from the cellarer and servants, and made sure that the leftovers were sent to the sick and aged brethren, *Fondation de Mortemer*, p. 159.

[38] *Vita Wulfstani*, p. 94. This particular section is missing from the folio and taken from the abridged version.

Eadmer describes how the archbishop toyed with his food, rather than eating it, so that he might listen more attentively to the reader, but did not condemn others for enjoying their food. On the contrary, Anselm would give them a friendly look and, filled with pleasure, raise his hand, bless them, and say, 'May it do you good'.[39] Members of the episcopate who had a regular, though not Benedictine, background might conform outwardly at table, to put guests at their ease. When Hugh of Avalon succeeded to the see of Lincoln in 1186, he relaxed the severity of the Carthusian diet he had observed as prior of Witham. Although Hugh never touched meat, even when sick, he often ate a little fish or drank a little wine either to strengthen his body or for the sake of his fellow diners. Hugh's biographer and chaplain, Adam of Eynsham, cites this as an example of Hugh's 'exquisite courtesy' and his ability to be all things to all men (I Corinthians 9:22).[40] Hugh also adapted his guest list. Whereas the Carthusians were vehemently opposed to any contact with women, Bishop Hugh, 'like other ecclesiastical dignitaries', occasionally invited devout matrons and widows to his table. His biographer argues that this should not be seen as a betrayal of the Carthusian ideal, but as a testimony to Hugh's exceptional character, since he, unlike his fellow men, was immune to the longings of the flesh. This emancipation from earthly desires apparently occurred on the eve of Hugh's promotion to Witham in 1179/80, when he received a vision of his former prior of the Chartreuse who removed burning coals from Hugh's loins, freeing him from earthly temptations; hence Hugh might safely receive women at his table.[41]

Whilst it is known that Benedictine abbots might offer guests meat, there is little evidence of what precisely they served at their tables in the twelfth and early thirteenth centuries.[42] Gerald of Wales's vivid account of his experiences at Christ Church, Canterbury in 1179 suggests that certainly on great occasions, the community and their guests might enjoy a sumptuous spread. Gerald was invited to dine with the prior to celebrate the feast of Holy Trinity, but was shocked at the abundance and variety of rich foods. He claimed that sixteen dishes were served and that there was so much exquisite food, the basic dishes

---

[39] *Vita Anselmi*, p. 78. Following his promotion from the abbacy of Bury to the see of Ely, Hugh allegedly retained the habit and behaviour of a monk, devoting himself as much to the spiritual table (the altar) as to the worldly table, and was hospitable, liberal and cheerful, Matthew Paris, *Historia Anglorum* 2, p. 305; *Chronica Majora* 5, pp. 454–5. Herbert of Bosham makes a similar case for Archbishop Becket and describes at length his various 'tables' – the maundy, altar, judicial court, feast table, *Materials for Becket* 3, pp. 198 ff.

[40] *Magna Vita* 1, p. 125.

[41] *Magna Vita* 1, pp. 48–52.

[42] Woolgar raises the possibility that the earliest surviving diet account, which dates from the late twelfth century and refers to the purchases made by a household in London, Windsor and Westminster, may be of Abbot Samson's household; if so this would shed some light on the kind of foods bought for the abbot's table. The list, however, is fragmentary and simply records purchases rather than consumption, *Household Accounts from Medieval England*, ed. C. M. Woolgar, British Academy Records of Social and Economic History 17–18 (London, 1992–93), 1, pp. 107–10. Items purchased include ale, wine, flour, garlic, mustard, fish, milk and apples.

('generals') were hardly touched.[43] The later Middle Ages are more fully documented. Surviving account rolls and customaries, and also archaeological evidence, suggest that the leading Benedictine abbots at this time enjoyed a rich and varied diet, akin to that of a great lord. For example, the account roll of the chaplain of Battle Abbey in 1520 records payments for dainties for the abbot's table.[44] The cellarer of Battle purchased cream and butter for the abbot and his guests, and it is likely that the swans, cygnets, dolphins, eels and other exotica listed in his accounts were for visitors.[45] When Edward II visited Battle in 1384, he feasted on oxen, pigs, swans, rabbits, herons, pheasants, capons, pike and bream, as well as bread and wine.[46] Cistercian accounts also suggest that by the later Middle Ages the abbots and their guests enjoyed fine fare. Abbot Greenwell of Fountains (1442–71) served figs, walnuts, pears, fish and oysters, as well as partridges, quails and venison.[47] His successors evidently dined just as finely, for excavations in the nineteenth century uncovered a hoard of meat bones as well as oyster, mussel and cockle shells.[48]

Although there is little comparable evidence for the twelfth and early thirteenth centuries, contemporary, non-monastic material may offer an insight into what was served at the abbot's table and also on important feasts when finer foods were enjoyed.[49] Two particularly important twelfth-century sources are Daniel of Beccles' *Urbanus* and Alexander of Neckam's wordlist, the *De Nominibus Utensilibus*.[50] Both works set out in detail how various foods should be prepared and served, and in what order they ought to be brought

43   *Speculum Ecclesiae*, pp. 39–41. Brewer suggests that Gerald's position as legate in Wales to Archbishop Richard, who was a former monk of the priory, may account for his honourable reception at Christ Church, *Speculum Ecclesiae*, p. 40. For the number of dishes served in Benedictine houses, see Harvey, *Living and Dying*, p. 11, and Knowles, 'Diet of the Black monks', pp. 279–82. For the monks of St Swithun's, who complained that the bishop of Winchester had denied them three of their thirteen dishes, see *Speculum Ecclesiae*, pp. 38–9.

44   E. Swift, 'The obedientiary rolls of Battle Abbey', *Sussex Archaeological Collections* 78 (1937), pp. 37–62 (pp. 45–6). For Ely in the later Middle Ages, see D. Owen, 'Ely 1109–1539: priory, community and town', *A History of Ely Cathedral*, ed. Meadows and Ramsay, pp. 59–76 (p. 66).

45   *Accounts of the Cellarers of Battle*, p. 19.

46   W. H. Blaauw, 'Visit of Edward II to Battle and other parts of Sussex, 1324', *Sussex Archaeological Society* 6 (1853), pp. 41–53 (p. 44). Neighbouring landholders sent presents to supplement the king's table; these included rabbits, swans and herons, wine, and also sweet wine, oxen, mutton, peacocks, and bream.

47   For example, see *Memorials of Fountains* 3, pp. 50 (figs), 51 (walnuts), 56 (pears), 89 (fish), 25 (oysters), 49 (quails), 14, 19 (partridges), 61 (venison).

48   Coppack, *Fountains Abbey*, p. 141. The table expenses for Sawley in 1381 included purchases of fowl, capons and fresh fish bought at Preston market, hogs' flesh, shellfish and geese, J. Harland, *Historical Account of the Cistercian Abbey of Salley* (London, 1853), p. 25. For further discussion of Cistercian hospitality in the later Middle Ages, see Kerr, 'Cistercian hospitality', forthcoming.

49   See above, p. 128 for Gerald of Wales' account of the fare at Christ Church, Canterbury, on the feast of Holy Trinity.

50   *Urbanus*, ed. Smyly; *De Nominibus utensilium*, pp. 177–90. The *De Nominibus* was Alexander's first grammatical work, but was more to instruct than to show off, and he grouped words according to their semantic fields, P. Lendinara, 'The *oratio de*

to the table. The *Urbanus* lists an array of meats and fowl, including pork, beef, mutton, venison, hare, roebuck and capon, which should be served first; these were followed by softer foods, such as pies, to give the teeth respite from chewing.[51] At the end of the meal napkins were brought containing spices, wafers and fruit.[52] Alexander of Neckam recommended pears and quinces, since grapes, cherries and apples should not be taken on an empty stomach or after meals.[53] On fast days fish was served instead of meat. Mullet, salmon, and conger were followed by lighter fish, such as perch, roach and pike.[54] The customary of Westminster Abbey, c. 1270, reveals that those dining in the refectory might enjoy flounder, haddock, bream and whelks; apples, plums, pears, cherries and nuts were brought from the garden.[55]

Whilst there is little specific evidence of the kinds of foods served to guests in the twelfth-century monastery, Jocelin of Brakelond reveals a little about their entertainment and explains that Abbot Samson occasionally hired harpists and page boys, but prudently discarded such expenses if they were not needed.[56] There is no shortage of evidence for the later Middle Ages, and the sources suggest that by this time it was fairly commonplace for heads of houses to engage minstrels and players.[57] The sixteenth-century account rolls of the chaplain of Battle Abbey record payments made to players from the abbot's privy purse and in 1536 the abbot of Crowland's fool was headhunted for the royal court.[58] The fifteenth-century accounts of the abbot of Fountains show that this Cistercian abbey in Yorkshire paid minstrels, players from Thirsk and

utensilibus ad domum regendum pertinentibus by Adam of Balsham', *AN Studies* 15 (1993), pp. 161–76 (pp. 174–5).

[51] He explains whether each dish should be carved, sliced or broken, accompanied with a sauce, gravy or a particular seasoning, *Urbanus*, lines 2563–7. Alexander is particularly informative about sauces and seasonings, *De Nominibus utensilium*, p. 183.

[52] *Urbanus*, lines 2569–73; line 1027 refers to fruit sent by the patron. Elsewhere Daniel mentions pears, apples and small figs, *Urbanus*, line 1022.

[53] *De Nominibus Rerum*, ch. 78 ('Of pears'), p. 175.

[54] *Urbanus*, lines 2600–3. For further discussion of this, including a list of guidelines for preparing the ideal feast compiled c. 1240 by the Franciscan, Bartholomaeus Anglicus, and Robert Grosseteste's rules for the countess of Lincoln, see Kerr, 'Food, drink and lodging', forthcoming.

[55] *Westminster Customary*, p. 76 lines 17–24; p. 124 lines 33–4. The gardener of Westminster was to provide apples on certain stated occasions, including St James' Day; at other times he was to provide large pears, cherries, plums and medlars, if they were to be had in the garden, p. 90 lines 37–8, p. 91 lines 1–11. For the arrangements at St Swithun's, Winchester, in the fourteenth century see *A Consuetudinary of the Fourteenth Century for the Refectory of the House of St Swithun in Winchester*, ed. G. W. Kitchin (London and Winchester, 1886), ch. 11 (pp. 18–19).

[56] *Jocelin*, p. 42.

[57] See S. Lindenbaum, 'Entertainment in English monasteries', *Le Théatre et la Cité dans l'Europe Médiévale*, ed. J. Claude Aubailly and E. E. Dubruck (Stuttgart, 1988), pp. 411–21.

[58] Swift, 'The obedientiary rolls', pp. 45–6; *L/P Henry VIII*: 10, no. 181 (p. 64). In 1427 the five-year-old Henry VI spent Christmas at Abingdon and the court was entertained by Jack Travail's players, Cox, *The Story of Abingdon* pt II, p. 89.

Ripon, a fool from Byland and 'a strange fabulist'.[59] Even Sawley, which was one of the poorest of the Yorkshire houses, spent 27s 4d on minstrels in the late fourteenth century.[60]

The monks' guests

The lack of centralisation amongst the Benedictines in the twelfth and early thirteenth centuries meant that the accommodation and dining arrangements for guests varied from house to house. It is helpful, therefore, to focus on two monasteries and a case study of Bury St Edmunds is followed by one of Abingdon. They are a testimony to the number of places where guests might be lodged and refreshed during their stay depending on who they were and their relationship with the community and, not least of all, on who else was present.

Case study 1: Bury St Edmunds

By the thirteenth century the convent's guests at Bury were looked after by one of two hostellers. An intern hosteller was chiefly responsible for Benedictine visitors and was assigned two houses for their care.[61] An extern hosteller entertained monks who were not of the Benedictine order, other regulars and also secular guests for whom the community was liable. It is not known where precisely these guest quarters were situated for little remains standing, and the site itself has been described as 'unintelligible'.[62] Moreover, the sources are riddled with ambiguity. The terminology is particularly problematic and it is difficult to know when to equate and when to differentiate certain buildings. For example, it seems, but is far from conclusive, that the 'interior hostel' should be identified with the 'great house' yet distinguished from the 'greater house'.[63] It has been suggested that the inner hostel for visiting Benedictines, which was effectively the Black hostelry, was adjacent to the refectory, to the north of the western range.[64] Whilst this remains conjectural, a location in or around the claustral area is most likely, since members of the order would have been more fully integrated than other visitors. St Albans also had a separate hospice for visiting Benedictines at this early stage, but it would

---

59   For example, *Memorials of Fountains* 3, pp. 17, 18, 19, 59, 60, 61. Abbot Thomas of Basingwerk (1480–c. 1522), who was allegedly 'given to hospitality', had 'a fine taste for minstrelsy', Williams, *Welsh Cistercians*, p. 69.

60   'Compotus of Sawley 1381', cited in F. Mullin, *A History of the Cistercians in Yorkshire* (Washington, 1932) p. 38.

61   This was the *hostilarius interior*, also known as the *hostilarius monachorum*, *Bury Customary*, pp. 25, 58.

62   Whittingham, 'Bury St Edmunds: plan, design and development', p. 169.

63   The terms used are *magna domus*, *domus maior* and *hostelaria intrinseca*, see *Bury Customary*, p. 60 line 1, p. 61 line 9; p. 61 line 6.

64   See above, p. 84 for the Black hostelry at Ely which is now a canon's residence.

not have been a feature of every house and in many cases members of the order would have simply been accommodated in the monks' dormitory. This would seem to have been the case when the Prior of Séez visited St Peter's Gloucester, with his monk companion.[65] In Cistercian houses visiting monks of the Order were seen as part of the wider family nexus and therefore joined the host community in the dormitory and followed every aspect of monastic observance. Benedictines visiting Bury might join the monks in the refectory – and their provision here is discussed later in the chapter – or else dine in the inside hostel or a private chamber with the cellarer, infirmarer or another great official.[66] This arrangement was presumably intended for guests dining outside regular hours or enjoying a more relaxed diet, perhaps with meat, and was fairly common.[67] Latecomers might, however, be refreshed in the refectory, along with obedientiaries and the bloodlet. On these occasions candles were provided by the sacrist and refectorer and, unless boys were present, guests were seated at the 'little table'.[68] A visiting abbot or cathedral prior presided in the fashion of the first sitting and was accorded a novice to serve him, but a conventual prior was tended kindly by the vice-refectorer.[69] A similar arrangement is set out in the later customary of Eynsham Abbey; an abbot dining at this later sitting was shown to the great table while other guests were seated at the first table.[70]

Just as visiting monks might dine in the refectory, members of the community were permitted, on occasion, to eat outside the refectory in the hostel or another private chamber if, for example, they had undergone bloodletting or were for some other reason entitled to a more satisfying diet. Whenever either the sacrist or chamberlain returned from a journey he might dine in this chamber and, if the prior was absent, was perhaps joined here by members of the community whom the prior would otherwise have indulged.[71]

---

[65] *Speculum Ecclesiae*, p. 34. This is also implied in the Eynsham Customary which states that the hosteller should first ask guests if they wished to see the dormitory so that they might visit the reredorters without any embarrassment, *Eynsham Customary*, ch. 19: 2 (506), p. 199 lines 28–30, see above, p. 104.

[66] *Bury Customary*, p. 61. The 'little chamber' mentioned here may have been attached to the extern hosteller's hall and was perhaps even the chamber where Cistercian guests were accustomed to eat; note the rather obscure reference to this chamber, also known as the 'cawetta', that stood beside 'the house of the hall of the monks' hosteller', *Bury Customary*, p. 61 lines 4–10. An earlier passage refers to Black monks dining in the refectory or other private places, *Bury Customary*, p. 27.

[67] For example, see *Westminster Customary*, p. 80 line 30 – p. 81 line 15; p. 83 lines 21–4; *St Augustine's Customary* (fourteenth-century), p. 137 lines 29–33.

[68] *Bury Customary*, p. 42. See below, pp. 144–5, for the refreshment of latecomers at Abingdon. This was evidently commonplace and similar arrangements are detailed in the *Westminster Customary*, p. 112 line 10; p. 80 lines 30–1.

[69] *Bury Customary*, p. 20 lines 10–20. The question of novice servers was a rather controversial one. For references to the separation of novices, or at least their isolation from seculars before they had made their profession, see the 1234 statutes of the house, Graham, 'A papal visitation', p. 731.

[70] *Eynsham Customary*, ch. 19: 3 (507), p. 201 lines 2–13.

[71] *Bury Customary*, p. 61 lines 10–15. The customs state that on account of guests and weak brothers the abbot, priors and custodians of the house could eat in chambers;

The Bury community evidently exploited this concession for the *Election of Abbot Hugh* describes one instance in the early thirteenth century when only six monks dined in the refectory and the rest enjoyed more appetising fare in private chambers.[72]

Benedictine abbots visiting Bury might be specially honoured by the abbot and received in his court, but were otherwise shown to the inner hostelry, along with other members of the order.[73] They were seemingly assigned a private chamber here for the customary states that any abbot of the order who was entertained in the monks' hostel should be shown first to the 'great house' and then escorted to his chamber for the drink known as the *potus*. He might be joined here by the prior of Bury or another monk of the house. Interestingly, whereas the treasurer was solely responsible for the lighting in the 'great house', the hosteller and he both provided this in the private chamber.[74] There was a similar procedure for welcoming conventual priors, although candles, referred to as *particata*, were only burnt if the prior of Bury was present.[75] This private chamber for visiting abbots is referred to also in connection with the Day of Absolution when a visiting abbot did not celebrate the maundy with the community, but in his own chamber.[76] The chamber where Nicholas of Tusculum stayed when he visited Bury for Christmas in 1213, should probably be distinguished from that where visiting Benedictines were accommodated, since Nicholas was a Cistercian and visiting as the papal legate. It would therefore have fallen on the abbot to provide for his entertainment. Given that there was a vacancy at this time, Nicholas may well have been assigned the abbot's chambers and indeed the archbishop of Trondheim was accommodated here during the vacancy preceding Samson's election in 1182.[77] The account of Nicholas's stay reveals little about the location of his lodgings and simply

---

in accordance with chapter 53 of the *Rule*, they could break their fast on account of guests, providing it was not a solemn feast, *Bury Customary*, pp. 49–50.

72 *Election of Abbot Hugh*, pp. 62–4. Gransden notes that this was a recurring problem at the house, *Bury Customary*, pp. xxvi–vii.

73 These Benedictine guests are mentioned specifically in details about the provision of candles, *Bury Customary*, p. 58. A short, mid-thirteenth-century customary of St Augustine's, Canterbury states that *auctentici* abbots might stay in the royal chamber here, and even priors if they were well known and beloved, *St Augustine's Customary* (c. 1250), p. 254 lines 16–19. The term *auctentici* is discussed below n. 125. Thompson, *St Augustine's Customary*, p. xiii, argues that the customary was probably written earlier than the mid-thirteenth century as marginal notes were added c. 1250, but that it was compiled after 1231. It may therefore have been written about the same time as the customary of Bury St Edmunds and was perhaps compiled c. 1234, the year that Edmund Rich confirmed their customs.

74 *Bury Customary*, pp. 59–60.

75 *Bury Customary*, p. 60. It is not clear what type of candles these were.

76 *Bury Customary*, p. 54. Abbots visiting Eynsham Abbey in the thirteenth or fourteenth century were evidently shown to a private chamber, for the customary states that the hosteller should not lead them to the parlour for the blessing and kiss, as was customary, but show them directly to their chamber, *Eynsham Customary*, ch. 19: 2 (506), p. 198 lines 8–9.

77 Jocelin, p. 15. It has been suggested that this was above the cellar, on the western range, Thomson, *Election of Abbot Hugh*, p. 27, n. 5. See also below, p. 172.

records that he was fittingly received and shown to a chamber to prepare for the day's ordinations.[78]

Visiting regulars who were not members of the Benedictine order were less fully integrated and certainly by the thirteenth century, when the customary was compiled, they were accommodated and refreshed in the guest-hall that was managed by the extern hosteller and his team.[79] The servants and households of Benedictine visitors, and also secular guests for whom the community was liable, were refreshed in the hall but were only accommodated if there was room; otherwise they stayed in the vill.[80] Distinguished seculars would usually have been entertained in the abbot's quarters or else received provisions in the vill.[81] Interestingly visiting Cistercians did not tend to eat in the guest-hall but in an adjoining chamber since they in theory followed a more restricted diet. Their exclusion may be attributable in part to the hostility engendered by the Cistercian abbot of Boxley, who, in 1232 defied the pope's ban to conduct visitations of St Augustine's Canterbury, Bury St Edmunds, Westminster Abbey and St Mary's, York. The abbot of Boxley and his party behaved with such violence at St Augustine's that the other houses refused to receive him. The customary of Westminster Abbey records that prior to this visitation the community had been accustomed to entertain a number of Cistercian guests, who slept in the dormitory and ate in the refectory; this changed following the events of 1232.[82] Still, the abbot of Boxley dined in the refectory of St Augustine's whenever he visited, but other Cistercians only ate here on the feast of St Augustine and were to be served the same as a Black monk.[83]

It is not clear where precisely the extern guest-hall was situated, but it was probably in the court and would certainly have been farther from the cloister than the intern hostel. Accordingly it could operate more or less independently and had its own kitchen and team of servants. The extern hosteller was to minister to his guests appropriately, and was free to honour whomsoever he pleased, provided he did not deplete the cellar.[84] The outer or forensic hostel at Ely stood to the east of the church and probably pre-dates the extension of the presbytery in 1240.[85]

There were clearly several places at Bury where guests might be refreshed depending on who they were and whether the abbot or the community was liable for their care. Whilst these arrangements were carefully defined they could be adapted. Thus, the abbot of Bury might honour Benedictine visitors and invite them to dine in his hall or chamber; laity and clerics might be invited to join the community in the refectory, particularly on a special

78   *Election of Abbot Hugh*, p. 27.
79   *Bury Customary*, pp. 6, 25.
80   *Bury Customary*, pp. 6, 7.
81   *Bury Customary*, p. 27. See above, pp. 57, 78 below, pp. 147, 180.
82   *Westminster Customary*, p. 87 line 27 – p. 88 line 2.
83   *St Augustine's Customary* (c. 1250), p. 258 lines 35–6.
84   *Bury Customary*, p. 7.
85   Dixon, 'The monastic buildings', pp. 145–6.

occasion such as the celebration of a feast.[86] The fact that the customary of the house is largely concerned with organisation within the conventual area means it reveals more about the set-up of the refectory than of the guest-hall, and of the arrangements for visiting prelates and Benedictine monks than for secular and lay guests. It is therefore useful to look more closely at the dining arrangements in Bury's refectory.

Dining arrangements in the refectory at Bury

It was extremely important where the monks and their guests sat, as well as the order in which they took their places and the manner in which they were served, for it was crucial to show visitors due deference without in any way compromising Bury's honour. The thirteenth-century customary of the house sets out the seating arrangements and appropriate protocol for certain situations. For example, it describes how diners should be seated in the presence of a bishop and what concessions ought to be made to this dignitary.[87] The precise nature of these arrangements is difficult to fathom, for there are gaps, ambiguities and seeming inconsistencies in the text. Notably, whilst it is likely that the great table and first table should be distinguished, and comparison with other customaries would certainly substantiate this, it is not explicit.[88] Nor is it clear if the prior's customary place was on the southern side of the great or first table.[89] These and other matters relating to the organisation of the refectory are considered.

The abbot of Bury was probably not a regular diner in the refectory, for he would have frequently been tied up on his manors or busy entertaining his household and guests in the abbatial lodgings. It would generally have been the prior or a sub-prior of the house who presided here. This is born out in the customary where the prior's, and not the abbot's position, is most greatly discussed. Whenever the abbot dined with the community he presided and did not even yield to a bishop or a distinguished Benedictine abbot.[90] Nevertheless, deference was shown to a bishop insofar as he was invited to give the blessing.[91] The abbot of Bury always occupied the northern side of the great table and the prior, seemingly, the southern side, but whether this was the great or first table is unclear. However, it would seem that the prior sat at

---

86   See, for example, *Election of Abbot Hugh*, p. 62.
87   *Bury Customary*, pp. 18–21.
88   I am grateful to Miss Barbara Harvey for her helpful comments on these table arrangements. The Eynsham customary refers to both the great table and the first table which suggests that they ought to be distinguished, *Eynsham Customary*, ch. 19: 2 (507), p. 201 lines 2–13.
89   The customaries of Westminster and St Augustine's suggest that the abbot and prior each had a side where they were accustomed to sit. The former describes this as a 'right and old custom', *Westminster Customary*, p. 111 lines 25–9; *St Augustine's Customary* (fourteenth-century), p. 169 lines 34–6.
90   *Bury Customary*, p. 20 line 33 – p. 21 line 1.
91   *Bury Customary*, p. 18 line 26 – p. 19 line 36.

the first table if the abbot of Bury presided.[92] Guests were seated in relation to the president, in accordance with their standing and also that of their fellow diners. Visiting abbots were shown equal honour and took their places at the great table at the same time; moreover, the service (*servicium*) was divided equally amongst them. This probably refers to the double ration of common dishes they received.[93] If any cathedral or conventual priors were dining when the abbot of Bury presided, they sat at the first table in order of the dignity of their church. Thus, the prior whose cathedral ranked first was placed on the abbot's side, that is, on the northern side of the table.[94] Regardless of where he sat, a cathedral prior received 'special service'. The meaning of this is not clear and while it may refer to how the meal was served, it more likely means a particularly fine meal that replaced everything in the ordinary meal.[95] On these occasions the prior of Bury did not yield his position, presumably this was on the southern side of the first table, and assumed the dignity of a cathedral prior for, as the customary boldly declares, 'he ought not to give his honour to another.'[96] Only in the prior's absence was a visiting prior permitted to take his place.[97] Any conventual priors who joined the community when the abbot was presiding were seated by the intern hosteller, who organised other visiting monks and monastic officials.[98]

It would normally have been the prior of Bury's responsibility to preside in the refectory, and he ceded only to a Benedictine abbot. Accordingly, if a bishop, episcopal prior or abbot of another order dined with the community in the abbot of Bury's absence, the prior of Bury sat at the northern side of the great table and the visiting prelate to his left, on the southern side.[99] Both received pittances which were brought to the table in several dishes but

92   See *Bury Customary*, p. 20 line 31. Whereas the Bury customary defines the abbot's and prior's places in relation to the north or south (or right or left), the later customaries describe their places in relation to the bell (*skilla*) and the Image of Majesty that marked the centre of the table and the seat of honour; for example, see *Westminster Customary*, p. 107 lines 16–29.

93   *Bury Customary*, p. 20 line 33 – p. 21 line 2. I am indebted to Miss Barbara Harvey for an explanation of the *servicium* in this context, and for sending me in advance of publication a copy of her article, 'Monastic pittances in the Middle Ages', *Food in Medieval England: diet and nutrition*, ed. C. M. Woolgar, D. Serjeantson and T. Waldron (Oxford, 2006), pp. 215–27.

94   *Bury Customary*, p. 20 lines 23–8. At Westminster Abbey, guests sat on the prior's side when the abbot presided in the refectory and on the abbot's side when the prior presided, *Westminster Customary*, p. 111 lines 25–33.

95   *Bury Customary*, p. 20 lines 30–2. I am grateful to Miss Barbara Harvey for this suggestion.

96   *Bury Customary*, p. 20 lines 24–32.

97   *Bury Customary*, p. 20 lines 32–3.

98   *Bury Customary*, p. 20 lines 6–8, 13–15.

99   *Bury Customary*, p. 18 lines 10–14. In chapter, the prior of Bury yielded only to his own abbot and also the abbot of St Benet of Hulme, with whom Bury had a special relationship, *Bury Customary*, p. 18. For the special relationship between the two houses, see R. H. C. Davis, 'The monks of St Edmund 1021–1148', *History* 40 (1955), pp. 227–39 (pp. 232–3), and A. Gransden, 'The legends and traditions concerning the origins of the abbey of Bury St Edmunds', *EHR* 100 (1985), pp. 1–24, esp. pp. 16–19. See below, p. 137, for the arrangements at Westminster and St Augustine's, Canterbury.

at the same time, for the sake of harmony.[100] Although the prior of Bury did not yield to a bishop, he showed the prelate deference by inviting him to give the various blessings. For practical and also symbolic reasons the prior himself sounded the bell or clapper before and after dinner, and gave the command for the pittances to be brought. He also made signs for the spoons and knives and did the same for his guest unless the bishop had been a member of the Benedictine order. Such being the case the prior intimated to him when he should make these signs and either he, or the prior, gave the appropriate order. The compiler of the customs concludes this section by noting that some held that the bishop should sit alone at the table, without the prior.[101] This concern to safeguard the host community's prominence – and pre-eminence – was not peculiar to Bury and similar measures were implemented elsewhere. At both Westminster Abbey and St Augustine's, Canterbury it was permitted to only a Benedictine abbot to sit alone at the bell known as the *skilla*; a bishop sat beneath the Image of Majesty and the prior, or his deputy from the house, sat with him and sounded the bell. No visiting prior was allowed to preside in the refectory at either Westminster or St Augustine's.[102] Concessions were granted to the priors of Bury St Edmunds, Worcester and Malmesbury, who were joined in fraternity, and to other great priors, for example of St Albans and Canterbury.[103]

Conventual and cathedral priors visiting Bury generally sat with the prior of the house, who presided.[104] The conventual prior was to sit at the head of the first table, on the northern side, but if two were present and the prior of Bury presiding at the table ('ad mensam'), one would sit on the northern side and the other to the south of Bury's prior. Whoever sat at the head of the first table was attended by the monk server and received the pittances which he then shared with those seated beside him. To do so, he made the appropriate nods and signs to the monk-server who distributed the dishes.[105]

---

[100] *Bury Customary*, p. 18 lines 12–18.

[101] *Bury Customary*, p. 18 lines 18–24. These practicalities are addressed also in the eleventh-century customaries for Cluny which state that a visiting abbot should be shown the respect normally reserved for their own abbot if he was absent, but if the visitor was ignorant of their customs he should not hold the Lord Abbot's place in the refectory or chapter, or extend the blessing to the reader. While a bishop might bless the reader, he was prompted by the prior, Herrgott, *Ordo Cluniacensis per Bernardum*, ch. 9 (p. 154).

[102] *Westminster Customary*, p. 107 lines 16–36; *St Augustine's Customary* (fourteenth-century), p. 166 lines 14–22; *St Augustine's Customary* (c. 1250), p. 254 lines 6–7.

[103] *Westminster Customary*, p. 107 line 36 – p. 108 line 17.

[104] *Bury Customary*, p. 20 lines 20–3.

[105] *Bury Customary*, p. 21 lines 2–13. In his set of rules for the countess of Lincoln, Robert Grosseteste advised that she order her dish to be 'refilled and heaped up', particularly with the light courses 'that you may courteously give from your dish to the right and left to all at high table and to whom else it pleases you that they have of the same as you had in front of you', rule 19, printed in *Walter of Henley and other Treatises on Estate Management and Accounting*, ed. D. Oschinsky (Oxford, 1971), pp. 388–415, treatise 3 (p. 405). M. Burger, 'The date and authorship of Robert Grosseteste's Rules for Household and Estate Management', *Historical Research* 74 (2001), pp. 106–16, has recently argued that the rules can only be dated before Grosseteste's death in 1253

These arrangements suggest that the prior of Bury may only have occupied the great table if an abbot, bishop or episcopal prior was present and perhaps also whenever the abbot of Bury presided; on such occasions he would have sat on the southern side. Otherwise, the prior sat at the first table on the southern side, even when presiding over the refectory. If, as this implies, the great table was only used when an abbot or prelate was present it must have lain empty more often than it was occupied.

Other monastic visitors dining in Bury's refectory, including claustral priors and superiors, were seated by the intern hosteller at the first table, with the senior monks of Bury. They retained this place in choir, in chapter and also at Collations if they attended. The organisation of these guests was highly complicated, for the hosteller was to make sure not only that everyone was accorded appropriate honour but that his own community was not overshadowed. Accordingly, he was to ensure that at least four of Bury's senior monks were seated first at this first table with any non-conventual prior who was visiting. The same applied in choir and at chapter unless the prior or precentor of Bury advised him otherwise.[106]

The Bury customary also sheds light on the nature of pittances distributed to guests. These were extra dishes served to supplement the basic allowances and might include fish, beans, eggs or vegetables.[107] At Bury, as elsewhere, all guests received pittances, which were also given to bolster sick and weak members of the community, to honour office-holders and to reward work within the convent. For example, whoever sang the daily mass received a share.[108] Pittances were brought to the president's table and then distributed, in order, to the various recipients. Benedictine abbots visiting Bury enjoyed an additional bonus for on the first day of their stay they received from the sacrist a measure of wine at dinner and of ale at supper, regardless of where they dined within the precinct – or, indeed, outside.[109] Abbots who were not of the Order only received this welcome gift if the sacrist decided to honour them in this way. However, it had recently been agreed that great Cistercian abbots visiting Bury, such as the abbots of Rievaulx, Fountains and Warden, should now receive a measure of wine, out of charity.[110]

---

and not, as previously, to c. 1240–42. Significantly, they are based on an earlier set of injunctions for Robert's episcopal household.

[106] *Bury Customary*, p. 21 lines 13–26. He was to do the same in choir and at chapter, unless the prior or precentor suggested otherwise on account of the guest's position, reputation or similar reason, lines 23–6.

[107] *Bury Customary*, p. 21 lines 30–1. For an extensive discussion of monastic pittances and their role in introducing new and better foods to the monastic diet, see Harvey, 'Monastic pittances'.

[108] *Bury Customary*, p. 21 lines 30–4; p. 22 lines 10–12. This was commonplace, see, for example, *Eynsham Customary*, ch. 18: 5 (452), p. 184, for the dish given by the kitchener to visiting regulars, and ch. 14: 10 (332), p. 186, for the measure of wine for the drink known as the *caritas*, whether they dined with or after the community.

[109] *Bury Customary*, p. 30, i.e. gifts, *xennia*, to bestow honour. Guests of the Irish monks of Tallaght would not have fared as well for ale was banned here; instead, water or milk was served with the evening meal, see O'Sullivan, *Hospitality in Ireland*, pp. 226–7.

[110] *Bury Customary*, p. 30.

The discussion of the organisation of the refectory has centred on the arrangements for visiting prelates and monks, but it is important to consider how accessible the refectory was to other guests. The customary is chiefly concerned with defining Bury's position *vis à vis* visiting prelates and makes little reference to seculars and laity. Whilst these guests were not prohibited from dining with the monks in the refectory, this was not, seemingly, encouraged and they were certainly not to dine here on a regular basis. There were greater restrictions regarding women who were in theory prohibited from the refectory. Statutes issued following the visitation of Bury in 1234 stipulated that no women should be led through the cloister to the refectory, infirmary or vestry. An exception might be made for noble ladies or good women, such as kinsfolk and those of whom no ill was suspected. They were to be refreshed ('shown honour') either by the custodians of the order or upon their instruction.[111] No equivalent clause appears in the 1234 statutes for Westminster, but a similar prescription occurs in the late-thirteenth-century customary of the house, and the ruling as a whole echoes Gregory IX's reforms of 1227–41.[112] The Bury statutes also impose restrictions on 'unknown persons' dining with the community, who were not to attend the convent's dinner unless they were clearly necessary and of service to the house.[113] An almost identical clause appears in the 1234 statutes for Westminster, which forbade ignoble laity and others ('laici ignobiles et alii') from entering the refectory unless the abbot was present.[114] The later customary of Westminster is more explicit and notes that whilst the refectorer should ensure that no laity, unknown or dishonest folk dined at the *skilla*, an exception might be made for those who were of use, such as the fishermen from the Thames who customarily dined with the convent when they offered the salmon of St Peter.[115] The origins of this custom are explained in Aelred of Rievaulx's *Life of St Edward the Confessor* which describes how St Peter appeared as a traveller to Eadric, a fisherman on the Thames, and asked for transport across the river. On the return journey Eadric had a good catch, and was told by the traveller to present the largest fish to Bishop Mellitus (d. 624) who, according to legend, had supported the foundation of an early church at Westminster and was to conduct the dedication ceremony. From then until the fourteenth

---

[111] Graham, 'A papal visitation', p. 731. The custodians of the order were the sub-prior, third or fourth priors.

[112] *Westminster Customary*, p. 170 line 31 – p. 171 line 3. Gregory underlined the importance of guarding the cloister, refectory, dormitory and choir, and of keeping women out of these places, but conceded that the abbot might make an exception for specific women who had just reason to enter. Thus, he might permit access to noble women or patrons at certain specific periods if their refusal might result in scandal. O'Sullivan's translation of these statutes are printed as the appendix to *The Register of Eudes of Rouen*, trans. S. M. Brown (London, 1964), pp. 737–46 (p. 742). These restrictions and exemptions are echoed in later statutes issued by the General Chapter of Canterbury, for example, in 1277, Pantin, *Chapters* 1, p. 72 (1272, v: i). It is not clear if they were corrective, preventative or emphatic.

[113] Graham, 'A papal visitation', p. 732.

[114] Graham, 'A papal visitation', p. 739.

[115] *Westminster Customary*, p. 103 lines 6–13.

century Eadric's descendants claimed the right to present the community with fish on St Peter's day, and the monks received a tithe of all fisheries on the Thames.[116]

These restrictions were largely intended to preserve silence and decorum in the refectory for outsiders would not have been familiar with the community's system of sign language that was used to communicate in the refectory and claustral area. The monks ate in silence and listened to a reading so that they might feed their souls as much as their bodies; necessary communication was made by signing.[117] The presence of visitors was therefore a potential distraction, although Gerald of Wales' rather acerbic remarks about the monks of Christ Church, Canterbury suggests that excessive signing could be just as disruptive as a little speech. Gerald, who dined with the community in 1179 to celebrate the feast of Holy Trinity, maintained that there was so much gesticulating in the refectory it was like a dumbshow.[118] The monks did make some allowances for certain notable visitors. At Bury St Edmunds, whoever was seated beside or ministered to a bishop or another distinguished guest might speak a little, to convey essential information.[119] According to the late-thirteenth-century customary of Westminster Abbey, the refectorer might address the king, queen, a bishop or another great Benedictine abbot, or indeed a great earl like the brother or son of the king; a little necessary speech was permitted to other seculars if no monks were present.[120] Concessions of this kind were not uncommon and suggest the importance of maintaining good relations with powerful guests. This is explicit in Archbishop Peckham's statutes for the Augustinian community at Haverfordwest in 1284, following his visitation of the priory. Peckham warned that the prior should not absent himself from the refectory or from Compline on account of guests unless it was to entertain a person of importance who might assist or injure the monastery.[121]

---

[116]   Aelred of Rievaulx, *The Life of St Edward the Confessor*, trans. J. Bertram (Southampton, 1993), bk 1: 13, pp. 51–3; 129–30.

[117]   *Rule of St Benedict*, ch. 38 (p. 104). The Superior was permitted to say a few words, if he wished. Anselm, evidently exploited Benedict's 'grudging sanction' to spiritual discourse at the table, Southern, *Vita Anselmi*, p. 7, n. 23. Bernard of Clairvaux's *Apologia* to William, written in 1125, complains of jokes and laughter at mealtimes, *Cistercians and Cluniacs, St Bernard's Apologia to Abbot William*, trans. M. Casey (Kalamazoo, 1970), p. 55.

[118]   See above pp. 128–9, for Gerald's account of Christ Church. Peter Abelard also warned of the excess of signing and cited St Gregory's *Moralia*, Abelard, *Epistolae*, ep. 8, col. 261; translated Radice, *Letters of Abelard and Heloise*, letter 7, p. 189.

[119]   *Bury Customary*, p. 19 lines 36–7, and p. 20 lines 1–4, states that the refectorer should not talk to any seculars if monks were present, unless to console them, and then only briefly and if necessary. However, this was permitted in the presence of a king, queen, bishop or another great Benedictine abbot, or indeed a great earl like the brother or son of the king.

[120]   *Westminster Customary*, p. 102 lines 23–36. For similar concessions made to the refectorer of St Augustine's, Canterbury, in the fourteenth century, see *St Augustine's Customary* (fourteenth-century), p. 163 lines 3–5.

[121]   F. G. Cowley, *The Monastic Order in South Wales, 1066–1349* (Cardiff, 1977), pp. 102–3; *Registrum Peckham* 3, pp. 782–4 (p. 785).

A later Cistercian example suggests that the restriction of laity and seculars from the refectory may have been for less lofty reasons. Injunctions issued following the visitation of Hailes in 1394 stipulated that no secular should be invited to dine in the convent on a regular basis lest something untoward occurred at the table that might detract from the honour of the Order. An exception was made if the secular in question was of good repute and some very great advantage would come of his presence.[122] It would seem that fear of scandal lay behind the injunction issued to Cluniac houses in England following the visitation of 1275, which prohibited the prior and convent from eating meat in the presence of seculars visiting the monastery or indulging in meaty feasts in the houses of laity.[123]

Case study 2: Abingdon Abbey

> He [Abbot Vincent] had built the fine tower of the church, and fittingly adorned the court with various and apt out-buildings, that is the hall of the guests with a chamber, a granary, a brew-house, a bake-house, a double stable, an almonry with three great towers.[124]

The *History of Abingdon* records that Abbot Vincent (1121–30) built a guest-hall with a chamber in the court, and reveals that from 1107 at least the abbots of Abingdon had their own chamber. The *De Obedientiariis* stipulates that the abbot should not yield this chamber to anyone other than the king or metropolitan. This suggests that Abingdon, unlike St Albans and St Augustine's, Canterbury had no royal suite at this time.[125] By the Dissolution in the sixteenth century, the abbot's lodgings at Abingdon were extensive and included 'two fair chambers called the king's and queen's chambers, a chapel with diverse and other chambers and houses of office'.[126] As previously noted in Chapter 2, the guest-hall at Abingdon is not mentioned in the customs of the house that were compiled c. 1220. It was suggested that this omission is perhaps attributable to the customary's concern with conventual affairs and with those entertained within the claustral area, rather than the abbot's guests who were ministered to by his gatekeeper (*janitor*) and the curtar in the

122 Harper-Bill, 'Visitation of Hailes', pp. 109–10.
123 *Charters and Records of Cluni* 2, pp. 124–7.
124 *History of Abingdon* 2, p. 341 (appendix, additions from MS B).
125 *History of Abingdon* 2, pp. 341, 339; *De Obedientiariis*, p. 339. See above, pp. 80–5, for further discussion of this accommodation at St Albans. The royal chamber at St Augustine's is mentioned in the short mid-thirteenth-century customary of the house which states that *auctentici* abbots might stay here and even priors if they were well known and beloved, *St Augustine's Customary* (c. 1250), p. 254 lines 16–19. The term *auctentici* is rather obscure, but it has been suggested by Miss Barbara Harvey that if it refers to abbots having authority, those who had retired from office were perhaps excluded from staying in the royal chamber. The ruling may also have been intended also to exclude abbots elect.
126 Cox, *The Story of Abingdon*, pt II, p. 115.

court or vill.[127] Distinguished guests would have been received in the abbot's quarters, and others in the court; the latter would have included the relatives, friends, knights and their men who visited to celebrate the Nativity of Mary, which was the abbey's patronal feast. Visiting monks were more fully integrated than other visitors, but it is not clear if the Black hostelry (*receptaculum monachorum*) mentioned in Robert of Carville's ordinances of 1245 was in use in the twelfth century or if fellow monks were at this time accommodated in the common dormitory.[128] There would certainly have been room for them here since Faritius's dormitory could accommodate about one hundred monks, yet in the late twelfth century there were, at most, about eighty monks.[129] Nor is it clear from the customary if the sheets, mantles and covers of dead monks that the chamberlain received for guests were intended specifically for the use of visiting monks or for guests in general.[130]

Where precisely a guest was received was clearly dependent on who he was and who else was visiting. The flexibility of these arrangements is made clear in Robert de Carville's prescriptions of 1245. These state that abbots, priors and other exalted religious persons for whom there ought to be greater and more honourable service should be shown to chambers in the abbot's court rather than the Black hostelry. However, if there was a large number of guests and it was not possible to accommodate them here ('outside'), they should instead be admitted 'within' and no apology was required.[131] Carville's ruling is also of interest regarding the perception of space. The number of grants permitting lay persons access to the claustral area underlines how this was often considered a privilege, yet for Benedictines who were accustomed to stay in the claustral area it was an honour to be entertained instead 'outside' in the abbot's quarters.

The refectory at Abingdon, as elsewhere, was reserved essentially for members of the convent and visiting monks. Although clerics and laity were not prohibited from dining here, they would probably not have done so on a regular basis; thus, the sources refer to the monks' relatives and friends dining in the court or the vill, when they visited on the Vigil of the Nativity

---

127 See above, p. 68–72. For provision for relatives of monks, who dined in the court or vill, see the customs relating to obedientiaries, *Chronicon de Abingdon* 2, p. 313; *De Obedientiariis*, pp. 350–1. This treatise reveals that the kitchener was to provide salt for the abbot's table and to salt the pork for those dining in the court; presumably this included guests and servants, p. 393.

128 *Two Cartularies of Abingdon* 2, no. C. 7 (p. 23). See above, p. 134, and below, p. 146, for the arrangements at Westminster Abbey.

129 A charter of 1194 x 1217 compelled the abbot to increase the community to eighty monks, *Two Cartularies of Abingdon* 1, no. L. 166 (p. 104), and 'De Abbatibus', ed. Stevenson, *Chronicon de Abingdon* 2, p. 287. The *History of Abingdon* 2, pp. 72–3, states that under Faritius numbers increased threefold.

130 *De Obedientiariis*, p. 388.

131 *Two Cartularies of Abingdon* 2, no. C. 7 (pp. 12–25). In 1219 it was decided that Benedictine monks should be entertained 'inside' unless they were abbots, who were entertained in the abbot's court, *Two Cartularies of Abingdon* 1, no. L. 167 (pp. 112–13).

of Mary.[132] The abbot himself may not have eaten regularly in the refectory since he, like other great abbots, would have frequently been away on his manors or at the royal court. Moreover, whenever the abbot was at home he generally would have dined at his feast table (*mensa convivium*) which was probably situated outside the refectory. He was certainly dining in a separate chamber by the mid-thirteenth century, as was commonplace in Benedictine and also Cistercian houses of the time.[133] The abbot would have shared this feast table with guests and members of his household. In accordance with chapter 56 of the *Rule of St Benedict*, he might invite some of the monks to join him here for a more nourishing meal.[134] The '*De abbatibus*' records that Abbot Faritius (1100–17) established the custom of inviting ten or twelve of the brethren to dine at his table each day. This is repeated in the customary of the house although it states that youths should not be left unattended in the refectory.[135]

On feast days and other special occasions the abbot would inevitably have joined the community in the refectory. Abbot John of St Albans (1195–1214) feasted joyfully with his brethren on the completion of the new refectory. At such times the abbot and any guests dining with him at the high table (*mensa consistorium*) were refreshed from the community's supplies.[136] An arrangement of this kind seems to have been fairly common and was prescribed, for example, at Westminster Abbey.[137] Guests who sat with the abbot or prior at the high table did not follow the community's procession to the church for grace but remained after dinner and were refreshed with a drink and a few words of consolation.[138] If guests were present the abbot did not join the post-dinner procession but stayed behind with his visitors. The prior only remained if he was dining with laity or clerics and might invite up to three members of the community to join them.[139] There were similar arrangements elsewhere.[140]

---

132 For example, *De Obedientiariis*, p. 350.
133 This is implied in a passage in the customary which lists the places where the kitchener of Abingdon should provide salt, for it distinguishes the refectory from the abbot's table, *De Obedientiariis*, p. 393. Clause iii of the Chatsworth MS, 71 E. fol. 165v, printed in Lambrick, 'Abingdon abbey', pp. 182–3 (p. 182), refers to the abbot dining in his chamber.
134 *De Obedientiariis*, p. 349. For a similar practice at Eynsham see *Eynsham Customary*, ch. 12: 24 (276), p. 136.
135 *De abbatibus*, p. 287; *De Obedientiariis*, p. 337.
136 *De Obedientiariis*, p. 348; GASA 1, p. 220. This is reiterated in a memorandum of c. 1245 that sets out the abbot's and brethren's perquisites and responsibilities; it reveals that the abbot had a barony to support his guests, but that he and his visitors were supplied from conventual supplies if they dined in the refectory, *Two Cartularies of Abingdon* 2, no. C. 405 (pp. 236–8). For a list of feasts when the abbot was in the refectory at Abingdon, see BL Cotton MS CIX fo. 187r. However, as noted earlier, it is not clear if the abbot's feast table was within the refectory at Abingdon in the early twelfth century.
137 'Statutes of Westminster', 1225, p. 222; *St Augustine's Customary* (fourteenth-century), p. 159 lines 34–5.
138 *De Obedientiariis*, p. 415.
139 *De Obedientiariis*, pp. 348, 362–3.
140 For example, see *Eynsham customary*, ch. 12: 23 (275), pp. 135–6.

Whenever the abbot or prior of Westminster Abbey presided in the refectory and was joined by guests, he led them to his chamber for the post-prandial beverage and grace. If another official such as the sub-prior or the third or fourth prior acted for him, guests were led to the hostel or, if this was full, to the long chamber that was next to the refectory. By the late thirteenth century the long chamber had been converted to the prior's chamber, and if the hostel was busy visitors were brought instead to the chapel of the Blessed Dunstan.[141] This update to the customs suggests that they were not simply derivative but working manuals. If anyone below the rank of fourth prior covered for the prior he was not permitted to lead guests out of the refectory or even talk to them, but had to minister to them in silence behind the refectory door.[142]

Visiting monks would have eaten in the refectory at Abingdon as a matter of course, whether they attended dinner with the convent or dined later with the servers. The customary sets out in some detail how they should be provided for and how this was affected by the time of their arrival. If a guest arrived before dinner, the hosteller notified the refectorer of his position so that he, in turn, could arrange the vessels appropriately and seat the visitor in accordance with his standing, either at the high table with the president or with the community.[143] Both the hosteller and refectorer ministered to the guest, and did so at whatever time he ate.[144] The hosteller procured their food and drink from the cellarer. He also acquired provisions for their servants who may have eaten in the hall.[145] The amount each guest received was dependent on his standing, but the arrangements for his refreshment were affected by the time of his arrival.[146] The customary made provision for every eventuality. If the visitor arrived before the convent had finished dining and it was not possible for him to enter the refectory, the hosteller showed him to the parlour while the refectory was swept. This particular custom may have been peculiar to Abingdon for it does not appear in the Eynsham customary. If the community had already dined and the guest was to eat with the servers, the hosteller notified the kitchener and refectorer before entering the refectory. When the prior carried out his post-dinner rounds, he might permit these latecomers

[141]   *Westminster Customary*, p. 112 lines 23–32. A similar arrangement is detailed in the fourteenth-century customary of St Augustine's, but whilst the abbot or prior led guests to his chamber after dinner, the sub-prior, third or fourth prior remained in the refectory with clerks and laity, and was joined by the hosteller; if he could not remain with guests, the sub-prior organised for another brother to join the hosteller and these guests, and to refresh them at the door of the refectory, in silence, *St Augustine's Customary* (fourteenth-century), p. 169 lines 34–6; p. 170 lines 1–8.

[142]   *Westminster Customary*, pp. 112–13.

[143]   *De Obedientiariis*, pp. 415, 403. A similar practice is detailed in the later customary of Eynsham, *Eynsham Customary*, ch. 19: 2 (506), p. 199 lines 20–8.

[144]   *De Obedientiariis*, p. 398.

[145]   *De Obedientiariis*, pp. 412, 413.

[146]   The Westminster Customary is more explicit; it states, that a conventual prior should receive the same as the prior of Westminster, namely, two loaves and a jug of ale at dinner and also supper if they were to have this; an abbot was to have three loaves at dinner and supper, *Westminster Customary*, p. 80 line 33 – p. 81 line 4.

to remain seated for a while at the table.[147] Those who dined with the community and sat with the abbot or prior stayed behind after dinner for the customary post-prandial consolation. If seated with the monks of Abingdon, they remained only if the abbot beckoned them to wait with the hosteller.[148] The Westminster Customary is more explicit and reveals that monks who had been professed at the house or were joined in fraternity sat with the brethren and celebrated grace with them in the choir; other monks sat with the abbot or senior members of the community and either remained with the president and hosteller after dinner, or joined the end of the procession and said grace outside the choir with the hosteller.[149]

The *De Obedientiariis* sheds some light on refreshment outside mealtimes. The post-Collations drink (*potus*) was offered to guests before they celebrated Compline in the chapter-house, and they were permitted a refill if they wished.[150] After Compline guests, and also members of the community who were recovering from bloodletting, were served drinks from the storeroom and offered up to four fills.[151] It is perhaps significant that the bishop of Salisbury's charter of 1219 permitted only three fills to pilgrims, poor clerks, sick laity and especially travellers, but as it is not known if his injunctions pre- or post-date the customs, it is not clear if the bishop sought to tighten up existing practices or if the monks sought to relax the episcopal ordinances.[152] The community dined later during Lent and therefore guests and the bloodlet were offered a drink before dinner, but were not allowed any bread at this time.[153]

Unfortunately the *De Obedientiariis* reveals little about dining arrangements for those who were refreshed outside the claustral area for, as previously mentioned, the customary is essentially concerned with conventual arrangements. Thus, whilst we know that the curtar provided for the monks' relatives and the knights and men of the shire who visited to celebrate the Nativity of St Mary, and who dined in either the court or the vill, it is not

---

147   *De Obedientiariis*, p. 415; 364.

148   *De Obedientiariis*, p. 349. For the arrangements at Eynsham, see *Eynsham Customary*, ch. 12: 22 (275), pp. 135–6. According to the twelfth-century customary of the Victorines, Paris, the brethren celebrated grace in the choir after dinner, whereas visiting canons said this outside the choir with the hosteller and visiting monks in the refectory, *Liber Ordinis*, pp. 62–3.

149   *Westminster Customary*, p. 83 lines 12–32. At St Augustine's, Canterbury visiting monks said grace outside the choir except the monks of Bury and others joined in fraternity, *St Augustine's Customary* (fourteenth-century), p. 139 lines 22–9.

150   *De Obedientiariis*, p. 414. According to the instructions compiled for novices at Christ Church, Canterbury, the community gathered in the refectory for a drink before Collations that took place in the chapter-house; this was followed by the *caritas* (usually a cup of wine) in the refectory; thereafter Compline was celebrated, *Instructio Noviciorum*, pp. 218–21. At Westminster Abbey, a measure of ale was provided at Collations for one visiting monk, but if there were two they shared this; three monks received two measures but four shared the two, *Westminster Customary*, p. 81 lines 5–13.

151   *De Obedientiariis*, p. 399.

152   *Two Cartularies of Abingdon* 1, no. L. 167 (pp. 112–13).

153   This was served by the cellarer and refectorer from the storeroom supplies, *De Obedientiariis*, p. 401.

clear what precisely they were given or indeed where in the precinct they were refreshed.[154] Their provisions would have been supplied by the various offices in the court including the dispensary, butlery and larder; a charter of 1219 ruled that whenever the curtar's servant deputised for him he should obtain necessities for guests from these offices, according to the number of visitors received.[155]

These case studies underline the variety of places where guests might be entertained during their stay at the monastery and suggest that this number increased throughout the period – and beyond. This was partly a response to developments on the religious front, chiefly the arrival and growth of the new religious orders. Benedictines visiting Bury St Edmunds in the late twelfth and early thirteenth centuries were not seemingly distinguished from other regulars, but by the mid-thirteenth century they were received 'within' by the intern hosteller while all other regulars, including Cistercian monks, were tended by the extern hosteller. As previously mentioned, the customary of Westminster Abbey suggests that the abbot of Boxley's antics in 1232 marked a watershed, for until then the community was wont to receive a large number of Cistercians who dined in the refectory and slept in the dormitory. By the late thirteenth century this was no longer the case; the few who visited were entertained in the outside hostel with other non-Benedictine regulars and friars. By this time visiting Benedictines were accommodated in a guest cell.[156] On account of the number of friars who regularly visited St Albans, the community built a hospice specifically for their use inside the gate of the new court. This was in situ shortly before 1247 and by 1251 the arrival of friars at the abbey was almost a daily custom.[157] Personal links and networks also had an impact and those visiting from houses joined in fraternity or from a cell of the house might be more fully integrated with the host community and accorded concessions. Whilst Westminster Abbey closed its doors to visitors after Compline, as was commonplace in religious houses, Benedictines who arrived after this time were admitted to the extern hostel and those from the house or joined in confraternity were admitted either at the sartry (tailor's workshop) or the door of the cellar.[158]

---

[154]   'Extract from the Rule of St Ethelwold', ed. Stevenson, *Chronicon de Abingdon* 2, p. 313; *De Obedientiariis*, pp. 350, 351.

[155]   *Two Chartularies of Abingdon* 1, L167 (p. 112).

[156]   *Westminster Customary*, p. 87 lines 1–3; p. 87 line 20 – p. 88 line 2. For similar arrangements see *Eynsham Customary*, ch. 19: 5 (516–20), p. 203; *St Augustine's Customary* (fourteenth-century) p. 141 line 30, p. 142 line 2. 'Passing monks' stayed in the *hostilaria* at St Augustine's, p. 103 lines 13–15.

[157]   *Chronica Majora* 4, p. 600; 5, p. 264. Not all friars stayed in this hospice, see above, p. 84.

[158]   *Westminster Customary*, p. 85 lines 14–19. Moreover, monks from Bury St Edmunds and those who shared in the fraternity of the house celebrated grace after dinner with the monks of Westminster in their choir; other Benedictines did so outside the choir, with the hosteller, p. 83 lines 24–32.

The sources also suggest that arrangements were flexible, and while halls and chambers were assigned specifically to guests, additional lodgings were put at their disposal if and when necessary. This was the advice given in the late thirteenth century to abbots hosting the General Chapter of Benedictines in Canterbury, who were to make free as many halls, chambers and houses as possible within the precinct, so that as many prelates as possible might be accommodated here, rather than in the vill. It was clearly expected that some at least might secure lodgings in the vill and they were also subject to restrictions regarding the number of men and horses they might bring.[159] Matthew Paris' account of the consecration of the church at Ely in 1252 is a further testimony to this flexibility, for he explains that everywhere was filled with visitors attending the ceremony; guests were accommodated in the monks' buildings, the bishop's lodgings and also with the townsfolk.[160]

Outside the precinct

Monastic hospitality extended beyond the abbey precinct, and visitors – both great and lowly – might be accommodated in the vill and receive provisions from the community. The curtar of Abingdon, who was a leading member of the abbot's household, provided for the crowds of men and knights of the shire who visited the abbey to celebrate feasts, and also the monks' relatives who dined in the court or the vill; similar provision was made in the later customaries of Eynsham and Westminster.[161] The external hosteller of Bury refreshed seculars who could not be accommodated in his hall, and the sacrist of the abbey was to provide bishops, barons and those of a similar standing who were residing in the vill with bread and wine at dinner, and ale and wax at supper. At his discretion, he might make similar gifts to other magnates, and both he and the cellarer gave gifts to nobles residing in the vill, according to their standing. They were to show particular honour to friends of the house, presumably, patrons, benefactors and those joined in confraternity.[162]

It is difficult to know what facilities the abbey had in the town for these guests and, indeed, what other lodgings were available to travellers for they would not have been wholly reliant on the monks' hospitality, at least, not in an urban setting such as Canterbury or Bury St Edmunds. Some distinguished

---

[159]   Pantin, *Chapters* 1, p. 104 (1279: clause viii:2).

[160]   *Chronica Majora* 4, p. 322. An interesting later example refers to the painted chamber at Worcester, in 1324, which stood next to the guest house. A certain clerk, John of Bitterley, was assigned the use of this room and a corrody on the understanding that should it be needed for a visiting magnate John would move, temporarily, to a chamber in the infirmary, *The White Book of Worcester: glimpses of life in a great Benedictine monastery in the fourteenth century*, trans. J. M. Wilson (Llanarch Press facsimile, 1999), no. 1039 (pp. 210–11).

[161]   *De Obedientiariis*, pp. 350–1; *Westminster Customary*, p. 88 lines 19–24; *Eynsham Customary*, ch. 19: 5 (520), p. 203 lines 22–36.

[162]   *Bury Customary*, pp. 32–3.

visitors may have had their own houses, while others, including pilgrims, may have stayed in a hospice, such as Eastbridge Hospital in Canterbury that was established for pilgrims travelling to the shrine of Thomas Becket. The miracle collections include a number of references to pilgrims staying with townsfolk, which suggests this was fairly common. Moreover, it could bring benefits. A baker of Rochester who entertained a pilgrim returning from Thomas Becket's shrine almost lost his hut when it caught fire but luckily his guest drove back the flames by holding out his phial of holy water from Canterbury.[163] Stories such as these may have encouraged householders to open their doors to pilgrims.

Whilst there is little explicit evidence, it is likely that the monastery owned houses in the vill that might be assigned to guests should the need arise. This is suggested in the account of Earl Richard of Chester's visit to Abingdon at Pentecost 1106, to confirm a charter regarding land in Wormsley. The *History of Abingdon* indicates that the abbey provided lodgings in the vill for the earl, his mother and the best of his barons.[164] A possible example of the kind of facilities the monastery may have provided for guests in the vill is Moyse's Hall in Bury St Edmunds, which is the oldest standing building in the town. This was built c. 1180 as a first-floor hall and chamber and today houses the town museum. It is generally thought to have been a synagogue or Jew's house, but Maltby suggests it may actually been intended as a hostelry for pilgrims who were unable to be accommodated in the abbey's guesthouse.[165] Whilst this remains speculative – and perhaps even nebulous – it is an interesting hypothesis.

Provision for guests' horses

Provision for guests' horses was intrinsic to monastic hospitality for most visitors would have arrived on horseback. This could be a considerable expense. It was no doubt to limit costs that Lanfranc stressed that the chamberlain should

---

163 *Materials for Becket* 2, pp. 186–7.
164 *History of Abingdon* 2, pp. 102–3. For the number of tenements Abingdon owned in the town, see C. J. Bond, 'The reconstruction of the mediaeval landscape: the estates of Abingdon abbey', *Landscape History* 1 (1979), pp. 59–75 (pp. 36–7); it is not clear if the community's guests were ever accommodated here.
165 M. E. Wood, 'Moyse's hall: a description of the building', *Archaeological Journal* 108 (1952), p. 165; H. J. M. Maltby, 'A history of the building and museum collection', *Archaeological Journal* 108 (1952), pp. 165–7 (p. 165). Grenville, *Mediaeval Housing*, p. 177, refers to the general and often erroneous attribution of stone houses to Jewish owners. The history of Moyse's hall and its Jewish connections has been discussed by R. Halliday, 'Moyse's Hall, Bury St Edmunds', *Suffolk Review: Bulletin of the Suffolk Local History Council* n.s. 25 (1995), pp. 27–44; E. R. Samuel, 'Was Moyse's Hall, Bury St Edmunds, a Jew's house?', *Jewish Historical Society of England – Transactions* 25 for 1973–75 (1977), pp. 43–7, who argues it was probably built or owned by a Jew but unlikely to have been a synagogue.

provide horseshoes only for visitors named by the abbot or prior.[166] Restrictions were also imposed at Cluny in the late eleventh century. According to the customs of the house, while the stabler (*connestabulus*) should not refuse horseshoes to any passer-by, he ought not give to anyone who had come for the market; indeed, nobody who had come for a market, a fair or a lawsuit was to be received at the guesthouse.[167] The curtar of Abingdon Abbey, who was a leading member of the abbot's household, supplied the horses of any of the monks' relatives who visited to celebrate the Nativity of Mary (8 September) on both the vigil and the day of the feast. The large number of knights and young men who visited Abingdon to celebrate the annual feasts received corrodies in court, which presumably included sustenance for their horses.[168] A similar arrangement was implemented at Bury St Edmunds, where the cellarer provided a prebend and hay for anyone lodging in the guest-hall or vill; this largely referred to non-Benedictine regulars and seculars for whom the community was liable.[169] Other than hay and horseshoes there is little specific evidence of what precisely these horses received. However, it is likely they were given oats, which were acknowledged as an important component of the horse's diet; indeed, Orderic Vitalis remarked that a horse which did not get its regular sester of oats would hardly be able to sustain its strength in western climes.[170] Later sources are more explicit and refer not only to oats and wheat but to malt, hempseed, 'horse-bread' and beans.[171] In 1381 the Cistercian monks of Sawley provided 2½ quarters of beans for the horses of those conducting a visitation of their house.[172] The community did not necessarily supply these provisions freely. Peter the Venerable (d. 1156) was clearly concerned that there should be sufficient oats for guests' horses, and thus ruled that the oats from the farm of Mazile should now be given to the procurator for guests' horses alone. However, they were expected to pay and

166 Lanfranc, *Constitutions*, ch. 88 (pp. 126–7). For the arrangements at the Cistercian abbey of Beaulieu, see *Account Book of Beaulieu*, p. 259.

167 *Ordo Cluniacensis per Bernardum*, ch. 12 (p. 157); Graham, *English Ecclesiastical Studies*, p. 37.

168 'Extract from Rule of Ethelwold', p. 313.

169 *Bury Customary*, p. 7. The late-twelfth-century list for rents due for the fabric at Abingdon refers to hay for the horse pertaining to the master of works, 'Rents to hosteller', ed. Stevenson, *Chronicon de Abingdon* 2, p. 329. Hay was also assigned for bedding and for use when bathing, ibid., p. 326.

170 *Orderic* 5, pp. 242–3. I am grateful to Briony Aitchison for this reference.

171 The chamberlain's accounts for Tewkesbury Abbey for 1351–52 mention malt, bran and hempseed that was bought for the horses, J. Bettey, 'The Benedictine foundation and monastic life', *Tewkesbury Abbey: history, art and architecture*, ed. R. K. Morris and R. Shoesmith (Almeley, 2003), pp. 41–52 (p. 48); F. W. Potto Hicks, 'A Tewkesbury compotus', *Transactions of the Bristol and Gloucestershire Archaeological Society* 55 (1933), pp. 249–55. Nigel Wireker's twelfth-century satire on the religious orders remarks on the fine horses of the Knights Templar that were 'wheat-fed and fat', *Mirror of Fools*, p. 60. C. M. Woolgar, *The Great Household in Late Medieval England* (London, New Haven, 1999), pp. 186–8, 191, refers to beans, bran, bread, hay, green fodder and oats.

172 T. Whitaker, *The History and Antiquities of the Deanery of Craven* (London, 1812), p. 51.

the procurator was warned that he should first have a guarantee from guests that they could pay, particularly from strangers.[173]

The abbot might himself accept responsibility for guests' horses, and in 1225 the abbot of Westminster agreed to provision the horses of anyone sent to lodge at the house.[174] At other times a portion of the monastery's revenues was allocated towards covering these costs. Abbot Randulph of Evesham (1214–29) conceded the chapel of Luttleton to the brethren of Evesham to sustain the horses of visiting religious with six or less horses; they had previously been supplied from his granary.[175] Statutes issued following the visitation of Bury in 1234 prescribed that the meadows and all the stores outside the vill of St Edmund should be assigned for the hay and prebends of guests; in addition, the tithes of Midhall, excepting that which was in demesne, were to be increased.[176] A list of rents to be paid to officials at Abingdon shows that specific revenues were allocated for shoeing the monks' horses and those of the poor and pilgrims.[177] Grants might be secured from the laity to help meet these costs and in the early thirteenth century, Ralf Francigena (c. 1215 x 1225) donated sixpence annually from land in Abingdon to the brethren's hostel (hostalarie) for the purchase of horseshoes. This was made with the agreement of Ralf's wife, Christine, and was to be increased to 12d p. a. upon her death.[178]

Not every monastery would have had stables set aside for the sole use of guests, but some of the larger houses such as St Albans were evidently well equipped. According to Matthew Paris the guest stables at St Albans could accommodate three hundred horses; even allowing for exaggeration, this indicates just what an undertaking the care of horses might be.[179] Tewkesbury Abbey had guest stables in the early thirteenth century, if not earlier, for the annals record that these were burnt down in 1255.[180] At Westminster Abbey a stabler was assigned specifically to minister to guests staying in the hostel of the court. At first it was the intern hosteller who made this appointment, but from Richard de Crokeley's abbacy (1246–58) this became

---

[173]   The oats from the farm of Mazille had hitherto supplied the abbot, prior, cellarer, procurator and guests, but as this pile had been plundered leaving little for visitors' horses, Abbot Peter ruled that they should now be given to the procurator for guests' horses alone, *Cistercians and Cluniacs: the Case for Cîteaux*, p. 214 n. 38.

[174]   *Walter de Wenlok*, p. 219.

[175]   Thomas of Marlborough, *History of Evesham*, ch. 421 (pp. 402–3); Appendix II B, pp. 556–7.

[176]   Graham, 'A papal visitation', p. 733.

[177]   'Rents of the hosteller', *Chronicon de Abingdon* 2, p. 329. Logically, it would seem that the rents were intended for the care of the poor and pilgrims, as well as for shoeing the monks' horses, for presumably the poor generally came on foot. However, the grammar indicates the above translation. For the dating of this see *History of Abingdon* 1, p. clxxix OMT, 2007.

[178]   *Two Cartularies of Abingdon* 1, no. L. 352 (pp. 226–7).

[179]   *Chronica Majora* 5, p. 344.

[180]   'Annals of Tewkesbury', *Annales Monastici* 1, p. 157. A later example is at Peterborough Abbey, where the sixteenth-century accounts record the purchase of a key for the hospice stable, *Accounts of the Obedientiaries of Peterborough Abbey*, p. 156.

the abbot's responsibility.[181] Guests would probably have had direct contact with the stabler but unfortunately the sources reveal little about his duties. Alexander of Neckam simply noted that the stabler should be faithful.[182] But there is more evidence for the Continent and no doubt stablers in England's monasteries had similar duties. The stabler of Cluny's role is set out in the eleventh-century customs for the house and these state how he should conduct himself with visitors. The brother accorded this title or, perhaps by this time, his lay assistant,[183] was to enter the refectory when guests started their meal and greet them modestly with the *Benedicite*. When the visitors responded 'The Lord be with you', the stabler was to reply, 'All that is in our service I offer you, and I will serve you with abundance'. When guests were leaving, the stabler was to ensure that their horses were newly shod and for this reason had a hammer to hand and stables located near the forge.[184]

Care for the sick

Take me to a nearby abbey where I know that the monks would do all in their power to heal me.[185]

Travellers who fell ill or were injured on their journey might seek hospitality at a nearby abbey to recuperate. The Cistercian monk, Caesarius of Heisterbach, tells of a priest who was attacked by Albigensian heretics and brought to recover at Cluny.[186] Of course guests might become sick during their stay at the monastery and require treatment. The monastic customaries and statutes make some provision for their care, but are chiefly concerned with how help should be sought and administered, and reveal little about the nature of ailments or treatments. A rather exceptional account is found in Benedict of Peterborough's 'Miracles of St Thomas', which describes the miraculous cure of a Yorkshire knight who was staying at the Cistercian abbey of Jervaulx. Benedict provides a detailed summary of the guest's afflictions and reveals that he was plagued by fevers and suffered severe pain in his kidneys. Moreover, a deformity from birth seemingly prevented him from straightening his fingers. Benedict also suggests that the monks of Jervaulx administered the holy water of St Thomas to members of the community and guests, to aid their recovery. Thus, when the knight learned of the number of monks and laity who had tasted the martyr's water and been successfully healed, he decided to follow

181   *Westminster Customary*, p. 72. This presumably refers to the hosteller of the court.
182   *De Sacerdos ad altare*, p. 265.
183   I am indebted to Miss Barbara Harvey for this suggestion.
184   *Ordo Cluniacensis per Bernardum*, ch. 12 (p. 157); *Udalrici Consuetudines* cols 634 – 778 (775); Graham, *English Ecclesiastical Studies*, p. 37.
185   The knight Melias to Sir Galahad, in the thirteenth-century romance, *The Quest of the Holy Grail*, trans. P. M. Matarasso (Harmondsworth, 1969), pp. 68–9. At the monastery, an old monk who had once been a knight, was brought to dress the wound.
186   Caesarius, *Dialogue on Miracles* 1, bk VIII: 5 (pp. 489–90).

their example. That night St Thomas seemed to appear to him in his sleep and by touching his head, hand and then the rest of his body, effected his cure. The following day the knight reported his experience to the abbot and showed how he could now straighten his fingers.[187]

The *De Obedientiariis* of Abingdon sets out the procedure to follow should a guest wish to be bloodlet, which suggests this was a common treatment administered to visitors, either as a curative or preventative. There is evidence that outsiders might visit a monastery specifically to receive this treatment. One notable example is Archbishop Thurstan (1114–40), who stopped off at the monastery of St-Martin-des-Champs, to be bled.[188] Any guest wishing to be bloodlet notified the hosteller, who then mediated his request to either the abbot or prior. The hosteller was expected to show the guest care and provide all that was customary; this presumably refers to the extra food and drink that was permitted to fortify anyone who had undergone this treatment.[189] Thomas of Marlborough's *History of Evesham Abbey* reveals that Nicholas of Tusculum, the papal legate who visited the abbey in 1213 to depose Abbot Norreys and oversee a successor, took four days in between the two events to be bloodlet and recuperate.[190] Members of the community were routinely bloodlet several times a year as a preventative measure, and more in case of sickness.[191] In addition to a more relaxed diet, the bloodlet followed a reduced schedule and were permitted to talk a little in the parlour. Jocelin of Brakelond describes how the monks of Bury would sit in groups at blood-letting time and 'reveal the secrets of their hearts' and chat with one another.[192]

Presumably sick guests were tended by the hosteller and infirmarer and ministered to in the secular hospice or in the secular infirmary if there was one. Facilities would inevitably have varied from house to house.[193] Marjorie Chibnall has raised the possibility that in 1134 the Empress Mathilda stayed in the guest quarters of Notre-Dame-du Pré, a cell of Bec, to recover from illness following a difficult childbirth, but she may instead have stayed in the

---

[187] 'Miracula Sancti Thomae Cantuariensis, auctore Benedicto, abbate Peterburgensis', ed. Robertson, *Materials for Becket* 2, pp. 21–281, no. LI (pp. 160–1). I am grateful to Dr Simone C. Macdougall for her help in interpreting this passage.

[188] *Chantor*, p. 70. For bloodletting in the monastery in general, see Harvey, *Living and Dying*, pp. 96–9. The monastic customaries and injunctions often discuss the duration of bloodletting and the number of sessions allowed per year, for example the Bury statutes of 1234, Graham, 'A papal visitation', p. 735.

[189] *De Obedientiariis*, p. 414. See also *Eynsham Customary*, ch. 19: 3 (511), p. 202 lines 6–7.

[190] Thomas of Marlborough, *History of Evesham*, ch. 500 (pp. 468–9).

[191] Peter the Venerable, abbot of Cluny, was accustomed to undergo bloodletting twice a month, see N. Siraisi, *Medieval and Early Renaissance Medicine* (Chicago and London, 1990), p. 115. I am indebted to Dr Simone C. Macdougall for drawing this to my attention and for reminding me of Jocelin of Brakelond's comments, below.

[192] *Jocelin*, p. 14.

[193] Jocelin's *Life of Waldef*, p. 133, records that each day the abbot of Melrose visited the infirmaries of the monks, lay-brothers, and also the poor and guests. For further discussion of Cistercian infirmaries, see D. Bell, 'The English Cistercians and the practice of medicine', *Cîteaux: Commentarii Cistercienses* 40:1–4 (1989), pp. 139–74.

priory or the royal residence adjacent to it.[194] However, some of the examples may refer rather to deathbed conversions, when one nearing the end would seek admittance to a religious house and die wearing the habit. This was seemingly the case at the Cistercian house of Strata Florida in 1222, when Prince Rhys, son of Guffydd was tended in the infirmary there.[195] Members of the order would likely have been treated in the monks' infirmary. When Gervase, a Cluniac monk of St Saviour's, Southwark, visited Bury St Edmunds to be healed through the powers of Saint Edmund, he was too ill to enter the church and was instead brought to the *cella infirmis* of the house.[196]

Guests who were ill were generally allowed to extend their visit if they sought permission. At Abingdon this meant they might remain longer than the statutory two nights but were expected, if able, to follow the community. This may indicate that these visitors were regulars.[197] When Archbishop Anselm visited Bury St Edmunds in 1107 to conduct various episcopal duties and consecrate a large cross, he fell seriously ill and remained with the monks for a week.[198] Henry III stayed for three weeks at Bury in 1252, on account of illness, and when Prince Edward fell sick at the dedication of Beaulieu in 1246 he recuperated there for three weeks.[199]

---

[194] M. Chibnall, 'The Empress Mathilda and Bec-Hellouin', *AN Studies* 10 (1988), pp. 35–48 (p. 39). Dr Liesbeth Van Houts (personal communication) thinks it likely that given Mathilda's generosity to the community she was probably cared for by the monks of Bec. It is perhaps most probable that she stayed in the royal residence and was spiritually tended by the monks of Bec. Penelope Johnson explains that the wealthy sick were admitted to the hospice of La Trinité, Vendôme, which also accommodated travellers on horseback, P. D. Johnson, *Prayer, Patronage and Power: the abbey of la Trinité Vendôme, 1032–1187* (New York, 1981), p. 160.

[195] *Brut Y Tywsysogion*, ed. J. Williams Ab Ithel, RS 17 (London, 1860), p. 310. For a Continental example, see *Orderic* 3, pp. 201–2. Knowles, *Monastic Order*, p. 477, discusses deathbed conversions in the infirmary.

[196] Samson of Bury's, '*De Miraculis Sancti Edmundi*', *Memorials of St Edmunds* 1, no. 19 (p. 203). When Hugh, bishop of Lincoln, arrived at the Cistercian house of Clairmarais to celebrate the Nativity of St Mary, he was taken to the infirmary where he stayed the night of the Vigil of the feast and was tended by two brothers who washed, dried and rubbed his feet, *Magna Vita* 2, pp. 178–9.

[197] *De Obedientiariis*, p. 413. If any guest at Eynsham wished to delay his departure on account of illness or bad weather the hosteller was to notify the abbot or prior who would show him mercy in accordance with the severity of his malady, *Eynsham Customary*, ch. 19: 3 (511), p. 202 lines 2–5. The postponing of departures is discussed in chapter 6.

[198] *Vita Anselmi*, p. 139, *Historia Nouorum*, p. 185.

[199] *Chronica Majora* 5, p. 304; *Annales Monastici* 2, p. 337.

Spiritual care

> In fortifying us with yesterday's repast, you restored not our stomach but our heart, and sent us away laden not with food but with divine services.[200]

Provision for the soul was integral to monastic hospitality. Guests received spiritual care throughout their stay, attending Mass and services in either the church or a chapel. Of course, a number of visitors came to the monastery specifically to celebrate a feast. When Queen Matilda found herself in the vicinity of Abingdon Abbey on the approach of Assumption Day (15 August), she diverted her route to observe this solemnity at the abbey.[201] A large crowd would have gathered at Abingdon to celebrate the Nativity of Mary (8 September), which was the abbey's patronal feast; the customary mentions the knights and men of the province, and also relatives of the monks who arrived on this occasion and were to receive provisions from the house.[202] Distinguished visitors might reside at the house for the festive period. The king's son, Henry, celebrated Easter at Abingdon in 1084 and kept Christmas at St Albans in 1115; he attended the dedication of the abbey church on 28 December.[203] Henry III visited St Albans in 1244, for the feasts of St Barnabas and St Thomas.[204]

Religious devotions

> The lord and his wife were well served and honoured in the abbot's chamber, and next morning went to hear mass.[205]

The *Rule of St Benedict* does not deal explicitly with religious observances for guests; Lanfranc's *Constitutions* simply state that the guestmaster should lead visiting monks to pray in the church.[206] It would, however, have been commonplace for guests to hear Mass, offer prayers and attend services. On special occasions, such as Ash Wednesday, Palm Sunday, Easter and the Purification of Mary (2 August), guests would have joined the community in the church.[207] They may also have listened to the abbot preach a sermon.

---

[200] Osbert de Clare, letter 42, of thanks to Abbess Adelidis of Barking, trans. Morton, *Guidance for Women*, p. 22. See above, pp. 33, 106–7.

[201] *History of Abingdon* 2, pp. 142–3; see above, p. 46, for the gift she gave on this visit.

[202] *De Obedientiariis*, p. 350; see also 'Extract from Rule of St Ethelwold', p. 313. For Continental examples see *Magna Vita* 2, pp. 177–8, *Vita Anselmi*, p. 104.

[203] *History of Abingdon* 2, pp. 16–19; GASA 1, p. 71, *Chronica Majora* 2, pp. 142–3. Continental examples include Orderic 2, pp. 196–8 and 6, p. 174; Torigni, *Chronicle*, pp. 117, 198, 320 (*Continuatio Beccensis*).

[204] *Chronica Majora* 4, pp. 358, 402.

[205] 'Yonec', in *Les Lais de Marie de France*, ed J. Reichner, CFMA 93 (Paris, 1966), pp. 102–19 (p. 117 lines 489–90).

[206] Lanfranc, *Constitutions*, ch. 90 (pp. 130–1).

[207] *Ecclesiastica Officia* 13: 23 (p. 88), 17: 4 (p. 96), 22: 24 (p. 108), 47: 5 (p. 142). See also the statutes issued by the General Chapter in 1210, Canivez, *Statutes* 1, 1210: 3 (p. 369).

Abbot Samson of Bury (1182–1211) preached to the people in English, in fact, in his native Norfolk dialect. He had a pulpit set up in the church for their benefit and also for ornamental purposes.[208] Guests at Cistercian houses probably heard Mass in the gatehouse chapel, although some guesthouses would have had their own chapels.[209] Visitors may have been shown to the porch at the west end of the church, which was known as the narthex or galilee. Part of this has been reconstructed at Fountains Abbey in Yorkshire.

Mass

The number of references to guests attending Mass during their stay, and in a wide range of sources, suggests that this was commonplace. King Stephen heard Mass when he visited St Albans during Robert's abbacy (1151–66), and when King John visited Bury in 1200, he heard Mass before his departure.[210] Marie de France's twelfth-century *lai*, 'Yonec', tells of a lord and his lady who stay at a monastery and hear Mass on the morning of their departure. The knights of the Arthurian romance, *La Queste*, hear Mass as a matter of course whenever they pass by or stay at a monastery.[211] Guests who had taken priestly orders would have expected to celebrate Mass during their stay. The hosteller of Abingdon Abbey was to ensure that these visitors received everything they required. If any visitor at Abingdon was unable to attend Mass, the hosteller, or another appointed by him, celebrated this and indeed all of the Hours on his behalf .[212] Roger of Llanthony's experience at Christ Church, Canterbury suggests that not every monastery was so accommodating. Gerald of Wales's version of events recounts how Roger sent his canon to prepare for him to say Mass in the church of Holy Trinity on the eve of his departure from Canterbury. To his amazement, the canon was informed that only Benedictines were permitted to celebrate the holy mysteries there and they ought instead to celebrate Mass with other clerks in the town. The tables were soon turned when a monk of Canterbury visited Llanthony, for he was sent into town to hear Mass with the monks of St Peter's.[213] The very fact that Gerald remarks upon Roger's experience at Christ Church, and that neither Roger nor his canon had seemingly anticipated a rebuff of this kind, implies that this was rather exceptional behaviour. It has been suggested that Canterbury's acquisition of the prestigious body of Thomas Becket may have made the monks of Christ Church more exclusive.[214] In contrast the Cistercians were renowned for their exclusiveness; Orderic Vitalis complained that they would not admit monks from other religious houses to their church

---

[208] *Jocelin*, p. 40.
[209] Williams, *Cistercians in the Early Middle Ages*, pp. 125, 202–3.
[210] GASA 1, p. 121; *Jocelin*, p. 117. For Continental examples, see Torigni, *Chronicle*, pp. 197, 198.
[211] 'Yonec', p. 117 lines 489–90; e.g. *La Queste*, pp. 52, 103, 268.
[212] *De Obedientiariis*, p. 413. Similar arrangements are detailed in the later customary of Eynsham *Customary*, ch. 19: 3 (509), p. 201 lines 31–2.
[213] *Speculum Ecclesiae*, pp. 81–2.
[214] I am indebted to Mr Peter King for this suggestion.

for Mass or the other offices.[215] By the thirteenth century it was evidently common for guests staying at St Augustine's, Canterbury to attend Mass at Christ Church before leaving the city. This perhaps refers to the early Mass that was celebrated for pilgrims at the shrine of St Thomas.[216] An interesting clause in the mid-thirteenth-century customary of St Augustine's refers to guests who had received the blessing for departure and therefore officially left the abbey, yet returned after hearing Mass at Christ Church hoping, it seems, for refreshment. As far as the monks of St Augustine's were concerned these visitors were no longer their responsibility and were not entitled to eat at the abbey that day.[217]

The canonical hours

To what extent were guests expected to follow the daily round of monastic observances, and did they join the community in the church or celebrate these in a chapel or altar elsewhere in the precinct? These are not easy questions to answer. Whilst the customaries make some provision for guests to celebrate the canonical hours, it is not clear if these arrangements were intended for all guests or, as seems more likely, for visiting regulars. On account of the liturgical differences amongst orders and indeed the Benedictines themselves, monk guests generally conducted their observances outside the choir, either in a side altar or a chapel. Those who were from a cell of the house or joined in confraternity often joined the host community in the choir. An arrangement of this kind is explicit in the later customaries of Westminster Abbey and St Augustine's, Canterbury, and functioned at Bec for visiting monks from St Étienne and Jumièges, and for canons visiting St Victor's, Paris; guest monks occupied the retrochoir at St Victor's.[218] In general, however, visiting monks

---

215 *Orderic* 4, pp. 326–7.
216 See Draper's discussion of the customary compiled in 1428 for the keepers of Becket's shrine but which, he argues, is likely indicative of earlier practice. The temporal keeper was responsible for ringing the bell and opening the doors to pilgrims for the early Mass; the doors were then closed after High Mass and a clerk carefully checked that no pilgrim, 'miscreant or rabid dog' was hidden, P. Draper, 'Enclosures and entrances in medieval cathedrals: access and security', *The Medieval Cathedral*, ed. J. Backhouse (Donington, 2000), pp. 76–88 (pp. 76–7).
217 *St Augustine's Customary* (c. 1250), p. 255 lines 6–8.
218 *Westminster Customary*, p. 83 lines 24–32; *St Augustine's Customary* (fourteenth-century), p. 139 lines 23–9; *Select Documents of the English Lands of the Abbey of Bec*, ed. M. Chibnall, CS, 3rd ser. 73 (London, 1951), charter no. 7, and Porée, *L'Histoire* 1, p. 482; *Liber Ordinis*, pp. 61–2. A later account of the 1254 union between St Augustine's, Canterbury, and Winchester stated that if either community required refuge they should be received by the other house and take their accustomed position in the choir, chapter-house, dormitory and refectory, *William Thorne, Chronicle of St Augustine's, Canterbury*, trans. A. H. Davis (Oxford, 1933), ch. 23 (pp. 230–1). This is explicit also in Robert of Torigni's letter of confraternity in 1172 between Cluny and Mont-Saint-Michel, see K. S. B. Keats-Rohan, 'Testimonies of the living dead: the martyrology-necrology and the necrology in the chapter book of Mont-Saint-Michel', *The Durham Liber Vitae and its Context*, ed. Rollason *et al.*, pp. 165–90 (pp. 183–4). For inter-house unions and confraternity which included the right to enter the

would have celebrated the Office outside the choir. The Black hostelry chapel at Bury St Edmunds, which was for visiting Benedictines, may have been situated in the south transept, or should perhaps be identified with the chapel over the cellarer's gate.[219] The intern hosteller of Bury, who was responsible for visiting monks, was one of three assigned to sing Matins from the book outside the choir.[220] This was presumably the 'book of pericopes for guests', a book of biblical passages selected for reading in church. This was also used by members of the community who for some reason could not attend the communal Hours, for example, anyone returning from a journey or the prior, should he miss Matins.[221] The library at Glastonbury Abbey had a breviary for guests which may have been part of Henry of Blois' (1126–71) collection.[222]

This section looks more closely at the provision made for guests at Abingdon to celebrate the Hours. However, as mentioned earlier, these arrangements may have been intended only for visiting regulars. On great feasts, particularly the main solemnities of Christmas, Easter, Pentecost and the Assumption, guests who were able[223] joined the community for Matins but left just before Lauds which they celebrated with the hosteller.[224] On other occasions they sang Matins with the hosteller outside the choir and sang fifteen psalms rather than the thirty sung in the choir.[225] A similar arrangement was observed at Eynsham but by the time when the customary was compiled in the thirteenth or fourteenth century, it had been decided that the hosteller should only sing Compline for guests staying in the dormitory.[226] If any visitor staying at Abingdon could not attend Matins, presumably if he was aged or unwell, the hosteller left the choir singing a verse from the liturgical book, celebrated the Office with him and then returned to take his place with the community. He did the same on feasts celebrated in copes and thus assimilated his monastic

other's choir, see Knowles, *Monastic Order*, pp. 472–5 (p. 474), and Burton, *Monastic and Religious Orders*, p. 163. For two surviving twelfth-century confraternity lists, see J. Burton, 'A confraternity list from St Mary's Abbey, York', *Revue Bénédictine* 89 (1979), pp. 325–33, and Tsurshima, 'The fraternity of Rochester'.

[219] M. R. James, *On the Abbey of St Edmunds at Bury* (Cambridge, 1895), pp. 140–1; A. B. Whittingham, 'Bury St Edmunds Abbey: the plan, design and development of the church and monastic buildings', *Archaeological Journal* 108 (1951), pp. 168–87 (p. 173). Whittingham also refers to the chapel of St Lawrence which was over the parlour or 'at the head of the guest hall' over the cellar, p. 176. Perhaps these should be equated and identified as the chapel that served the convent's guests who were not members of the Order, chiefly, non-Benedictine regulars.

[220] *Bury Customary*, p. 25 lines 10–13.

[221] This book is mentioned in the Abingdon customary, see *De Obedientiariis*, pp. 356, 377. The book of guests is mentioned also in the Eynsham Customary which states that the sacrist should supply candles for guests and whoever else sang from this book; if the prior missed matins, he was to sing this from the book of guests, *Eynsham Customary*, ch. 12: 2 (445), p. 182, ch. 14: 10 (332), p. 153.

[222] *English Benedictine Libraries*, B37: 12 (p. 163).

[223] 'Expeditus' presumably refers to their agility and state of health.

[224] *De Obedientiariis*, p. 412. These four feasts are specified in the customary of Eynsham, *Eynsham Customary*, ch. 19: 3 (508), p. 201 lines 22–5.

[225] *De Obedientiariis*, p. 411.

[226] *Eynsham Customary*, ch. 19: 3 (508), p. 201 lines 14–27, 19: 3 (514), p. 202 lines 24–6.

duties with the demands of his office.[227] Unless guests had to leave early to start on their journey they returned to rest immediately after hearing Matins.[228]

The *De Obedientiariis* sheds some light on guests attending Collations, which was the daily spiritual reading that was followed by a drink and then Compline. The hosteller of Abingdon was to lead guests to Collations only after the first verse of the Bible had been delivered. Once this was over, they waited at the door of the chapter-house and were then led to the parlour for the post-Collations drink; they received one or two fills, depending on their wish.[229] The monks of Abingdon probably were refreshed in the refectory, as was the case at Bury St Edmunds and Christ Church, Canterbury.[230] After the Collations drink, Compline was sung to guests in the same order as in the choir; at Eynsham this was only required for guests staying in the dormitory.[231] The hosteller of Abingdon was also expected to recite the Night Office (Vigils) for visitors. The intern hosteller of Westminster Abbey was bound 'by right and ancient custom' to spend the night in the guest cell with any monk who arrived alone and was not from a cell of Westminster, to celebrate the night devotions with him.[232]

There were various other spiritual services provided for guests, notably the blessing for sins on the journey given upon their arrival and departure. This was not simply bestowed upon guests but was given to any member of the community who was leaving or returning from a journey.[233] Any abbot who was visiting Bury St Edmunds on the day of Absolution conducted the maundy independently in a separate chamber and, as previously mentioned, the cellarer provided food that was to be distributed to the poor.[234] Guests who died during their stay were generally accorded the right of burial at the monastery. At Bury St Edmunds, a visiting monk was to be buried according to the monastic custom, although the brethren were not on this occasion given candles in their hands. The compiler of the Bury customary refers to a monk of Westminster Abbey who had died there and been buried in this

---

[227]   *De Obedientiariis*, p. 412.

[228]   *De Obedientiariis*, p. 411.

[229]   *De Obedientiariis*, p. 414. For similar arrangements, see *Eynsham Customary*, ch. 19: 3 (514) p. 202 lines 14–26. For details of the Collations drink, see Knowles, *Monastic Order*, p. 457.

[230]   *Bury Customary*, p. 44 lines 6–7; *Instructio Noviciorum*, pp. 218–21.

[231]   *De Obedientiariis*, p. 414; *Eynsham Customary*, ch. 19: 3 (514), p. 202 lines 24–6.

[232]   *De Obedientiariis*, p. 411; *Westminster Customary*, p. 87 lines 20–7.

[233]   *De Obedientiariis*, p. 412. The customary sets out various times when this should be given. Similar provisions are made in the *Rule of St Benedict*, in relation to brothers setting out and returning from a journey, *Rule of St Benedict*, ch. 67 (p. 172); for a later example see the customary of Eynsham Abbey, *Eynsham Customary*, ch. 19: 7 (522), pp. 204–5.

[234]   *Bury Customary*, p. 54 lines 1–8; see above, p. 131 below p. 181. For discussion of absolution, including when this occurred and the format, see *The Catholic Encyclopaedia*, ed. C. G. Hebermann, E. A. Pace, C. B. Pallen, T. J. Shahan, J. J. Wynne, 15 vols (London, 1907–56), 1, pp. 61–6.

way.[235] The romance literature suggests that those nearing death might be brought to a nearby monastery to receive the last rights and burial.[236] Whilst the Cistercians had a rather hands-off approach to outsiders, they did from the outset permit burial to any guest who died during his visit. The twelfth-century customary of the order sets out in detail how a guest nearing death should be tended. The exact procedure depended on his standing. For example, priests and religious who died in the hospice were taken to the choir, unless the abbot ruled otherwise, but the chant was reserved for elevated persons; seven psalms were said after the burial of any Cistercian monk, novice or lay-brother, and the bow after the *Clementissime* was reserved for members of the Order.[237]

Religious ceremonies

> It was announced beforehand and gladly learnt that from the furthest regions counsellors, persons of the highest ecclesiastical ranks and innumerable classes of men would come ... All the bishops of Normandy, all the abbots and other religious men congregated there. The knights of the realm were present ... The most celebrated counsellors of the French kingdom were there, and a great many dignitaries of that realm; clerics, monks from the nearby provinces, numberless types of men flocked thither.[238]

Guests might visit the monastery specially to celebrate a feast or vigil, or to attend a translation, dedication, installation or consecration. Throughout the twelfth century it became increasingly popular to encourage these visitors with the promise of indulgence, that is, the remission of punishment from temporal sins.[239] Theobald of Canterbury (1138–61) offered an indulgence of twenty days to anyone who visited Reading Abbey on either the Feast of the Invention (3 May) or the Exaltation of the Holy Cross (14 September); a piece of this relic was supposedly housed at the abbey.[240] Not everyone who visited on these occasions would have benefited from the community's hospitality, but it seems that those who attended dedications were generally well provided for during their stay. Some or all of the expenses might be borne by the king, a patron or the bishop. In 1164, Henry II procured for the monks and guests

---

[235] *Bury Customary*, p. 53 lines 19–22.

[236] For example, see *La Queste*, pp. 153–4.

[237] *Ecclesiastica Officia*, 101 (pp. 292–4). Bernard of Clairvaux's account of Malachy's death and burial at Clairvaux, sheds considerable light on this procedure, albeit for a distinguished figure and a member of the Order, *De Vita et Rebus Gestis S. Malachiae, Hiberniae Episcopi*, PL 182.1073–1118 (1114 ff.)

[238] Gilbert Crispin's account of the consecration of Bec in his *Vita Herluini*, ch. 106, translated Vaughn, *The Abbey of Bec and the Anglo-Norman State*, p. 83.

[239] For a more extensive discussion of indulgences, see chapter 5 of Webb's *Pilgrimage in Medieval England*, pp. 93–109.

[240] RAC 1, no. 183 (p. 148); see, too, nos 184–201 (pp. 148–56). D. M. Stenton, *English Society in the Early Middle Ages, 1066–1307*, 4th edn (Harmondsworth, 1965), p. 226, explains that the bishops issued these indulgences to reward Reading's hospitality. For accounts relating to Bury and St Albans see *Feudal Documents*, charter no. 171 (p. 153); GASA 1, p. 92.

who gathered to celebrate the Hallowing of Reading Abbey. The ceremony was conducted by Archbishop Thomas Becket and the festivities lasted for three days. Unfortunately Robert of Torigni's account of the event does not describe what they ate, or where.[241] Those who attended the dedication of the conventual church of St Albans on 28 December 1115 feasted in the palace of the court. The guest list on this occasion was impressive and included Henry I with his queen and his heir, the archbishop of Rouen, the bishops of London, Durham, Lincoln and Salisbury, as well as abbots, earls and other secular dignitaries.[242]

Most accounts of dedications are rather uninformative and simply provide a checklist of distinguished guests.[243] An exceptionally detailed, though slightly later, account is Matthew Paris's description of the dedication of Ely on St Lambert's Day (17 September) 1252 which he himself attended. This was a magnificent occasion that was conducted with great pomp and ceremony. A number of dignitaries were present including the king. Everyone who visited was granted an indulgence, and this boon was extended to anyone who visited on the coming days. After the spiritual observances had been celebrated in the church, guests were richly entertained in the royal palace, which Bishop Hugh had built in his court at Ely. The bishop provided a festive banquet of rich delicacies for the crowds of guests but his generosity was such that, in spite of the vast numbers, he was said to have lamented the lack of visitors.[244]

Another informative account relates to Normandy and the dedication of Bec on 23 October 1077. Gilbert Crispin's record of events, written some forty years later, describes the preparations involved in staging a celebration of this kind.[245] He explains that invitations were sent to ecclesiastical persons of the highest rank, to counsellors who lived far away, and to all kinds of men; moreover great sums of money were collected to sustain them. Accordingly, all the bishops, abbots and religious men of Normandy were present, as well as the nobles of the duchy, the most eminent counsellors of France, clerks, monks and men of all kinds. The king and queen were detained by business and unable to attend, but Matilda generously marked the occasion and sent the community great gifts. The vast crowd that assembled was so great that only a few of the older monks were present, and whilst everyone managed to squeeze into the church the procession could hardly move without colliding and the doors to the church were wrenched off. This is described as a jubilant and emotional occasion and the customary post-ceremonial feasting magnificent, lasting from morning until late at night. Interestingly the feast was held in the refectory rather than the abbot's chambers or indeed a hall in the court, and we can perhaps infer that no meat was served on this occasion. Guests

---

[241] Torigni, *Chronicle*, p. 221.

[242] *GASA* 1, pp. 70–1; *Chronica Majora* 2, pp. 142–3. See, too, Torigni, *Chronicle*, p. 96.

[243] Examples include the accounts of dedications of the new church at Christ Church, Canterbury, in May 1130, and of the female house at Godstow in 1138, Torigni, *Chronicle*, p. 117, *English Episcopal Acta* 1, no. 33 (pp. 20–2).

[244] *Chronica Majora* 4, p. 322.

[245] *Vita Herluini*, ch. 105–7 (pp. 83–4). For the compilation of this, c. 1117/18, see Vaughn, *Abbey of Bec*, p. 63.

were served in a succession of sittings and through God's Providence, everyone was abundantly refreshed that day and for many succeeding days.[246] On the third day Lanfranc departed leaving the community much aggrieved. Herluin honoured the archbishop by accompanying him for two miles and they made an emotional farewell.[247]

In addition to translations and dedications, crowds might visit the monastery to attend installations and consecrations. Jocelin of Brakelond's detailed account of Samson's installation at Bury in 1182, sets out what precisely this entailed, for he records who was present and describes the nature of entertainment provided. His assertion that over one thousand people attended is probably more emphatic than literal. Jocelin explains that the clerks and knights who attended the ceremony in the church joined the community in the chapter-house where the king's charters were read and business discussed. On this occasion Samson formally requested their future advice in matters of government. The post-ceremonial feasting was held in the abbot's chambers which were perhaps more suited than the refectory to the scale and solemnity of the occasion, but may have been chosen as meat could be served here.[248]

---

246 The host's ability to sufficiently provide for his guests as testimony to God's Providence emerges as somewhat of a topos, e.g. *Vita Wulfstani*, pp. 55, 59. See also *Life of Waldef*, pp. 136–8.

247 *Vita Herluini*, p. 107. This is also recorded in *Gesta Normannorum 2*, p. 70. See, too, Innocent II's visit to St Denis for Easter, 1131, *Oeuvres Complètes de Suger*, ed. A. Lecoy de la Marche (Paris, 1867), p. 138. The significance of a personal escort is discussed in the following chapter.

248 *Jocelin*, p. 25.

5

Provision for guests:
entertainment and interaction

Communication with the brethren

Let no one except the guestmaster associate or converse with guests. But if a monk happens to meet or see them, after humbly greeting them and asking their blessing, let him pass on, explaining that he is not permitted to talk with guests.[1]

The *Rule of St Benedict* makes it clear that conversation between monks and guests should be avoided. Nevertheless monks ought to be polite to any visitors they should happen to meet. For practical purposes a little necessary conversation was permitted to the guestmaster and anyone else who had a legitimate reason to speak with visitors. Over time the monastery's relationship with its patrons and benefactors, the regular arrival of messengers and of people seeking advice and conducting business, meant that interaction (and conversation) was an inevitable part of daily life in the monastery, but one that had to be monitored and controlled. Accordingly there were set procedures for guests to follow should they wish to speak with a member of the community. It was essential that permission was first sought from the abbot or prior. This was generally effected through the guestmaster, who mediated between guests and the convent. According to Lanfranc's *Constitutions*, any relative or stranger wishing to speak with either the abbot, the prior or a claustral monk, should inform the guestmaster who would intimate this to the abbot or prior. If permission for the meeting was given, the guestmaster then notified the monk concerned and escorted him to meet his visitor. This was probably in the outer parlour, on the western range. If permission was withheld, the brother who had been requested was not to be informed of the matter, presumably to prevent

---

1   *Rule of St Benedict*, ch. 53 (p. 136).

any ill feeling.[2] A similar procedure would have been observed in other houses and at Abingdon the hosteller sought authorisation from the prior.[3]

Meetings with female relatives were more strictly monitored. Statutes issued following the visitation of Bury in 1234 sought to ensure that these encounters were conducted in open places, and forbade any monk to meet with female relatives or strangers either at the green door or the cross, or any other hidden / 'secret' places.[4] The green door here mentioned was seemingly the great door at the upper end of the choir in the fifth bay of the presbytery.[5] To prevent rumours arising, the monks were forbidden to converse with nuns or female recluses, and might only speak with women within the precinct of the cemetery if another brother was present as a witness. Moreover they might not meet with their guests at dinner or supper, at the time assigned to the post-Collations drink or during their after-dinner nap (*meridian*).[6]

An early testimony to family meetings, in this case to a young monk meeting with his mother, is Eadmer's rather touching account of Archbishop Lanfranc's generosity to a monk of Christ Church, Canterbury. This sheds light on the form and frequency of these meetings but also offers a rare glimpse of the prelate's humanity and, not least of all, raises the possibility of a theft at Christ Church. Eadmer, who was himself a monk of Christ Church and may in fact be recounting his personal experience, explains that this particular monk was accustomed to receive thirty shillings each year from Lanfranc.[7] He was given this in six instalments and duly passed five shillings to his mother on each of her visits. This transfer of money was evidently conducted with great discretion, so much so that on one occasion the monk thought he had successfully dropped the money pouch into his mother's hands, but she, alas, was preoccupied and failed to notice; unbeknown to them both the money fell to the ground. Mother and son departed as usual and it was only later that they realised what had happened. Fearing that Lanfranc would punish him for his carelessness the monk returned to the cloister in great distress. Lanfranc sought to comfort rather than chastise, and assured his young charge that the

2 Lanfranc, *Constitutions*, ch. 90 (pp. 130–1).
3 *De Obedientiariis*, p. 414. See *Westminster Customary*, p. 81 line 32 – p. 82 line 6; *St Augustine's Customary* (fourteenth-century), p. 138 lines 8–21; *Eynsham Customary*, ch. 19: 3 (513), p. 202 lines 8–13.
4 Graham, 'A papal visitation', p. 731.
5 James, *On the Abbey of St Edmunds*, p. 160; Whittingham, 'Bury St Edmunds', p. 172. The estimate of weekly expenses mentions that a guard manned this door; the door is mentioned also in an account of the fire in 1465, James, *On the Abbey of St Edmunds*, p. 160. *Bury Customary*, p. 12 line 29, states that whenever the prior or sub-prior waited in the vestry before Mass, he should enter the church via the green door and pass to the altar.
6 Graham, 'A papal visitation', p. 734. Similarly, Archbishop Peckham's injunctions issued to Christ Church, Canterbury, in 1279 specified that visiting nuns might speak with the monks in the public parlour or hall, both of which were freely accessible, *Registrum Peckham* 1, no. 261 (p. 345).
7 *Historia Nouorum*, pp. 13–14. Southern follows Knowles' hypothesis that the monk was in fact Eadmer, R. Southern, *St Anselm and his Biographer: a study of monastic life and thought, 1059–c. 1130* (Cambridge, 1963), p. 231; Knowles, *Monastic Order*, p. 109.

lost money had surely found its way to a needier person. He also gave the monk seven shillings for his mother but warned him not to reveal anything of the gift or the giver.

Relatives would not only have visited the abbey to meet family members but might also come to celebrate a feast or another important event. The curtar of Abingdon provided for the monks' relatives and their horses when they visited to celebrate the Nativity of Mary both on the vigil and the day of the feast.[8] This was the abbey's patronal feast which lasted a week, and would have attracted a number of visitors. It was presumably for this reason that less rigid restrictions were imposed. Thus, while the sacrist generally removed anyone who stood or sat in the convent's sight, this was not enforced on the Vigil of St Mary.[9] In 1219 the curtar was warned to receive these guests with respect, which suggests that they may have previously been welcomed rather less warmly or courteously than was appropriate. This was evidently the case at Bury St Edmunds, for in 1234 the community was enjoined to receive relatives, in particular the relatives of claustral monks, more honourably than before.[10]

Distinguished visitors, largely visiting prelates, might well address the monks or offer informal advice in the cloister. When Abbot Anselm stayed with the monks of Christ Church, Canterbury in 1079, shortly after his consecration to the abbacy of Bec, he spoke with the brethren in the chapter-house and cloister.[11] Hugh of Lincoln edified the monks of Eynsham 'by the wine of his good humour and the excellent fare of his kindliness' when he stayed with the community for eight days after recovering his rights of patronage there.[12] The fact that these venerable men mingled with the community was a sign of their humility, and the fact they were able to do so was a testimony to their authority.[13] The visit of a foreigner might engender a lively and informative discourse. When an Armenian archbishop visited St Albans in 1228 he was asked about the celebration of the Three Conceptions in his country and also quizzed about the 'wandering Jew' who was said to have known Jesus and was still alive. The monks hardly anticipated their guest's answer for the archbishop replied that he himself had met this Jew. When an Angevin abbot, Lambert, visited Bury the monks asked the reason for his devotion to Edmund; he explained that on one occasion when he was wind-bound at Barfleur, he had evoked the saint and was soon able to set sail.[14]

---

8   *De Obedientiariis*, p. 351; *Two Cartularies of Abingdon* 1, no. L. 167 (pp. 112–13); *De Obedientiariis*, p. 350. See, too, 'Customs relating to the obedientiaries', ed. Stevenson, *Chronicon de Abingdon* 2, p. 313.

9   *De Obedientiariis*, p. 379.

10   Graham, 'A papal visitation', p. 736. For a later example see Henry Wakefield's visitation of Tewkesbury in 1378, *Tewkesbury Abbey: history, art and architecture*, p. 48.

11   *Vita Anselmi*, pp. 48–50; see above, p. 47.

12   *Magna Vita* 2, p. 42.

13   Examples include Archbishop Lanfranc's participation at Bec in 1077, *Vita Herluini*, p. 105, and Thomas Becket's involvement with the brethren of Christ Church, Canterbury, *Materials for Becket* 3, p. 39; see above, pp. 47–8.

14   *Chronica Majora* 3, p. 161; Samson of Bury, *De Miraculis Sancti Edmundi*, no. 7 (pp. 176–8).

Even the Cistercians, who were renowned for their exclusiveness, clearly allowed some interaction between the monks and their guests. In his *History of English Affairs*, the Yorkshire Augustinian, William of Newburgh, recounts how he had often seen the old monk, Wimund, former bishop of the Isles, when visiting his neighbouring Cistercians at Byland Abbey. Elderly and blind, Wimund, had recounted his colourful past to William who recorded the monk's 'most audacious acts as well as his merited misfortunes' in his history.[15] The *Chronicle of Melrose Abbey* describes how one monk of the house, Adam of Lennox, was renowned for his great holiness and accordingly received visits from a number of nobles who sought to make confession and receive his blessing. Adam was said to spend most of his days sitting by the door of the church, reading his Psalter and giving bread to the poor, so it was presumably here or in the parlour that he met with his guests.[16] Visitors might come to seek spiritual advice or counsel on matters relating to the religious life, perhaps about joining the religious life or founding a community. A well-known example is Christina of Markyate, who regularly visited St Albans to meet with Abbot Geoffrey (1119–46). In 1252 Isabella of Arundel received papal permission to enter the Cistercian abbey of Waverley, to consult with the abbot; it is thought that this was about the foundation of Marham Priory.[17]

Greater restrictions were enforced between nuns and their guests or, at least, there were greater attempts to control access. A notable case is King John's visit to the double foundation of Fontevrault where his mother, Eleanor of Aquitaine, was buried. His visit is recounted by Adam of Eynsham in his biography of Hugh of Lincoln.[18] Adam explains that John arrived at the house with a throng of nobles and knocked at the door of the choir, for he wished to see the tombs and commend himself to the prayers of the community. The abbess was not herself present and as nobody was permitted to see the convent or enter the enclosure without her, John was told to wait for her return. The nuns requested the king not to take offence at their response but to admire their adherence to the statutes; thereupon they closed the door and returned to the cloister.[19] Adam himself regarded this as a memorable and worthy example and, perhaps surprisingly, the king was also said to have been impressed and on this occasion announced his intent to confer great favours

---

15   *The History of William of Newburgh*, trans. J. Stevenson (Llanerch facsimile, Felinfach, 1996), bk 1 ch. 22 (p. 430). Wimund's story is recounted in ch. 24 (pp. 431–2).

16   'The Chronicle of Melrose', trans. J. Stevenson, *Medieval Chronicles of Scotland: the chronicles of Melrose and Holyrood* (Llanerch facsimile, Felinfach, 1988), pp. 7–124 (p. 96).

17   *Life of Christina of Markyate*, pp. 140, 158. *Annales Monastici* 2, p. 345. According to the *Life* of Boso, the fourth abbot of Bec, Boso answered the enquiries of everyone who sought his advice, according to their need, *Vita Venerabilis Bosonis Abbatis Beccensis Quarti*, PL 150. 723–32 (730, 726).

18   *Magna Vita* 2, pp. 138–9.

19   The customs of Fontevrault differ slightly: if a rich man or Christian pilgrim wished to see the cloister when the abbess was not there, the nuns should hide away and be guarded; the church doors would then be opened and the great prioress or cellaress, along with two or three of the brothers, would introduce the men inside and show them the cloister, chapter, monastery and refectory, PL 162. 1081.

on the house. The Gilbertine nuns were to avoid conversing with visitors, but might speak with male relatives at the large window or guesthouse gate. With the prioress's consent nobles or the advocate of the house might speak at the little window.[20]

Male visitors were not denied hospitality in the nunneries and the French clerk, Garnier, describes how he visited Thomas Becket's sister, the abbess of Barking, to gather information for a verse life he was writing about the martyr.[21] Goscelin of St Bertin acquired material for his lives from oral as well as written sources. At Barking he gleaned much from the sacrist, Judith, and at Wilton he chatted to those more familiar than he with English history.[22] The presence of male visitors and their contact with the nuns had to be carefully monitored, and restrictions of this kind are invariably included in injunctions issued following visitation of the house; these date from the thirteenth century. In 1252, the nuns of Marrick Priory, Yorkshire, were instructed that they should not sit outside the cloister with visitors after curfew or remain alone with them. This was presumably to make sure there was no conversation with visitors in the parlour after Compline, when the parlour door was closed.[23] The presence of Robert de Hilton's household at Swine Priory was a cause of anxiety to Archbishop Giffard, c. 1267, for he feared that harm might come of their wandering too freely in the cloister and parlour, and holding 'suspicious' conversations with the nuns and sisters.[24] Archbishop Peckham voiced similar concerns following his visitation of Romsey Abbey in 1287. He ruled that no nun might converse with any man except in the parlour or at the side of the church by the cloister. To prevent any scandals arising, a nun might only speak with a man if she had two companions as witnesses who would either be edified by her useful words or would hinder any evil ones.[25]

---

[20] 'Incipiunt capitula de quatvor procuratoribus', Dugdale, *Monasticon*, 6: 2, p. li: XXXIV.

[21] *Vie de Sainte Thomas*, lines 16–19; see above, p. 24.

[22] C. H. Talbot, 'The Liber Confortatorius of Goscelin of St Bertin', *Analecta Monastica* 3, *Studia Anselmiana* 37 (Rome, 1955), pp. 1–117 (p. 9); see, too, Morton's translation of Goscelin's lives of the abbesses of Barking, *Guidance for Women*, pp. 139–55 (p. 146). Goscelin also visited Ramsey and Ely.

[23] These injunctions are in the BL, Egerton charter 406. For a summary of the injunctions see *VCH York* 3, ed. W. Page (Westminster, 1913), p. 117. The visitation is discussed by Tillotson, *Marrick Priory*, pp. 17–21, Burton, *Yorkshire Nunneries*, p. 52, n. 123, and Powers, *English Nunneries*, p. 401, n. 1.

[24] Swine was visited in 1267/8 by Archbishop Giffard, *Register of Giffard*, pp. 146–8. For similar rulings at Romsey, see *Registrum Peckham* 3, no. 666 (p. 928).

[25] *Registrum Peckham* 2, no. 508 (p. 664). Similar restrictions were imposed at Barking Abbey in 1279, *Registrum Peckham* 1, no. 70 (pp. 81–6); for his rulings at Godstow see *Registrum Peckham* 3, no. 610 (p. 848).

Tours and recreation

The splendour of the buildings attracts the eye and captivates the minds of visitors.[26]

Visitors who were curious to see around the abbey and perhaps view its collection of treasures might be offered a tour of the monastic buildings; some might even be shown inside the claustral buildings. It was generally the hosteller who was responsible for escorting guests around the monastery, and the customs of Cluny actually outline the route he should take when showing new *confratres* around the house.[27] These guided tours prevented outsiders from wandering around the monastery at will and would therefore have helped to minimise the disruption to monastic life. Lanfranc enjoined the guestmaster to check that the monks were not in the cloister before he escorted visitors around the buildings. Furthermore he was to make sure that nobody entered the cloister unsuitably attired, that is, barefoot, wearing riding boots or spurs, or wearing only drawers.[28] Similar arrangements are detailed in the later customaries of St Mary's, York, Westminster and Eynsham which also accord the hosteller a supervisory role and mention a custodian who was to guard the cloister door.[29] These restrictions suggest that the exclusion of outsiders from certain areas of the precinct was not so much to delineate sacred space than to minimise contact between the monks and outsiders and disruption to religious observances. The canons of St Victor's, however, seem to have been more concerned with presenting guests a positive impression of the buildings for the guestmaster was to check that offices were open and fit to be seen before showing visitors around. Moreover, guests were not to be brought to the infirmary or kitchen where they might encounter chaos or unpleasantness.[30] Tours might be offered to help guests who were unfamiliar with the layout of the precinct find their bearings, in particular visiting monks who were lodged in the claustral area. Tours of this kind are specifically mentioned in the late-thirteenth-century customary of Westminster Abbey but were probably commonplace at an earlier date and in other houses.[31]

---

26 William of Malmesbury, c. 1125, on Tewkesbury Abbey, *William of Malmesbury's Chronicle of the Kings*, ed. J. A. Giles (London, 1847), p. 433.

27 *Ordo Cluniacensis per Bernardum*, ch. 9 (p. 154); *Udalrici Consuetudines*, col. 765.

28 Lanfranc, *Constitutions*, ch. 90 (pp. 131–3).

29 *St Mary's Customary*, p. 96; *Westminster Customary*, p. 170 lines 8–30; *Eynsham Customary*, ch. 19: 10 (518), p. 203 lines 14–16; ch. 19: 12 (541), p. 211 lines 14–25. *Westminster Customary*, p. 170 lines 8–30 states that according to ancient custom four servants should monitor the cloister and ensure that no secular person entered when the brothers were at chapter, in the refectory, washing feet or shaving; nobody was permitted to enter wearing spurs, or barefoot unless the king was present.

30 *Liber Ordinis*, p. 61.

31 *Westminster Customary*, p. 80 lines 19–23. The hosteller was to show visiting monks, who did not know the abbey, around the cloister, and if there was time might lead them through the court and the whole monastery.

Visitors might admire the architecture or view interesting treasures and relics. In his *Life of St Ethelberga*, Goscelin of St Bertin (c. 1035–c. 1107) mentions a stone at Barking Abbey that depicted how Danes who had looted the abbey, had met their fate. In his *Life of St Edith* he remarks on the wonderful needlework displayed by the nuns and also the rich decorations, hangings, sculptures, and gold and silver vessels.[32] The eulogy to Euphemia, abbess of Wherwell (d. 1257), refers to the precious stones, reliquaries and crosses she gave to the church.[33] The nine canons from Laon who travelled with relics of Mary through the south-east of England in 1113, to raise money to restore their church, stopped off with the nuns of Wilton where they were shown the grave of Bede and beside this the tomb of the poetess, Muriel, a former nun of the abbey.[34] The sacrist might inform interested guests about relics, altars, treasures and tombs that were in the chapter-house and church. The sacrist of Westminster was permitted to speak in church to point out a relic or miracle, but was to do so briefly and quietly.[35] It has been suggested that some local histories may even have been written to educate monks for the 'pilgrim trade', so that they, in turn, could inform visitors of the history of their monastery and of its altars, ornaments and treasures.[36]

In the twelfth-century *lai*, *Yonec*, the abbot entreats his guests to tour the abbey after dinner. He shows the lord and his lady the dormitory, refectory and also the chapter-house where they view many treasures, including fine gold candelabra and a magnificent tomb.[37] Walter Map's rather scathing account of monks suggests that tours of this kind were reserved for favoured guests, to secure their goodwill and generosity. Map denounces monks as the most discriminating of hosts and describes how they warmly received knights and those who had wasted their patrimony; having entertained them sumptuously, they then displayed the treasures of the house, leading their guests to the various altars and informing them of who was the patron of each.[38] Map also suggests that the monks used these tours as a public relations exercise. He claims that they displayed their frugal larders hoping to impress visitors and secure favourable reports of their abstemious ways. But, as Map bitterly remarks, this was done before they had broken their fasts and stocked the larders.[39] Distinguished visitors would no doubt have been given a personal

---

[32]   *Vita et translatio S. Ethelburgae* 1: 15, ed. M. L. Colker, Jocelyn of St Bertin, 'Life and miracles of St Ethelburga', *Studia Monastica* 7 (1965), pp. 398–417 (p. 414); *Vita S. Edithae* ch. 11, 16, ed. Wilmart, pp. 69, 79.

[33]   A translation of this eulogy is printed as appendix D in Spear, *Leadership in Medieval Nunneries*, pp. 217–18 (p. 218).

[34]   For their account of this visit, see Herman of Laon's 'De Miraculis', in PL 156. 983, ch. 14 'De febricitante curato apud Wittoniam abbatiam sanctimonialium'. For discussion of Muriel, see J. Tatlock, 'Muriel, the earliest English poetess', *Publications of the Modern Language Association of America* 48 (1933), pp. 317–21.

[35]   *Westminster Customary*, pp. 51–2.

[36]   A. Gransden, *Historical Writing in England, c. 550–c. 1307* (London, 1974), pp. 284–5.

[37]   *Yonec*, lines 472–6.

[38]   Map, *De Nugis*, p. 84. For further references to guests viewing treasures pertaining to the house, see *Gesta Normannorum* 2, p. 244, and *Orderic* 4, pp. 71–2.

[39]   Map, *De Nugis*, p. 84.

tour by the abbot or abbess. They might, however, be left to their own devices and William Rufus (1087–1100) evidently amused himself in the cloister at Romsey Abbey when he visited the convent to win the affections of Matilda of Scotland, who was then only twelve years old. While her aunt, who was the abbess of Romsey, cleverly placed a veil on the young girl's head to protect her from the king who was 'young and untamed', Rufus entered the cloister to admire the roses and other flowering herbs.[40] In addition to viewing the buildings or the monastery's treasures, guests might use the community's library to conduct research. Between them the monks Orderic Vitalis and William of Malmesbury visited Crowland, Thorney, Worcester and Glastonbury to gather information for various lives and histories.[41] Orderic was invited to Crowland by Abbot Geoffrey of Orleans, a former monk of St Évroul, to write the history of the foundation of the house and also to record an account of the death of Earl Waltheof, whose body was buried in the abbey and was said to have been working miracles. Orderic was also asked to abbreviate the lengthy life of St Guthlac, a hermit of Crowland, which had been written by Felix.[42] The French clerk, Garnier, visited the abbess and nuns of Barking Abbey to gather information for his verse *Life* of Thomas Becket, for the abbess of Barking was none other than Becket's sister. Garnier also stayed with the monks of Christ Church for almost a year to conduct his research.[43]

During their stay guests might enjoy the fresh air and relax in the garden.[44] By the thirteenth century the hosteller at St Albans had a little garden within a three-sided cloister, and this was presumably made available to guests. The *Gesta Abbatum* reveals that the garden was surrounded by a wattle-work wall to prevent free access.[45] The sacrist of Bury St Edmunds, Robert de Gravely,

40 I am indebted to Professor Robert Bartlett for the source of this reference, Hermann of Tournai, *Liber de restauracione monasterii sancti Martini Tornacensis*, trans. L. Nelson, *The Restoration of the Monastery of Saint Martin of Tournai* (Washington DC, 1996), pp. 31–3.

41 For Orderic's visits to Crowland, Thorney and Worcester, see *Orderic* 2, pp. xxxix, 188; for William of Malmesbury's visits to Glastonbury and Worcester, see R. Thomson, *William of Malmesbury* (Woodbridge, 1987), pp. 4, 5, and *Vita Wulfstani*, p. ix.

42 *Orderic* 2, pp. 524–5. See Chibnall, *World of Orderic Vitalis*, pp. 36, 107. Orderic returned to St Évroul with a copy of the *Life of Guthlac*, to edify the monks there.

43 For Garnier's visit to Christ Church, Canterbury, see *Vie de Sainte Thomas*, lines 1–9, esp. 7–8; for his visit to Barking Abbey, see lines 16–19 and above, p. 23–4. In the late fifteenth century the antiquary, William Worcester, visited Glastonbury Abbey to obtain bibliographical details of contemporary chronicles relating to Arthur. There he spoke with the monk, Dom Murelege, about chronicles and acts of King Arthur, and was shown a list of certain acts and other documents; he was entertained that day in the abbot's hall at the invitation of the abbot's secretary, William of Worcester, *Itineraries*, p. 261.

44 T. McLean, *Mediaeval Gardens* (London, 1981), pp. 258–9, discusses monastic vineyards and parks and explains that hostellers might keep gardens which served functional and decorative purposes, i.e. guests could walk and refresh themselves here, p. 36.

45 GASA 1, p. 290; see above, p. 83–4.

bought the vineyard across the river from the infirmary c. 1211, which he enclosed for the comfort of the infirm and bloodlet.[46]

It is likely that some visitors whiled away their time playing board games, cards and dice. Whilst there is little explicit evidence for the twelfth and early thirteenth centuries, later references and indeed surviving artefacts, probably reflect earlier practice. Excavations at Kirkstall Abbey recovered a chess piece and also a stone with a game scratched on it; a stone board for a game similar to Tic Tac Toe or Nine Mens Morris, was found at Byland Abbey. When Henry VIII stayed at Abingdon for almost three weeks in 1518 to escape the sweating sickness in London, the royal party amused themselves during Holy Week by playing cards and dice, and picking off arrows over the screen in the hall.[47] Guests might also go hunting during their stay. King John stayed at the Cistercian house of Flaxley, Gloucestershire, on several occasions in 1207–14 and enjoyed hunting in the locality.[48] He built a hunting lodge near to Romsey Abbey, close to the New Forest, which Henry III granted to the abbess in 1221 to accommodate the sick; this was still in use during Edward I's reign.[49] When Henry VI spent Christmas 1433 at Bury St Edmunds, he was able to ride through the gates of the vineyard to the open fields and hunting ground.[50]

Confraternity and the chapter-house

> Some rich man seeking fraternal association with the monastery would arrive with a large sum of money ... by which their necessities could be supplied for many days to come.[51]

Those wishing to be admitted to the confraternity of a monastery were formally welcomed at a ceremony and on this occasion were likely entertained by the community. But guests might be offered the chance, or actively encouraged, to join the confraternity during their stay. Walter Map's satirical remarks suggest that as part of their preferential treatment, distinguished guests might be enrolled as *confratres* in the hope that this would secure their benefaction

---

[46] 'Gesta Sacristarum', Memorials of Bury 2, pp. 289–98 (p. 293). For the guestmaster's great garden at Westminster Abbey see, J. Harvey, 'Westminster Abbey: the infirmarer's garden', Garden History 20: 2 (1992), pp. 97–115 (pp. 97–8).

[47] L/P Henry VIII: ii pt 2, no. 4043 (p. 1249). James IV played and lost at cards when he spent Christmas at Melrose in 1496, R. Fawcett and R. Oram, Melrose Abbey (Stroud, 2004), p. 54.

[48] The Cartulary and Historical Notes of the Cistercian Abbey of Flaxley, ed. A. W. Crawley-Boevey (Exeter, 1887), p. 53.

[49] Rotuli Litterum Clausaurum 1, ed. T. D. Hardy (London, 1833), p. 479 b; R. Luce, Pages from the History of Romsey and its Abbey (Winchester, 1948), p. 43.

[50] Whittingham, 'Bury St Edmunds', p. 180. James V (1513–42) stayed at Melrose Abbey when hunting in the Borders in November 1539, Annales Monastici 2, p. 345.

[51] Eadmer's description of the monastery of Bec in his Vita Anselmi, pp. 47–8.

for the house.[52] To be received as a *confrater* was highly desirable, and whilst the benefits varied from house to house the recipient was generally accorded a share in the monks' prayers and perhaps the right to take the habit and receive burial within the precinct.[53] Ralph Basset, who had been admitted within the fraternity of Abingdon, was buried in the chapter-house there.[54]

The twelfth- and thirteenth-century sources reveal little about the format of these enrolment ceremonies in England but the customaries and chronicles both indicate that they were usually conducted in the chapter-house. Lanfranc's *Constitutions* state that seculars seeking fraternity should be introduced to chapter by the guestmaster. Gilbert of Mountchesney was admitted to the confraternity of Abingdon in its chapter-house.[55] The new *confrater* might make a gift to the community to cement this new relationship and in the late twelfth century, Turstin and his wife made a grant in the chapter-house at Abingdon to mark their reception as *confratres*.[56] Confraternity might of course be granted to a donor in recognition of his or her generosity.[57] The reception of *confratres* is described at length in the later customaries of Westminster and St Augustine's, Canterbury.[58] These show that the format of the ceremony and also the benefits accorded, varied depending on the recipient's sex and identity. At Eynsham Abbey, for example, monks seeking fraternity were received in chapter with the customary bowing, prostrating, kissing and prayer, but the community rose to greet an abbot and remained standing until he was seated. Seculars, canons and other regulars were received through the book, that is, the applicant received in his hand the book of the Gospels; women, however,

---

52 Map, *De Nugis*, pp. 84–5.
53 For an outline of unions and confraternity among houses and between individuals, see Knowles, *Monastic Order*, pp. 472–9. Individual studies of confraternity rolls include Tsurushima, 'Fraternity of Rochester' and 'Forging unity'. See also Wardrop, *Fountains Abbey*; *Durham Liber Vitae and its Context*, ed. Rollason, Piper *et al.*.
54 *History of Abingdon* 2, pp. 246–9.
55 Lanfranc, *Constitutions*, ch. 90 (pp. 130–1); *History of Abingdon* 2, pp. 226–9. See, too, Angenendt's discussion of the procedure for receiving *confratres* at Cluny, A. Angenendt, 'How was a confraternity made? The evidence of charters', *Durham Liber Vitae and its Context*, ed. Rollason *et al.*, pp. 207–20, esp. pp. 214 ff.
56 'Rents due to the hostillar', p. 330. For the reception of the priest, Geoffrey, into the confraternity of Ramsey Abbey, 1134–60, see *Chronicon Ramesiensis*, no. 305 (p. 272). Additional examples of grants made in chapter include *Chronicon Ramesiensis*, nos 248 (p. 237), 255 (pp. 240–1); *Orderic* 3, pp. 122–3, 174–7 and 4, pp. 136–9. For discussion of patronage and gift-giving more generally, see Cownie, *Religious Patronage*, pp. 152–71; for gift-giving ceremonies and objects as symbols, see Hudson, *Land, Law and Lordship*, ch. 5, esp. pp. 162–6, M. Clanchy, *From Memory to Written Record, England, 1066–1307*, 2nd edn (Oxford, 1993), pp. 38–40, and Chibnall, *World of Orderic*, pp. 34–5.
57 Steve White's analysis of the *Laudatio Parentum* in western France similarly shows that a gift was sometimes given in return for fraternity, but fraternity might instead be offered as reciprocity for a gift received, White, *Custom, Kinship*, p. 33.
58 *Westminster Customary*, p. 232 line 15 – p. 234 line 4; *St Augustine's Customary* (fourteenth-century), pp. 291–7. For the procedure at Cluny, see H. E. J. Cowdrey, 'Unions and confraternity with Cluny', *JEH* 16 (1965), pp. 152–62; *Udalrici Consuetudines*, cols 765–6.

did not kiss the abbot's hand unless this was conceded out of reverence.[59] This latter point is also stated in Lanfranc's *Constitutions*, although his instructions generally pertain to religious men seeking fraternity.[60]

Whilst access to the chapter-house was restricted, and outsiders were forbidden to enter here or even the cloister when a chapter meeting was in progress, it was clearly not demarcated as a sacred spot.[61] Men and women of all ranks might enter the chapter-house to enrol as a *confrater* or to bestow a gift,[62] or to bear testimony to a miracle they had experienced at the abbey's shrine. Samson of Bury's *De Miraculis de Sancti Aedmundi* describes how a clerk of Lichfield who was miraculously saved him from drowning by the saint, reported this to the older monks of Bury in their chapter-house.[63] They might also enter the chapter-house to listen to a sermon. When the papal legate, Nicholas of Tusculum, visited Bury in December 1213 he preached to a crowd in the community's chapter-house, but dismissed them to address the community on private matters.[64] The chapter-house was often used to host important ecclesiastical or state councils. In August 1184 Henry II held a council at Reading Abbey to elect a new archbishop of Canterbury. This was attended by the leading magnates and prelates, including John, archbishop of Dublin, the duke of Saxony, bishops of the provinces, and all the monks of Christ Church. The following year he received and gave audience to the patriarch of Jerusalem in Reading's chapter-house. The patriarch was hoping to persuade Henry to undertake a crusade to the Holy Land. Richard I held a Council of the Realm here in 1191, and on 6 December 1213 King John gathered an assembly at Reading to discuss compensation following the interdict.[65] It is hardly surprisingly that Reading had one of the finest chapter-houses in the country.[66]

---

59   *Eynsham Customary*, ch. 19: 10 (526–31), pp. 207–9. At Cluny the *Rule of St Benedict*, a missal or chapter-book might be placed on the altar with the charter to give this act greater force, Angenendt 'How was a confraternity made?', p. 216.

60   Lanfranc, *Constitutions*, ch. 90 (pp. 130–1).

61   It was presumably for this reason that the sub-prior of Abingdon (or the third prior if he was holding chapter) was to close the parlour door and other doors before chapter, *De Obedientiariis*, p. 367. For similar arrangements see *Westminster Customary*, p. 170, and *St Mary's Customary*, p. 95.

62   See Lanfranc, *Constitutions*, ch. 108 (pp. 170–1); *Eynsham Customary*, ch. 11 (526–531), pp. 207–9. Women were not, however, permitted to enter the chapter-house at La Trinité, Vendôme in the late eleventh and early twelfth centuries, and made their offerings instead in the parlour (*auditorium*) which was seemingly located in the western wall of the forecourt, Johnson, *Prayer, Patronage and Power*, pp. 29; 35, n. 63.

63   Samson of Bury, *De Miraculis de Sancti Edmundi*, no. 16 (pp. 195–6).

64   *Election of Abbot Hugh*, pp. 26–35 (pp. 26–9); see above, p. 113. Cheney, *Episcopal Visitation*, pp. 54–103, discusses the general procedure on such visits.

65   Gervase, *Chronicle* 1, p. 311; J. B. Hurry, *The Octocentenary of Reading Abbey* (London, 1921), p. 50; *Gesta Regis Henrici Secundi Benediciti Abbatis. The chronicle of the Reigns of Henry II and Richard I, 1169–1192, known commonly under the name of Benedict of Peterborough*, ed. W. Stubbs, 2 vols, RS 49 (London, 1867), 1, pp. 317–18.

66   Hurry, *Reading Abbey*, pp. 31–3. The refectory might also be used to host events of this kind and in 1466 parliament met in the refectory at Bury St Edmunds to try Humphrey, duke of York, Whittingham, 'Bury St Edmunds', p. 178.

Clearly, it was the chapter meetings rather than the building itself that were marked as private. Outsiders might enter the chapter-house at appropriate times but were forbidden to attend the chapter meetings; indeed, the content of these meetings was not to be revealed. There were exceptions. When Henry II visited St Albans in 1182/4 with Walter of Coutances, bishop of Lincoln, he humbly requested to enter the chapter-house and attend the meeting as a *confrater* and essentially a monk of the abbey.[67] Henry attended the chapter meetings at Christ Church, Canterbury on several occasions during the dispute between Archbishop Baldwin and the monks of Holy Trinity. On 14 December 1184, for example, he entered the chapter-house alone after the sermons and writings, and took his place amongst the brethren as if he was a member of the community.[68] King John was evidently less inclined to attend chapter meetings, a point that he himself made after entering the chapter-house at Bury in November 1214, to discuss the disputed election of Hugh of Northwold. Whilst this may have been an acknowledgement of the inappropriateness for outsiders to attend the chapter, John may instead have been referring to his recent excommunication. Significantly he was unaccompanied by any layman save the earl of Winchester and also Philip de Ulecotes, who carried his sword before him.[69]

The departure

At the arrival and departure of guests let Christ – who indeed is received in their person – be adored in them by bowing the head or even prostrating on the ground.[70]

Whereas there is considerable information for the reception of guests, there is relatively little regarding their departure. The *Rule of St Benedict* simply states that Christ should be received in guests on their arrival and departure, that is, the brethren should bow or prostrate themselves before them. The Abingdon customary stipulates that guests should receive the blessing upon arrival and departure, and sets out arrangements for anyone leaving early.[71] It also reveals that visitors were not to leave the cloister without the guestmaster's permission and were to be escorted by him, a means, no doubt, of maintaining control and preserving decorum.[72] As previously suggested these clauses may refer specifically to monastic guests staying in the claustral area rather than visitors residing in the court.

---

67 GASA 1, p. 197. See also Knowles, *Monastic Order*, p. 476.
68 Gervase, *Chronicle* 1, p. 322. For his visit in February, 1187, see pp. 353–4.
69 *Election of Abbot Hugh*, p. 118. John was excommunicated from November 1209 to May 1213, R. Turner, *King John* (Harlow, 1994), pp. 164–8.
70 *Rule of St Benedict*, ch. 53 (p. 134).
71 See above, p. 158.
72 *De Obedientiariis*, p. 414. See, too, *Westminster Customary*, p. 82 lines 82–4.

The Abingdon customary sheds little light on the departure itself. Other sources suggest that guests might be offered the services of an escort on their journey. This was both an act of courtesy and a practicality, for it provided guidance to strangers through unfamiliar territory.[73] It may not have been obligatory for the monastery to provide an escort for guests – and this is not explicitly prescribed in the customaries or statutes – but it was seemingly expected that, as a mark of respect, those of a certain standing would be honoured accordingly. Gerald of Wales complained when during his struggle for St David's the abbot of Whitland ordered that at no house subject to him should Gerald receive the escort of a monk, a lay-brother or even a *garcio* (groom) of the house, not even if the way was dark or deserted. Gerald was appalled at this slight to his dignity claiming the monks were withholding a boon 'which kind hearts are not wont to deny even to foreign travellers'.[74] When the legate, Nicholas of Tusculum, left Bury St Edmunds in 1213 he was given a dignified send-off and accompanied by the leading men of the community. They included the prior, the abbot-elect and sacrist of Bury, and the party stayed overnight at a manor belonging to the house. When Archbishop Lanfranc left Bec following the dedication of the ceremony, Abbot Herluin accompanied him for two miles.[75]

In the mid-twelfth century Peter the Venerable, abbot of Cluny, complained that their openness to outsiders had disrupted the spiritual life of the house and almost converted the cloister into a public street. Peter acknowledged that outsiders had a right to visit parts of the abbey and agreed that they should attend some of the monastic services such as high Mass, but argued that certain areas should be set aside for the exclusive use of the monks. The restoration of the cloister to the monks therefore formed part of his reform programme for Cluny which was inaugurated before c. 1146.[76] Bernard of Clairvaux's remark in 1128 that the cloister at St Denis hitherto frequented by knights, tradesmen and women had now returned to the monks, suggests that similar measures had been taken there by Abbot Suger at the start of the twelfth century.[77]

---

[73]   For the practical importance of this, see the arrangements for the abbot of St Alban's visit to Tynemouth priory: six squires were enfeoffed of the abbey to escort him there and back, GASA 1, pp. 264–5.

[74]   *De jure et statu*, p. 202, trans. Butler, *Autobiography of Gerald*, p. 226. In 1196 the Cistercian monks of Aigubelle, France, were reprimanded for refusing to guide an abbot in a strange land, Waddell, *Twelfth-Century Statutes*, 1196: 31 (pp. 362–3). According to a fourteenth-century Irish account, St Senán's guesthouses in Kilrush provided bread, protection and an escort for anyone who required it, O'Sullivan, *Hospitality in Ireland*, p. 150.

[75]   *Election of Abbot Hugh*, p. 34; *Vita Herluini*, p. 107. The provision of an escort by lay hosts is discussed in Kerr, 'Welcome the coming', forthcoming.

[76]   Statute 23, cited by Constable, *Cluniac Studies*, essay 3, p. 134. Leclercq, explains that although visitors were usually allowed to enter and watch the monks' choir at Cluny, they were kept out of the claustral buildings, J. Leclercq, 'Hospitality and monastic prayer', *Cistercian Studies* 8:1 (1973), pp. 3–24 (p. 9).

[77]   *Sancti Bernardi Opera*, ed. J. Leclercq and H. Rochais, 8 vols (Rome, 1957–77), 8, *Epistolae*, ep. 78. However, Bernard's remarks were based on hearsay rather than his

The extent to which visitors were integrated within the precinct and interacted with the brethren clearly varied according to the customs of the house or order, and depending also on the occasion, the guest's identity and his or her relationship with the community.[78] But in theory outsiders were largely kept apart from the brethren and access to the cloister was restricted. Thus, custodians were appointed to preserve the quietude of the cloister and the guestmaster was to monitor who entered and to escort them within.[79] Herbert de Losinga, bishop of Norwich (1090–1119), insisted upon conventual silence in the cloister except at certain stated times when a little appropriate conversation might be permitted.[80] This concern for privacy may have led to the insertion of double-splayed windows in the western range of Norwich Cathedral Priory, in an attempt to restrict guests' and lay people's view of the cloister.[81]

Given that in theory if not in practice access to the cloister and interaction with the monks was restricted, it is striking and even puzzling to note Orderic Vitalis's approval of life at Maule Priory, a cell of St Évroul, in the early twelfth century. Orderic explains that the knights of the priory frequented the cloisters discussing practical as well as speculative matters; instead of criticising this social intercourse Orderic hopes for its continuance.[82] It is not so surprising that this intercourse took place, but Orderic's commendation is rather perplexing and seems at odds with the monastic ideal of the solitude of the cloister and, indeed, with the policies of Peter the Venerable, Suger of St Denis and Bernard of Clairvaux. A possible explanation for this disparity may lie with our interpretation of the term *claustrum*, which can refer to the monastic enclosure as a whole and not specifically the inner claustral area.[83] However, we can perhaps only conclude that the quietude of the cloister was rather ambiguous, that discourse with outsiders was acceptable on certain occasions but the extent of tolerance varied from house to house.

own observances, G. Constable, 'Suger's monastic administration', *Abbot Suger and St Denis: a symposium*, ed. P. Lieber Gerson (New York, 1986), pp. 17–32 (p. 19).

78   Henry I, for example, held a long session in the cloister of St Évroul when conducting his visitation at Candlemas, 1113, *Orderic* 6, pp. 174–5. Additional examples include *Vita Anselmi*, p. 50, *Vita Herluini*, p. 105.

79   See above, pp. 66, 76–7.

80   *Epistolae Herberti de Losinga*, ed. R. Anstruther, Caxton Society 5 (Brussels, 1846), ep. 48. See, too, ep. 23, and ep. 57.

81   Heywood citing Franklin, S. Heywood, 'The Romanesque building', *Norwich Cathedral*, ed. Atherton *et al.* (London, 1996), pp. 73–115 (p. 108).

82   *Orderic* 3, pp. 206–7. This book was written c. 1127–30 at the latest, ibid., p. xiv. According to Chibnall, *World of Orderic*, p. 90, monks 'willingly' gave pastoral advice to lay benefactors who frequented their cloister, and had discussions with parish clergy from the locality. See also R. W. Church, *Saint Anselm* (London, 1870), pp. 52–3.

83   Chibnall explains that 'claustrum' can refer to the entire enclosure, the buildings and cloisters, or simply the claustral area, *Orderic* 1, p. 267; see also 6, p. 174, n. 3.

Conclusion

The nature of surviving evidence makes it difficult to evaluate how precisely guests were entertained and the extent to which they interacted with the monastic community throughout the twelfth and thirteenth centuries. Analysis is dependent largely on the customaries which record what was prescribed rather than practised, and deal with procedures. Accordingly, they shed little light on how the guest quarters were furnished, how visitors spent their day and their overall satisfaction. It is likely, however, that the nature of entertainment varied considerably depending on the guest's identity and relationship with the community, the reason for the visit and on who else was visiting at the time. Facilities would have differed from house to house, and each monastery might review and modify its policies according to its financial state, the relationship between abbot and convent and, not least of all, between the community and its guest. Patrons and *confratres* might be permitted greater access within the precinct and have more involvement with the community; they might also receive gifts during their stay. Monastic hospitality may have become more accessible to women who were traditionally subject to greater restrictions within the precinct. Concessions were now granted to certain females, effectively noble women and kinsfolk, who were permitted to enter the claustral area for refreshments. This ostensibly more open policy may have been in response to external pressure, and was perhaps an attempt by the monasteries to attract female benefactors, but may simply reflect earlier practice that was now formalised and consigned to writing. The nature of hospitality at this time was affected also by developments in the religious life. The increasing number and popularity of the new religious orders meant that a visiting Benedictine might be distinguished from other regulars who were now entertained apart from the community. The larger houses might have separate lodgings each for the Benedictines, Cistercians and friars.

Ideally, the host community was to accord its guests appropriate honour without compromising the monastery's standing or resources. Inevitably this was not always the case. Unfortunately there are few surviving records of the guests' experiences, and it is difficult to gauge if they perceived significant differences between the entertainment offered by the Benedictines and Cistercians or between large and small houses, and if they noted changes over time. But it is clear that some monasteries, such as Reading and St Swithun's, Winchester, were more greatly renowned for their hospitality than others. It is likely that standards varied considerably from house to house and also within each house. While guests entertained by the abbot would have fared well, enjoying fine food and perhaps musical accompaniment, others would have received more basic provision, having necessities rather than luxuries.

6

The financial implications of hospitality

... This house was founded by him [Henry I] ... in a place well suited to provide lodging for almost all travellers to the more populous cities of England. In it he established monks of Cluny who are at this time a distinguished exemplar of holy life and a model of inexhaustible and delightful hospitality. One can see there, as nowhere else, how the guests who arrive at all hours get more provisions than the inmates.[1]

Hospitality was a basic part of the monastery's financial outlay but it could be an expensive one, particularly by the twelfth century when monasteries felt that they were more greatly burdened with guests than their predecessors.[2] It is, however, difficult to estimate the actual cost of administering hospitality at this time. The later Middle Ages is better served and obedientiary rolls dating from the late thirteenth century record payments relating to guests. For example, the chamberlain of Abingdon's rolls for 1428–29 list payments for various items of furniture and also tools purchased for the hospice; the treasurer's rolls for 1375–76 reveal that he bought utensils for the hospice and paid for its door to be made. The hosteller of Peterborough's expenses in 1498–99 included 'necessary expenses', for the refreshment of servants in the hostel, for repairs, the purchase of candles and cord for curtains.[3] While there is little evidence of this kind for the preceding period, the earlier sources can nonetheless shed some light on the relative expense of entertainment in the monastery. In 1238 the Cluniacs of Bermondsey Priory attributed their impoverishment to heavy legatine exactions and extensive hospitality, but claimed that as their house was a 'gazingstock' to the king and kingdom, they could not reduce hospitality without causing scandal or a commotion. Bermondsey was located

1   William of Malmesbury on Reading Abbey, *Gesta Regum* 1, p. 746.
2   See above, p. 5–6.
3   *Accounts of Obedientiars of Abingdon*, pp. 110, 29, 27; *Account Rolls of Obedientiaries of Peterborough*, p. 35. See, too, *Accounts of the Cellarers of Battle*. An early, and in many ways exceptional set of accounts, relates to the obedientiary and manorial officials of Bury. This dates from the mid-thirteenth century and has recently been discussed by P. D. A. Harvey, 'Mid-thirteenth-century accounts from Bury St Edmunds', *Bury St Edmunds: Medieval Art, Architecture, Archaeology and Economy*, ed. A. Gransden, British Archaeological Association Conference Transactions 20 (Leeds, 1998), pp. 128–138. Whilst this sheds light on estate farming at this time, it contributes little to our understanding of hospitality.

about half a mile off the main London to Dover road, and would have been a popular stopping-off point for travellers. Moreover, the monks were obliged to entertain the earl of Gloucester and his heirs whenever they visited the priory.[4] Irrespective of any spiritual and worldly benefits that might be accrued through receiving guests, hospitality could be costly, particularly for communities that had demanding patrons or, like Bermondsey and St Swithun's, Winchester, were located on a thoroughfare.[5] Monasteries which were centres of pilgrimage or had a popular attraction might also be overwhelmed by visitors. In the fourteenth century the Cistercians of Meaux Abbey, Yorkshire, were inundated with crowds of local women who flocked to the abbey to see the miracle-working cross there.[6] Nevertheless, the pilgrim trade could be extremely lucrative and might be promoted by houses requiring financial aid to complete building work or undertake repairs, or simply to enhance the abbey coffers.[7] Abbot Baldwin (1065–97) of Bury St Edmunds fervently encouraged the cult of St Edmund which helped finance the splendid new Romanesque church, and Samson, as sub-sacrist of the abbey, used a portion of the offerings at the shrine to support the building and restoration of the church.[8] The offerings made to William of Perth's shrine at Rochester helped restore the community's fortunes in the thirteenth century and supported the rebuilding of the cathedral. The monks of Christ Church, Canterbury, profited greatly from Becket's shrine, particularly in 1220, the year of the translation.[9]

Orderic Vitalis's memorable account of Mabel Talvas, the wife of Roger of Montgomery, vividly describes how she and her vast entourage would descend on the monks of St Évroul demanding hospitality. On one occasion Mabel went too far and arrived with one hundred knights. When warned by the abbot to restrain this vanity she simply threatened to bring an even larger retinue on her next visit. The Hand of God, however, intervened to administer

---

4   Graham, *English Ecclesiastical Studies*, pp. 100–1. The earls of Gloucester were important benefactors of the priory.

5   St Swithun's, Winchester, would have been the first hostelry that nobles and merchants came upon after arriving at Southampton, Kitchin, *Compotus Rolls*, p. 10.

6   *Chronica de Melsa* 3, pp. 35–6; see also above, p. 107.

7   Reading and St Albans both sought to promote pilgrimage to their abbeys in the twelfth century, Kemp, 'The hand of St James', pp. 10–11; Stil, *Abbot and the Rule*, pp. 16–17. Reading had a substantial relic collection and a late-twelfth-century list that is incomplete cites 240 relics, which includes the hand of St James, the foreskin of Christ and pieces of the Virgin's hair, Kemp, 'Hand of St James', p. 3; Hurry, *Reading Abbey*, pp. 127–8. For how the collection was assembled see D. Bethall, 'The making of a twelfth-century relic collection', *Popular Belief and Practice*, ed. G. J. Cuming and D. Baker, *Studies in Church History* 8 (Cambridge, 1972), pp. 61–72.

8   Gransden, 'Separation of portions', p. 395; 'The cult of St Mary at Beodericisworth and then in Bury St Edmunds Abbey to c. 1150', *JEH* 55: 4 (2004), pp. 627–53 (pp. 638–9).

9   H. Loxton, *Pilgrimage to Canterbury* (Newton Abbot, London, Vancouver, 1978), p. 155; C. E. Woodruff, 'The financial aspect of the cult of St Thomas of Canterbury, as revealed by a study of the monastic records', *Archaeologia Cantiana*, 14 (1932), pp. 13–32, esp. 16–19, 22–3, 26–9.

justice and Mabel was struck down with illness.[10] A similar offender in the late thirteenth century was Agnes de Vesci, who was patron of the Gilbertine Priory of Watton. Agnes allegedly descended upon this community with a great crowd of women and animals, and left only at the king's insistence.[11] Whilst there are no such colourful examples for twelfth-century England, there are certainly indications that patrons at this time could be just as demanding. The compiler of the *Liber Benefactorum* of Ramsey Abbey, for example, mentions sons who, seeking to exploit their fathers' patronage, exploited the monks' hospitality.[12]

> Let it be known to all that out of consideration for the 'honest' way of life of the monks of Reading and their pious reception of guests, we confirm the grant of 40 shillings per annum from the church of Rowington and the tithe from their demesne there, to support the administration of hospitality at the house.[13]

Hospitality was regarded as a fundamental part of the monastery's outlay, and one which required adequate resources. When Ralph of Rochester was appointed head of the cathedral priory in the late twelfth century he was shocked to discover that no income had been earmarked for the accommodation of travellers and considered this deficiency a scandal (*scandalum*).[14] As one of the thirteen abbots elect in 1182, Samson of Bury urged the other twelve to swear that whoever succeeded to the abbacy would return the churches of the convent's demesne to provide for hospitality. Ironically, when Samson was himself elevated to the abbacy he retracted this vow, arguing that it would endanger the legacy of the abbacy.[15] That hospitality was integral to the life and economy of the monastery and had to be provided for accordingly is implied in a number of charters, such as Earl William of Gloucester's confirmation of various tithes and revenues to Tewkesbury Abbey (1148 x 83) where it appears amongst the *necessitates* of the house.[16] In the late twelfth century Pope Clement III conceded Reading Abbey the right to assign certain of its churches, when vacant, to support its basic needs, namely the maintenance of the monks, their guests and the poor.[17] A similar bull permitted the monks of St Peter's, Westminster to appropriate the tithes and

---

[10] *Orderic* 2, pp. 54–7. *Gesta Normannorum* 2, p. 118, describes Mabel as a small woman, a gossip, inclined to doing harm, shrewd and witty, as well as cruel and avaricious.

[11] Golding, *Gilbert*, pp. 320–1.

[12] 'Liber Benefactorum', *Chronicon Ramensiensis*, ch. 23, pp. 46–7.

[13] From Hubert Walter's inspeximus and confirmation of Bishop Henry of Worcester's charter, c. April / October 1195, *English Episcopal Acta* 3, no. 584 (p. 237).

[14] Flight, *Bishops*, pp. 217–18. It was probably to redress this deficiency that Ralph initiated Celestine III's confirmation of various parish churches and the altar of St Nicholas for the use of hospitality in August 1191, ibid., appendix B, no 113 (p. 260). The charter is printed in *Papsturkunden* 2, no. 264 (pp. 457–8).

[15] *Jocelin*, pp. 19, 63.

[16] *Earldom of Gloucester Charters: The Charters and Scribes of the Earls and Countesses of Gloucester to AD 1217*, ed. R. B. Patterson (Oxford, 1973), no. 288 (p. 181).

[17] 1191 x 1198, *RAC* 1, no. 155 (p. 134).

revenues of their churches, whenever they fell vacant, to sustain these three groups.[18] The arrangements for establishing Ely as a see, c. 1109 are equally revealing, for the monks had complained that contrary to the old agreement Bishop Hervey's initial proposals for the division of lands made no allowances for the administration of hospitality.[19] In response Hervey conceded that revenues from Stretham should be assigned to support guests.[20] The monks of Glastonbury voiced a similar complaint following the union of their abbey with the bishopric of Bath and the reconstitution of their house as a cathedral priory. They maintained that the division of revenues in 1219 had decreased their resources for hospitality and other pious works, and sought papal help. Subsequently, on 25 May 1219, Honorious III conceded that they receive the full fruits of their advowsons for six years.[21]

The financing of hospitality was not simply a matter of providing food and lodging for visitors. It meant buying utensils and equipment for the guest chambers, supplying candles and wax tablets for practical and devotional reasons, and providing for the visitors' horses and entourage. Moreover, the monastery might provision nobles and their households staying in the vill, or part-finance their costs making them gifts of food, drink and other supplies. When Hugh de Neville, earl of Essex, stayed at Abingdon in 1207 his household expenses were covered by the abbot; at Salisbury his costs were met by the bishop.[22] Barons and bishops staying in the vill of Bury St Edmunds received from the sacrist bread and wine at dinner, and ale and wax at supper. Magnates might be similarly provided for while nobles received gifts from the cellarer and sacrist, presumably to boost their household supplies without draining the monastery's coffers.[23] Monks visiting Westminster Abbey on either Palm Sunday or the Feast of All Saints received stockings and boots when these were distributed to the community. Some guests had specific

---

18   For the delegation Abbot Walter sent to the papal *curia* in 1189 concerning this earlier bull see *Westminster Abbey Charters, 1066–c. 1214*, ed. E. Mason, London Rec. Soc. 25 (London, 1988), no. 178 (p. 87). See, too, *Papsturkunden* 1, 201 (pp. 470–3), and E. Mason, *Westminster Abbey and its People, c. 1250–1216* (Cambridge, 1996), p. 63.

19   *Liber Eliensis*, p. 261. For the monks of Rochester's complaint during Gilbert's episcopacy, 1198–1205, see *Select Cases from the Ecclesiastical Courts of the Province of Canterbury, c. 1200–1300*, ed. N. Adams and C. Donahue, SS 95 (London, 1981), no. A 15: 2 (p. 41).

20   *Liber Eliensis*, pp. 262–3.

21   *Glastonbury Cartulary* 1, no. 150 (p. 104). For the final agreement in November 1220, see no. 149 (pp. 102–4). Most of those who wrote to the pope on the monks' behalf referred to the priory's inability to support pilgrims and the poor; see, for example, nos 128, 131, 132, 133, 134, 136, 137 (pp. 80–6).

22   Woolgar, *Household Accounts* 1, pp. 110–16 (p. 114). Whilst it is not explicit it seems that Hugh stayed in the vill of Abingdon and not at the abbey. Hugh, who was Master of the royal hounds and chief justice of the forests was an important advisor to King John.

23   *Bury Customary*, pp. 32–3. Indeed, in 1301 the archbishop of Canterbury ruled that judges should no longer stay at the monasteries when attending courts, but might receive presents to boost their supplies. He claimed they had unfairly exploited the monasteries by demanding hospitality for themselves and their men for four and even eight days, *White Book of Worcester*, no. 53 (pp. 16–17).

requirements. It was noted earlier that abbots staying at Bury St Edmunds on the day of Absolution were given all they needed to celebrate the maundy. Those in priestly orders who visited Abingdon received everything they required to celebrate the Mass.[24] The fifteenth-century obedientiary accounts of Abingdon reveal that by this time at least it was common for guests to receive gifts; in 1420–21 small gifts of money were made to travelling monks and to scholars visiting Abingdon.[25]

The community might receive a donation to support a particular aspect of hospitality, such as lighting in the hospice or the care of guests' horses.[26] Robert de Lacy is recorded as granting land to the monks of Pontefract (1108 x 1114) for the maintenance of their own horses and those of their guests. This is an early example and its authenticity has been questioned, but there are plenty of similar grants from the late twelfth century.[27] It was noted in Chapter 4 that Ralf Francigena donated sixpence annually from land in Abingdon to the brethren's hostel for the purchase of horseshoes.[28] Bishop William of Ely confirmed £20 yearly from the church of Meldreth to buy utensils and other necessities for the community's guesthouse at Ely (February 1197 x February 1198).[29] The tithes from the three Littletons were earmarked for purchasing bowls, basins and towels for the guest cell at Evesham;[30] the chapel of Luttleton and everything pertaining to it was assigned by Abbot Randulf (1214–29) for the prebends of religious men with up to six horses lodged at the abbey.[31] From 1234 the hay and prebends for guests staying at Bury were to be supplied from the meadows and all the stores outside the vill of St Edmund and by increasing the tithes of Midhall, except for that which was in demesne.[32]

Grants were sometimes made to enable communities renowned for their exemplary hospitality to continue their good work or, conversely, to help improve hospitality at houses faced with difficult times. In recognition of the hospitality and works of charity administered by the abbot and monks of Abingdon, Hugh of Lincoln confirmed various tithes and pensions in the

---

24   *Westminster Customary*, p. 82 lines 30–3; *Bury Customary*, p. 54 lines 1–8; *De Obedientiariis*, p. 413. According to the rules of the Cistercian Order, the prior and *uestiarius* were to provide visiting monks with a habit, cowl and socks at their bed, Stephen of Lexington, *Letters From Ireland 1228–29*, trans. B. O'Dwyer (Kalamazoo, 1982), ep. 80 (p. 165).

25   *Accounts of Obedientiaries of Abingdon*, pp. 110, 92. 10 shillings were given to a travelling Cistercian and 6s 8d to a scholar from Bury, *Accounts of Obedientiaries of Abingdon Abbey*, p. 92.

26   But see above, p. 149–50 for the implication that guests visiting Cluny were expected to pay for the oats which the community supplied.

27   *EYC* 3, no. 1485 (pp. 177–9).

28   *Two Cartularies of Abingdon* 1, no. L. 352 (pp. 226–7); see above, p. 150.

29   *English Episcopal Acta* 3, no. 454 (pp. 115–16).

30   Thomas Marlborough, *History of Evesham*, pp. 402–3; 'Customs reissued by Abbot Randulf', printed as appendix B, Thomas Marlborough, *History of Evesham*, pp. 556–7;

31   *Chronicon de Evesham*, ed. Macray, p. 263, n. 2, inserted Harl. 3763 (fourteenth-century); see also above, p. 150.

32   Graham, 'A papal visitation', p. 733.

archdeaconry of Oxford to help support travellers and the indigent at the abbey.[33] Hubert Walter's *inspeximus* of April x October 1195 acknowledged the noteworthy hospitality administered by Reading Abbey and confirmed various revenues granted by his predecessor to assist the care of guests.[34] Hubert confirmed Dover Priory's rights in the church of St Lawrence of Hougham to help the monks recover from destruction caused by a recent fire at the house, and to support the heavy burden of hospitality. His charter reveals that the brethren had been inundated with religious and other men, an influx that can surely be attributed to the priory's coastal location.[35] In the early thirteenth century Hugh of Hereford granted Morville Priory the chapel of Astley to improve upon hospitality. Morville had been established as a dependency of Shrewsbury in 1138 specifically to provide hospitality.[36]

A substantial number of requests to appropriate revenues were claimed on the grounds of hospitality.[37] Tithes were originally intended for pastoral duties and their acquisition by monasteries was a matter of some controversy.[38] That so many appropriations were made to support hospitality and also charity suggests that they were considered an appropriate alternative, and were seen as a legitimate way for monks to acquire these revenues – whether or not they were used as intended. In April 1201 Hubert of Salisbury confirmed to Reading Abbey nine marks annually from two portions of the church of Thatcham and thirty-four shillings and one penny yearly from a third portion, as well as various woods and meadows, to support the house and foster hospitality.[39]

The request to make an appropriation was often accompanied by a plea of hardship. Moved by the poverty of Shrewsbury Abbey, which provided hospitality for all who sought it, Alexander Stavensby, bishop of Coventry

---

[33] *Two Cartularies of Abingdon* 2, no. C. 48 (pp. 73–5), 1197 x 1200. See also *Select Documents of Bec*, no. 6. (p. 4).

[34] *English Episcopal Acta* 3, no. 584 (p. 237). Bishop Herbert of Salisbury also remarked on Reading's reputation for hospitality and charity, and on 18 April 1201 confirmed various revenues to sustain this work, *RAC* 2, no. 1114 (pp. 259–60). See above, p. 25, for Silvester of Worcester's confirmation of his predecessor's gifts.

[35] 1210 x 1219, *English Episcopal Acta* 3, no. 446 (pp. 107–8). Cistercian houses on coastal routes were similarly aggrieved. See Canivez, *Statutes* 1, 1220: 22 (p. 521), for restrictions imposed on abbots from England and Ireland staying at Whitland Abbey, S. Wales. For dispensation sought from Basingwerk and Margam, on account of their location and the influx of guests, see Williams, *Welsh Cistercians*, p. 144; Cowley, *Monastic Order*, pp. 204–5, and above, p. 6.

[36] *Chartulary of Shrewsbury Abbey* 2, no. 347 (p. 313). For its foundation by Bishop Robert of Hereford, see no. 334 (pp. 303–4).

[37] I.e. the transfer of tithes and revenues from parish churches to monastic houses, generally with the proviso that the monastery should provide for the vicar of the parish, see C. Platt, *The Parish Churches of Mediaeval England* (London, 1981), p. xiii, and R. H. Snape, *English Monastic Finances in the Later Middle Ages* (Cambridge, 1926), pp. 78–9.

[38] For controversy regarding the monastic acceptance and exemption from tithes see G. Constable, *Monastic Tithes From their Origins to the Twelfth Century* (Cambridge, 1964), and B. R. Kemp, 'Monastic possessions of parish churches in England in the twelfth century', *JEH* 31 (1980), pp. 133–60, esp. pp. 141 ff.

[39] *RAC* 2, no. 1114 (pp. 259–60).

and Lichfield, granted the abbey half the greater tithes of Wellington in July 1232.[40] The appropriation of tithes to sustain hospitality was not peculiar to the Benedictines and was common amongst other religious. The Cistercians were officially prohibited from receiving tithes and were to live off their own labours rather than those of others but might receive tithes to support guests, pilgrims and the poor.[41] Thurstan, archbishop of York, stipulated that the monks of Fountains Abbey should spend the revenues and tithes of their churches only on guests, pilgrims and the poor.[42] Matilda de Percy, countess of Warwick responded to Sawley's plight and granted the monks the revenues of the church of Tadcaster that they might uphold their duties and receive the poor and pilgrims.[43] There are a number of examples relating to the Augustinian Canons. In c. 1185 x 88 Richard of Ilchester confirmed that the canons of Southwick Priory should appropriate the revenues of their churches to support themselves and the hospitality of the house, as long as provision was made for the vicars.[44] In 1195, Godfrey de Lucy confirmed the appropriation of St Nicholas' church, West Boarhunt, to Southwick Priory to support hospitality, on the understanding that forty shillings should be set aside annually for the vicar.[45]

Revenues that had been appropriated for hospitality were not always used as intended. The abbot and monks of Reading Abbey complained to Honorius III that various churches appropriated to them for hospitality and other pious causes had been put to different uses by certain abbots and other individuals. In July 1217 the pope issued a mandate to the abbots of St Albans, Evesham and Thame to effect the restoration of these churches to their intended purpose and to induct the abbot and convent into corporal possession of the same.[46] When Innocent III heard that benefices accorded to Westminster Abbey to sustain the chapter and poor had been assigned to clerks on occasion, at the insistence of certain magnates, he issued a bull ordering that other churches intended for hospitality and pious works should not be used in any other way (24 April, 1199). This bull was likely in response to the sacrist's appeal against Abbot William's methods to clear financial, and perhaps also personal obligations following the crisis of 1190–91 when the community agreed to pay King John the princely sum of £1000 for his support in ousting William de Longchamp's candidate from the abbacy.[47] The Cistercians were also guilty of

---

40 *Cartulary of Shrewsbury Abbey* 1, no. 63 (p. 66). The lesser tithes, altarage, renders of tenants, tithes of mills and pensions of chapels were to be reserved for the vicars. Also see the visitors' injunctions for Bury in 1234, Graham, 'A papal visitation', p. 733.

41 For the prohibition of tithes, see clause 9 of the 'Institutes of the General Chapter', in Waddell, *NLT*, p. 460.

42 *Memorials of Fountains* 1, p. 21.

43 This is discussed by Burton, *Monastic Order in Yorkshire*, pp. 196–7.

44 *English Episcopal Acta* 8, no. 176 (pp. 132–3).

45 *English Episcopal Acta* 8, no. 243 (pp. 187–8). Additional examples include EYC 1, no. 26 (pp. 36–7); for the canons of Nostell (1164 x 1181), see EYC 3, no. 1481 (pp. 174–5) and for the canons of Bridlington (1200 x 1213) see 3, no. 1344 (p. 63).

46 *RAC* 2, no. 697 (p. 34).

47 *Westminster Abbey Charters*, no. 185 (pp. 89–90). This crisis was the consequence of the vacancy at Westminster following the death of Abbot Walter in September 1190.

misdirecting these revenues or, at least, allegations of this nature were made. A particularly colourful, if partial example, is the rector of St Keverne's petition to the legate, Otto, in 1235 regarding the monks of Beaulieu Abbey. The rector vehemently objected to Beaulieu's request to appropriate his church of St Keverne in Cornwall to support the administration of hospitality at the abbey. He argued that the monks already received £1000 p. a. and required no extra rents, especially as they were in a desert place and supposedly had no need for visitors. He also claimed that the community hardly ever admitted a single guest and that these revenues were instead used for debauchery in the house.[48]

Restrictions: length of stay, number of retainers

His progresses were attended by a thousand horses and sometimes more; under the pretence of legation he extorted entertainment from all the monasteries throughout England; from small houses that could not support the burden of his entertainment he exacted a certain sum ... as for the larger ones, he preyed upon them like a locust.[49]

The expense of financing hospitality could be controlled by restricting how long guests might stay. The *Rule of St Benedict* states that stranger monks should be allowed to visit for as long as they wished, providing they adhered to the customs of the house.[50] Benedict does not, however, specify how long other guests might remain. The twelfth- and thirteenth-century sources are rather mixed. Chronicles often praise houses where guests might stay indefinitely and present this as a testimony to the community's success, but the customaries and statutes are more pragmatic and invariably set a fixed time

---

William de Longchamp, who took control attempted to have his candidate nominated but the monks of Westminster managed to oust him with John's support – and paid the price; this sum was to be paid off over seven years, Mason, *Westminster Abbey and its People*, pp. 66–7.

48   Cited in R. A. R. Hartridge, *A History of Vicarages in the Middle Ages* (Cambridge, 1930), p. 224.

49   William Longchamp, chancellor, legate and bishop of Ely, described by William of Newburgh, *Historia Rerum Anglicarum, Chronicles of the Reigns of Stephen, Henry II and Richard I*, ed. R. Howlett, 4 vols, RS 82 (London, 1882–89), 1, p. 334, trans. Stevenson, *History of William of Newburgh*, p. 578.

50   *Rule of St Benedict*, ch. 61 (p. 154). This is reiterated in the late-thirteenth-century Westminster customary where it is described as an 'ancient custom', *Westminster Customary*, p. 86 lines 24–8. It might, however, lead to problems and in 1218 the General Chapter of Cîteaux ruled that no Cistercian monk or lay-brother visiting London should stay more than three days at Stratford Langthorne; additional restrictions were issued the following year, Canivez, *Statutes* 1, 1218: 41, 1219: 11 (pp. 493, 505).

limit.[51] Guests visiting Abingdon were allowed accommodation for two nights and were to leave after they had eaten on the third.[52]

This seems to have been fairly standard although at nunneries such as Marrick Priory in Yorkshire, and probably also smaller houses where resources were limited, visits were often restricted to one night.[53] William of Malmesbury describes how a cripple seeking a cure at his abbey stayed at Malmesbury for four nights. Whilst William refers to the cripple as a guest ('hospes') he may have stayed in the town rather than at the abbey, or perhaps in the church where he kept vigil on his final night.[54] Interestingly, monasteries in Ireland seem to have extended hospitality for three days and nights, perhaps after the example of St Columba who instructed the monks of Iona to receive the crane that would shortly visit them and tend the bird as a guest for three days and three nights.[55] Most visitors who arrived at the monastery would have required accommodation simply for a night or two as a stopover on their journey, or to attend a feast or ceremony at the house.[56] But at times they may have needed to extend their visit on account of illness or adverse weather conditions. Such being the case, they were required to seek permission from the abbot or prior and might be liable for the additional costs. At Abingdon, the abbot, prior and curtar were all notified if any guest had to delay his departure. The visitor was administered to freely for the first day of his extended stay but was, it would seem, expected to reciprocate thereafter. There was a similar arrangement at the Cistercian abbey of Beaulieu, Hampshire, in the late thirteenth century where relatives visiting the community were liable for their expenses if they

[51] The foundation charters of Greek monasteries suggest that a three-night stay was generally permitted to convents and monasteries joined in a network, see K. N. Ciggar, *Western Travellers to Constantinople, the West and Byzantium, 962–1204* (Leiden, New York, 1996), pp. 41–2.

[52] *De Obedientiariis*, p. 413. For similar arrangements, see *Eynsham Customary*, ch. 19: 3 (511), p. 202 lines 1–5; the late-thirteenth-century account book of the Cistercian abbey of Beaulieu, *Account Book of Beaulieu*, p. 271. According to the fourteenth-century customary for the refectory of St Swithun's, Winchester, the monks' mothers, fathers, brothers or sisters who visited from afar should receive the same allowances of bread, beer and meat as the monks for three days and up to three times a year, *Consuetudinary of St Swithun*, ch. 21 (p. 24). For attempts to control the duration of relatives' visits at Cistercian houses, see Canivez, *Statutes* 1, 1210: 12 (p. 371).

[53] Tillotson, *Marrick Priory*, p. 20. There were similar arrangements in the Gilbertine houses, although patrons here were permitted to remain for three days, Golding, *Gilbert*, pp. 228, 320. Following his visitation of Nun Appleton, Yorkshire, in 1281 Archbishop Wickwane voiced his concern at the number of seculars visiting the house and the length of time they were staying, for while he did not object to the nuns offering 'decent hospitality' for a night or two, he feared that long visits might cripple the community financially and lead to scandal, Burton, *Yorkshire Nunneries*, p. 32.

[54] *Gesta Pontificum*, pp. 418–19.

[55] O'Sullivan, *Monastic Hospitality in Ireland*, pp. 143–4; pp. 212–13.

[56] For example, in 1189, John of Anagni stayed overnight with the monks of Christ Church on his return home, Diceto, *Opera Historica* 2, p. 72. The privileges allegedly accorded to Glastonbury by Ine, 725 AD, stipulated that the bishop should only stay one night at the abbey's manors of Pilton and Greinton unless detained by weather or sickness, *De Antiquitate*, pp. 98–102 (p. 100). The likelihood that this charter was a twelfth-century forgery makes it more and not less relevant.

exceeded the permitted allowance of two days, three or four times a year.[57] This would seem to suggest a more discerning attitude to monastic hospitality which was given freely but not indefinitely.

The monastery might host more long-term guests. The French cleric, Garnier, stayed with the monks of Christ Church, Canterbury for more than a year at their expense, to research his verse life of Thomas Becket.[58] By the later Middle Ages it was common for the Welsh bards to stay at the Cistercian abbeys. In return for this hospitality they might address poems of praise to their generous hosts. For example, Gutun Owain (fl. 1460–90), 'herald, bard and historian' addressed a verse to Abbot John ap Richard of Valle Crucis c. 1455.[59]

Patrons of the house were usually permitted a longer visit and might even claim unlimited hospitality. In the late twelfth century Bishop Hugh of Coventry maintained that as patron of Buildwas Abbey, which had been founded by his predecessors, he should be able to visit the community whenever he wished. In return for this unrestricted hospitality and as a friendly gesture he granted the monks a lodging in Lichfield.[60] Hugh of Lincoln stayed with the monks of Eynsham Abbey for eight days in 1196 after successfully reasserting his rights of patronage there. Hugh's biographer cites this as a testimony to the bishop's interest in and devotion to Eynsham, and maintains that the brethren were honoured that Hugh deigned to spend so much time with them.[61] Long-staying guests could, however, take their toll, and Matthew Paris complained that Henry III's three-week stay at Bury St Edmunds was a considerable burden to the house.[62] A number of charters and letters were issued reprimanding prelates whose visits were onerous and financially draining. In the late eleventh century Archbishop Lanfranc admonished Peter of Chester for staying with his retinue at Coventry for eight days and exhausting the monks' supplies.[63]

---

[57] *De Obedientiariis*, p. 413; Talbot, 'The account book of Beaulieu', p. 195.

[58] *Vie Saint Thomas*, lines 18–19; see also above, p. 169.

[59] L. S. Knight, 'Welsh monasteries and education', *Archaeologia Cambrensis* 20 (1920), pp. 257–75 (p. 269); he also stayed at Basingwerk and Strata Florida, and wrote over fifteen poems praising Cistercian abbots. David ab Owain, who presided over Strata Marcella, Strata Florida and Aberconwy (c. 1485–1513) attracted most attention and was mentioned by thirteen poets, Williams, *Welsh Cistercians*, p. 145.

[60] Dugdale, *Monasticon* 5, p. 359. See Wood, *English Monasteries*, p. 102. Buildwas was originally a Savignac foundation.

[61] *Magna Vita* 2, p. 42. Conversely, Adam presents Hugh's visit to the Cistercian house of Clairmarais as a testimony to Hugh's consideration since he was concerned not to burden the community and visited with only one monk and one lay-brother, and instructed the rest of his retinue to remain at their lodgings in the town with the horses, *Magna Vita* 2, p. 178.

[62] *Chronica Majora* 5, p. 304. Gransden, 'The abbey of Bury St Edmunds and national politics', pp. 85–6, explains that Matthew was exaggerating and Henry stayed for about two weeks; still this would have been a significant undertaking for the monastery.

[63] Lanfranc, *Letters*, ep. 27 (pp. 110–13). The letter is dated 29 August 1072 x 25 December 1085. Cheney, *Episcopal Visitation*, pp. 119–21, explains that while there was no fixed length of stay, and there was great variation regarding the frequency and duration of visitations, these usually lasted a night and a day.

As this particular visit marked the culmination of Peter's attempt to take over the property of Coventry it is hardly surprising that the monks complained of their guest to Lanfranc, but it is significant that the archbishop reproached Peter specifically for the length of his visit.[64]

The cost of entertaining a distinguished guest could be vast, especially if he or she arrived with a sizeable retinue. A key way to control expenses was to limit the number of horses and attendants permitted to visitors.[65] At the Third Lateran Council of 1179, Alexander III issued restrictions regarding the size of retinue each ecclesiastical office was allowed, for he was concerned that their visits were unduly taxing. Accordingly, archbishops were not to exceed forty or fifty horses, bishops were permitted twenty to thirty, cardinals twenty to twenty-five, archdeacons five to seven and deans two.[66] Alexander urged all dignitaries to exercise discretion and to travel with fewer horses if they were accustomed to do so, or if the place was poor. He also prohibited travelling with hounds or hawks and ruled that nobody should demand sumptuous entertainment but accept gratefully whatever his hosts could provide. Nevertheless problems continued and the statutes were reissued and reformulated. Hubert Walter, for example, reissued the dictates in 1200, and in 1225 the Benedictine Chapter General for the Canterbury Province stipulated that those on visitation should not exceed twelve horses; in 1277 it was agreed that if, out of necessity, this was exceeded, the visitor was liable for the extra.[67]

A colourful account of William de Longchamp's notorious journey around the religious houses in England in 1190, in his capacity as legate, suggests that he flagrantly disregarded the papal bull of 1179. William, who was also bishop of Ely and chancellor of England, reputedly moved like lightning through the kingdom, leaving the entire country in a state of distress.[68] Roger of Howden vividly describes the legate's entourage of men, horses, dogs and birds, and claims that any monastery where he stopped overnight was depleted of three years' savings.[69] According to William of Newburgh the legate and his train of 1000 horsemen preyed on larger houses 'like a locust' but offered smaller monastic communities, who could ill afford this hospitality, the chance to

---

[64] Gibson, *Lanfranc*, p. 147.
[65] See Snape, *Monastic Finances*, pp. 16–17, for Gregory IX's revision of the Cluniac Rule in 1238 imposing restrictions on the number of attendants.
[66] These restrictions are cited in Gervase, *Chronicle* 1, pp. 291–2; Howden, *Chronicle* 2, pp. 173–4; William of Newburgh, *Historia Rerum* 1, p. 216. In 1235, it was agreed that the bishop of Chichester and up to twenty-five horses might receive hospitality from Battle Abbey once every three years, Cheney, *Episcopal Visitation*, p. 42.
[67] Howden, *Chronicle* 4, pp. 130–1; Pantin, *Chapters* 1, pp. 20, 87, clause xxiv: 2. In 1253 Innocent IV stated that an abbot should travel with ten horses, Snape, *Monastic Finances*, p. 17. For an interesting Continental parallel see C. Potts, *Monastic Revival and Regional Identity in Early Normandy* (Woodbridge, 1997), p. 48: in return for his grant of lands in alms to St Étienne, Caen, Robert of Belfour received the society of the house and was permitted to stay there for one night, four times a year, so long as he did not come with a multitude of men.
[68] Devizes, *Chronicon*, p. 13.
[69] Howden, *Chronicle* 3, p. 72.

buy him off for five or eight marks.[70] Whilst few visitors would have been quite so taxing, the burdens of episcopal and legatine visitations remained a problem. In the early thirteenth century Thomas of Marlborough complained that bishops were wont to arrive with great retinues demanding refreshment for themselves and stabling for their horses. The community was often required to hand over revenues and gifts that it could ill afford, and, to make matters worse, might be visited as often as the bishop deemed necessary.[71] Matthew Paris complained that whilst abbots should provide spiritual sustenance for those whom they visited, they were generally more concerned with their own nourishment. He cites the example of a former abbot of the house, Abbot Simon (1166–83), who had exhausted the supplies at Tynemouth Priory to such an extent during his visitation that, out of sheer desperation, the monks presented him with their plough oxen and suggested he might like to eat them also.[72]

Exceptional events and visitors

Very large sums of money were gathered together for receiving all kinds of people, whereby the text was fulfilled, 'God will set aside a plentiful rain for his heirs' (Psalm 68:9) ... The consecration was performed most sumptuously and satisfied all their desires, nor did it contract any debts for the future.[73]

The cost of entertaining guests on ceremonial occasions hosted by the community was considerable and Gilbert Crispin marvelled that the monks of Bec incurred no debt for the future following their magnificent reception of visitors attending the consecration of the abbey in 1077.[74] Abbot Suger of St Denis estimated that c. 1000 *sous* was needed to buy sheep for the feast celebrating the consecration of the choir in 1144, but the recent sheep plague in the Parisis may mean this was an unusually high figure.[75] The entertainment of distinguished visitors could be equally oppressive and might leave the community saddled with debts. On his return to York in 1120 Archbishop Thurstan received an apology from the people of France that they had not previously received him with due honour. They explained that the expense of entertaining the pope had depleted their resources.[76]

---

70   William of Newburgh, *Historia Rerum* 1, p. 334.
71   Thomas Marlborough, *History of Evesham*, pp. 258–9 (ch. 255). Significantly, William of Malmesbury commended Ralph of Séez who, unlike other Norman prelates, was careful not to burden houses with persistent requests, *Gesta Pontificum*, p. 127.
72   GASA 1, pp. 264–5; Vaughan, *Chronicles of Matthew Paris*, pp. 41–2.
73   Sally Vaughn's translation of ch. 106 of the *Vita Herluini* in her *Abbey of Bec*, p. 83.
74   Vaughn, *Vita Herluini*, ch. 106 (p. 83).
75   *Oeuvres Complètes*, p. 231. Luckily for St Denis the Cistercians spared them the cost of the sheep, see L. Grant, *Abbot Suger of St Denis: church and state in early twelfth-century France* (London, 1998), p. 217.
76   *Chantor*, p. 91. Indeed, when Innocent II visited the Cistercian house of Fossanova, France, in 1108, he had an entourage of two hundred men, Williams, *Cistercians in the*

The cost of hosting celebrations and entertaining dignitaries was not necessarily borne by the community. The monastery might receive outside help and in 1164 Henry II provided for the monks of Reading and their guests who attended the dedication of St Mary's. The lavish hospitality enjoyed by everyone present at the dedication of Ely on 17 September, 1252 was financed by the bishop.[77] The accounts for the treasurer of Christ Church, Canterbury show that the community bore some of the costs for the banquet celebrating Thomas Becket's translation in 1220, but most of the expenses would have been met by the archbishop and indeed the feast was held in his palace.[78] Outside help was probably more forthcoming for coronations, crown wearings and other events when the monastery was essentially used as a venue. Archbishop Hubert Walter financed the coronation of John and Isabella.[79] As we noted earlier, the food and drink for Richard I's second coronation at St Swithun's, Winchester in 1194 may have been provided by the citizens of London and Winchester, who served from the butlery and kitchen respectively.[80] Official meetings and general chapters could be equally expensive and restrictions were issued to reduce costs. The Fourth Lateran Council of 1215 limited the number of horses permitted to those attending the provincial chapters of the Benedictine order to six mounts and eight persons. To reduce expenses further visiting prelates were enjoined to lead the common life and share the costs.[81] It was particularly important for the Cistercians to enforce restrictions on abbots attending the General Chapter at Cîteaux since all abbots were expected to be present. It has been estimated that by the late twelfth century there would have been about three hundred abbots arriving at the mother-house; as each was permitted to bring one companion, numbers would have risen to about five hundred.[82] Cîteaux would have been stretched to its limits at this time and, not surprisingly, no other travellers were to be entertained while the assembly was gathered.[83] The Cistercians also received

Early Middle Ages, p. 127. For the magnificence of Innocent II's reception at Cluny in 1130, see *Orderic* 6, pp. 418–21.

[77] Torigni, *Chronicle*, p. 221; *Chronica Majora* 4, p. 322; for J. A. Giles's translation see *Matthew Paris's English History, 1225–1273*, 3 vols (London, 1852–54), 2, pp. 515–18.

[78] R. Eales, 'The political setting of the Becket translation of 1220', *Martyrs and Martyrologies*, ed. D. Webb, *Studies in Church History* 30 (Oxford, 1993), pp. 127–39 (p. 138).

[79] Gervase, *Chronicle* 2, p. 410. For an indication of the expense of coronations, see J. W. F. Hill, *Medieval Lincoln* (Northampton, 1948), p. 182, who discusses Henry II's second coronation at Lincoln, and Eales, 'Political setting', p. 135, for Henry III's second coronation at Westminster Abbey, 17 May, 1220.

[80] Howden, *Chronicle* 3, p. 248; above, pp. 123–4. For the honour to be accrued from such privileges, see Richardson, 'Coronation', p. 131, and P. E. A. Schramm, *History of the English Coronation*, trans. L. G. Wickham Legg (Oxford, 1937), pp. 62–4.

[81] *Decrees of the Ecumenical Councils*, ed. N. P. Tanner, 2 vols (London and Washington, 1990), 1, pp. 240–1 (clause 12).

[82] Clause 44, 'Institutes of the General Chapter', *NLT*, pp. 475–6; Waddell, *Twelfth-Century Statutes*, pp. 290–1. T. Coomans, 'L'accueil du chapitre général au Moyen Age', *Pour une histoire monumentale de l'abbaye de Cîteaux 1098–1998* (Brecht, 1998), pp. 154–64, considers the difficulties of providing hospitality during the General Chapter.

[83] Waddell, *Twelfth-Century Statutes* 1188: 1 (p. 147).

external help to cope with financing the General Chapter. An interesting example is Richard I's grant to Cîteaux of the church of Scarborough at the time of the General Chapter to help sustain the visiting abbots gathered for the three-day event.[84]

The entertainment of visiting dignitaries could be equally onerous and might merit external assistance. When the papal legate, John of Anagni, visited Canterbury in 1189 he was solemnly received by the bishops and the community of Christ Church in the monks' court and entertained at the archbishop's expense.[85] However, the financial assistance that Bury St Edmunds received from King John in 1213 when the legate, Nicholas of Tusculum, spent Christmas at the abbey is probably associated with the vacancy here. The *Election of Abbot Hugh* describes how the prior and sacrist of Bury had been travelling to London to pay their dues to the king when they learned of Nicholas's imminent arrival. They returned quickly to prepare for his visit, bringing with them the money owing to the king which was presumably used to defray the cost of entertaining the legate.[86]

Guests might themselves subsidise their visit. Peter of Blois' letter complaining of the poor reception he had received at Wallingford Priory reveals that his servants were sent ahead of him to prepare for his arrival and brought with them various necessities; presumably this included food, drink, wax and perhaps fodder.[87] King John sent three hogsheads of wine to Abingdon Abbey to prepare for his arrival on 15 July 1215, and in 1241 Henry III sent ahead wine from Bristol to supply the royal party during his stay at Malmesbury Abbey.[88] Henry instructed his local sheriffs to provide wax for a large number of tapers in preparation for his stay at Bury St Edmunds

---

[84] *EYC* 1, no. 365 (pp. 286–7). Farrer remarks on the timing of this gift, which was given a few weeks before Richard's coronation. For a detailed discussion, see C. H. Talbot, 'Cîteaux and Scarborough', *Studia Monastica* 2 (1960), pp. 95–158.

[85] Gervase, *Chronicle* 1, p. 482. The legate was initially prohibited from visiting Canterbury and upon his arrival at Dover stayed for thirteen days at the archbishop's expense, Diceto, *Opera Historica* 2, p. 72. Continental examples *Orderic* 6, pp. 42–3, and *Vie de Saint Thomas*, lines 2636–7, 3786–8.

[86] *Election of Abbot Hugh*, p. 26. *Bury Customary*, p. xvi. This refers to the 400 marks that the convent agreed to pay John in 1211, in return for control of the abbatial and conventual resources during the vacancy; this sum was to be paid over the course of the year but had still not been paid by May 1214 when John himself assumed control of both portions and granted the convent basic subsistence, Gransden, 'Separation of revenues', p. 375. See above, p. 133, for the archbishop of Trondheim's accommodation in the abbot of Bury's houses during the vacancy of 1180–82; on the king's orders he received ten shillings daily from the abbatial revenues, a total of £94 10s. Interestingly, the *History of Abingdon* 2, pp. 16–19, complains that when Prince Henry stayed at Abingdon at Easter 1084, during the vacancy, Robert d'Oilly supplied the household from the monastery's resources and not just the royal revenues.

[87] Peter of Blois, *Epistolae*, ep. 29; see above, p. 107. Geoffrey of La Trinité–Vendôme's complaint of his poor reception at Pin Priory reveals that he had his own supplies of bread and wine but not of provender for the horses, *Goffridi, Abbatis Vindocinensis, Opera Omnia, PL* 157. 151–2.

[88] Cox, *The Story of Abingdon*, pt II, p. 17; *Calendar of Liberate Rolls Preserved in the Public Record Office* (London, 1916–), 2, *Henry III, 1240–45*, p. 65.

and St Albans Lent 1242.[89] While the arrival of distinguished guests and the staging of prestigious events could be lucrative, the higher income would have been largely balanced by the greater outlay on these occasions.[90] Nevertheless, in return for its generosity the community might secure a grant, a concession or goodwill. Following his three-day stay at Abingdon in 1234 Henry III ordered that four oaks should be taken from the royal forest of Brill, Bucks., for the monks to construct a huge cross at the abbey. After his visit to Bury in 1251 he sent oaks to the sacrist to repair the belfry at the abbey.[91] Lanfranc, archbishop of Canterbury, was extremely generous to his former house of Bec, and when he visited the community in 1077 to consecrate the new abbey church, contributed extensively to the hospitality of the house.[92]

The cost

The sources show that hospitality was an integral part of monastic life and the abbey's economy, and had therefore to be adequately provided for; revenues were thus set aside and extra help harnessed when needed. It is, however, difficult if not impossible, to calculate just how much the community spent on hospitality or what percentage of the monastery's revenues this represented for as noted earlier most household accounts date from the late thirteenth century.[93] The late-twelfth-century receipts for the Abingdon hosteller are limited in what they reveal. They are simply concerned with the purchase of horseshoes for monks, pilgrims and the poor, and make no mention of utensils and fuel for the guesthouse or food for visitors, which were presumably supplied by other obedientiaries.[94] Henry de Sully's inquisition of Glastonbury's manors in 1189 is more revealing and shows that the hosteller received one mark for the guesthouse from the church of Winfrod. Five shillings of this went on his servant's wages, leaving about eight shillings for the guesthouse.[95] Still it is

89   *Calendar of Liberate Rolls 2, Henry III, 1240–45*, pp. 114, 115.
90   See Woodruff, 'Financial aspect', p. 16, for the high takings at Becket's shrine in the year of John's coronation at Canterbury.
91   Cox, *The Story of Abingdon*, pt II, pp. 22, 252; *Close Rolls Henry III 1247–1251*, 1251 (p. 423), cited in A. Gransden, 'The abbey of Bury St Edmunds and national politics in the reigns of King John and Henry III', *Monastic Studies 2*, ed. Loades, pp. 67–86 (p. 85). Following his stay at Abingdon in 1290, Edward I granted the monks permission to hold an eight-day fair in June, Cox, *The Story of Abingdon*, pt II, p. 44. For Edward II's gifts to Battle see, Blaauw, 'Visit of Edward II', p. 44.
92   Ch. 8 *Vita Lanfranci*, ed. M. Gibson, *Lanfranco di Pavia e l'Europe del secolo xinel lx centenario della morte* (1089–1989), Pavia 21–24 September, 1989, ed. G. D'Onofrio (Rome, 1993), pp. 659–718 (p. 691); see also *PL* 150. 45.
93   For example, the late-thirteenth-century Durham accounts reveal that the guestmaster received £272 2s 2d p.a. although only c. £250 was allocated for running the guesthouse for the hosteller bought his own clothing and supplied pittances for the monks, Moorman, *Church Life*, pp. 281–2.
94   'Rents of the hosteller', *Chronicon de Abingdon 2*, pp. 329–32.
95   *Inquisition of Glastonbury*, p. 8.

unlikely that this sum represents the complete expenditure on guests for, as mentioned in previous chapters, the hosteller often received supplies of food, ale, candles and necessities from other obedientiaries; moreover, the hosteller's guests represented only a percentage of all the monastery's visitors, since the abbot and perhaps also the almoner of the house were responsible for certain guests.

Records of appropriations granted to sustain hospitality – or promised, for they may never have been received – are similarly incomplete.[96] Whilst these indicate that hospitality was an important part of the monastery's outlay, they represent only a part of the revenue set aside for the care of guests. An agreement between the abbot and convent of Westminster in 1225 granted the church of Staines and half the church of Wheathampstead with everything pertaining to them, a rent of ten pounds from Ockendon, eight pounds from Westminster and half the herbage of Westminster to sustain guests staying at the house when the king was at Westminster; presumably these men were stationed at the abbey when the royal court was at the palace.[97] Hugh of Reading's notification of the foundation of the hospice at the gate of the abbey (1189 x 93) records that it was to receive the fulling mill of Leominster and the chapel of Gilbert Martel to provide for 'passing guests' who could not be received in the 'upper house', but Hugh does not specify how much this amounted to.[98] Similarly the bishop of Exeter's grant to St Nicholas' Priory, Exeter to appropriate the church of Pinhoe and all pertaining to it, simply records that this was for the hospitality of the house with no indication of the sum involved.[99] Moreover hospitality was sometimes only one of several uses to which the appropriation was made. In 1166 x 79 Alexander III agreed that the abbot and monks of Reading might increase the pensions of the churches assigned to them for guests, the poor and other such uses. Bishop Hugh of Coventry (February 1188 x March 1198) conceded that upon the deaths of the present incumbents the profits of the church of Baschurch should be used to support guests, pilgrims and the poor at Shrewsbury Abbey; the monks were always to provide a suitable parson and to supply him with an appropriate endowment to carry out his duties.[100]

---

[96]   Note Harvey's discussion of the problems the abbot of Westminster incurred when securing tithes from the abbey's churches, to support the poor and guests, *Westminster Abbey and its Estates*, pp. 48–52. In appendix 3 Harvey lists all the churches appropriated by Westminster, and the delays and problems involved to secure them, pp. 402–12.

[97]   *Walter de Wenlok*, p. 218. Harvey explains that Bishop Hugh of Lincoln, probably Hugh of Grenoble (1186–1200), granted the abbot and convent a pension of thirty marks from the churches of Oakham and Hambleton for entertaining guests; in the early thirteenth century, twenty-one marks of this was assigned to the infirmarer, p. 218 n. 1.

[98]   *RAC* 1, no. 224 (pp. 185–6).

[99]   November 1193 x March 1194, *English Episcopal Acta* 3, no. 458 (pp. 118–19).

[100]   *RAC* 1, no. 150 (p. 133); *Cartulary of Shrewsbury Abbey* 1, no. 71 (pp. 70–1). Additional examples include *The Cartulary of Worcester Cathedral Priory*, ed. R. R. Darlington, PRS, new ser. 38 (London, 1968), nos 332 and 391; *The Charters of Norwich Cathedral Priory*, ed. B. Dodwell, 2 vols, PRS, new ser. 40, 46 (London, 1974–85), 1, no. 154. For Welsh examples, see Cowley, *Monastic Order*, p. 175.

Whilst grants and appropriations made to support hospitality do not enable us to calculate the actual cost of entertaining guests, it is possible to estimate the proportion of the monastery's revenue spent on guests from the Pipe Rolls, which record the income received by the king during vacancies. The entry for Westminster Abbey in 1174–75 reveals that the receipts from the abbey's farms in Essex and Hertfordshire totalled £408 15s 4d, and that £18 12s 4d of this sum was assigned to sustain guests and servants of the court and to repair the buildings in the court.[101] Of the revenues going to the exchequer from Abingdon in 1184–85, £10 12s 9d was set aside to provide 'relish' (*companagium*) for the guests and servants of the court, and for wages for the latter. Part of this text is missing and it is therefore impossible to calculate the total income for this year.[102] In 1186–87 the total income from Glastonbury's farms and rents was £233 11s 2d and of this £22 9s 7d was assigned to support servants, guests and custodians for nineteen weeks. This may have been particularly generous since the earl of Cornwall's son, William, was staying at the abbey.[103] The Pipe Roll of 1207 records that when the papal legate, John de Ferentino, visited England in 1206 Ramsey Abbey spent forty shillings on his lodging. It is not clear if this was the cost of entertaining the legate at the abbey or the sum paid in *lieu* of hospitality rendered.[104] Forty shillings seems to have been an accepted figure and appears in a number of fixed payments.[105]

The care of guests' horses could be considerable. The Pipe Rolls give an indication of the cost of maintaining horses and custodians, although the sum charged does not necessarily represent the cost involved. Thus, neither the 55s 7d assigned from Ramsey Abbey in 1211 to support fifteen of the king's horses and custodians for half a year nor the £4 9s 5d allocated from Peterborough's revenues in 1211 to provide for fourteen of the king's horses and custodians, included the purchase of hay and oats.[106] The accounts for Westminster Abbey in 1174–75 record that £4 13s 9d was assigned to provide fodder, hay and herbage for the king's horses and also for Philip, the custodian, and the abbot's horses and keepers, but give no indication of the number of

---

[101] PR, 21, H.II, PRS, old ser. 22, pp. 79–80. From these figures Harvey calculates that the total rents from the Essex and Hertfordshire lands may have been c. £218 p.a., and that if these lands constituted c. 29.5 per cent of the abbey's net income, the abbey's total income would have been c. £739. But Harvey underlines that these figures are probably rather 'generous' and that we should regard this as a maximum, Harvey, *Westminster Abbey*, pp. 56–7.

[102] PR, 31, H.II, PRS, old ser. 34, p. 29. 'Companagium' – this was something given to accompany the bread, see *Mediaeval Latin Dictionary*, p. 402.

[103] PR, 33, H.II, PRS, old ser. 37, pp. 27–8.

[104] PR, 9, John, PRS, new ser. 22, p. 111.

[105] For example, *English Episcopal Acta 6*, no. 164 (p. 128); *Westminster Abbey Charters* no 324 (pp. 172–3). For discussion of procurations, see W. E. Lunt, *Financial Relations of the Papacy with England to 1327*, 2 vols (Cambridge, MA, 1939–62), 1, pp. 532–40; G. V. Scammell, *Hugh du Puiset, Bishop of Durham* (Cambridge, 1956), p. 197; Cheney, *Episcopal Visitation*, pp. 104 ff.

[106] PR, 13, John, PRS, new ser. 28, pp. 269–71 (p. 270); PR 13 John, pp. 271–2 (p. 272).

horses involved.[107] Provender for guests' horses was not necessarily given freely and, as noted in chapter 4, visitors to Cluny were to pay the procurator for supplies of oats.

Times of hardship

> I have been to several places that had been seized by the king – no guest or poor people were made welcome there. I myself was turned away from the door by the porter – from what he said I gathered that charity was not at home. The king took away everything except the barest necessities. Monk, cook, servant, squire and serving lad, they all received their exact ration of bread, for the king's servants were in the house. And they, when they left, caused such destruction that you would not have been able to find any provisions, no, not the least little capon.[108]

Hospitality could be onerous and for this reason might be legitimately abandoned or reduced in times of hardship and political upheaval.[109] When Walter de Lucy succeeded to the abbacy of Battle in 1139 the country was in a state of anarchy and, faced with a shortage of resources, Walter was unable to devote anything to the hospitality of the house. Once peace had been restored under Henry II, Walter recovered the abbey's goods and was able to revive 'the old and proper customs',

> so that to everyone who knocked the door was opened and no one requesting the gift of hospitality was refused; everyone had good manners shown to him according to his rank or station.[110]

Gervase of Canterbury describes how the monks of Christ Church suffered under the tyranny of Archbishop Theobald in the mid-twelfth century and were half-starved; charity and hospitality ceased with guests now excluded from the court and the poor driven out. There were similar scenes during Baldwin's archiepiscopate at the end of the century and also at Evesham, under the tyranny of Abbot Norreys (1190–1213).[111]

Whilst hospitality might justifiably be curtailed or withheld in difficult times, those who managed to sustain guests when faced with hardship were celebrated for their achievement. Abbot Martin of Peterborough (1125–55) is commended by the chronicler of the house, for he held his abbacy 'with great labour' during the troubles of Stephen's reign, yet found everything necessary

---

[107] PR, 21, H. II, PRS, old ser. 22, p. 80.
[108] *Vie de Sainte Thomas*, pp. 66–7.
[109] From 1218 Cistercian abbots conducting visitation were permitted to send guests away, if they felt the house was overly oppressed, Canivez, *Statutes* 1, 1218: 83 (p. 502). For further discussion see Kerr, 'Cistercian hospitality', forthcoming.
[110] *Battle Chronicle*, pp. 260–1; see also above, p. 39.
[111] E.g. Gervase, *Chronicle* 1, pp. 53–4, 332, 394–5, 400. Garnier refers to this also in his *Vie Saint Thomas*, lines 2486–505.

for the brethren and guests.[112] Matthew Paris praises Abbot John of Hertford (1235–55) who faced 'the worst possible persecutions, losses and insults' yet managed to maintain the customary standards of generosity and hospitality, both internally and externally.[113] Abbot John of Fountains (c. 1205–9) was similarly lauded for, in spite of King John's persecution of the Cistercian Order, he refreshed the poor, received guests and sustained the whole house.[114]

Conclusion

The late-twelfth- and early-thirteenth-century sources considered in this chapter show evidence of a more discerning attitude to hospitality at this time. While the idea of hospitality freely given was still promoted – the twelfth-century accounts of Earl Brihtnoth's experiences at Ramsey and Ely, discussed earlier, stress Abbot Wulfsey's reluctance to receive the earl and all his men with Ely's willingness to entertain the entire troop – restrictions were imposed to reduce the potential cost of hospitality and its burden on the monastery's resources.[115] Guests were often limited as to how long they might stay at the community's expense and should they receive permission to postpone their departure would likely be liable for the additional costs.[116] It may previously have been expected that the monastery would shoulder the household expenses of most if not all visitors who stayed within the precinct and in the vill but now, it would seem, only a few were provided for in full and most received gifts of provisions to subsidise rather than cover their expenses. This can perhaps be seen as a prelude to the later tendency to discriminate between the lord and his household and provide only for the former.[117] These conclusions would seem to concur with Barbara Harvey's suggestion that by the late twelfth century monastic hospitality was more discriminating and that lords accordingly, found travel increasingly difficult. She argues that by the late thirteenth century aristocratic guests were effectively 'paying guests', and that the 1275 Statute of Westminster prohibiting all save the patron from demanding hospitality at the monastery's cost was probably a formal recognition of earlier practice.[118] While the aristocratic guest of the late twelfth century was not, perhaps, a 'paying guest' and the idea of open

---

[112] *Candidus*, p. 105. Hugh later adds that Martin provided in abundance for the monks and guests, p. 122.

[113] GASA 1, p. 320 translated by Vaughan, *Chronicles of Matthew Paris*, p. 77.

[114] *Memorials of Fountains* 1, p. 127.

[115] See above, pp. 44–5.

[116] Similar arrangements were negotiated between lords and their tenants to ensure the lord received his due but the tenant was not exploited. A well known example is the agreement between Ivo of Deene and the abbot of Westminster in 1215, F. M. Stenton, *The First Century of English Feudalism, 1066–1166*, 2nd edn (Oxford, 1961), pp. 267–9. For further discussion see Kerr, 'Food, drink and lodging', forthcoming.

[117] Harvey, 'The aristocratic consumer', p. 24 and Woolgar, *Great Household*, p. 21 who notes similar developments in lay households.

[118] Harvey, 'The aristocratic consumer', pp. 23–4.

hospitality remained important, there was clearly a conscious effort at this time to control the expense of hospitality or, at least, to consign these restrictions to writing. Few would have now expected to receive unlimited hospitality and might be liable for some of their own expenses.

Hospitality was integral to monastic life and was not to be neglected without good reason. Nor was it to be excessive, lest this overstretched the community. Prudent administration was recommended and the monks were to entertain visitors according to their resources. This is explicit in a number of statutes, notably those issued by the Benedictine province of Canterbury in 1219 which stipulated that monks should welcome everyone who visited them with charity and joy, and receive all visitors warmly, in accordance with the regulations and also the ability of the house.[119] It was clearly vital to combine the spirit of generosity with sensible management.

---

[119]   Pantin, *Chapters* 1, 1219: 10 (p. 10). Additional examples include, York 1221: 13 (p. 234); Canterbury 1249: 14 (p. 39). Cistercian abbots were similarly urged to exercise prudence, Waddell, *Twelfth-Century Statutes*, 1196: 53 (p. 370).

Conclusion

In 1224, shortly after the first Franciscans arrived in England, two of the four friars who had travelled from Canterbury to London progressed to Oxford. They were Brothers Richard of Ingworth and Richard of Devon, and their journey was made at the end of October.[1] They are probably the friars referred to in the late fourteenth century by Bartholomew of Pisa in his account of how the Franciscans earned respect in England and, more specifically, amongst the monks of Abingdon who had shown them an inhospitable welcome on their journey to Oxford.[2] Bartholomew describes how the two Franciscans took a wrong turn on their way to Oxford. Night was falling and the weather inclement – heavy rains had caused the rivers to overflow. Lest they perished from cold, hunger or the wild beasts that lurked in the forest, the men decided to seek shelter at a nearby manor belonging to Benedictine monks. This was about six miles from Oxford and is thought to have been Abingdon's grange of Culham or perhaps even Great Milton.[3] Upon their arrival the friars gently knocked at the gate and for the love of God humbly requested the porter for lodging. From their dishevelled appearance and foreign accents the monks assumed that their visitors were entertainers; anticipating a lively evening ahead they welcomed their arrival. The monks soon realised their mistake and that these rather earnest guests would scarcely contribute to an evening of jollity. Accordingly, they turned the friars out to brave the elements. One of the young monks however was moved by pity. He persuaded the porter to let the strangers in, refreshed them charitably, sheltered them in the hay-loft and recommended himself to their prayers before returning to his own lodgings. That night the young monk had a dream in which Christ appeared sitting on a tribunal to pass judgement on the prior and his three companions who

---

[1] The other two friars were Brothers Henry and Melioratus, E. Hutton, *The Franciscans in England, 1224–1538* (London, 1926), p. 37. Little notes that Bartholomew inaccurately mentions that four friars made the journey, A. G. Little, *The Grey Friars in Oxford*, Oxford Historical Society 20 (Oxford, 1892), p. 2, n. 1.

[2] E. Hutton, *The Franciscans in England, 1224–1538* (London, 1926), pp. 37–40. For Anthony Wood's account in his 'Survey of the Antiquities of the City of Oxford', see Dugdale, *Monasticon* 6: 3, p. 1524. While Wood's version is derived from Bartholomew it differs in places; for example, he maintains that when the young monk awoke from his dream he found his companions dead, see Little, *The Grey Friars*, p. 2.

[3] Culham was about a mile from Abingdon.

had so heartlessly turned the friars away. The offenders were brought before a friar who asked Christ that he be avenged,

> Remember, O Lord, that these persons have refused the common reliefs of life and Thy servants, who have abandoned all worldly pleasures to gain souls for whom Thou hast suffered death; relief which they would have bestowed upon buffoons.[4]

Christ asked the prior to what order he belonged and was told the order of St Benedict, and verified this with the saint, who happened to be seated beside him. But Benedict declared these monks were over-throwers of his order for he had commanded that in all of his houses the doors should be ever open to strangers. Sentence was duly passed and in the dream it seemed that all three offenders – the prior, sacrist and dispenser – were hanged on a neighbouring elm tree. Christ then turned to the young monk and posed the same question. Fearing that a similar fate might befall him the monk answered that he belonged to the order of St Francis. Francis, who was also present, confirmed this and ran to embrace the monk as one of his own. When the young Benedictine awoke from his dream he rushed to check the condition of his companions. They were alive but seemed to have suffered in their sleep and were extremely afraid when they heard the substance of their companion's dream. Bartholomew explains that when news of this spread it earned respect for the Franciscans throughout the country and particularly at Abingdon. Indeed, the young monk who had helped the friar was said to have later joined the Franciscans at Oxford.

Whatever element of truth there is to this story it would have highlighted to contemporaries the importance of extending a warm welcome to strangers. Regardless of what restrictions were imposed to reduce the potential burden of hospitality it was clearly important to receive guests kindly. Not least the account shows how hospitality functioned beyond the monastery precinct and the vill, for monks might entertain visitors on their manors and granges and at their urban properties. Later evidence suggests that communities might operate rather like a medieval service station in providing supplies for travellers to purchase on their journey.[5] This is an area that merits further exploration for the light it may shed on the true extent of the monastery's role in the community and more generally on the nature of travel.

---

4   Hutton, *The Franciscans in England, 1224–1538*, p. 39.
5   For example, James I granted the Cistercian monks of Kinloss the right to bake bread in an old brewery that stood on their lands and to cook flesh and fish when required, that they might sell this to travellers and others, *Records of the Monastery of Kinloss*, ed. J. Stuart (Edinburgh, 1872), p. xxxviii.

The impact of monastic hospitality

No traveller left without a night's lodging, meat, drink and money; he was not asked from where he came or to where he would go. Thus, they fed the hungry and gave drink to the thirsty, clothed those who needed clothing, and comforted the sick, sore and lame, and helped strangers to lodging within their gates.[6]

At the time of the Dissolution of the religious houses tribute was paid to their remarkable contribution to hospitality and cited in their defence against closure. Robert Aske, a leading figure in the Pilgrimage of Grace who argued for the continuance of the monasteries, maintained that hospitality had disappeared with their closure, since the monks alone could afford shelter and refuge to pilgrims, corn dealers and travellers in the remote and barren parts of the North.[7] A wide range of visitors benefited from the monks' services which might include spiritual care, guidance and medical provision, as well as food and lodging. Moreover, the administration of hospitality itself offered a forum for cultural exchange where information and ideas might be shared and texts disseminated. It might even lead to the foundation of a new house if guests were suitably impressed during their stay. It was alleged that when Bishop Sigurd of the ancient see of Bergen visited the Cistercian abbey of Fountains during Henry Murdac's abbacy (1144–53), he was so struck with the way of life there that he urged the abbot to send a colony of his monks to Norway. As a consequence in 1146 a group of Fountains' monks established a community at Lyse.[8]

Although monks had retreated from the world they clearly did not live in a vacuum; they were influenced by developments beyond the monastery and shared some of the concerns of their neighbours. Analysis has shown that monastic hospitality was driven by ideals that were integral to the Benedictine Order and the Christian way of life. Nevertheless, social, political and economic developments might have a considerable impact on how hospitality was perceived and administered in the monasteries. It was likely to be curtailed in times of famine and warfare, and as noted earlier twelfth-century ideas on humanism may have increased the importance of showing guests courtesy and

---

[6]   BL, Add. MS 5813, fol. 5, p. 1. For a transcription, see Michael Sherbrook, 'The fall of the religious houses', p. 94. Sherbrook was rector of Wickersley, some five miles west of the Cistercian abbey of Roche. His father and uncle both witnessed the spoliation of the abbey in 1538, which is described pp. 123–6. Sherbrook completed his account in the 1590s, but may actually have begun writing c. 1567.

[7]   A. Savine, *English Monasteries on the Eve of the Dissolution* (London, 1909), p. 241. See also R. W. Dunning, 'The last days of Cleeve Abbey', *The Church in Pre-Reformation Society: essays in honour of F. R. H. Du Boulay* (Woodbridge, 1985), pp. 58–67 (p. 59) and Kerr, 'Cistercian hospitality', forthcoming.

[8]   'Narratio de fundatione Fontanis monasterii', pp. 89–90, translated A. W. Oxford, *The Ruins of Fountains Abbey* (London, 1910), appendix 1, pp. 127–230. A similar situation led to the foundation of St Pancras at Lewes in 1077 following William of Warenne's visit to Cluny in 1075, R. Graham, 'Life at Cluny in the eleventh century', in her *English Ecclesiastical Studies*, p. 40.

extending a personal welcome. It is perhaps significant that a late twelfth-century depiction of St Cuthbert's reception at Old Melrose shows Abbot Boisil warmly embracing his visitor (above, p. 101), whereas an earlier illustration is less intimate, showing Cuthbert dismounting while the abbot looks on from a distance.[9] Whilst urban growth would have increased the number of people visiting towns and requiring accommodation, the monasteries here may have been less burdened than those in a remote location where there were few other options available to travellers. It is difficult to know precisely what provision there was at this time in the towns, but there is evidence for visitors staying with locals or in hospices, or in their own townhouses, particularly in London and Winchester where the court gathered, and where markets were held. Moreover, there are indications that monasteries in urban settings may now have been more discerning, for example, refusing hospitality to anyone travelling to the markets or the courts.[10]

The arrival of the new religious orders brought competition for patronage which perhaps encouraged the Benedictines to exercise greater discrimination in the twelfth century, preferring those who would in turn support them. Men and women may accordingly have been compelled to offer patronage in the hope of securing a special welcome from their community. Unfortunately there is little explicit evidence to strengthen this hypothesis, but further research on the smaller houses may in future shed greater light on this. Significantly, the arrival of the new orders introduced a new category of guest which might affect how visiting religious were now distinguished and provided for within the precinct. Thus, as noted in chapter 2, Benedictine guests might be entertained apart from visiting Cistercians and other religious, and a hospice might be established specifically for mendicant visitors. Another significant, albeit slightly later, development is the emergence of the universities. Houses such as Abingdon and Eynsham which lay on the main route to Oxford or Cambridge were likely popular stopping-off points for students travelling to their place of learning, especially monk scholars; later sources suggest that they might receive a gift of money from the host community.[11]

The twelfth century marks a significant stage in the development of monastic hospitality. While current ideas on courtesy and etiquette may have heightened the importance of welcoming guests warmly, concerns about the cost of hospitality and fear for the monastery's resources meant that few were able to offer unlimited hospitality. Restrictions were imposed and consigned to writing, and open hospitality probably referred more to the spirit in which

---

9   BL Yates Thompson MS 26, fol. 16 (c. 1180s) and Oxford University College MS 165, p. 23. For the dating of these two manuscripts and comparison of the scenes, see Marner, St *Cuthbert*, pp. 39, 41; he suggests that the importance of friendship at this time may explain the difference, p. 44.

10   See above, p. 149, for the practice at Cluny.

11   See, for example, Kirk, *Accounts of Obedientiaries of Abingdon*, p. 92. Eynsham Abbey was evidently a popular and appropriate stopping-off point for students travelling to the university at Oxford. In 1331 Edward III petitioned the pope (John XXII) on Eynsham's behalf, that the community might appropriate the church of Tetbury to help support the hospitality of the house, *White Book of Worcester*, no. 1240 (p. 267).

guests were received than the terms on which they might stay. Later, it seems, greater limitations were imposed leading to the injunction of 1275 formally prohibiting all, save the patron, from demanding hospitality at the monastery's expense. The twelfth century is also an interesting time in England for the development of prescriptive sources, particularly, the customaries which date from this time and are indicative of a growing concern to write down and codify past and existing practice. They reveal the discussion and debate that this often incited, and the tensions that might exist within the monastic community, especially between the abbot and convent, over the administration of hospitality.

The analysis of Benedictine hospitality can reveal much about the organisation of the monastery. It underlines the complexity and also the fluidity of arrangements, which were discussed and adapted to suit the changing needs of the community and to meet the expectations of outsiders. It also sheds light on a number of related topics such as patronage, pilgrimage, charity and fraternity, and the nature of social ties that functioned at the time. Monastic hospitality was clearly a significant part of medieval life which benefited the monks and their neighbours. It was intrinsic to the order and as such was an important step in the monks' journey to salvation. Yet it also provided a way for individual communities, and the order at large, to survive in a changing world. It gave the monks a role in society that was recognised and valued by their contemporaries, who might subsequently be drawn to take the monastic habit or found a new house, or perhaps to support a particular community as a patron. Through exercising hospitality and adhering to the ideals of the order, the monks might preserve the past in the present and build for the future. There were of course potential problems and the entertainment of guests could be disruptive and financially damaging. However, properly managed, hospitality could provide a way for monks to keep the Benedictine spirit alive while responding to the new challenges and demands of contemporary society.

Appendix 1

Jocelin of Brakelond, monk of Bury St Edmunds

The identity of Jocelin of Brakelond, a monk of Bury St Edmunds who compiled a chronicle of the house, has fuelled debate over the years. It has been argued that he should in fact, be equated with Jocellus, the cellarer, whom he mentions in his chronicle. This was the opinion of R. H. C. Davis who in 1954 maintained that charters witnessed by 'Jocelin the cellarer' in 1198 and 1200/1 reveal that Jocelin of Brakelond was actually Jocellus the cellarer, whose sense of humility and modesty caused him to assume this pseudonym.[1] For Davis this explained Jocelin's extensive knowledge of the cellarer's affairs and his concern to vindicate the office. Davis' interpretation has been accepted by Scarfe and Thomson,[2] and Scarfe argued that Jocellus was, in fact, 'a transparent pseudonym' combining Jocelin and *celerarius*.[3] In short, the Davis camp argues that Jocelin of Brakelond was demoted from the cellar to the sub-cellar c. 1200–1, where he officiated as guestmaster and sub-cellarer; Davis suggests that these two posts were joined, but Scarfe implies that the one official held both offices.[4] This may well be so, but as Gransden argues, there is no evidence that this was the case.[5] Bernard McGuire's more tentative interpretation is convincing. He suggests that it is likely, though not conclusive, that Jocelin was appointed guestmaster when Jocellus was assigned to the cellar in 1197, and that he remained there during the cellarer's demotion and reinstatement.[6] This seems more plausible for, as is suggested in chapter 2, Jocelin's detailed knowledge of the cellar and his concern to vindicate the office may be indicative of the close working relationship between the cellarer and guestmaster, rather than proof that he was the cellarer.[7] Accordingly, we

---

[1] *Kalendar of Samson*, pp. li–lvi. Davis' argument is summarised by N. Scarfe, 'Jocelin of Brakelond's identity: a review of the evidence', *Proceedings of the Suffolk Institute of Archaeology and History* 39 (1997), pp. 1–5 (p. 1), and B. P. McGuire, 'The collapse of a monastic friendship: the case of Jocelin of Brakelond and Samson of Bury', *JMH* 4 (1978), pp. 369–97 (p. 374).

[2] N. Scarfe, *Suffolk in the Middle Ages* (Woodbridge, 1986), pp. 99–109; Scarfe, 'Jocelin of Brakelond's identity', p. 1, and Thomson, *Chronicle of Abbot Hugh*, p. xvii.

[3] Scarfe, *Suffolk in the Middle Ages*, p. 100.

[4] Scarfe, *Suffolk in the Middle Ages*, pp. 105–7, esp. p. 106.

[5] Gransden, *Historical Writing*, p. 383, n. 15, *Bury Customs*, p. xxii, n. 5.

[6] McGuire, 'Collapse of a monastic friendship', p. 376.

[7] See above, p. 62.

should perhaps read Jocelin's account as a defence of a colleague rather than self-vindication, and the name 'Jocellus' as a nickname to differentiate two Jocelins working in close quarters, and not a pseudonym for the author.[1]

1 McGuire, 'Collapse of a monastic friendship', p. 375, seems to suggest as much.

Appendix 2

The Waterworks Plan of Christ Church, Canterbury

The Waterworks Plan of Christ Church, Canterbury (above, p. 4) is a unique remnant of the Middle Ages for it is the only known plan of a western monastery prior to the sixteenth century.[2] It depicts the monastery's hydraulic system, which was central to Prior Wibert's building programme of 1155–67 and may have been intended as a guide for repairs and extensions. It shows the layout of the precinct in the mid-twelfth century, but is probably representative of the monastery as it was until the Dissolution, for the conventual buildings were renovated but not rearranged.[3] The buildings are not, however, shown to scale. For example, whilst the toilet block (*necessarium*) and dormitory are detached in the drawing, the ruins at this point are joined; the door between the guesthouse and kitchen is huge in comparison to the other buildings and would be about twelve metres by fifteen metres.[4] Furthermore, the plan shows little of the interior layout of the buildings and says little of their use.

The plan shows that the prior's quarters lay to the NE of the church, by the infirmary buildings, and were separated from the court by a wall and gate.[5] The prior would presumably have welcomed here more noteworthy guests, such as distinguished ecclesiastics, nobility and others whom he wished to honour and were not received by the archbishop.[6] The prior's lodgings are described as the old and new chambers (*camera*) of the prior but would probably have

---

[2]   The map of St Gall, c. 820, was only intended as an ideal and was never actualised. For a brief comparison of the two plans see W. Urry, 'Canterbury, Kent, c. 1153', *Local Maps and Plans From Mediaeval England*, ed. R. A. Skelton and P. D. A. Harvey (Oxford, 1986), pp. 43–58 (pp. 47–8); for a more detailed analysis of the St Gall plan, see Price, *Plan of St Gall*.

[3]   Braunfels, *Monasteries*, p. 164. Braunfels attributes the plan's survival to the fact that it was bound in the Eadwine Psalter.

[4]   R. Willis, *The Architectural History of the Conventual Buildings of the Monastery of Christ Church in Canterbury* (London, 1869), p. 126. Woodman, 'Waterworks', pp. 171, 174–6, also discusses the accuracy and limitations of the plan.

[5]   The prior's own household would have been based here, Smith, *Canterbury Cathedral Priory*, p. 30. The prior's quarters were altered extensively over the years; for the complicated and elaborate construction of these quarters in the later Middle Ages, see Dobson, 'The monks of Canterbury in the later Middle Ages', p. 92.

[6]   Willis, *Architectural History*, pp. 94–5. Lanfranc's archiepiscopal palace is not shown in the plan.

been comprised of a series of rooms or a suite, rather than a single chamber. The term *camera* could seemingly apply to a wide range of lodgings from the humble cell where Abbot Suger of St Denis read, wept and contemplated 'as the hours allowed',[7] to the abbot of Peterborough's chamber which was large enough to accommodate his honorial court in 1133.[8]

The *domus hospitum* stood to the NW of the cloister, and adjoined the cellarer's range. In later documents it is sometimes described as the cellarer's hall and was presumably run in a similar way to the convent's guesthouse at Bury St Edmunds.[9] In the absence of explicit evidence it is generally assumed that middling guests were entertained here by the cellarer.[10] No doubt the decision as to who should be received in the *domus hospitum* depended on the monks' requirements at a given time and on who else was staying at the house. If, however, the division of guests at Christ Church was similar to that at Bury, it is likely that at least part of the *domus hospitum* was assigned to visiting regulars. Benedictines visiting Christ Church in the twelfth century may have stayed with the host community in the dormitory.

The *domus hospitum* formed a private court with the kitchen and parlour, and was convenient to the stables, kitchen and the cellarage beneath the refectory.[11] The Waterworks plan is not the only source of evidence for the *domus hospitum* which is mentioned in the rental of 1165. There are also Norman remains, albeit scant.[12] The east end wall stands to its full height and from this it has been calculated that the outer length would have measured about forty metres, and the distance between the walls at the southern end around eight metres.[13] The *domus hospitum* has recently been the subject of archaeological research and restoration work is ongoing.[14] It is known that the hall was built over an undercroft of seven bays and entered from the transverse staircase, towards the south.[15] It was ornately decorated and would have been a particularly fine building in the twelfth century.[16]

---

7   Peter the Venerable was amazed at how humble Suger's cell was, *Oeuvres Complètes*, pp. 392–3; Grant, *Abbot Suger*, p. 251; Constable, 'Suger's monastic administration', p. 19. See also Bernard's letter to Suger, *Epistolae*, ep. 309 (p. 229).
8   King, *Peterborough Abbey*, p. 31.
9   Willis, *Architectural History*, p. 38. 'For convenience sake', Willis refers to this court as 'the cellarer's court', p. 115.
10 Urry evidently thought that distinguished visitors stayed here and was thus puzzled at how so many could have been accommodated in what was a relatively small building, Urry, 'Canterbury, Kent', p. 53.
11 Willis, *Architectural History*, p. 38.
12 W. Urry, *Canterbury Under the Angevin Kings* (London, 1967), rental B (1163–7), nos 23, 51, 84. Various rents in the city were appointed to the upkeep of the guesthouse and almonry, Smith, *Canterbury Cathedral*, p. 14.
13 Willis, *Architectural History*, pp. 125–6.
14 J. Bowen, 'The *Domus hospitum*', in 'Interim report on work carried out in 1987 by the Canterbury Archaeological Trust', *Archaeologia Cantiana* 104 (1988), pp. 326–7.
15 Bowen, '*Domus hospitum*', p. 327. The south vestibule seems to have contained a flight of steps which led the visitor through ornamented doors from the cellarer's court to the floor of the hall, Willis, *Architectural History*, p. 135. Presumably the eastern entrance led to the *locutorium*.
16 Tim Tatton-Brown, personal communication.

The *aula noua* stood at the main gate to the court, in the NW corner, and was therefore situated on the edge of the precinct, between the menial and monastic buildings.[17] Despite the wealth of architectural knowledge, there is no documentary evidence to explain who exactly stayed here, but this too probably changed over time, in accordance with the monastery's needs. Its location in the precinct and similarity with the hall at Eastbridge hospital in Canterbury's High Street, where pilgrims were provided with food and lodging for 4d, has led to the assumption that 'the lowest class of pilgrims or persons who craved hospitality' were accommodated in the *aula nova*.[18] There are other possibilities. St John's hospice at the gate of Reading Abbey was built for pilgrims and other guests not admitted to the upper house, as well as for twenty-six resident poor.[19] Odo of Battle (1175–1200) was credited with building a hospice outside the gate of his abbey for those who were not permitted to lodge within the precinct, and hospices at the gates of Cluny and la Trinité, Vendôme welcomed guests on foot – those on horseback were received within the precinct.[20] As noted above, the retinues of monks visiting Abingdon Abbey may have stayed at St John's hospital, by the abbey gate.[21] A hospice for mendicants was built at the gate of St Albans.[22]

Much of the *aula noua* survives and the building has been well documented by architects and art historians.[23] Although it has been mostly rebuilt since the twelfth century, the original staircase remains and this is now supported on a multi-foil laver.[24] The hall was built on a raised vaulted substructure which was reached by an external staircase. The entire building measured about fifty

17 For a reconstruction of the precincts, see T. Tatton-Brown, *Canterbury History and Guide* (Stroud, 1994), p. 26. The *aula noua* was evidently built around at the same time as the Norman entrance gateway, Willis, *Architectural History*, pp. 144–5. It is generally thought that the almonry, which had been newly constructed by 1161, stood adjacent to the *aula noua*, Willis, *Architectural History*, pp. 12, 15.

18 Willis, *Architectural History*, pp. 148, 15. Edward Fitz Odbold founded the hospital at Eastbridge, c. 1180, and endowed it with land and tithes from mills. The hospital was dedicated to St Thomas of Canterbury and was intended to provide one night's lodging for twelve poor pilgrims visiting the shrine at Christ Church. The hospital still functions as an almshouse belonging to the archbishop. For details of this hospital, see the various pamphlets issued by the Eastbridge Trustees. See, too, Tatton-Brown, *Canterbury History*, p. 97, and Urry, *Canterbury*, pp. 193, 19. For Archbishop Stratford's reforming statutes of 1342, see *Literae Cantuarienses, The Letter Books of the Monastery of Christ Church, Canterbury*, ed. J. B. Shepperd, 3 vols, RS 85 (London, 1887–89), 2, no. 719 (pp. 251–2).

19 See also above, p. 27. A resident chaplain oversaw the management of St John's, *RAC* 1, nos 203 (pp. 157–8), 224 (pp. 185–6).

20 *Battle Chronicle*, pp. 306–7; Evans, *Monastic Life at Cluny*, pp. 92–3; Johnson, *Prayer, Patronage and Power*, p. 160.

21 See above, pp. 84–5, 146.

22 *Chronica Majora* 4, p. 600.

23 E.g. Woodman and Kahn describe the bays and the sculptures; Bowen, has written on the architecture, see above. Awaiting publication: M. Sparks, 'The *aula noua*, documentary evidence', J. Bowen, 'The architecture of the *Aula Noua*', and D. Kahn, 'The sculpture of the *Aula Noua*', *Excavation in the Cathedral Precincts 1: The Aula Noua, Almonry Chapel and Lanfranc's Dormitory*, Canterbury Archaeological Trust.

24 Kahn, *Canterbury*, p. 105.

metres by fourteen metres externally, and forty-eight metres by twelve metres internally; the hall itself was about eight metres broad. The body of the hall occupied the western part and had a side aisle to the east.[25] The *aula noua* in the plan is seemingly shown in 'abbreviated form'. Architectural and archaeological research indicates that it was larger and more ornate than the plan suggests. For example, although there were originally nine bays, the plan shows only the major elements of the façade, namely, five bays, an open arcaded basement and a staircase projecting from the middle.[26] A possible explanation for this disparity is that the building had probably not been completed when the plan was compiled. Moreover, it was perhaps intended that the plan should be a reflective rather than accurate representation of the buildings.[27]

---

[25] Willis, *Architectural History*, pp. 145–6.
[26] Woodman, 'Waterworks', p. 174, argues that the plan is more concerned with the proportion of the form than the number of bays and windows, pp. 174–6; Kahn, *Canterbury*, p. 195.
[27] Willis, *Architectural History*, p. 147.

Bibliography

Unpublished works

London, British Library
MSS Cotton Claudius B vi, C ix
MS Cotton Otho cxi
MS Harleian 1005
MS Harleian 2977
MS Harleian 3763
MS Yates Thompson 26

Trinity College Cambridge
MS 17.1

Hildesheim, St Godehard
St Albans Psalter

Theses

Kerr, J. 'Monastic hospitality: the Benedictines in England c. 1070–c. 1245', Ph.D. thesis, University of St Andrews, 2000
McFadden, G. J., 'An edition and translation of the *Life of Waldef*, Abbot of Melrose, by Jocelin of Furness', Ph.D. thesis, University of Columbia, 1952

Published works

Primary sources
The Account Book of Beaulieu Abbey, ed. S. F. Hockey, CS, 4th ser. 16 (London, 1975)
Account Rolls of the Obedientiaries of Peterborough, ed. J. Greatrex, Northamptonshire Rec. Soc. 33 (Northampton, 1984)
Accounts of the Cellarers of Battle Abbey, 1275–1513, ed. E. Searle and B. Ross (Sydney, 1967)
Accounts of the Obedientiars of Abingdon Abbey, ed. R. E. G. Kirk, CS, new ser. 51 (London, 1892)
Adam of Eynsham, *Magna Vita Sancti Hugonis*, ed. and trans. D. Douie and D. H. Farmer, 2 vols, Nelson's Medieval Texts (London, 1961–62); repr. OMT (Oxford, 1985)
Adam du Petit Pont, '*De Utensilibus*', in *Teaching and Learning Latin in 13th-century England* 1, ed. T. Hunt (Cambridge, 1991), pp. 165–76
Aelred of Rievaulx, '*De Institutione Inclusarum*', *Opera Omnia* 1, *Opera Ascetic*, ed. A. Hoste and C. H. Talbot, CCCM 1 (Turnhout, 1971), pp. 635–82
—— *Treatises and Pastoral Prayer*, ed. M. Pennington (Kalamazoo, 1971)

—— 'De Spiritali Amicitia', Aelredi Rievallensis, Opera Omnia 1, pp. 279–350; trans. M. E. Laker, On Spiritual Friendship (Kalamazoo, 1977)

—— 'Speculum Caritatis', Opera Omnia 1, pp. 3–161; trans. E. Connor, Mirror of Charity (Kalamazoo, 1990)

—— The Life of St Edward the Confessor, trans. J. Bertram (Southampton, 1993)

Alexander of Neckam, De Naturis Rerum et De Laudibus Diuinae Sapientiae, ed. T. Wright, RS 34 (London, 1863)

—— 'De Nominibus utensilium', in Teaching and Learning Latin in 13th-century England 1, ed. T. Hunt (Cambridge, 1991), pp. 177–90

—— 'De Sacerdos ad altare', in Teaching and Learning Latin 1, ed. Hunt, pp. 250–73

Annales Furnesiensis, ed. T. Beck (London, 1844)

Annales Monastici, ed. H. R. Luard, 5 vols, RS 36 (London, 1864–69)

Anselm, The Letters of Saint Anselm of Canterbury, trans. and annotated W. Fröhlich, 3 vols (Kalamazoo, 1990–94)

Augustine, On Christian Charity, ed. and trans. D. W. Robertson Jr (New York, 1958)

—— Concerning the City of God against the Pagans, trans. H. Bettenson (Harmondsworth, 1984)

—— The Rule of St Augustine, trans. R. Canning (Kalamazoo, 1984)

Bartholomeus Anglicus, Bartholomew of England, De Proprietatibus Rerum ['On the properties of things'], On the Properties of Things, John Trevisa's Translation of Bartholomaeus Anglicus, De Proprietatibus Rerum, A Critical Text, ed. M. C. Seymour, 3 vols (Oxford, 1975–88)

Basil, The Ascetic Works of Basil, trans. and intro. W. K. L. Clarke (London, 1925)

'Benedict of Peterborough', Gesta Regis Henrici Secundi Benediciti Abbatis. The chronicle of the Reigns of Henry II and Richard I, 1169–1192, known commonly under the name of Benedict of Peterborough, ed. W. Stubbs, 2 vols, RS 49 (London, 1867)

Bernard of Clairvaux, De Vita et Rebus Gestis S. Malachiae, Hiberniae Episcopi, PL 182. 1073–1118

—— St Bernard's Apologia to Abbot William, trans. M. Casey (Kalamazoo, 1970)

—— Sancti Bernardi Opera 8: Epistolae, ed. J. Leclercq and H. Rochais (Rome, 1977)

—— The Letters of Saint Bernard of Clairvaux, trans. B. S. James, with new intro. and bibliography B. Kienzle (Surrey, 1998)

Bernard of Cluny, Consuetudines, Ordo Cluniacensis per Bernardum Saeculi XI Scriptorem, ed. M. Herrgott, Vetus Disciplina Monastica (Paris, 1726), pp. 133–374

The Book of St Gilbert, ed. and trans. R. Foreville and G. Keir, OMT (Oxford, 1987)

The Book of William Morton, Almoner of Peterborough 1448–1467, ed. P. I. King, trans. W. T. Mellows, intro. C. N. L. Brooke, Northamptonshire Rec. Soc 16 (Northampton, 1954)

Borough Customs, ed. M. Bateson, 2 vols, Selden Society 18, 21 (London, 1904–6)

British Borough Charters, 1216–1307, ed. A. Ballard and J. Tait (Cambridge, 1923)

Brut y Tywysogyion or The Chronicle of the Princes, ed. J. Williams Ab Ithel, RS 17 (London, 1860)

Caesarius of Heisterbach, Dialogus Miraculorum, ed. J. Strange, 2 vols (Cologne, Brussels, Bonn, 1851)

—— The Dialogue on Miracles, trans. H. von E. Scott and C. C. S. Bland, 2 vols (London, 1929)

Calendar of Liberate Rolls Preserved in the Public Record Office (London, 1916–)

'Carta Caritatis Prior' in Narrative and Legislative Texts from Early Cîteaux, ed. and trans. C. Waddell (Cîteaux, 1999), pp. 274–82, 441–52

'Carta Caritatis Posterior' in Narrative and Legislative Texts from Early Cîteaux, ed. and trans. C. Waddell (Cîteaux, 1999), pp. 373–94, 498–505

Cartae et Alia Munimenta Quae ad Dominium de Glamorgan Pertinent, ed. G. T. Clark (Cardiff, 1910)

The Cartulary and Historical Notes of the Cistercian Abbey of Flaxley, ed. A. W. Crawley-Boevey (Exeter, 1887)

The Cartulary of the Cistercian Abbey of Old Wardon, Bedfordshire, ed. G. H. Fowler (Manchester, 1931)

The Cartulary of Shrewsbury Abbey, ed. U. Rees, 2 vols (Aberystwyth, 1975)

The Cartulary of Worcester Cathedral Priory, ed. R. R. Darlington, PRS, new ser. 38 (London, 1968)

The Charters of the Anglo-Norman Earls of Chester, c. 1071–1237, ed. G. Barraclough, Rec. Soc of Lancashire and Cheshire 126 (Stroud, 1988)

Charters and Customals of the Abbey of Holy Trinity, Caen, ed. M. Chibnall, Records of Social and Economic History, new ser. 5 (London, 1982)

Charters and Documents Illustrating the History of the Cathedral, City, and Diocese of Salisbury in the Twelfth and Thirteenth Centuries, selected W. H. Rich Jones, ed. W. D. Macray (London, 1891)

Charters and Records Illustrative of the Ancient Abbey of Cluni, from 1077 to 1534, ed. G. F. Duckett, 8 vols (Lewes, 1888)

Charters of the Honour of Mowbray, 1107–1191, ed. D. E. Greenway, Records of Social and Economic History, new ser. 1 (London, 1972)

The Charters of Norwich Cathedral Priory, ed. B. Dodwell, 2 vols, Pipe Roll Soc., new ser. 40, 46 (London, 1974–85)

Chrétien de Troyes, *Erec et Enide*, ed. M. Roques, CFMA 80 (Paris, 1952)

—— *Cligés*, ed. A. Micha, CFMA 84 (Paris, 1957)

—— *Chrétien de Troyes, Arthurian Romances*, trans. W. W. Kibler (Harmondsworth, 1991)

The Chronicle of Battle Abbey, ed. and trans. E. Searle, OMT (Oxford, 1980)

The Chronicle of Bury St Edmunds, 1212–1301, ed. and trans. A. Gransden, Nelson's Medieval Texts (London, 1964)

The Chronicle of the Election of Hugh, Abbot of Bury St Edmunds and Later Bishop of Ely, ed. and trans. R. M. Thomson (Oxford, 1974)

'The Chronicle of Melrose' in *Medieval Chronicles of Scotland: the chronicles of Melrose and Holyrood*, trans. J. Stevenson (Llanerch facsimile, Felinfach, 1988), pp. 7–124

The Chronicle of St Mary's, York, ed. H. H. E. Craster and M. E. Thornton, SS 148 (Durham, 1933)

Chronicles of the Reigns of Stephen, Henry II and Richard I, ed. R. Howlett, 4 vols, RS 82 (London, 1884–89)

Chronicon Abbatiae de Evesham ad annum 1418, ed. W. D. Macray, RS 29 (London, 1863)

Chronicon Abbatiae Ramensiensis, ed. W. D. Macray, RS 83 (London, 1886)

Chronicon de Lanercost, 1201–1346, ed. J. Stevenson (Edinburgh, 1839)

—— *The Chronicle of Lanercost, 1201–1346* tr. H. E. Maxwell (Glasgow, 1913; Llanerch facsimile, Felinfach, 2001)

Chronicon Monasterii de Abingdon, ed. J. Stevenson, 2 vols, RS 2 (London, 1858)

Chronica Monasterii de Melsa, a fundatione usque ad annum 1396, auctore Thoma de Burton, abbate. Accedit continuation ad annum 1406 a monacho quodam ipsius domus, ed. E. A. Bond, 3 vols, RS 43 (London, 1866–68)

Collections for a History of Staffordshire: Burton Abbey, ed. I. H. Jeayes, Staffordshire Rec. Soc (Kendal, 1937)

Compotus Rolls of the Obedientiaries of St Swithun's, Winchester, ed. G. W. Kitchin (Winchester, 1892)

A Consuetudinary of the Fourteenth Century for the Refectory of the House of St Swithun in Winchester, ed. G. W. Kitchin (London and Winchester, 1886)

Consuetudines Beccenses, ed. M. P. Dickson, Corpus Consuetudinum Monasticarum 4 (Siegburg, 1967)

Corpus Iuris Canonici, ed. A. Friedberg, 2 vols (Leipzig, 1879–81)

Councils and Synods with Other Documents Relating to the English Church 871–1204, 1, ed. D. Whitelock, M. Brett and C. N. L. Brooke (Oxford, 1981)

The Customary of the Benedictine Abbey of Bury St Edmunds in Suffolk, ed. A. Gransden, HBS 99 (Chichester, 1973)

The Customary of the Benedictine Abbey of Eynsham in Oxford, ed. A. Gransden, Corpus Consuetudinum Monasticarum 2 (Siegburg, 1963)

The Customary of the Cathedral Priory Church of Norwich, ed. J. B. L. Tolhurst, HBS 82 (London, 1948)

The Customary of St Augustine's, Canterbury, and St Peter's, Westminster, ed. E. M. Thompson, 2 vols, HBS 23, 28 (London, 1902–4)

Daniel of Beccles, *Urbanus Magnus Danielis Becclesiensis*, ed. J. Gilbart Smyly (Dublin, 1939)

'*De Abbatibus Abbendoniae*', ed. Stevenson, Chronicon Monasterii de Abingdon 2, pp. 267–95

'*De Obedientiariis Abbendoniae*', ed. Stevenson, Chronicon Monasterii de Abingdon 2, pp. 335–417

Decrees of the Ecumenical Councils, ed. N. Tanner, 2 vols (London and Washington, 1990)

Documents Illustrating the Activities of the General and Provincial Chapters of the English Black Monks, 1215–1500, ed. W. A. Pantin, 3 vols, CS, 3rd ser. 45, 47, 54 (London, 1931–37)

Documents Illustrative of the Rule of Walter de Wenlok, Abbot of Westminster, 1283–1307, ed. B. F. Harvey, CS, 4th ser. 2 (London, 1965)

Documents Illustrative of the Social and Economic History of the Danelaw, ed. F. M. Stenton, Records of the Social and Economic History of England and Wales 5 (London, 1920)

'*Dum manducatis*', in S. Gieben, 'Robert Grosseteste and mediaeval courtesy books', *Vivarium* 5 (1967), pp. 47–78 (52)

Eadmer, *Historia Nouorum in Anglia*, ed. M. Rule, RS 81 (London, 1884)

—— *Historia Nouorum in England: history of recent events in England*, trans. G. Bosanquet (London, 1964)

—— *The Life of St Anselm, Archbishop of Canterbury*, ed. and trans. R. W. Southern, Nelson's Medieval Texts (London, 1962), 2nd edn, OMT (Oxford, 1972)

Earldom of Gloucester Charters: the charters and scribes of the Earls and Countesses of Gloucester to AD 1217, ed. R. B. Patterson (Oxford, 1973)

Early Charters of the Cathedral Church of St Paul, London, ed. M. Gibbs, CS, 3rd ser. 58 (London, 1939)

Early Yorkshire Charters, vols 1–3, ed. W. Farrer (Edinburgh, 1914–16); index to vols 1–3, ed. C. T. and E. M. Clay; vols 4–9, ed. C. T. Clay, YAS Rec. Ser., extra ser. (Edinburgh, 1935–65)

Les Ecclesiastica Officia Cisterciens du xiième Siècle, ed. D. Choisselet and P. Vernet (Reiningue, 1989)

—— *The Ancient Usages of the Cistercian Order [Ecclesiastica Officia]*, Guadalupe Translations (Lafayette, 1998)

Ecclesiastical Documents I: a brief history of the Bishoprick of Somerset from its foundation to 1174, ed. J. Hunter, CS, old ser. 8 (London, 1840)

Ely Ordinances and Visitation Records: 1241–1515, ed. S. Evans, Camden Miscellany xvii, CS, 3rd ser. 64 (1940)

English Episcopal Acta 1, Lincoln, 1067–1185, ed. D. M. Smith (London, 1980)

English Episcopal Acta 2, Canterbury, 1162–90, ed. C. R. Cheney and B. E. A. Jones (London, 1986)

English Episcopal Acta, 3, Canterbury, 1193–1205, ed. C. R. Cheney (London, 1986)

English Episcopal Acta 5, York, 1070–1154, ed. J. E. Burton (London, 1988)

English Episcopal Acta 6, Norwich, 1070–1214, ed. C. Harper-Bill (London, 1990)

English Episcopal Acta 7, Hereford, 1079–1234, ed. J. Barrow (London, 1993)

English Episcopal Acta 8, Winchester, 1070–1204, ed. M. J. Franklin (London, 1993)

English Episcopal Acta 14, Coventry and Litchfield, 1072–1154, ed. M. J. Franklin (London, 1997)

English Historical Documents 2, 1042–1189, ed. D. C. Douglas and G. W. Greenaway (London, 1981)

English Historical Documents 3, 1189–1327, ed. H. Rothwell (London, 1975)

English Lawsuits from William I to Richard I, ed. R. C. van Caenegem, 2 vols, SS 106, 107 (London, 1990–91)

Epistolae Herberti de Losinga, Osberti de Clara et Elmeri, ed. R. Anstruther, Caxton Society 5 (Brussels, 1846)

Eynsham Cartulary, ed. H. E. Salter, 2 vols, Oxford Historical Society 49, 51 (Oxford, 1908–9)

Feudal Documents from the Abbey of Bury St Edmunds, ed. D. C. Douglas, Records of the Social and Economic History of England and Wales 8 (London, 1932)

'The Foundation of Byland Abbey', Dugdale, *Monasticon*, 5, pp. 349–54

'The Foundation of Jervaulx Abbey', Dugdale, *Monasticon*, 5, pp. 568–74

'The Foundation of Kirkstall Abbey', ed. E. K. Clark, *Thoresby Society Miscellany* 2 (Leeds, 1895), pp. 169–208

The Fountains Abbey Lease Book, ed. D. J. H. Michelmore, YAS Rec. Ser. 140 (Leeds, 1981)

Gaimar, *L'Estoire des Engleis*, ed. A. Bell, 3 vols, ANTS 14–16 (London, 1960)

Garnier, *La Vie de Sainte Thomas le Martyr, par Guernes de Pont-Sainte-Maxence*, ed. E. Walberg (Lund, 1922)

—— *Garnier's Becket*, trans. J. Shirley (Llanerch repr., Felinfach, 1996)

Geoffrey of Burton, *Life and Miracles of St Modwena*, ed. and trans. R. Bartlett, OMT (Oxford, 2002)

Geoffrey of Monmouth, *The Historia Regum Britannie of Geoffrey of Monmouth, 1, Bern Burgerbibliothek, MS 568*, ed. N. Wright (Cambridge, 1985)

—— *A History of the Kings of Britain*, trans. L. Thorpe (Harmondsworth, 1966)

Gerald of Wales, *Giraldi Cambresensis Opera*, ed. J. S. Brewer, J. F. Dimock, and G. F. Warner, 8 vols, RS 21 (London, 1861–91)

—— *The Journey Through Wales / The Description of Wales*, trans. L. Thorpe (Harmondsworth, 1978)

—— *The History and Topography of Ireland*, trans. J. O'Meara (rev. Harmondsworth, 1982)

—— *The Autobiography of Giraldus Cambrensis*, ed. and trans. H. E. Butler, intro. C. H. Williams, guide to reading J. Gillingham (Woodbridge, 2005)

Gervase of Canterbury, *Opera Historica*, ed. W. Stubbs, 2 vols, RS 73 (London, 1879–80)

—— *The History of the Archbishops of Canterbury*, trans. J. Stevenson, The Church Historians of England 5, pt 1 (London, 1858), pp. 293–348

Gervase of Louth Park, *The Testament of Gervase of Louth Park*, ed. C. H. Talbot, *Analecta Sacri Ordinis Cisterciensis* 7 (1951), pp. 32–45

The Gesta Normannorum Ducum of William of Jumièges, Orderic Vitalis and Robert of Torigni, ed. and trans. E. M. C. van Houts, 2 vols, OMT (Oxford, 1992)

'Gesta Sacristarum', in *Memorials of St Edmund's Abbey*, ed. T. Arnold, 3 vols, RS 96 (London, 1896), 2, pp. 289–98

Gesta Stephani, ed. K. R. Potter, OMT (Oxford, 1976)

The Great Chartulary of Glastonbury, ed. A. Watkin, 3 vols, Somerset Rec. Soc 59, 63, 64 (Frome, 1947–56)

Gilbert Crispin, *Vita Domni Herluini Abbatis Beccensis Liber Domni Gisleberti Abbatis de Simoniacis*, ed. J. A. Robinson, *Gilbert Crispin, Abbot of Westminster: a study of the abbey under Norman rule* (Cambridge, 1911), pp. 87–110

The Gilbertine Institutiones, Dugdale, *Monasticon* 6: 2, xxix–lviii

Goffridi, Abbatis Vindocinensis, *Opera Omnia*, PL 157

Goscelin of St Bertin, *Vita S. Edithae*, ed. A. Wilmart, 'La Légende de Sainte Édith en prose et ver par le moine Goscelin', *Analecta Bollandiana* 56 (Brussels, Paris, 1928), pt 1, pp. 1–101; pt 2, pp. 265–307

—— *Vitae sancti Ethelburgae Virginis*, ed. M. L. Colker, 'Jocelyn of St Bertin, The Life and miracles of St Ethelburga', in 'The texts of Jocelyn of Canterbury which relate to the history of Barking Abbey', M. Colker, *Studia Monastica* 7 (1965), pp. 383–460 (399–434)

—— 'The *Liber Confortatorius* of Goscelin of St Bertin', ed. C. H. Talbot, *Analecta Monastica* 3, ed. M. M. Lebreton, J. Leclercq, C. H. Talbot, *Studia Anselmiana* 37 (Rome, 1955), pp. 1–117; trans. M. Otter, *Goscelin of St Bertin, The Book of Encouragement and Consolation* (Cambridge, 2004)

Guigues, *Consuetudines*, PL 153. 631–760

Henry, Archdeacon of Huntingdon, *Historia Anglorum, The History of the English People*, ed. and trans. D. Greenway, OMT (Oxford, 1996)

Herman of Laon, '*De Miraculis*', PL 156. 983

Hermann of Tournai, '*Herimanni Liber de restauracione monasterii sancti Martini Tornacensis*', ed. G. Waitz, Monumenta Germaniae Historica Scriptores 14 (Hannover and Berlin, 1883), pp. 274–317

——— *The Restoration of the Monastery of Saint Martin of Tournai*, trans. with intro. L. H. Nelson (Washington DC, 1996)

Hildegard of Bingen, *Explanation of the Rule of St Benedict*, trans. with intro., notes and commentary H. Feiss, Peregrina Translation Series (Toronto, 1998)

Historia Ecclesiae Abbendoniensis: the history of the church of Abingdon, ed. and trans. J. Hudson, 2 vols OMT (Oxford, 2002, 2007)

Household Accounts from Medieval England, ed. C. M. Woolgar, Records of Social and Economic History 17–18 (London, 1992–93)

Hugh Candidus, *The Chronicle of Hugh Candidus, a Monk of Peterborough*, ed. W. T. Mellows, OMT (Oxford, 1949)

——— *The Peterborough Chronicle of Hugh Candidus*, trans. C. and W. T. Mellows (Peterborough, 1941)

Hugh the Chantor, *The History of the Church of York, 1066–1127*, ed. and trans. C. Johnson (Edinburgh, 1961), rev. M. Brett, C. N. K. Brooke, M. Winterbottom, OMT (Oxford, 1990)

Hugh of St Victor, *De Sacramentis, On the Sacraments of the Christian Faith*, ed. and trans. R. J. Deferrari (Cambridge, Mass., 1951)

Idungus, *Le Moine Idung et Ses Deux Ouvrages; 'Argumentum super quatuor questionibus' et 'Dialogus duorum monachorum'*, ed. R. B. C. Huygens (Spoleto, 1980)

——— trans. J. F. O'Sullivan, 'A dialogue between a Cistercian and a Cluniac', *Cistercians and Cluniacs: the case for Cîteaux* (Kalamazoo, 1977), pp. 3–141

Inquisitio Comitatus Cantabrigiensis Subiicitur Inquisitio Eliensis, ed. N. E. S. A. Hamilton (London, 1876)

Inquisition of the Manors of Glastonbury Abbey, ed. J. Jackson (London, 1882)

Ipomedon: Poème de Hue de Roteland, ed. A. J. Holden (Paris, 1979)

'*Instructio Noviciorum*' in *The Monastic Constitutions of Lanfranc*, rev. D. Knowles and C. Brooke (Edinburgh, 2002), pp. 198–221

Jerome, *Hieronymus Stridonensis: S. Eusebii Hieronymi Stridonensis Presbyteri 'Apologia Aduersus Libros Rufini, Missa ad Pammachium et Marcellam, Liber Tertius, uel Ultima Responsio S. Hieronymi Aduersus Scripta Rufini*, PL 23. 415–514

Jocelin of Brakelond, *The Chronicle of Jocelin of Brakelond*, ed. and trans. H. E. Butler (Edinburgh, 1949)

——— *Chronicle of the Abbey of Bury St Edmunds*, trans. D. Greenway and J. Sayers (Oxford, 1989)

John Chrysostom, *Homilies on the Acts of the Apostles and the Epistle to the Romans*, trans. Stephens *et al.*, ed. P. Schaff, The Nicene and Post-Nicene Fathers, first ser. 11 (New York, 1889)

John Flete, 'History of Westminster Abbey', in *Notes and Documents relative to Westminster Abbey no. 2: Flete's History of Westminster Abbey*, ed. J. A. Robinson (Cambridge, 1909)

John of Ford, *De vita beati Wulrici anachoretae Haselbergiae*, ed. Dom. M. Bell, Somerset Rec. Soc 47 (Frome and London, 1933)

John of Glastonbury, *The Chronicle of Glastonbury Abbey: an edition, translation and study of John of Glastonbury's Cronica Siue Antiquitates Glastoniensis Ecclesie*, ed. J. P. Carley, trans. D. Townsend (Woodbridge, 1985)

John of Salisbury, *Ioannis Saresberiensis Episcopi Carnotensis Policratici*, ed. C. C. J. Webb, 2 vols (Oxford, 1909)

——— *Ioannis Saresberiensis Episcopi Carnotensis Metalogicon*, ed. C. Webb (Oxford, 1929)

——— *Historia Pontificalis, Memoirs of the Papal Court*, ed. and trans. M. Chibnall, OMT (Oxford, 1956)

—— *The Letters of John of Salisbury*, ed. W. J. Millor and C. N. L. Brooke, 2 vols, OMT (Oxford, 1979)

John of Worcester, *The Chronicle of John of Worcester*, ed. and trans. P. McGurk, 3 vols, OMT (Oxford, 1995–98)

Jordan Fantosme, *Chronicle*, ed. and trans. R. C. Johnston (Oxford, 1981)

Kalendar of Abbot Samson of Bury St Edmunds and Related Documents, ed. R. H. C. Davis, CS, 3rd ser. 84 (London, 1954)

'The Lai d'Haveloc', in *The Birth of Romance: an anthology, four twelfth-century Anglo-Norman romances*, trans. J. Weiss (London, 1992), pp. 141–58

Lanfranc, *The Letters of Lanfranc, Archbishop of Canterbury*, ed. and trans. H. Clover and M. Gibson, OMT (Oxford, 1979)

—— *The Monastic Constitutions of Lanfranc*, rev. D. Knowles and C. Brooke (Edinburgh, 2002)

The Leges Edwardi, in B. O'Brien, *God's Peace and King's Peace: the laws of Edward the Confessor* (Philadelphia, 1999)

Letters and Papers Foreign and Domestic in the Reign of Henry VIII, arranged and catalogued J. S. Brewer, J. Gairdner and R. H. Brodie, 22 vols (London, 1862–1932)

The Libellus de Diuersus Ordinibus et Professionibus qui sunt in Aecclesia, ed. and trans. G. Constable and B. Smith, OMT (Oxford, 1972)

Liber Eliensis, ed. E. O. Blake, CS, 3rd ser. 92 (London, 1962)

Liber Eliensis: a history of the Isle of Ely from the seventh century to the twelfth century, trans. with notes Janet Fairweather (Woodbridge, 2005)

Liber Ordinis S. Victoris Parisiensis, ed. L. Jocqu and L. Mills, CCCM 61 (Turnhout, 1984)

The Life of Christina of Markyate, a Twelfth-Century Recluse, ed. and trans. C. H. Talbot, rev. edn OMT (Oxford, 1987)

Literae Cantuarienses, The Letter Books of Christ Church, Canterbury, ed. J. B. Shepperd, 3 vols, RS 85 (London, 1887–89)

Marie de France, *Les Lais de Marie de France*, ed. J. Reichner, CFMA 93 (Paris, 1966)

—— *The Lais of Marie de France*, trans. G. S. Burgess and K. Busby (Harmondsworth, 1986)

Materials for the History of Thomas Becket, ed. J. C. Robertson, 7 vols, RS 67 (London, 1875–85)

Matthew Paris, *Chronica Majora*, ed. H. R. Luard, 7 vols, RS 57 (London, 1872–84), trans. J. A. Giles, *Matthew Paris's English History, 1225–1273*, 3 vols (London, 1852–54)

——*Historia Anglorum*, ed. F. Madden, 3 vols, RS 44 (London, 1866–69)

—— *Gesta Abbatum Monasterii Sancti Albani*, ed. H. T. Riley, 3 vols, RS 28 (London, 1867–69)

The Memorials of the Abbey of St Mary of Fountains, ed. J. S. Walbran, J. Raine and J. T. Fowler, 3 vols, SS 42, 67, 130 (Durham, 1863–1918)

The Memorials of St Anselm, ed. R. W. Southern and F. S. Schmitt (London, 1969)

The Memorials of St Edmund's Abbey, ed. T. Arnold, 3 vols, RS 96 (London, 1890–96)

Michael Sherbrook, 'The fall of religious houses', ed. A. G. Dickens, *Tudor Treatises*, YAS Rec. Ser. 125 (Wakefield, 1959), pp. 89–142

The Miracles of Saint Aebbe of Coldingham and Saint Margaret of Scotland, ed. and trans. R. Bartlett, OMT (Oxford, 2003)

Monastic Chancery Proceedings, ed. J. S. Purvis, YAS Rec. Ser. 88 (Wakefield, 1934)

Monasticon Anglicanum, ed. Sir William Dugdale, rev. J. Caley, H. Ellis, B. Bandinel, 6 vols in 8 (London, 1817–30)

Nigel Wireker, *Nigel de Longchamp's Speculum Stultorum*, ed. J. H. Mozley and R. R. Raymo (Berkley and Los Angeles, 1960); trans. J. H. Mozley, *A Mirror for Fools: the Book of Burnel the Ass, by Nigel Longchamp* (Oxford, 1961)

'Narratio de fundatione Fontanis monasterii', ed. Walbran, *Memorials of Fountains* 1, pp. 1–129; trans. A. W. Oxford, *The Ruins of Fountains Abbey* (London, 1910), appendix 1, pp. 127–230

Narrative and Legislative Texts from Early Cîteaux, ed. and trans. C. Waddell (Cîteaux, 1999)

The Obedientiaries of Westminster Abbey and their Financial Records c. 1275–1500, ed. B. Harvey, Westminster Record Series 3 (Woodbridge, 2002)

The Observances in Use at the Augustinian Priory of St Giles and St Andrew at Barnwell, Cambridgeshire, ed. and trans. J. W. Clark (Cambridge, 1897)

Odo of Deuil, *De Profectione Ludouici VII in Orientem*, ed. and trans. U. Berry (New York, 1948)

Orderic Vitalis, *The Ecclesiastical History of Orderic Vitalis*, ed. and trans. M. Chibnall, 6 vols, OMT (Oxford, 1969–80)

The Ordinal of the Holy Trinity, Fécamp, ed. D. Chadd HBS 112 (London, 2002), pp. 379–88

Osbert de Clare, *The Letters of Osbert of Clare, Prior of Westminster*, ed. E. W. Williamson (Oxford, 1929); letter 42, trans. V. Morton in *Guidance for Women in Twelfth-Century Convents* (Cambridge, 2003), pp. 15–49

'A papal visitation of Bury St Edmunds and Westminster in 1234', R. Graham, *EHR* 27 (1912), pp. 728–39

Papsturkunden in England, ed. W. Holzmann, 3 vols (Berlin and Göttingen, 1930–52)

The Paraclete Statutes: Institutiones Nostrae, ed. C. Waddell (Trappist, Kentucky, 1987)

Patrologia cursus completes, series Latina, ed. J. P. Migne *et al.*, 221 vols (Paris, 1844–64)

Peter Abelard, *Petri Abelardi, Epistolae*, PL 178. 113–379

—— *The Letters of Abelard and Héloise*, ed. and trans. B. Radice (Harmondsworth, 1974)

Peter of Blois, *Opera Omnia*, ed. I. A. Giles, 4 vols (Oxford, 1846–47)

Peter de Celle, *Selected Works*, trans. H. Feiss (Kalamazoo, 1987)

Peter the Venerable, *The Letters of Peter the Venerable*, ed. G. Constable, 2 vols (Cambridge, Mass., 1967)

La Queste del Saint Graal, ed. A. Pauphilet, CFMA 33 (Paris, 1923)

The Quest of the Holy Grail, trans. P. M. Matarasso (Harmondsworth, 1969)

'Quisquis es in mensa', in C. H. Haskins, *Studies in Mediaeval Culture* (Oxford, 1929), p. 79

Ralph of Coggeshall, *Chronicon Anglicanum*, ed. J. Stevenson, RS 66 (London, 1875)

Ralph of Diceto, *Opera Historica*, ed. W. Stubbs, 2 vols, RS 86 (London, 1876)

Raoul de Cambrai, ed. and trans. S. Kay (Oxford, 1992)

Reading Abbey Cartularies, ed. B. R. Kemp, 2 vols, CS, 4th ser. 31, 33 (London, 1986–87)

'Le Récit de la Fondation de Mortemer', ed. J. Bouvet, *Collectanea Ordinis Cisterciana Reformatorum*, 22 (1960), pp. 149–68

Records of the Monastery of Kinloss, ed. J. Stuart (Edinburgh, 1872)

Regesta Regum Anglo-Normannorum, 1066–1154
    1. *1066–1100*, ed. H. W. C. Davis, with the assistance of R. J. Whitwell (Oxford, 1913)
    2. *1100–1135*, ed. C. J. Johnson and H. A. Cronne (Oxford, 1956)
    3. *1135–1154*, ed. H. A. Cronne and R. H. C. Davis (Oxford, 1968)
    4. *Facsimiles of Original Charters and Writs of King Stephen, the Empress Mathilda, and Dukes Geoffrey and Henry*, ed. H. A. Cronne and R. H. C. Davis (Oxford, 1969)

Reginald of Coldingham / Durham, *Reginaldi Monachi Dunelmensis Libellus de Admirandis Beatis Cuthberti Virtutibus*, ed. J. Raine, SS 1 (Durham, 1835)

—— *De Vita et Miraculis S. Godrici, Hermitae de Finchale Auctore Reginaldo Monacho Dunelmensis*, ed. J. Stevenson, SS 20 (Durham, 1847)

The Register of Archbishop Greenfield, Lord Archbishop of York, 1306–15, pt 4, ed. W. Brown and A. H. Hamilton, SS 152 (Durham, 1937)

The Register of Archbishop Walter Giffard, Lord Archbishop of York, 1266–79, ed. W. Brown, SS 109 (Durham, 1904)

The Register of Eudes of Rouen, trans. S. M. Brown (London, 1966)

The Register of William Wickwane, Lord Archbishop of York, 1279–1285, ed. W. Brown, SS 114 (Durham, 1907)

The Registrum Antiquissimum of the Cathedral Church of Lincoln, ed. C. W. Foster and K. Major, 10 vols, Lincoln Rec. Soc (Hereford, 1931–73)

Registrum Epistolarum Fratris Johannis Peckham Archiepiscopi Cantuariensis, ed. C. T. Martin, 3 vols, RS 77 (London, 1882–85)

Registrum Roberti Winchelsey 2, transcribed and ed. R. Graham, Canterbury and York Society 52 (London, 1956)

La Règle du Maître, ed. P. B. Corbett, H. Vanderhoven, F. Masai (Brussels and Paris, 1953)

Regularis Concordia Anglicae Nationis Monachorum et Sanctimonialium, ed. and trans. T. Symons (Edinburgh, 1953)

Richard of Devizes, *Chronicon Richardi Diuisiensis De Tempore Regis Richardi Primi*, ed. and trans. J. Appleby (London, 1963)

Robert of Torigni, *Chronica Roberti de Torigneio, Abbatis Monasterii Sancti Michaelis in Periculo Maris*, ed. Howlett, *Chronicles and Memorials of Stephen, Henry II and Richard I*, 4, pp. 81–315; trans. J. Stevenson, *The Chronicle of Robert de Monte* (Llanerch repr., 1991)

—— *Continuatio Beccensis* (additions to Robert of Torigni's chronicle for the years 1157–60), ed. R. Howlett, *Chronicles of the Reigns of Stephen, Henry II and Richard I*, 4, pp. 317–27

Roger of Howden, *Chronica Rogeri de Houedene*, ed. W. Stubbs, 4 vols, RS 51 (London, 1868–71)

Roger of Wendover, *Liber qui dictiur Flores Historiarum ab anno Domini MCLIV annoque Henrici Anglorum regis Secundi primo*, ed. H. G. Hewlett, 3 vols, RS 84 (London, 1886–9)

Rolls of the Justices in Eyre for Lincolnshire and Worcestershire, ed. D. M. Stenton, SS 53 (London, 1934)

The Romance of Horn, ed. M. K. Pope, 2 vols, ANTS 9–10, 12–13 (London, 1955–64)

Rotuli Litterum Clausaurum in Turri Londinensi 1, ed. T. D. Hardy (London, 1833)

Rule of Fontevrault (Fontis Ebraldi), PL 162. 1079–82

The Rule of the Master, trans. L. Eberle (Kalamazoo, 1977)

The Rule of St Benedict, ed. and trans. D. O. Hunter Blair, 5th edn (Fort Augustus, 1948)

Samson of Bury, 'De Miraculis Sancti Aedmundi', ed. T. Arnold, *The Memorials of St Edmund's Abbey*, ed. T. Arnold, 3 vols, RS 96 (London, 1890–6), 1, pp. 107–208

Select Cases from the Ecclesiastical Courts of the Province of Canterbury, c. 1200–1300, ed. N. Adams and C. Donahue, SS 95 (London, 1981)

Select Charters and Other Illustrations of English Constitutional History from the Earliest Times to the Reign of Edward I, ed. H. W. C. Davis, 9th edn (Oxford, 1948)

Select Documents of the English Lands of the Abbey of Bec, ed. M. Chibnall, CS, 3rd ser. 73 (London, 1951)

Simeon of Durham, *Opera Omni Historia Ecclesiae Dunhelmensis*, ed. T. Arnold, 2 vols, RS 75 (London, 1882)

—— *Simeon of Durham, A History of the Kings of England* (Llanerch repr., Felinfach, 1987)

Sir Christopher Hatton's Book of Seals, ed. L. C. Loyd and D. M. Stenton, Northamptonshire Rec. Soc (Oxford, 1950)

'Stans puer ad mensam', in Gieben, 'Robert Grosseteste', pp. 61–2

Statuta Capitulorum Generalium Ordinis Cisterciensis ab Anno 1116 ad Annum 1786, ed. J. M. Canivez, 8 vols (Louvain, 1933–41)

Statuts, Chapitres Généraux et Visites de L'Ordre de Cluny, ed. G. Charvin, 9 vols (Paris, 1965–)

Stephen of Lexington, *Registrum Epistolarum Abbatis Stephani de Lexinton*, ed. B. Griesser, *Analecta Sacri Ordinis Cisterciensis* 2 (1946), pp. 1–118

—— *Letters From Ireland, 1228–29*, trans. B. O'Dwyer (Kalamazoo, 1982)

Suger, *Oeuvres Complètes de Suger*, ed. A. Lecoy de la Marche (Paris, 1867)

—— *Abbot Suger: on the abbey church of St Denis and its art treasures*, 2nd edn, G. Panofsky-Soergel (Princeton, 1979)

A Thirteenth-Century Register: Odo, Archbishop of Rouen, ed. C. Jenkins, *Church Quarterly Review* 150 (1925–26), pp. 80–123

Twelfth-Century Statutes from the Cistercian General Chapter, Latin text with English notes and commentary, ed. C. Waddell (Brecht, 2002)

Thomas of Kent, *The Anglo-Norman Alexander, Le Roman de Toute Chevalerie*, ed. B. Foster, 2 vols, ANTS 29–31, 32–3 (London, 1976–7)

Thomas of Marlborough, *History of the Abbey of Evesham*, ed. and trans. J. Sayers and L. Watkiss, OMT (Oxford, 2003)

Two Cartularies of Abingdon Abbey, ed. C. F. Slade and G. Lambrick, 2 vols, Oxford Historical Society, new ser. 32, 33 (Oxford, 1990–92)

Two Cartularies of the Priory of St Peter's of Bath, ed. W. Hunt, 2 vols, Somerset Rec. Soc 52, 53 (1893)

Udalricus, *Udalrici Cluniacensis Consuetudines*, PL 149. 663–778

Visio Thurkilli: Relatore, et Videtur, Radulpho de Coggeshall, ed. P. G. Schmidt (Leipzig, 1978)

The Vision of MacConglinne: a Middle-Irish wonder tale, ed. and trans. K. Meyer, intro. W. Wellner (Llanerch Press facsimile, Felinfach, 1999)

Visitations and Chapters of the Order of Cluny, ed. G. F. Duckett (Lewes, 1893)

Visitations of English Cluniac Foundations, ed. G. F. Duckett (London, 1890)

Vita Gundulfi: the life of Gundulf, Bishop of Rochester, ed. R. Thomson (Toronto, 1977)

Vita Lanfranc, ed. M. Gibson in *Lanfranco di Pavia e l'Europe del secolo xinel lx centenario della morte* [1089–1989], Pavia, 21–24 September 1989, ed. G. D'Onofrio (Rome, 1993), pp. 659–718

Vita Venerabilis Bosonis Abbatis Beccensis Quarti, PL 150. 723–32

Wace, *A History of the British*, text and trans. J. Weiss (Exeter, 1999)

Walter Daniel, *The Life of Aelred of Rievaulx*, ed. and trans. F. M. Powicke, repr. OMT (Oxford, 1950)

Walter Map, *The Latin Poems Commonly Attributed to Walter Mapes*, coll. and ed. T. Wright, CS, old ser. 16 (London, 1841)

—— *De Nugis Curialium*, ed. and trans. M. R. James, rev. C. N. L. Brooke and R. A. B. Mynors, OMT (Oxford, 1983)

The Waltham Chronicle, ed. and trans. L. Watkiss and M. Chibnall, OMT (Oxford, 1994)

Westminster Abbey Charters, 1066–c. 1214, ed. E. Mason, London Rec. Soc 25 (London, 1988)

William of Malmesbury, *Willelmi Malmesbiriensis Monachi Gesta Pontificum Anglorum*, ed. N. E. S. A. Hamilton, RS 52 (London, 1870)

—— *The Vita Wulfstani of William of Malmesbury*, ed. R. R. Darlington, CS, 3rd ser. 40 (London,1928)

—— *The Early History of Glastonbury by William of Malmesbury, De Antiquitate Ecclesiae Glastoniensis*, ed. and trans. J. Scott (Woodbridge, 1981)

—— *Polyhistor Deflorationum*, ed. H. Testroet Ouellette (Binghamton, 1982)

—— *Life of Wulfstan of Worcester*, trans. J. H. F. Peile (Llanerch repr., 1996)

—— *Historia Nouella*, ed. E. King, trans. K. R. Potter, OMT (Oxford, 1998)

—— *Gesta Regum Anglorum*, ed. and trans. R. A. B. Mynors, R. M. Thomson and M. Winterbottom, OMT (2 vols; Oxford, 1998–99)

William of Newburgh, *Historia Rerum Anglicarum, Chronicles of the Reigns of Stephen, Henry II and Richard I*, ed. R. Howlett, 4 vols, RS 82 (London, 1882–89); trans. J. Stevenson, *The History of William of Newburgh* (Llanerch facsimile, Felinfach, 1996)

Winchester Cathedral Cartulary, ed. A. W. Goodman (Winchester, 1928)

William Thorne, *Chronicle of St Augustine's, Canterbury*, trans. A. H. Davis (Oxford, 1933)

William of Worcester, *Itineraries*, trans. J. Harvey (Oxford, 1969)

Secondary sources

Aird, W., *St Cuthbert and the Normans: the church of Durham, 1071–1153* (Woodbridge, 1998)

Alexander, J.W., 'Herbert of Norwich, 1091–1119: studies in the history of Norman England', *Studies in Mediaeval and Renaissance History* 6 (1969), pp. 115–232

Anderson, F., 'St Pancras Priory, Lewes: its architectural development to c. 1200', *AN Studies* 11 (Woodbridge, 1989), pp. 1–35

Angenendt, A., 'How was a confraternity made? The evidence of charters', *The Durham Liber Vitae and its Context*, ed. D. Rollason et al. (Woodbridge, 2004), pp. 207–20

Appleby, J., *The Troubled Reign of King Stephen* (London, 1969)

Ashdown, M., *English and Norse Documents Relating to the Reign of Ethelred the Unready* (Cambridge, 1930)

Baldwin, J.W., *Aristocratic Life in Medieval France: the romances of Jean Renart and Gerbert de Montreuil, 1190–1230* (Baltimore, 2000)

Barlow, F., *Thomas Becket* (London, 1986)

Barnes, G. D., *Kirkstall Abbey, 1147–1539: an historical study*, Thoresby Society 58 (Leeds, 1985)

Bartlett, R. J. B, *England Under the Norman and Angevin Kings, 1075–1225* (Oxford, 2000)

Bauer, N., 'Monasticism after dark: from dormitory to cell', *American Benedictine Review* 38 (1987), pp. 95–114

Bell, D.N., 'The English Cistercians and the practice of medicine', *Cîteaux: Commentarii Cistercienses. Revue d'histoire cistercienne/A Journal of Historical Studies* 40: 1–4 (1989), pp. 139–74

Bennett, J. M., 'Conviviality and charity in mediaeval and early modern England', *Past and Present* 134 (1992), pp. 19–41

Benton, J. F., 'Suger's life and personality', *Abbot Suger and Saint Denis: a symposium*, ed. P. Lieber Gerson (New York, 1986), pp. 3–16

Berger, J. M., *Die Geschichte der Gastfreundschaft im hochmittelalterlichen Münchtun* (Berlin, 1999)

Berman, C., 'Cistercian nuns and the development of the Order: the Cistercian abbey of Saint-Antoine-des-Champs outside Paris', *The Joy of Learning and the Love of God: studies in honour of J. Leclercq*, ed. E. R. Elder (Kalamazoo, 1995), pp. 121–56

Bethell, D., 'The foundation of Fountains Abbey and the state of St Mary's, York, in 1132', *JEH* 17 (1966), pp. 11–27

—— 'The making of a twelfth-century relic collection,' *Popular Belief and Practice*, ed. G. J. Cuming and D. Baker, *Studies in Church History* 8 (Oxford, 1972), pp. 61–72

Biddle, M., 'Season festivals and residence: Winchester, Westminster and Gloucester in the tenth to twelfth centuries', *AN Studies* 8 (Woodbridge, 1985), pp. 51–72

Binns, A., *Dedications of Monastic Houses in England and Wales, 1066–1216* (Woodbridge, 1989)

Blaauw, W.H., 'Royal journeys in Sussex, from the Conquest to Edward I', *Sussex Archaeological Society* 2 (1849), pp. 132–60

—— 'Visit of Edward II to Battle and other parts of Sussex, 1324', *Sussex Archaeological Society* 6 (1853), pp. 41–53

Blair, P., 'Hall and chamber: English domestic planning, 1000–1250', *Manorial Domestic Buildings in England and N. France*, ed. G. Meirion-Jones and M. Jones (London, 1993), pp. 1–21

Bond, C. J., 'The reconstruction of the mediaeval landscape: the estates of Abingdon abbey', *Landscape History* 1 (1979), pp. 59–75

Bonde, S., and Maines, C., 'The archaeology of monasticism: a summary of recent work in France, 1970–87', *Speculum* 63 (1988), pp. 794–825

Borias, A., 'Christ and the monk', *Monastic Studies* 10 (New York, 1974), pp. 97–129

Bowen, J., 'The *Domus hospitum*; Interim report on work carried out in 1987 by the Canterbury Archaeological Trust', *Archaeologia Cantiana* 104 (1987), pp. 326–7

Brakspear, H., *Waverley Abbey* (Guildford, 1905)

—— 'The abbot's house at Battle', *Archaeologia* 83 (1933), pp. 139–66

—— and St John Hope, W. H., 'The Cistercian abbey of Beaulieu in the county of Southampton', *Archaeological Journal* 63 (1906), pp. 129–86

Braunfels, W., *Monasteries of Western Europe: the architecture of the orders*, trans. A. Laing (London, 1972)

Bredero, A. H., *Cluny et Cîteaux au douzième siècle: l'histoire d'une controverse monastique* (Amsterdam, 1985)

Bremner, R. H., *Giving: charity and philanthropy in history* (New Brunswick and London, 1996)

Brentano, R., 'Samson of Bury revisited', *Vita Religiosa im Mittelalter: Festschrift für Kaspar Elm zum 70. Geburtstag*, ed. F. J. Felten and N. Jaspert, Berliner Historische Studien 31; Ordensstudien 13 (Berlin, 1999), pp. 79–85

Brooke, C., 'St Albans: the great abbey', *Cathedral and City: St Albans ancient and modern*, ed. R. Runcie (London, 1977), pp. 43–70

Brown, S., 'Leavetaking in the twelfth century', *History* 79 (1994), pp. 199–215

Bruckner, M. T., *Narrative Invention in Twelfth-Century French Romance: the Convention of Hospitality, 1160–1200* (Lexington, 1980)

Bruhl, C., 'Zur Geschichte der Procuratio canonica vornehmlich im 11. und 12. Jahrhundert', *Aus Mittelalter und Diplomatik* 1 (Hildesheim, Munich and Zurich, 1989), pp. 323–35

Brundage, J. A., *Mediaeval Canon Law* (London, 1995)

Bucknell, P., *Entertainment and Ritual, 600–1600* (London, 1979)

Burger, M., 'The date and authorship of Robert Grosseteste's *Rules for Household and Estate Management*', *Historical Research* 74 (2001), pp. 106–16

Burnley, D. *Courtliness and Literature in Mediaeval England* (London, 1998)

Burton, J. E., *The Yorkshire Nunneries in the Twelfth and Thirteenth Centuries* (York, 1979)

—— 'A confraternity list from St Mary's Abbey, York', *Revue Bénéndictine* 89 (1979), pp. 325–33

—— *The Monastic and Religious Orders in Britain, 1000–1300* (Cambridge, 1994)

—— *Kirkham Priory from Foundation to Dissolution*, Borthwick Papers 86 (York, 1995)

—— *The Monastic Order in Yorkshire, 1069–1215* (Cambridge, 1999)

—— 'The "Chariot of Aminadab" and the Yorkshire priory of Swine', *Pragmatic Utopias: Ideals and communities, 1200–1630*, ed. R. Horrox and S. Rees Jones (Cambridge, 2001), pp. 26–42

—— and Wilson, C., *St Mary's Abbey, York* (York, 1988)

Bussby, F., *Winchester Cathedral, 1079–1979* (Southampton, 1979)

Butler, C., *Benedictine Monachism: studies in Benedictine life and rule* (London, 1919)

Butler, L., 'The archaeology of rural monasteries in England and Wales', *The Archaeology of Rural Monasteries*, ed. R. Gilchrist and H. Mytum, BAR British Series 203 (Oxford, 1989), pp. 1–28

—— and Given-Wilson, C., *Mediaeval Monasteries of Great Britain* (London, 1979)

Bynum, C. W., '*Docere et exemplum*: an aspect of twelfth-century spirituality', *Harvard Theological Studies* 31 (1979)

—— *Holy Feast and Holy Fast: the religious significance of food to mediaeval women* (Berkeley, 1986)

Carlin, M. and Rosenthal, J. T., ed., *Food and Eating in Mediaeval Europe* (London, 1998)

Cassidy-Welch, M., *Monastic Spaces and their Meanings: thirteenth-century English Cistercian monasteries* (Turnhout, 2001)

Castora, J., 'The Cistercian Order as portrayed in the *Speculum Ecclesiae* of Gerald of Wales', *Analecta Cisterciansia* 53 (1997), pp. 73–97

Cheney, C. R., 'The papal legate and English monasteries in 1206', *EHR* 46 (1931), pp. 443–52

—— 'King John and the Papal Interdict', *Bulletin of the John Rylands Library* 31 (1948), pp. 295–317

—— 'King John's reaction to the Interdict in England', *TRHS*, 4th ser. 31 (1949), pp. 129–50

—— *Episcopal Visitation of the Monasteries in the Thirteenth Century*, 2nd edn (Manchester, 1982)

Cheney, M., *Roger, Bishop of Worcester, 1164–79* (Oxford, 1980)

Chibnall, M. G., 'Les relations entre Jumièges et l'Angleterre, du xi au xiii siècles', *Jumièges Congrès Scientifique du xiii eme centenaire*, 2 vols (Rouen, 1955), 1, pp. 269–75

—— *The World of Orderic Vitalis, Norman Monks and Norman Knights* (Oxford, 1984)

—— *Anglo-Norman England, 1066–1166* (Oxford, 1986)

—— 'The Empress Mathilda and Bec-Hellouin', *AN Studies* 10 (Woodbridge, 1988), pp. 35–48

—— 'Monastic foundations in England and Normandy, 1066–1189', *England and Normandy in the Middle Ages*, ed. D. Bates and A. Curry (London, 1994), pp. 37–49

Church, R. W., *Saint Anselm* (London, 1870)

Clanchy, M. T., *England and Its Rulers, 1066–1272* (London, 1983)

—— *From Memory to Written Record, England, 1066–1307*, 2nd edn (Oxford, 1993)

Clark, E., 'Social welfare and mutual aid in the mediaeval countryside', *Journal of British Studies* 33 (1994), pp. 381–406

Coffin, L. D., 'Hospitality: an orientation to Benedictine spirituality', *American Benedictine Review* 39 (1988), pp. 50–71

Coldstream, N., 'Architecture from Beaulieu to the Dissolution', *Cistercian Art and Architecture in the British Isles*, ed. C. Norton and D. Park (Cambridge, 1986), pp. 139–59

Colvin, H. M., *The White Canons in England* (Oxford, 1951)

Constable, G., *Monastic Tithes, from their Origins to the Twelfth Century* (Cambridge, 1964)

—— *Cluniac Studies* (London, 1980)

—— 'Suger's monastic administration', *Abbot Suger and St Denis: a symposium*, ed. P. Lieber Gerson (New York, 1986), pp. 17–32

—— *Three Studies in Mediaeval Religious Social Thought* (Cambridge, 1995)

—— *Culture and Spirituality in Medieval Europe* (Hampshire, 1996)

—— *The Reformation of the Twelfth Century* (Cambridge, 1996)

Cook, G. H., *English Monasteries in the Middle Ages* (London, 1961)

Coomans, T., 'L' accueil du chapitre général au Moyen Age', *Pour une histoire monumentale de l'abbaye de Cîteaux, 1098–1998*, ed. M. Plouvier *et al.* (Brecht, 1998), pp. 154–64

Coppack, G., 'The interface between estate and monastery', *L'Espace Cistercien*, ed. L. Pressouyre (Paris, 1994), pp. 415–25

—— *The White Monks: the Cistercians in Britain, 1128–1540* (Stroud, 1998)

—— *Fountains Abbey: the Cistercians in northern England* (Stroud, 2003)

—— and Fergusson, P., *Rievaulx Abbey* (London, 1994)

—— and Gilyard-Beer, R., 'Excavations at Fountains Abbey in N. Yorkshire, 1979–80: the early development of the church', *Archaeologia* 108 (1986), pp. 147–88

—— *Fountains Abbey, Yorkshire*, English Heritage Guide (London, 1993)

Cormier, R. J., 'Mediaeval courtly literature, royal patronage and world harmony III', *Anuario de Estudios Medievales* 21 (1991), pp. 277–90

Corpus of Mediaeval Library Catalogues 3: the libraries of the Cistercians, Gilbertines and Premonstratensians, ed. D. N. Bell (London, 1992)

Corpus of Mediaeval Library Catalogues 4: English Benedictine Libraries: the shorter catalogues, ed. R. Sharpe, J. P. Carley, R. M. Thomson, A. G. Watson (London, 1996)

Coss, P., *Lordship, Knighthood and Locality: a study of English society, c. 1180–1280* (Cambridge, 1991)

Coulton, G. G., *Five Centuries of Religion*, 4 vols (Cambridge, 1923–50)

—— *Life in the Middle Ages*, 4 vols, 2nd edn (Cambridge, 1928–30)

Courtney, P., 'Excavations in the outer precinct of Tintern abbey', *Medieval Archaeology* 33 (1989), pp. 99–143

Cowdrey, H. E. J., 'Unions and confraternities with Cluny', *JEH* 16 (1965), pp. 152–62

Cowley, F. G., *The Monastic Order in South Wales, 1066–1349* (Cardiff, 1977)

Cownie, E., 'Gloucester Abbey, 1066–1135: an illustration of religious patronage in Anglo-Norman England', *England and Normandy in the Middle Ages*, ed. D. Bates and A. Curry (London, 1994), pp. 143–57

—— *Religious Patronage in Anglo-Norman England* (Woodbridge, 1998)

Cox, D. C., *The Chronicle of Evesham* (Evesham, 1904)

Cox, M., *The Story of Abingdon: Part 2, medieval Abingdon, 1186–1556* (Abingdon, 1996)

Cram, L., *Reading Abbey* (Reading, 1988)

Cramer, P., *Baptism and Change in the Early Middle Ages c. 200–c. 1150* (Cambridge, 1993)

Crehan, J. H., 'The supper of the Lord', *Downside Review* 89 (1971), pp. 296–301

Crook, J., and Fletcher, J. M., 'The date of the pilgrim's hall, Winchester', *Proceedings of the Hampshire Field Club and Archaeological Society* 40 (1984), pp. 130–3

Crosby, E. U., *Bishop and Chapter in Twelfth-century England: a study of the Mensa Episcopalis* (Cambridge, 1994)

Davis, H. W. C., 'The chronicle of Battle abbey', *EHR* 29 (1914), pp. 426–34

Davis, R. H. C., 'The monks of St Edmund, 1021–1148', *History* 40 (1955), pp. 227–39

Delatte, P., *The Rule of St Benedict, A Commentary*, trans. J. McCann (London, 1959)

Denholm-Young, N., *Collected Papers of N. Denholm-Young* (Cardiff, 1969)

Dickinson, J., *The Origins of the Austin Canons* (London, 1950)

Dictionary of Mediaeval Latin from British Sources, prepared by R. E. Latham and D. R. Howlett (Oxford, 1975–)

Dictionary of National Biography, ed. H. C. G. Matthew and B. Harrison (Oxford, 2004)

Dictionnaire de l'Ancien Français: le moyen age, ed. A. J. Greimas (Paris, 1995)

Dixon, P., 'The monastic buildings at Ely', *A History of Ely Cathedral*, ed. P. Meadows and N. Ramsay (Woodbridge, 2003), pp. 143–56

Dobson, B., 'The monks of Canterbury in the later Middle Ages, 1220–1540', *A History of Canterbury Cathedral*, ed. P. Collinson, N. Ramsey and M. Sparks (Oxford, 1995), pp. 69–157

Dodwell, B., 'The monastic community', *Norwich Cathedral: church, city and diocese, 1096–1996*, ed. I. Atherton, E. Fernie, C. Harper-Bill, H. Smith (London, 1996), pp. 231–54

Donkin, R. A., 'The urban property of the Cistercians in mediaeval England', *Analecta Sacri Ordinis Cisterciensis* 15 (1959), pp. 104–31

—— *The Cistercians: studies in the geography of medieval England and Wales* (Toronto, 1978)

Dowdy, M., *The Monastic Setting of Ely* (London, 1977)

Draper, P., 'Enclosures and entrances in medieval cathedrals: access and security', ed. J. Backhouse, *The Medieval English Cathedral: papers in honour of Pamela Tudor-Craig*, Proceedings of the 1998 Harlaxton Symposium (Donington, 2000), pp. 76–88

Dugdale, W., *Monasticon Anglicanum*, ed. Sir William Dugdale, rev. J. Caley, H. Ellis, B. Bandinel, 6 vols in 8 (London, 1817–30)

Duggan, A., 'The cult of St Thomas Becket in the thirteenth century', *St Thomas Cantilupe, Bishop of Hereford: essays in his honour*, ed. M. Jancey (Hereford, 1982), pp. 21–44

Dunning, R. W., 'The last days of Cleeve Abbey', *The Church in Pre-Reformation Society: essays in honour of F. R. H. Du Boulay*, ed. C. M. Barron and C. Harper-Bill (Woodbridge, 1985), pp. 58–67

Eales, R., 'Royal power and castles in Norman England', *The Ideals and Practice of Medieval Knighthood* 3, ed. C. Harper Bill and S. Harvey (Woodbridge, 1990), pp. 49–78

—— 'The political setting of the Becket translation of 1220', *Martyrs and Martyrologies*, ed. D. Webb, *Studies in Church History* 30 (Oxford, 1993), pp. 127–39

—— and Sharpe, R., ed. *Canterbury and the Norman Conquest: churches, saints and scholars, 1066–1109* (London, 1995)

Elder, E. R., ed., *The New Monastery, Texts and Studies on the Earliest Cistercians* (Kalamazoo, 1998)

Elkins, S., *Holy Women of Twelfth-Century England* (Chapel Hill, 1988)

Evans, J., *Monastic Life at Cluny, 910–1157* (London, 1931)

Farmer, D. H., 'Two biographies of William of Malmesbury', *Latin Biography*, ed. T. A. Dorey (London, 1967), pp. 157–76

—— *Saint Hugh of Lincoln* (London, 1985)

Fergusson, P., 'The first architecture of the Cistercians in England and the work of Abbot Adam of Meaux', *Journal of the British Archaeological Association* 136 (1983), pp. 74–86

—— *Architecture of Solitude: Cistercian abbeys in twelfth-century England* (Princeton, 1984)

—— '*Porta patens esto*. Notes on early Cistercian gatehouses in the north of England', *Mediaeval Architecture and its Intellectual Context: studies in honour of Peter Kidson*, ed. E. Fernie and P. Crossley (London, 1990), pp. 47–60

—— 'Aelred's abbatial residence at Rievaulx abbey', *Studies in Cistercian Art and Architecture* 5, ed. M. P. Lillich (Kalamazoo, 1998), pp. 41–58

Finucane, R. C., *Miracles and Pilgrims: popular beliefs in mediaeval England*, rev. edn (Basingstoke, 1995)

Flight, C., *The Bishops and Monks of Rochester, 1076–1214* (Maidstone, 1997)

Fosbroke, T. D., *British Monachism or Manners and Customs of Monks and Nuns of England* (London, 1817)

France, J., 'The cellarer's domain – evidence from Denmark', *Studies in Cistercian Art and Architecture* 5, ed. M. P. Lillich (Kalamazoo, 1998), pp. 1–40

Gasquet, F., *English Monastic Life* (London, 1904)

—— *Henry III and the Church: a study of his ecclesiastical policy and of the relations between England and Rome* (London, 1905)

Gibson, M., *Lanfranc of Bec* (Oxford, 1978)

—— 'Normans and Angevins, 1070–1220', *A History of Canterbury Cathedral*, ed. P. Collinson, N. Ramsey and M. Sparks (Oxford, 1995), pp. 38–68

—— 'The image of Lanfranc', *Lanfranco di Pavia e l'Europe del secolo xinel lx centenario della morte* [1089–1989], Pavia, 21–24 September, 1989, ed. G. D'Onofrio (Rome, 1993), pp. 21–8

Gieben, S., 'Robert Grosseteste and mediaeval courtesy books', *Vivarium* 5 (1967), pp. 47–74

Gilchrist, R., 'The archaeology of mediaeval English nunneries: a research design', *The Archaeology of Rural Monasteries*, ed. R. Gilchrist and H. Mytum, BAR British Series 203 (Oxford, 1989), pp. 251–60

—— *Gender and Material Culture: the archaeology of religious women* (London, 1994)

—— *Contemplation and Action: the other monasticism* (London, 1995)

—— *Norwich Cathedral Close: the evolution of the cathedral landscape* (Woodbridge, 2005)

—— and Mytum, H., ed., *Advances in Monastic Archaeology*, BAR British Series 227 (Oxford, 1993)

Gillingham, J., 'From *civilitas* to civility: codes of manners in medieval and early modern England', *TRHS* 6: 12 (2002), pp. 267–89

Gilyard-Beer, R., 'Fountains abbey: the early buildings, 1132–50', *Archaeological Journal* 125 (1968), pp. 313–19

Glixelli, S., 'Les contenances de table', *Romania* 21 (1947), pp. 1–40

Golding, B., 'Hermits, monks and women in twelfth-century France and England: the experience of Obazine and Sempringham', *Monastic Studies*, ed. J. Loades (Bangor, 1990), pp. 127–45

—— 'Gerald of Wales and the monks', *Thirteenth-Century England* 5, ed. P. R. Coss and S. D. Lloyd (Woodbridge, 1995), pp. 53–64

—— *Gilbert of Sempringham and the Gilbertine Order, c. 1130–c. 1300* (Oxford, 1995)

Goodwin, A., *The Abbey of St Edmundsbury* (Oxford, 1931)

Graham, R., 'The relation of Cluny to some other movements of monastic reform', *Journal of Theological Studies* 15 (1914), pp. 179–95

—— *English Ecclesiastical Studies, Being Some Essays in Mediaeval History* (London, 1929)

—— *An Essay on the English Monasteries* (London, 1939)

Gransden, A., *Historical Writing in England c. 550–c. 1307* (London, 1974)

—— 'A democratic movement in the abbey of Bury St Edmunds in the late twelfth and early thirteenth centuries', *JEH* 26 (1975), pp. 25–39

—— 'Baldwin, abbot of Bury St Edmunds, 1065–97', *AN Studies* 4 (Woodbridge, 1982), pp. 65–7

—— 'The legends and traditions concerning the origins of the abbey of Bury St Edmunds', *EHR* 100 (1985), pp. 1–24

—— 'The abbey of Bury St Edmunds and national politics in the reigns of King John and Henry III', *Monastic Studies* 2, ed. J. Loades (Bangor, 1991), pp. 67–86

—— ed., *Bury St Edmunds: medieval art, architecture, archaeology and economy*, British Archaeological Association Conference Transactions 20 (Leeds, 1998)

—— 'The cult of St Mary at Beodericisworth and then in Bury St Edmunds Abbey to c. 1150', *JEH* 55: 4 (2004), pp. 627–53

—— 'The separation of portions between abbot and convent at Bury St Edmunds: the decisive years, 1278–1281', *EHR* 119: 481 (2004), pp. 373–406

Grant, L., *Abbot Suger of St Denis: church and state in early twelfth-century France* (London, 1998)

Greatrex, J., 'St Swithun's Priory in the later Middle Ages', *Winchester Cathedral: 900 years, 1093–1993*, ed. J. Crook (Chichester, 1993), pp. 129–66

—— 'Benedictine observance at Ely: the intellectual, liturgical and spiritual evidence considered', *A History of Ely Cathedral*, ed. P. Meadows and N. Ramsay (Woodbridge, 2003), pp. 77–93

Greenaway, G., *The Life and Death of Thomas Becket, Chancellor of England and Archbishop of Canterbury* (Folio Society, Bristol, 1961)

Greene, J. P., *Mediaeval Monasteries* (Leicester, 1992)

Greer, R. A., 'Hospitality in the first five centuries of the church', *Monastic Studies* 10 (New York, 1974), pp. 29–48

Grenville, J., *Mediaeval Housing* (London, 1997)

Halliday, R., 'Moyse's Hall, Bury St Edmunds', *Suffolk Review: Bulletin of the Suffolk Local History Council*, new ser. 25 (1995), pp. 27–44

Hammond, P. W., *Food and Feast in Mediaeval Society* (Stroud, 1993)

Hare, J., 'The buildings of Battle abbey: a preliminary survey', *AN Studies* 3 (1980), pp. 78–95

—— *The Eastern Range and the Excavation of 1978–80* (London, 1985)

Hare, M., 'Kings, crowns and festivals: the origins of Gloucester as a royal ceremonial centre', *Transactions of the Bristol and Gloucestershire Archaeological Society* 115 (1997), pp. 41–78

Harland, J., *Historical Account of the Cistercian Abbey of Salley* (London, 1853)

Harper-Bill, C., 'Herluin, abbot of Bec and his biographer', *Religious Motivation: biographical and sociological problems for the church historian*, ed. D. Baker, *Studies in Church History* 15 (1978), pp. 15–26

—— 'The piety of the Anglo-Norman class', *AN Studies* 2 (Woodbridge, 1980), pp. 63–77

—— 'Cistercian visitation in the late Middle Ages: the case of Hailes Abbey', *Bulletin of Historical Research* 53 (1980), pp. 103–14

Harris, M. E., 'Lanfranc and Anselm', *Benedict's Disciples*, ed. D. H. Farmer (Leominster, 1980), pp. 154–74

Hartridge, R. A. R., *A History of Vicarages in the Middle Ages* (Cambridge, 1930)

Harvey, B., *Westminster Abbey and its Estates in the Middle Ages* (Oxford, 1977)

—— *Monastic Dress in the Middle Ages: precept and practice*, William Urry Memorial Trust (Canterbury, 1988)

—— *Living and Dying in England c. 1100–1540: the monastic experience* (Oxford, 1993)

—— 'The aristocratic consumer in England in the long thirteenth century', *Thirteenth-century England* 6, ed. M. Prestwich, R. H. Britnell and R. Frame (Woodbridge, 1997), pp. 13–37

—— 'Monastic pittances in the Middle Ages', *Food in Medieval England: diet and nutrition*, ed. C. M. Woolgar, D. Serjeantson and T. Waldron (Oxford, 2006), pp. 215–27

Harvey, J., 'Westminster Abbey: the infirmarer's garden', *Garden History* 20: 2 (1992), pp. 97–115

Harvey, P. D. A., 'Mid-thirteenth-century accounts from Bury St Edmunds', *Bury St Edmunds: Medieval art, architecture, archaeology and economy*, ed. A. Gransden, British Archaeological Association Conference Transactions 20 (Leeds, 1998), pp. 128–38

—— and Skelton, R. A., ed., *Local Maps and Plans from Mediaeval England* (Oxford, 1986)

Haseldine, J., 'Friendship and rivalry: the role of *amicitia* in twelfth-century monastic relations', *JEH* 44 (1993), pp. 390–414

Haskins, C. H., *Studies in Mediaeval Culture* (Oxford, 1929)

Hassall, W. O., *They Saw it Happen: an anthology of eye-witness' accounts of events in British History 55 BC–1485 AD* (Oxford, 1957)

Hatcher, J. and Miller, E., *Mediaeval England: rural society and economic change, 1086–1348* (London, 1978)

Heal, F., 'The idea of hospitality in early modern England', *Past and Present* 102 (1984), pp. 66–93

—— *Hospitality in Early Modern England* (Oxford, 1990)

Heale, M., *The Dependent Priories of Medieval English Monasteries*, Studies in the History of Medieval Religion 22 (Woodbridge, 2004)

Henisch, B. A., *Fast and Food: food in mediaeval society* (London, 1976)

Heron, *Table and Tradition: towards an ecumenical understanding of the Eucharist* (Edinburgh, 1983)

Heywood, S., 'The Romanesque building', *Norwich Cathedral: church, city and diocese, 1096–1996*, ed. I. Atherton, E. Fernie, C. Harper-Bill, H. Smith (London, 1996), pp. 73–115

Hill, B. D., *English Cistercian Monasteries and their Patrons in the Twelfth Century* (London, 1968)

Hill, J. W. F., *Mediaeval Lincoln* (Northampton, 1948)

Hill, M. C., *The King's Messengers, 1199–1377: a contribution to the history of the Royal Household* (London, 1961)

Hills, G., 'The antiquities of Bury St Edmunds', *Journal of the British Archaeological Association* 21 (1865), pp. 32–56, 104–40

Holdsworth, C., 'Christina of Markyate', *Medieval Women*, ed. D. Baker, *Studies in Church History subsidia* 1 (Oxford, 1978), pp. 185–204

Hollis, S., ed. with W. R. Barnes, R. Hayward, K. Loncar and M. Wright, *Writing the Wilton Women: Goscelin's legend of St Edith and Liber Confortatorius*, Medieval Women: Texts and Contexts 9 (Turnhout, 2004)

Hollister, C. W., 'Courtly culture and courtly style in the Anglo-Norman world', *Albion* 20 (1988), 1–17

Holmes, U. T., *Daily Living in the Twelfth Century, based on the Observations of Alexander of Neckham in London and Paris* (Madison, 1952)

Holton-Krayenbuhl, A., 'The infirmary complex at Ely', *Archaeological Journal* 154 (1997), pp. 118–73

—— 'The prior's lodgings at Ely', *Archaeological Journal* 156 (1999), pp. 294–341

Howell, M., *Regalian Rights in England* (London, 1962)

—— 'Abbatial vacancies and the divided *mensa* in mediaeval England', *JEH* 33 (1982), pp. 173–92

Hudson, J. G. H., *Land, Law and Lordship in Anglo-Norman England* (Oxford, 1994)

Huerre, D., 'Monastic hospitality and the conversion of the monk', *American Benedictine Review* 44 (1993), pp. 249–57

Hunt, R. W., 'The preface to the *Speculum Ecclesiae*', *Viator* 8 (1977), pp. 189–213

—— *The Schools and the Cloister: the life and writings of Alexander Nequam (1157–1217)*, rev. M. Gibson (Oxford, 1984)

Hurry, J. B., *Reading Abbey* (London, 1901)

—— *Henry Beauclerc and Reading Abbey* (London, 1917)

—— *The Octocentenary of Reading Abbey* (London, 1921)

Hutchinson, C., *The Hermit Monks of Grandmont* (Kalamazoo, 1989)

Hutton, E., *The Franciscans in England, 1224–1538* (London, 1926)

Iogna-Prat, D., 'Coutumes et statuts Cluniensis comme sources historiques (c. 990–c. 1200)', *Revue Mabillon* 64 (1992), pp. 23–48

Jaeger, C., *The Origins of Courtliness: civilising trends and the formation of courtly ideals, 939–1200* (Philadelphia, 1985)

—— 'Humanism and ethics in the School of St Victor in the early twelfth century', *Mediaeval Studies* 55 (1993), pp. 51–79

—— *The Envy of the Angels: cathedral schools and social ideals in mediaeval Europe* (Philadelphia, 1994)

—— *Scholars and Courtiers: intellectuals and society in the medieval West*, Variorum Collected Studies Series (Aldershot, 2002)

James, M. R., *On the Abbey of St Edmunds at Bury* (Cambridge, 1895)

Jamroziak, E., *Rievaulx Abbey and Its Social Context, 1132–1300: memory, locality and network* (Turnhout, 2005)

Jansen, V., 'Architecture and community in mediaeval monastic dormitories', *Studies in Cistercian Art and Architecture* 5, ed. M. P. Lillich (Kalamazoo, 1998), pp. 59–94

Jared, L. H., 'English ecclesiastical vacancies during the reigns of William I and Henry I', *JEH* 42 (1991), pp. 362–93

John, E., 'The division of the *mensa* in early English monasteries', *JEH* 6 (1955), pp. 143–55

Johnson, P. D., *Prayer, Patronage and Power: the abbey of la Trinité Vendôme, 1032–1187* (New York, 1981)

—— *Equal in Monastic Profession: religious women in Medieval France* (Chicago, 1991)

Kahn, D., *Canterbury Cathedral and Its Romanesque Sculpture* (London, 1991)

Keats-Rohan, K. S. B., 'Testimonies of the living dead: the martyrology-necrology and the necrology in the chapter book of Mont-Saint-Michel', *The Durham Liber Vitae and Its Context*, ed. D. Rollason *et al.* (Woodbridge, 2004), pp. 165–90

Kemp, B., 'Monastic possession of parish churches in England in the twelfth century', *JEH* 31 (1980), pp. 133–60

—— 'The seals of Reading abbey', *Mediaeval Studies* 14 (1988), pp. 139–62

—— 'The hand of St James at Reading', *Reading Mediaeval Studies* 16 (Reading, 1990)

Kerr, J., 'Monastic hospitality: the Benedictines in England c. 1070–c. 1245', *AN Studies* 23 (Woodbridge, 2001), pp. 115–54

—— 'The open door: hospitality and honour in twelfth- / early-thirteenth-century England', *History* 87 (2002), pp. 322–35

—— 'Cistercian hospitality in the later Middle Ages', *Monasteries and Society in the later Middle Ages*, ed. J. Burton and K. Stöber, (forthcoming, Woodbridge, 2008)

—— 'Food, drink and lodging: hospitality in twelfth-century England', *Haskins Society Journal* 18, ed. S. Morillo (forthcoming, Woodbridge, 2007)

—— 'Welcome the coming and speed the departing guest', *JMH* (forthcoming)

Kerry, C., *A History of the Municipal Church of St Lawrence, Reading* (Reading, Derby, 1883)

King, E., *Peterborough Abbey, 1086–1310: a study in the land market* (Cambridge, 1973)

—— 'The Anarchy of Stephen's reign', *TRHS* 5th ser. 34 (1984), pp. 133–53

King, G. G., 'The Vision of Thurkill and St James of Compostella', *The Romanic Review* 10 (1919), pp. 38–47

Kissan, B. W., 'Lanfranc's alleged division of lands between archbishop and community', *EHR* 54 (1939), pp. 285–93

Kite, E., ed., *Memorials of Wilton and other Papers* (Devizes, 1906)

Klukas, A., 'The architectural implications of the *Decreta* of Lanfranc', *AN Studies* 6 (Woodbridge, 1984), pp. 136–71

Knowles, D., 'Essays in monastic history 3: the Norman monasticism', *Downside Review* 50 (1932), pp. 33–48

—— 'Essays in monastic history 4: the growth of exemption', *Downside Review* 50 (1932), pp. 201–31, 396–436

—— *The Religious Houses in Mediaeval England* (London, 1940)

—— *The Religious Orders in England*, 3 vols (Cambridge, 1948–59)

—— 'Les relations monastiques entre la Normandie et l'Angleterre', *Jumièges Congrès Scientifique du xiii-eme centenaire*, 2 vols (Rouen, 1955), 1, pp. 261–7

—— 'The reforming decrees of Peter the Venerable', *Petrus Venerabilis, 1156–1956: studies and texts commemorating the eighth centenary of his death*, ed. G. Constable and J. Kritzeck, *Studia Anselmiana* 40 (Rome, 1956), pp. 1–20

—— The Historian and Character, and Other Essays, collected and presented to him by his friends, pupils and colleagues on the occasion of his retirement as Regius Professor of Modern History in the University of Cambridge, ed. C. N. L. Brooke and G. Constable (Cambridge, 1963)

—— The Monastic Order in England: a history of its development from the times of St Dunstan to the Fourth Lateran Council, 940–1216, 2nd edn (Cambridge, 1963)

—— Christian Monasticism (Hampshire, 1969)

—— and Brooke, C. N. L., and London, V. C. M., The Heads of Religious Houses in England and Wales, 940–1216 (London, 1972)

—— and Hadcock, R. N., Mediaeval Religious Houses, England and Wales, 2nd edn (Harlow, 1971)

Koenig, J, New Testament Hospitality: partnership with strangers as promise and mission (Philadelphia, 1985)

Kristeva, J., Strangers to Ourselves, trans. L. S. Roudiez (New York, 1992)

Labarge, M. W., Mediaeval Travellers: the rich and restless (London, 1982)

Lambrick, G., 'Abingdon abbey administration', JEH 17 (1966), pp. 159–83

—— and M. Biddle, J. N. L. Myers, 'The early history of Abingdon, Berkshire, and its abbey', Mediaeval Archaeology 12 (1968), pp. 26–9

Lawrence, C. H., Mediaeval Monasticism, 2nd edn (London, 1989)

Leclercq, J., 'Hospitality and monastic prayer', Cistercian Studies 8: 1 (1973), pp. 3–24

Legge, M. D., Anglo-Norman in the Cloisters (Edinburgh, 1950)

—— Anglo-Norman Literature and Its Background (Oxford, 1963)

Lekai, L. J., The White Monks: a history of the Cistercian Order (Okauchee, Wis., 1953)

—— The Cistercians: ideals and reality (Kent, Ohio, 1977)

—— 'Ideals and reality in early Cistercian life and legislation', Cistercian Ideals and Reality, ed. J. R. Sommerfeldt (Kalamazoo, 1978), pp. 4–29

Lendinara, P., 'The oratio de utensilibus ad domum regendum pertinentibus by Adam of Balsham', AN Studies 15 (Woodbridge, 1993), pp. 161–76

Lennard, R. V., Rural England, 1086–1135: a study of social and agrarian conditions (Oxford, 1959)

Léotaud, A., 'Monastic officials in the Middle Ages', Downside Review 56 (1938), pp. 391–409

Leyser, K., 'Frederick Barbarossa, Henry II, and the hand of St James', EHR 90 (1975), pp. 481–506

Liddesdale Palmer, R., English Monasteries in the Middle Ages (London, 1930)

Lindenbaum, S., 'Entertainment in English monasteries', Le Théâtre et la Cité dans L'Europe Médiévale, ed. J. Claude Aubailly and E. E. Dubruck (Stuttgart, 1988), pp. 411–21

Little, A. G., The Grey Friars in Oxford, Oxford Historical Society 20 (Oxford, 1892)

Loades, D., ed., The End of Strife (Edinburgh, 1984)

Lobel, M. D., The Borough of Bury St Edmunds: a study of the government and development of a monastic town (Oxford, 1935)

Loxton, H., Pilgrimage to Canterbury (Newton Abbot, London, Vancouver, 1978)

Luce, R., Pages from the History of Romsey and its Abbey (Winchester, 1948)

Lunt, W. E., Financial Relations of the Papacy with England to 1327, Studies in Anglo-Papal Relations During the Middle Ages 1, 2 vols (Cambridge, Mass., 1939–62)

Maltby, H. J. M., 'A history of the building and museum collection', Archaeological Journal, 108 (1952), pp. 165–7

Marner, D., St Cuthbert: his life and cult in medieval Durham (Toronto, 2000)

Mason, E., 'Timeo Barones et Donas Ferentes', Religious motivation: biographical and sociological problems for the church historian, ed. D. Baker, Studies in Church History 15 (Oxford, 1978), pp. 61–75

—— 'Pro statu et incolumnitate regni mei: royal monastic patronage, 1066–1154', Religion and national identity, ed. S. Mews, Studies in Church History 18 (Oxford, 1982), pp. 99–117

—— St Wulfstan of Worcester, c. 1008–95 (Oxford, 1990)

—— 'Westminster Abbey and the monarchy between the reigns of William I and John', JEH 41 (1990), pp. 199–216

—— *Westminster Abbey and its People, c. 1250–1216* (Cambridge, 1996)

Matthew, D., *The Norman Monasteries and their English Possessions* (Oxford, 1962)

Mauss, M., *The Gift: forms and functions of exchange in archaic societies*, trans. W. D. Halls (London, 1990)

Mayr-Harting, H., 'Hilary, bishop of Chichester, 1147–1169, and Henry II', *EHR* 78 (1963), pp. 209–24

McGuire, B. P., 'The collapse of a monastic friendship: the case of Jocelin of Brakelond and Samson of Bury', *JMH* 4 (1978), pp. 369–97

McLean, T., *Mediaeval English Gardens* (London, 1981)

Mead, W. E., *The English Feast* (London, 1931)

Milis, L. *Angelic Monks and Earthly Men: monasticism and its meaning to mediaeval society* (Woodbridge, 1992)

Moore, E. W., 'Mediaeval English fairs: evidence from Winchester and St Ives', *Pathways to Mediaeval Peasants*, ed. J. A. Raftis (Toronto, 1981), pp. 283–99

Moorhouse, S., 'Monastic estates: their composition and development', *The Archaeology of Rural Monasteries*, ed. R. Gilchrist and H. Mytum, BAR British Series 203 (Oxford, 1989), pp. 29–85

Moorman, J. R. H., *Church Life in England in the Thirteenth Century* (Cambridge, 1945)

Morey, A., 'Chapters of the English Black monks', *Downside Review* 49 (1931), pp. 420–9

—— 'The conflict of Clairvaux and Cluny', *Downside Review* 50 (1932), pp. 87–107

Morton, V., *Guidance for Women in Twelfth-Century Convents* (Cambridge, 2003)

Mullin, F., *A History of the Cistercians in Yorkshire* (Washington, 1932)

Neilson, N., *Customary Rents* (Oxford, 1910)

Newman, M., *The Boundaries of Charity: Cistercian culture and ecclesiastical reform, 1098–1180* (Stanford, California, 1996)

Nicholls, J. W., *The Matter of Courtesy: medieval courtesy books and the Gawain poet* (Cambridge, 1985)

Nichols, J. A., 'The internal organization of English Cistercian Nunneries', *Cîteaux* 30 (1979), pp. 23–40

—— 'Cistercian nuns in twelfth- and thirteenth-century England', *Hidden Springs: Cistercian monastic women*, ed. J. A. Nichols and L. Shanks, 2 vols (Kalamazoo, 1995), 1, pp. 49–62

O'Brien, B., *God's Peace and King's Peace: the laws of Edward the Confessor* (Philadelphia, 1999)

Ohler, N., *The Mediaeval Traveller*, trans. C. Hillier (Woodbridge, 1989)

The Oxford Dictionary of Saints, ed. D. H. Farmer, 3rd edn (Oxford, 1992)

The Oxford Dictionary of the Christian Church, ed. F. L. Cross, 3rd edn (Oxford, 1997)

Orme, N., *From Childhood to Chivalry: the education of the English kings and aristocracy, 1066–1530* (London, 1984)

O' Sullivan, C. M., *Hospitality in Medieval Ireland, 900–1500* (Dublin, 2004)

Owen, D., 'Ely, 1109–1539: priory, community and town', *A History of Ely Cathedral*, ed. P. Meadows and N. Ramsay (Woodbridge, 2003), pp. 59–76

The Oxford Companion to the Bible, ed. B. M. Metzger and M. D. Coogan (New York and Oxford, 1993)

Parisse, M., *Les Nonnes au Moyen Age* (Clamecy, 1983)

Peifer, C., 'What does it mean to live "According to the *Rule*"?', *Monastic Studies* 55 (1968), pp. 19–44

Peters, T., 'Elements of the *Chanson de Geste* in an Old French Life of Becket: Garnier's *Vie de Saint Thomas le Martyr*', *Olifant* 18 (1993–94), pp. 278–88

Philp, B., *Excavations at Faversham, 1965: the royal abbey, Roman villa and Belgic farmstead* (Bromley, 1968)

Pitt-Rivers, J., *The Fate of Shechem: essays in the anthropology of the Mediterranean*, Cambridge Studies in Social Anthropology 19 (Cambridge, 1977)

Platt, C., *The Monastic Grange in Mediaeval England* (London, 1969)

—— *The Abbeys and Priories of Mediaeval England* (London, 1984)

Porée, A. A., *Histoire de l'Abbaye du Bec*, 2 vols (Évroux, 1901)

Power, E., *Medieval English Nunneries, c. 1275–1535* (Cambridge, 1922)

Preston, A. E., *The Church and Parish of St Nicholas Abingdon and Other Papers*, Oxford Historical Society 99 (Oxford, 1935)

Price, L., *The Plan of St Gall in Brief* (University of California, Berkeley, CA, and London, 1982)

Quiney, A., 'Hall or chamber? That is the question: the use of rooms in post-Conquest houses', *Architectural History Journal of the Society of Architectural Historians of Great Britain* 42 (1999), pp. 24–46

Rahtz, P., *Glastonbury* (London, 1993)

Rampton, M., 'The significance of the banquet scene in the Bayeux tapestry', *Medieualia et Humanistica,*, new ser. 21 (1990), pp. 33–45

Rawcliffe, C., 'On the threshold of eternity': care for the sick in East Anglian monasteries', *East Anglia's History: studies in honour of Norman Scarfe*, ed. C. Harper-Bill, C. Rawcliffe, R. G. Wilson (Woodbridge, 2002), pp. 41–72

Reece, S., *The Stranger's Welcome: oral theory and the aesthetics of the Homeric hospitality scene* (Kalamazoo, 1993)

Reeves, C., *Pleasure and Pastimes in Mediaeval England* (Stroud, 1995)

Reyerson, K. L., 'The way of Mary and that of Martha: conceptions of monastic life at Savigny, 1112–80', *The Mediaeval Monastery*, ed. A. MacLeish (Minnesota, 1988), pp. 34–42

Richardson, H. G., 'The coronation in mediaeval England', *Traditio* 16 (1960), pp. 111–202

Rigg, A. G., *A History of Anglo-Latin Literature, 1066–1422* (Cambridge, 1992)

Robinson, J., A., 'Lanfranc's monastic *Constitutions*', *Journal of Theological Studies* 10 (1909), pp. 375–88

—— *Gilbert Crispin, Abbot of Westminster: a study of the abbey under Norman rule* (Cambridge, 1911)

Robuck, J., *St Augustine's Abbey, Canterbury* (London, 1997)

Roffe, D., 'The Historia Croylandsensis: a plea for reassessment', *EHR* 110 (1995), pp. 93–108

Rollason, D., *et al.*, ed., *The Durham Liber Vitae and its Context*, ed. D. Rollason, A. Piper, M. Harvey and L. Rollason (Woodbridge, 2004)

Rosenwein, B. H., *To be the Neighbor of St Peter: the social meaning of Cluny's property, 909–1049* (Ithaca and London, 1989)

Rosser, G., *Mediaeval Westminster, 1200–1540* (Oxford, 1989)

—— 'Going to the fraternity feast: commensality and social relations in late medieval England', *Journal of British Studies* 33 (1994), pp. 430–40

Rowling, M., *Everyday Life of Mediaeval Travellers* (London, 1971)

Royal Commission on Historical Monuments London 1: Westminster Abbey (London, 1924)

Rubin, M., *Charity and Community in Mediaeval Cambridge* (Cambridge, 1986)

Samuel, E. R., 'Was Moyse's Hall, Bury St Edmunds, a Jew's house?', *Jewish Historical Society of England – Transactions* 25 for 1973–75 (1977), pp. 43–7

Saltman, A., *Theobald, Archbishop of Canterbury* (London, 1956)

Salzman, L. F., *Building in England down to 1540: a documentary history* (Oxford, 1952)

Savine, A., *The English Monasteries on the Eve of the Dissolution* (London, 1909)

Scaglione, A., *Knights at Court* (Oxford, 1991)

Scammell, G. V., *Hugh du Puiset, Bishop of Durham* (Cambridge, 1956)

Scarfe, N., *Suffolk in the Middle Ages* (Woodbridge, 1986)

—— *Jocelin of Brakelond* (Leominster, 1997)

—— 'Jocelin of Brakelond's identity: a review of the evidence', *Proceedings of the Suffolk Institute of Archaeology and History* 30 (1997), pp. 1–5

Schmidt, P. G., 'The vision of Turkhill', *Journal of Warburg and Courtauld Institute* 41 (1978), pp. 50–64

Schofield, J., *The Building of London from the Conquest to the Great Fire* (London, 1984)

Schramm, P. E., *A History of the English Coronation*, trans. L. G. Wickham Legg (Oxford, 1937)

Schroll, M. A., *Benedictine Monasticism as Reflected in the Warnefrid-Hildemar Commentaries on the Rule* (New York, 1941)

Searle, E., *Lordship and Community: Battle Abbey and its Banlieu, 1066–1538* (Toronto, 1974)

Seasoltz, R. K., 'Monastic hospitality', *American Benedictine Review* 25 (1975), pp. 427–59

Siraisi, N., *Mediaeval and Early Renaissance Medicine: an introduction to knowledge and practice* (Chicago and London, 1990)

Slade, C. F., 'Reading', in *Historic Towns, 1*, ed. M. D. Lobel (London and Oxford, 1969)

Smith, D. M., and London, V. C. M., *The Heads of Religious Houses in England and Wales 2, 1216–1377* (Cambridge, 2001)

Smith, R. A. L., 'The central financial system of Christ Church, Canterbury, 1186–1512', *EHR* 55 (1940), pp. 353–69

—— 'The financial system of Rochester Cathedral priory', *EHR* 56 (1941), pp. 586–95

—— *Canterbury Cathedral Priory: a study in monastic administration* (Cambridge, 1943)

Snape, R. H., *English Monastic Finances in the Later Middle Ages* (Cambridge, 1926)

Southern, R. W., *Saint Anselm and his Biographer: a study of monastic life and thought, 1059–c. 1130* (Cambridge, 1963)

—— *Medieval Humanism and Other Studies* (Oxford, 1970)

—— *Saint Anselm: a portrait in a landscape* (Cambridge, 1990)

Spear, V., *Leadership in Medieval English Nunneries* (Woodbridge, 2005)

Stalley, R., *The Cistercian Monasteries of Ireland: an account of the history and architecture of the White Monks in Ireland from 1142 to 1540* (London and New Haven, 1987)

Stenton, F. M., *The Early History of Abingdon Abbey* (Reading, 1913)

—— *Norman London: an essay* (London, 1934)

—— *The First Century of English Feudalism, 1066–1166*, 2nd edn (Oxford, 1961)

Stewart, D. J., *On the Architectural History of Ely Cathedral* (London, 1868)

Stewart-Brown, R., *The Serjeants of the Peace in Mediaeval England and Wales* (Manchester, 1936)

Stil, M., *The Abbot and the Rule: religious life at St Albans, 1290–1349* (Aldershot, 2002)

Stratham, M., 'The medieval town of Bury St Edmunds', *Bury St Edmunds: medieval art, architecture, archaeology and economy*, British Archaeological Association Conference Transactions 20 (Leeds, 1998), pp. 98–110

Sweeting, R. W. D., *The Cathedral Church of Ely* (London, 1924)

Swift, E., 'The obedientiary rolls of Battle Abbey', *Sussex Archaeological Collection* 78 (1937), pp. 37–62

Talbot, C. H., 'The account book of Beaulieu Abbey', *Cîteaux de Nederlanden* 9 (Westmalle, 1958), pp. 189–210

—— 'Cîteaux and Scarborough', *Studia Monastica* 2 (1960), pp. 95–158

Tatlock, J., 'Muriel, the earliest English poetess', *Publications of the Modern Language Association of America* 48 (1933), pp. 317–21

Tatton-Brown, T., 'The great hall of the Archbishop's palace', *Art and Architecture at Canterbury before 1220*, British Archaeological Association Conference Transactions 5 (Leeds, 1982), pp. 112–19

—— 'Three great Benedictine houses in Kent: their buildings and topography', *Archaeologia Cantiana* 100 (1985), pp. 171–88

—— *Canterbury History and Guide* (Stroud, 1994)

Taunton, E. L., *The English Black Monks of St Benedict*, 2 vols (London, 1897)

Thomson, R. M., 'The library of Bury St Edmunds abbey in the eleventh and twelfth centuries', *Speculum* 47 (1972), pp. 617–45

—— *The Archives of the Abbey of Bury St Edmunds*, Suffolk Records Society 21 (Woodbridge, 1980)

—— 'The obedientiaries of St Edmund's Abbey', *Proceedings of the Suffolk Institute of Archaeology and History* 35 (1983), pp. 91–103

—— *William of Malmesbury* (Woodbridge, 1987)

Thompson, E. M., *The Carthusian Order in England* (London, 1930)

Thompson, M., *The Mediaeval Hall: the basis of secular domestic life, 600–1600 AD* (Aldershot, 1995)

—— *Mediaeval Bishops' Houses in England and Wales* (Aldershot, 1998)

Thompson, S., *Women Religious: the founding of English nunneries after the Conquest* (Oxford, 1991)

Tillotsan, J. H., *Marrick Priory: a nunnery in late mediaeval Yorkshire*, Borthwick Papers 75 (York, 1989)

Townsend, J., *A History of Abingdon* (repr., Trowbridge and London, 1970)

Tsurushima, H., 'The fraternity of Rochester Cathedral priory c. 1100', *AN Studies* 14 (Woodbridge, 1992), pp. 313–37

—— 'Forging unity between monks and laity in Anglo-Norman England: the fraternity of Ramsey Abbey', *Negotiating Secular and Ecclesiastical Power: Western Europe in the Central Middle Ages*, ed. A. A. Bijsterveld, H. Teunis, A. Wareham (Turnhout, 1999), pp. 133–46

Turner, E., 'Battel Abbey', *Sussex Archaeological Collections* 17 (1865), pp. 1–56

Turner, R., *King John* (Harlow, 1994)

Urry, W., *Canterbury Under the Angevin Kings* (London, 1967)

—— 'Canterbury, Kent, c. 1153', *Local Maps and Plans From Mediaeval England*, ed. R. A. Skelton and P. D. A. Harvey (Oxford, 1986), pp. 43–58

Van Houts, E. M. C., 'The *Gesta Normannorum Ducorum*: a history without an end', *AN Studies* 3 (Woodbridge, 1981), pp. 106–18

—— 'Normandy and Byzantium in the eleventh century', *Byzantion* 55 (1985), pp. 544–59

—— 'Robert of Torigni as a genealogist', *Studies in Mediaeval History presented to R. Allen Brown*, ed. C. Harper-Bill, C. J. Holdsworth, J. Nelson (Woodbridge, 1989), pp. 215–33

Vaughan, R., *Matthew Paris* (Cambridge, 1958)

—— *Chronicles of Matthew Paris: monastic life in the thirteenth century* (Stroud, 1984)

Vaughn, S., *The Abbey of Bec and the Anglo-Norman State, 1034–1136* (Woodbridge, 1981)

Victoria History of the Counties of England (London, 1900–)

Vinogradoff, P., *Villainage in England: essays in English medieval history*, rev. edn (Oxford, 1927)

Ward, B., *Miracles and the Mediaeval Mind: theory, record and event, 1000–1215* (London, 1982)

—— *Signs and Wonders: saints, miracles and prayers from the fourth century to the fourteenth century* (London, 1992)

Ward, H. L. D., 'The Vision of Thurkhill, probably by Ralph of Coggeshall', *British Archaeological Journal* 31 (1875), pp. 420–59

Wardrop, J., *Fountains Abbey and its Benefactors, 1132–1300* (Kalamazoo, 1987)

Warren, W. L., *King John* (London, 1961)

—— *Henry II* (London, 1973)

Warrilow, J., 'Cluny: *silentia claustri*', *Benedict's Disciples*, ed. D. H. Farmer (Leominster, 1980), pp. 118–38

Webb, D., *Pilgrimage in Medieval England* (London, 2000)

Westlake, H. F., *Westminster Abbey*, 2 vols (London, 1923)

Whitaker, T., *The History and Antiquities of the Deanery of Craven* (London, 1812)

White, G. H., 'The household of the Norman kings', *TRHS*, 4th ser. 30 (1948), pp. 127–55

White, S., *Custom, Kinship and Gifts to Saints: the Laudatio Parentum in Western France, 1050–1150* (Chapel Hill, London 1988)

Whitney, M. P., 'Largesse, queen of mediaeval virtues', *Vassar Mediaeval Studies*, ed. C. Fiske (New Haven, 1923), pp. 181–215

Whittingham, A. B., 'Bury St Edmunds Abbey: the plan, design and development of the church and monastic buildings', *Archaeological Journal* 108 (1952), pp. 168–87

—— *Bury St Edmunds Abbey*, Ancient monuments and historic buildings (London, 1971; repr. 1992)

Williams, A., 'The Anglo-Norman abbey', *English Heritage Book of St Augustine's Abbey Canterbury*, ed. R. Gem (London, 1997), pp. 50–66

Williams, D. H., 'Layfolk within Cistercian precincts', *Monastic Studies* 2, ed. J. Loades (Bangor, 1991), pp. 87–117

—— *The Cistercians in the Early Middle Ages* (Leominster, 1998)

—— *The Welsh Cistercians* (Leominster, 2001)

Williams, E. A., 'A bibliography of Giraldus Cambrensis c. 1147–c. 1223', *The National Library of Wales Journal* 12 (1961–62), pp. 97–140

Williams, W., 'A dialogue between a Cluniac and a Cistercian', *Journal of Theological Studies* 31 (1930), pp. 164–75

Willis, R., *The Architectural History of the Conventual Buildings of the Monastery of Christ Church in Canterbury* (London, 1869)

Winzen, D., 'Conference on the reception of guests', *Monastic Studies* 10 (1974), pp. 55–63

Wolff, R. E., 'Caesarius of Heisterbach's *Dialogue on Miracles*: report of the translator', *Heaven and Earth: Studies in Mediaeval Cistercian History* 9, ed. E. R. Elder (Kalamazoo, 1983), pp. 102–13

Wood, M. E., 'Norman domestic architecture', *Archaeological Journal* 92 (1935), pp. 167–242

—— 'Moyse's hall: a description of the building', *Archaeological Journal* 108 (1952), p. 165

Wood, S. M., *English Monasteries and their Patrons in the Thirteenth Century* (Oxford, 1955)

Woodman, F., 'The Waterworks drawing of the Eadwine Psalter', *The Eadwine Psalter: text, image and monastic culture in twelfth-century Canterbury*, ed. M. Gibson, T. A. Heslop, R. W. Pfaff (London, 1992), pp. 168–77

Woodruff, C. E., 'The financial aspect of the cult of St Thomas of Canterbury as revealed by a study of the monastic records', *Archaeologia Cantiana* 14 (1932), pp. 13–32

Woolgar, C. M., *The Great Household in Late Medieval England* (London, New Haven, 1999)

Wormald, F., ed., *The St Albans Psalter (Psalter Albani)* (London, 1960)

Wrathmell, S., *The Guest-house at Kirkstall Abbey: a guide to the mediaeval buildings and the discoveries made during recent excavations* (Yorkshire, 1987)

Wright, T., *A History of Domestic Manners in England During the Middle Ages* (London, 1862)

Yates, R., *History and Antiquities of the Abbey of St Edmund's, Bury*, 2nd edn (London, 1843)

Index

Individuals are listed under their first name
References to illustrations are in bold

Other volumes in
Studies in the History of Medieval Religion